▷ Book is ∧ repetitive ∧ reiterating
points. Succinctness and
editing ▷ stretching the reader's
∆would have helped.

+ verbose + sometimes

+

▷ Exhaustive analysis, yes. Engaging
read for initiates, no.

▷ Reads in part like a memoir
of his time + studies in Brazil

RELOCATING THE SACRED

SUNY series, Afro-Latinx Futures
———————
Vanessa K. Valdés, editor

RELOCATING THE SACRED

AFRICAN DIVINITIES AND BRAZILIAN CULTURAL HYBRIDITIES

Niyi Afolabi

SUNY
PRESS

Published by State University of New York Press, Albany

For information, contact State University of New York Press, Albany, NY
www.sunypress.edu

Library of Congress Cataloging-in-Publication Data

Name: Afolabi, Niyi, author.
Title: Relocating the sacred : African divinities and Brazilian cultural hybridities /
    Niyi Afolabi.
Other titles: SUNY series, Afro-Latinx futures.
Description: Albany : State University of New York Press, 2022. | Series:
    SUNY series, Afro-Latinx futures | Includes bibliographical references
    and index.
Identifiers: LCCN 2022009663 | ISBN 9781438490717 (hardcover : alk. paper) |
    ISBN 9781438490731 (ebook)
Subjects: LCSH: Yoruba (African people)—Brazil—Rites and ceremonies. |
    Syncretism (Religion)—Brazil. | Democracy—Brazil. | Racism—Brazil. |
    Brazil—Religion—African influences.
Classification: LCC BL2590.B7 A36 2022 | DDC 299.60981—dc23
LC record available at https://lccn.loc.gov/2022009663

10 9 8 7 6 5 4 3 2 1

To Funmilayo Afolabi,
Wherever you are.

Contents

Preface   ix

Introduction   1

Part I: Mapping the Sacred

Chapter 1   Bahia: Yoruba Diasporic Domain of Activating
the Sacred   25

Chapter 2   Pierre Verger and Yoruba Ritual Altars in Brazil   49

Chapter 3   Matriarchs of Candomblé: Mãe Stella de Oxóssi,
Mãe Beata de Yemonjá, and Mãe Valnizia Bianch   79

Part II: The Sacred in Literary Manifestations

Chapter 4   Jorge Amado and Vasconcelos Maia: The Sea/River
as Iemojá/Oxum's Domain   109

Chapter 5   Abdias Nascimento and Nelson Rodrigues:
The Fallen Angel as Betrayal of Blackness   135

Chapter 6   Zora Seljan and Alfredo Dias Gomes: Sacred
Feminine Solidarities and Sango's Revenge   159

Chapter 7   Raul Longo and Robson Pinheiro: Afro-Brazilian
             Deities in Literary Rituals   181

Chapter 8   Cléo Martins and Chynae: Oiá and Oxossi in
             Invocations and Encounters   207

Part III: Hybridities in Afro-Brazilian Culture

Chapter 9   Filhos de Gandhi and Cortejo Afro: Candomblé in
             the Carnivalesque Frame   233

Chapter 10   Give Us This Day Our Daily Acarajé   265

Conclusion   281

Notes   285

Bibliography   315

Index   339

Preface

For almost three years now (2019–2022), the Covid-19 pandemic raged on uncontrollably, killing millions of people worldwide. Research travel became almost impossible due to necessary preventive medical restrictions. For those of us whose research is negatively impacted without the benefit of ethnographic fieldwork in Brazil, one is compelled to sustain scholarly productivity nonetheless by resorting to alternative methodologies in order to complete a book project that has been in hibernation for a while. *Relocating the Sacred* was born in this unusual context. I have always been fascinated by African spirituality because as youngsters growing up in Nigeria, we were not encouraged by our parents to assimilate indigenous African religions due to colonial mentality that denigrated our African cultural values by imposing alien religions on us. At home, in church, as well as at school, we were expected to sing and pray to God but not to the Yoruba pantheon whose presence among us was more interactively visible through communal ritual performances and celebrations than Christianity. Yet, from Anglican to Methodist mission schools, we sang "Nearer my God to thee" from *Songs of Praise* but could not cite a single verse from Yoruba sacred Ifá divination system in which are located divine and moral codes of ideal human character. It took visiting Brazil as a university student to realize with so much chagrin, that by giving us the Bible as the singular truth of salvation and redemption, British colonialism stripped us of fundamental African spiritual knowledge systems that are worth preserving, learning, and practicing as they do in the African diaspora. The de-alienating process of seeing and appreciating African deities being openly venerated and celebrated on the streets of Bahia-Brazil, gave me something to think about. Against this background, *Relocating the Sacred* serves as an opportune medium to excavate

ix

some of the terrains in which African deities have been relocated and
hybridized in Brazil in ritual altars, literature, and Afro-Brazilian popular
forms such as in music, festivals, and culinary arts. I do hope that my
future research into African spirituality in Brazil will draw me closer to
sacred Afro-Brazilian mysteries that remain camouflaged, marginalized,
and invisible even in plain sight.

I am indebted to a number of individuals and institutions who
facilitated this book by virtue of their contributions through insightful
conversations with me over several years in Brazil or through their
scholarly or creative works. I thank Mãe Stella de Oxóssi, Camafeu de
Oxóssi, Pierre Verger, Felipe Fanuel Xavier Rodrigues, Lisa Earl Castillo,
Lande Onawale, Miriam Alves, Esmeralda Ribeiro, Alberto Pitta, Ana
Rita Santiago, Elizandra Batista de Souza, Aulo Barreti Filho, and
Vagner Gonçalves da Silva, among others. I thank the Warfield Center
for African and African American Studies as well as the Department
of African and African Diaspora Studies at the University of Texas at
Austin for continuing to support my research on Afro-Brazilian studies.
Equally deserving of my acknowledgment are the following entities:
Centro de Estudos Afro-Orientais (Universidade Federal da Bahia),
Fundação Jorge Amado, Fundação Pierre Verger, and Ilê Axê Opo
Afonjá. Of special significance is the honorific book subvention I was
awarded by the Office of the Vice President for Research, Scholarship
and Creative Endeavors at the University of Texas at Austin, especially
Liza Scarborough, who supervised the application process. I am grateful.
Last but not least, the editorial team at State University of New York
Press deserves my gratitude for their meticulous work on making the
final product the best it could be. I am particularly grateful to Vanessa
K. Valdés, Rebecca Colesworthy, Timothy J. Stookesberry, Eileen Nizer,
and Matthew Phillips. *Relocating the Sacred* invites the reader to an
academic exercise in spiritual self-discovery and decolonial consciousness
as manifest in the multilayered works explored between the sacred and
the syncretism of the sacred in Brazil.

Introduction

Relocating the Sacred

In 1982, I was one of seven privileged Nigerian students from the University of Ife (now Obafemi Awolowo University) who participated in the study abroad program at the University of São Paulo, Brazil. Sometime in late November of the same year, I was performing my customary sociocultural immersion by strolling through the city of São Paulo. I ran into an older Afro-Brazilian man who was in town for one of those annual Afro-Brazilian congresses that took place to commemorate the death of Zumbi dos Palmares, the Afro-Brazilian leader who was killed by the Portuguese colonial invaders of the Palmares maroon settlement (*Quilombo dos Palmares*) on November 20, 1695. After some fraternal greetings, Antônio Carlos dos Santos, an iconic personality who is popularly known in Salvador and within the Black movement as "Vovô," gave me his business card and invited me to visit Bahia. I noticed that the name of his carnival organization, Ilê Aiyê (House of the world), was written in Yoruba, my native language.[1] When the semester ended, I made a trip to Bahia that transformed my life spiritually, culturally, and professionally. The overwhelming two-week research sojourn felt like two years. In the last twenty years, I have since returned to Bahia to uncover more of the cultural convergences and divergences between Africa and Brazil.

While in Bahia, I decoded the many striking influences of Yoruba religion, culture, and language in Brazil. Beyond the enchanting use of Yoruba words in building names, such as the "Edifício Ogum" (Ogun building), "Oxumare Center" (mini-shopping center called "Rainbow"), and the "Casa de Yemanjá" (Yemoja house), as well as in popular songs

1

by Gerônimo, I noticed that the spirit of the Osun goddess reigns over the entire city ("É d'Oxum" [Belongs to Osun]) and the traditional Yoruba bean cake (*akara*) is popularly sold on the streets as acarajé. I soon came to learn that Yoruba orisa influenced the Afro-Brazilian religion of Candomblé, as well as the many Afro-Brazilian carnival groups, such as Ilê Aiyê, Olodum (Celebrant), Orunmila (Father of divination), Okambi (Progenitor or child of Okan), Araketu (People of Ketu), Badauê (Power of unity), and Filhos de Gandhi (Children of Gandhi), among others.[2] The influence of Yoruba was everywhere.

My culture shock reached an ecstatic crescendo in Bahia when I visited Ilê Axé Opo Afonja, one of the oldest Afro-Brazilian temples. I was there to conduct an ethnographic interview about Afro-Brazilian carnival. To my surprise, my scheduled research participant was not only an active member of one of the Afro-Bahian carnival organizations in which I was interested, but he was also an initiate of the sacred temple I had visited. What was to be a secular encounter became inadvertently religious. Three decades since that defining encounter, I no longer remember the name of my interviewee. Yet, two things occurred during that fortuitous interview that I have been reflecting on for many years. First, while I was expecting him to speak Portuguese, he offered me coffee in Yoruba: "Omo Oxum, se wa mu omi dudu?" (Child of Osun [Nigerian] would you care for a cup of coffee?). I was not only shocked but started perspiring uncontrollably. I was speaking Portuguese, and my Brazilian interviewee was responding in a millennial Yoruba liturgic language that contemporary Yoruba speakers like me no longer use. By calling me "Omo Oxum," he was identifying me as both a devotee of Osun, a Nigerian goddess, and as a Nigerian, because Osun is one of the most well-known rivers in Nigeria. He then invited me to visit the houses of many different orisas (deities), including Osun (Goddess of sweet rivers and fertility), Yemoja (Sea goddess or mermaid), Sango (God of thunder), Ogun (God of iron and justice), Oya (Goddess of the wind), Obatala (God of divination), and Esu (God of the crossroads).

My Afro-Brazilian host could not help but notice my trepidation. I was not comfortable entering the sacred houses that had been opened for me, even as a Yoruba, a Nigerian, and an African. Nor did I offer the expected verbal venerations (*orikis*) to these deities. As I swiftly removed myself from the sacred spaces and altars, I explained that I was not yet initiated into the secrets of Yoruba religiosity and could not perform sacred rituals reserved for the elders. But this was only partially true. In actuality, I was dealing with the impact of the British colonial mentality that had almost "erased" my Yoruba consciousness and pride. In other words, it took my research visit to Brazil, and Bahia especially, to rediscover the richness of my Yoruba identity and to rid myself of the remaining relics of the colonial brainwashing that had forced many of us to abandon our Yoruba deities (orisas, or orixás in Brazil) and thereafter embrace Christianity as colonized Africans under the tutelage of imposed foreign religions. Even after independence, many Africans still suffer from the ravages of European coloniality. Through religious syncretism, Brazil has preserved African religious culture for many centuries, despite the hardships and horrors of enslavement. It is against this background that I can relate to Brazil as a site where sacred Yoruba traditions have been relocated through the Middle Passage.

This book brings a critical perspective to the relocation of Yoruba sacred practices in the diaspora and in so doing challenges the racial democracy myth in Brazil. Why do these African cultural practices persist amidst the onslaught of globalization? Within a context of ongoing racial discrimination and demonization of Blackness, what roles exist for identifiable religious-cum-sacred rituals? My claim is that the tension between the theory of racial democracy and the practice of white supremacy in Brazil opens the space for syncretism of cultures, including African sacred practices. Turning to three location(s) of culture—to borrow from Homi Bhabha—that is, ritual altars, literature, and carnival, I argue that the syncretism of African sacred practices offers a technology for grappling with enduring racisms, provides a strategy of resistance against white hegemonic power, and serves as a tool in the ongoing efforts toward decolonization.

By the sacred, I am referring to all Yoruba religious rites that have blended into Brazilian popular culture over the years through syncretism. In my argument, relocation operates at two main levels. At the diasporic level, it relates to the Atlantic crossing of the Middle Passage, while, at the cultural level, it informs how the sacred has become hybridized, popularized, and commercialized as a strategy of religious negotiation, political resistance, and economic survival. By examining relocation as it relates to sacred rites of African religious culture in Brazil, this study argues that "racial democracy" in Brazil is an inherently contradictory idea. That is because racial democracy is premised on celebrating the hybridization of African divinities in Brazilian popular and expressive cultures while also denying the collateral existence of racial discrimination, which is temporarily camouflaged by miscegenetic rituals and festive performances. Studies on religious syncretism and hybridized festivals in Brazil coalesce on the primacy of the popularization of the sacred.[3] While it is facile to study these expressive cultures separately, comparative studies of the popularization of the sacred must also grapple with the fact that cultural producers either deny the presence of the sacred in their production or strategically use symbologies to hide the more obvious examples. In either case, an absent presence (racism) shapes cultural expressions under threat of limited funding opportunities, which compel producers to succumb to dominant political pressures and manipulative sponsorships. In other words, hybridizations serve as a safety valve to launch resistance or negotiations without upsetting the racist status quo. Many of these strategies are characterized by the acceptance of co-optation as an inevitable compromise for pursuing political ideas, which are ultimately traded for cultural symbologies in the name of social survival.

Relocating the Sacred: African Divinities and Brazilian Cultural Hybridities is divided into three parts, each of which maps the location of the sacred: the first in Afro-Brazilian ritual altars, the second in literature, and the third in carnival culture. This study argues that, whether in literature or hybrid cultural manifestations, such as the carnival or musical performances, the sacred emerges in intricate alternative spaces as the oppressive memory of slavery and racial discrimination. In the shadow of colonialism and enslavement, Africanism ceases to be a matter of the clear demarcation of authentic identity. Instead, given the reality of miscegenation and identity crisis in Brazil, Africanism must necessarily be thought of as plural.

Theorizing Relocation of the Sacred

To understand the relocation of the sacred, it is imperative to first appreciate what constitutes a sacred space. In the Afro-Brazilian context, relocation is doubly manifest as both the forcible removal from Africa and the affirmation of Afro-spiritual identity through negotiations with hybridity, cultural identity, and self-preservation.[4] Claudia Moser and Cecilia Feldman (2014) argue that the location in which rituals are enacted foundationally impacts ritual practices themselves. They suggest that "a sacred space does not exist *a priori* but is the outcome of actions, intentions, and recollections—it is the result of past and present interactions among humans, material implements, architecture, and landscape."[5] While there is bound to be disagreements about what constitutes "authenticity" once a sacred or ritualized action is relocated, we can at least agree that religious practices are conditioned by local social contexts that define their meanings and politics depending on the aspirations of their devotees over many years of adaptations and shifting continuities. For example, in his case study of Hinduism, Vijay Agnew (2005) insists that the dynamic acculturation to new social contexts following dislocation gives flavor to the new diasporic culture. He argues that rituals evolve, and their cultural manifestations are not fixed—"change resists petrification and allows the religion to meet the spiritual and emotional needs of its devotees over time."[6] In other words, the practice of Hinduism in the diaspora is mediated by the reality of race and racism. Likewise, the relocation of Yoruba religion and its adaptation into Candomblé in Brazil shares some of the same characteristics of the diasporic soul highlighted by Agnew.

Combining the religious aspects of Yoruba deities with Catholicism and some Amerindian influences, Candomblé evolved in Brazil between the sixteenth and nineteenth centuries and fully emerged with the founding of the first *terreiro* (temple) in the nineteenth century. Understood by its Brazilian devotees as the veneration of the orixás (Yoruba deities), Candomblé is an Afro-Brazilian religious tradition that is practiced mainly in Salvador da Bahia, Brazil, but with some variations in other Latin American countries, such as Argentina, Uruguay, Paraguay, and Venezuela. By syncretizing Catholic saints with Yoruba deities, Candomblé emerged as a religion of resistance against the horrors of enslavement. Practitioners sought to draw strength from their ancestral divinities, as well as from a Supreme Creator called Olodumaré. Devotees have their selected orixás, which regulate their destinies and serve as guardian protectors of their daily activities. The ceremonies include music and dance, through which some devotees are possessed by the descending deities. Like African religious traditions, Candomblé ceremonies may also include offerings of gifts and animal sacrifices. Rachel Harding (2000) theorizes that Candomblé has been an alternative space of citizenship and identity for Afro-Brazilians, and the circle dance within Candomblé ceremonies serves to create "new, more elastic boundaries—of community, of refuge, of transformation. . . . [T]he structures of community engendered by shared dance, especially in the circle, were prime sites for the recreation of black identity toward a pan-African emphasis in the New World."[7] Through this negotiation of citizenship and identity, Afro-Brazilians deploy the relocation of the sacred from Africa to Brazil as a form of political agency toward self-transformation in spite of the lasting traumas of enslavement. Dance, drumming, ritual ceremonies, and annual festivals embody the memory of Africa through its relocation.

The Brazilian domains of the relocation of the sacred are multispatial and extensive. The Candomblé houses alone are just one of the major spaces of the sacred, and they serve as living museums for religious, memorial, archival, historical, architectural, artistic, musical, culinary, ritualistic, festive, linguistic, moral, entrepreneurial, medicinal, and social organizational contents.[8] Given that the forced Atlantic migration and enslavement of Africans took place under traumatic circumstances, there was neither the opportunity nor the luxury for the enslaved to bring along with them any material belongings. However, through the oral traditions with which they were already familiar and in which they had been socialized in Africa, the enslaved were able to draw on the power of memory to reconstruct most of the sacred activities, which served as a way to cope with the traumas of enslavement. Through this painstaking process, the enslaved simultaneously rehumanized themselves through cultural relics and preserved themselves against the breaking of their spirits. Over the years, relocated sacred spaces that used to look rather basic in their architectural design are now quite elaborate and gigantic. The influx of renovation funds to the major Candomblé houses in Bahia and elsewhere during the tenure of Gilberto Gil as minister of culture in the new millennium permitted Afro-Brazilians to renovate and modernize old structures. Such renovations have also impacted what has become known as heritage tourism, as African Americans and other curious tourists flock to Brazil to better understand African cultural and historical resonances in South America.

In her critical excavation of Candomblé in sacred and secular spaces in Salvador, Heather Shirey (2009) provides one of the most extensive elaborations (at least since the works of Pierre Verger) of how relocation "transform[ed] the Orixás." Succinctly covering both sacred and public (or secularly relocated) spaces, Shirey exposes a city that is engrossed with the manifestation and preservation of the sacred:

> In the streets and plazas of Salvador da Bahia, Brazil, representations of the *orixás*, the deities of the African-Brazilian religion of Candomblé, are visible throughout the city, Mural

paintings appear on walls and signs where they blend in with advertisements and graffiti, allowing motorists to contemplate the entire pantheon of *orixás* while filling up the gas tank. A sculpture of Exú, the guardian of the crossroads and the *orixá* who oversees all forms of communication, is positioned, most appropriately, in front of the city's central post office; a painted mermaid associated with Yemanjá overlooks the sea; and on the Dique do Tororó, a large lake and recreation zone in the middle of the city, a group of *orixá* statues dances in a circle on the surface of the water.[9]

Shirey's study, combining ethnography, participant observation, and qualitative methods, was conducted between 1998 and 2002. For her study, she had the opportunity to interview some of the artists behind these visual representations of Candomblé across the city, including Tatti Moreno, who created the permanent installation of African deities on the Dique do Tororó. Her study also allowed the devotees of different Candomblé communities or nations (Nagô, Jejé, and Angola) to compare notes on the detailed differences between their forms of sacred structure, empowerment, and possession trance. In addition to analyzing the historic evolution and complexity of Candomblé through the works of Roger Bastide (2009), Melville J. Herskovits and Frances S. Herskovits (1958), Ruth Landes (1994), Roger Sansi (2007), Stephen Selka (2005), and Jim Wafer (1991), Shirey critiques the monumental representation of the orixás in the public realm for their simplicity and for homogenizing and secularizing sacred altars that are now deprived of their ritualistic practices. Perhaps even more interesting is Shirey's description of the public protest by Pentecostal churches against the official inauguration of these sacred sculptures.[10] These protests signal the problematic side of the relocation of the sacred from Africa to the Western world, where Christianity still reigns supreme.

Of significant impact to the relocation thesis is a recent exhibition (and attendant catalogue) that focuses on the sacred artistry of the orixás in Salvador da Bahia. In *Axé Bahia: The Power of Art in Afro-Brazilian Metropolis* (2017), edited by Patrick A. Polk, Roberta Conduru, Sabrina Gledhill, and Randal Johnson, Bahia is rendered through painstakingly illustrated artistic works, as well as through analyses by a score of prominent scholars. Prominent among these analyses is the characterization of Bahia as a kind of "Black Rome," where the relics of Africa are visible throughout the city. The monumental work documents festival cycles, such as Festa de Yemanjá (Yemoja festival) and the Lavagem do Bomfim (Washing of the Good-End Church), which culminate in the national carnival celebrations in February or March. It also describes the creative artistry of ancestrality in the production of emblems of the orixás; capoeira martial performances; the exploration of the orixás in Brazilian popular music; Black presence in Afro-Bahian carnival; the inspired and syncretic artistry of Candomblé; and the interlocking agency of art, beauty, and vital force, among others. Collectively, *Axé Bahia* demonstrates that the city of Salvador is the quintessential reservoir of African religiosity and cultural preservation in Brazil. Each essay could easily be expanded into a book of its own. In one such essay, Patrick Polk provides an analysis of a painting by Carybé. As if answering the question posed in the title of his essay—"Have You Been to Bahia?"—Polk offers a global vision of what a newcomer needs to know:

> The Church of Bomfim dominates the high ground to the right. Some residents watch a capoeira match while others go about their business carrying goods to and from market. Nearby a Candomblé initiation is underway. Musicians, one playing a *berimbau* and another holding a guitar, crowd up against a contemplative Baiana sitting cross-legged on an expanse of Portuguese tile. It is also a spirit-filled domain with the Afro-Brazilian orixá Yemanjá floating just beneath its waters in mermaid form while other orixás join with Jesus and Catholic saints to hold court and battle demons in the sky above.[11]

Polk's overall description of the domain of the sacred is extensive and comprehensive, reflecting the major images and themes of relocation in the Afro-Brazilian experience from slavery to the present.

As Afro-Brazilian sacred artistry recuperates from its dislocation from Africa, so too do other cultural manifestations, such as music, dance, carnival, culinary arts, capoeira, medicine, literature, and cinema, use memory to relocate the sacred. Music is a powerful example—not only is it therapeutic and soothing, but it also has the emotive power to express deep feelings that may otherwise be permanently silenced due to trauma and pain. In the context of the musical veneration of the orixás, the complex dynamics of the Yoruba liturgic language (from

Nigeria, Benin, and Togo) have been diluted with Portuguese and, at times, even Kimbundu (from Angola). Within the Candomblé rituals, singing, drumming, and dancing challenge the preservation of authenticity because the songs are orally transmitted from one generation to the next rather than written down for posterity. With the advent of modern technology and efforts to record these chants or sacred songs, popular musicians as well as the Candomblé houses are beginning to document these invaluable treasures through CD and DVD recordings.[12] Relocation of the sacred in this instance takes place as a form of documentation of African sacred songs within Brazilian sacred space, as well as as a form of commercialization through popular music. Studies by José Jorge de Carvalho (1999a, 1999b, 2004), Luciano da Silva Candemil (2019), and Christopher Dunn (2017) trace the history and manifestations of Afro-Brazilian ritual music from their origins as Vissungos, Jongos, and Alabês, through to the many variations of Cantos Sangrados, Tambores de Axé, Samba, and Axé music.[13] These studies also painstakingly analyze the social contexts and meanings of ritual music as it translates the aspirations of Afro-Brazilian communities to a wider audience. Through these recordings, supplicants venerate the orixás and request protection for their communities as well as for necessary improvements in their social life. This collaboration between the African originators of the musical culture and their Brazilian appropriators has a documentary value for the relocation of the sacred from Africa to Brazil.

Of central importance to the relocation thesis is the prominence of carnival in Brazil. After soccer, carnival is a national phenomenon and serves as a reset button for all Brazilians after a year of social struggle and racial tension. Often mixed with music, local color, extravagantly decorated floats, and historical and transnational themes, carnival is the greatest show on earth and a unique opportunity for locals and state tourist organizations alike to benefit economically from the influx of global revelers. However, contrary to the marketing of Rio carnival as the only carnival that exists, there are many carnival celebrations in Brazil, and it is worth mentioning a few: Carnaval carioca, the most extravagant and touristic celebration, held in Rio; Frevo, a very fast variation in which revelers dance with small umbrellas on the streets of Recife-Pernambuco; and Afro-Bahian carnival, the one with the most visible African presence, in which African deities are often on display in a strategic enactment of political negotiation that Christopher Dunn has termed a "stage for protest."[14] On a consistent annual basis, carnival groups (blocos afros and afoxés), including Ilê Aiyê, Olodum, Cortejo Afro, Filhos de Gandhy, Ara Ketu, among others, draw inspiration from African religious motifs to resist and politically negotiate with a hostile and racist environment. Afro-Bahian carnival is often a strategically hybrid or masked process, one that showcases pride in African cosmologies during weeks-long festive parades. Afro-Bahian carnival serves to preserve African cultural values that were relocated during the Middle Passage. The annual ritual empowers the most Africanized and concentrated diasporic population in the Americas. The reenactment of African deities, kingdoms, kings, pharaohs, queens, heroes, heroines, and colonial rebellions captures the inherent spiritual desire of Afro-Brazilians to validate their religious traditions through pride, memory, and cultural performance.

The mixture of races, religiosities, festivals, and expressive arts serves as the driving force for the relocation and effervescence of Africa in Bahia. The Baianas (also Baianas de Acarajé), robed in the white-laced spiritual garments of Candomblé and adorned with colorful beads, turbans, and good-luck charms, suggest an image of Bahia as a land of warmth and hospitality. But beyond this symbolic representation, the Baianas are the face of religiosity and cuisine in Bahia, as they sell acarajé on street corners and invite tourists to take pictures with them for a fee. Due to their historical significance to local color as an embodiment of the merging of the sacred and the profane, the Baianas participate in religious events and festivals, such as Lavagem do Bomfim (Washing of the Lord of Good End Church), and have their own wing, called Ala das Baianas, within each school of samba during the national carnival celebrations, especially in Rio de Janeiro and São Paulo. The relocation of the sacred comes alive in annual Bahian religious syncretic festivals in which the orixás are honored, as in the festival of the sea goddess, or Yemanjá, which corresponds to Catholic Our Lady of Conception or Virgin Mary. Similarly, Iansã, the goddess of winds and storms, is honored as Catholic Santa Bárbara during the *Festa* de Santa Bárbara. Meanwhile, Oxalá, the patron deity of the universe, is honored during the Catholic Lord of Good End festival. Of special significance is the Good Death Festival (Festa da Boa Morte) in the city of Cachoeira, which celebrates the ascension of Virgin Mary to heaven, the procession of which is exclusively reserved for Afro-Brazilian women who are over the age of fifty. This sampling of Africa-derived religious festivals and expressive and culinary arts that have been fully integrated within Afro-Bahian cultural identity would be incomplete without mentioning capoeira. A mix of martial arts and dance that is now practiced all over the world, capoeira symbolizes the history of the struggle for freedom from enslavement and now transcends its Angolan rootedness to have become a manifestation of the Afro-Bahian identity.[15] With its myriad manifestations of the sacred in the popular realm, Bahia remains the quintessential zone for the activation of the sacred in the daily life of Brazilians.

Affirmation of Afro-Spiritual Identities

Any discussion of the relationship between spirituality and cultural identity in Brazil is inextricably linked to questions of racial identity, especially when discussing the African influences on Brazilian heritage. While religious syncretism manifests in both sacred and popular spheres, racial mixture is even more problematic as a strategy for negotiating power, as when racial heritage was covertly masked under the guise of religious interconnectedness to preserve African cultural identity. In other words, while both frameworks (religious syncretism and racial mixture) assert sameness despite diversity, they often silence the identitarian foundations that are necessary for African cultural identity to assert its true value and pride. The efforts of Afro-Brazilian religions to deploy syncretism to survive the hardships of enslavement and to preserve African cultural values are not only strategic but also praiseworthy. The challenge remains, however, for Afro-Brazilian subjects to reconcile Euro-Brazilian and Afro-Brazilian identities. Ethnoreligious identity politics in Brazil offer a case study in how Afro-Brazilians cope with the many facets of their identity as they negotiate both the sacred and the African. Studies by Stefania Capone (2010), Stephen Selka (2007), and Vagner Gonçalves da Silva (2014) offer some insight into the complexities and contradictions of the quest for racial and ethnic identity within a problematic national and political context. While these approaches vary, whether focusing on multiple religions, a specific religion, or overlapping religious affiliations, they coalesce on the primacy of identity as a structuring motif in the configuration of belonging regardless of religious affinity. Selka, for example, unveils the underlying contradictions between Blackness and Brazilian religions and how these relationships shape what is left of political affluence (albeit an affluence that is subsumed under cultural politics). Meanwhile, Silva argues that the relationship between black cultural identity and religion are relics of African symbologies in Brazilian heritage. This fact is further confirmed in Capone's study, which illustrates how Candomblé remains the zone of tradition and power despite the controversial authenticity and purity of the African-derived Brazilian religion. Afro-spiritual identity subscribes to the politics of identity even when masked by popular, cultural, or festive manifestations.[16]

Stephen Selka's study *Religion and the Politics of Ethnic Identity in Bahia* (2007) examines the thriving intersections of Afro-Brazilian religion, race, and social mobilization. By drawing out the many connections and conflicts among devotees of Candomblé, promoters of identity politics during community festivals, and Afro-Brazilian Evangelicals, whose resistant attitude condemns Candomblé as "devil worship," Selka succeeds in placing race and "racial democracy" at the heart of both the search for alternative identities and a Black consciousness movement in the collective struggle against racism.[17] Selka's contributions to the debate on religiosity and Afro-Brazilian identity can be summed up as follows: (1) Blackness and religiosity have contradictory relationships; (2) racial identity in Brazil is historically cultural rather than political; (3) religion is inseparable from racial, cultural, and political identities; (4) Brazilian racial ideology often puts adherents of Catholicism, Candomblé, and Evangelicalism in conflict with each other despite their common Black identity; and (5) individuals and communities tend to negotiate Blackness and religious affiliations in contradictory forms. Beyond these theoretical and anthropological ruminations, Selka establishes a fundamental relationship between Candomblé and Afro-Brazilian identity, especially when he describes how this relationship has become part of daily life in Bahia:

> Candomblé terreiros enjoy all the legal rights of any other religion. One example of this openness is the ubiquity of Candomblé symbols and images throughout the city. At a public park in the center of town (Duque de Tororó), for example, large statues representing the different Candomblé orixás are displayed in the middle of a lake. Smaller versions of each statue are found at different places on a path around the water along with explanations of the characteristics of each orixá and the Catholic saint(s) with which they are identified.[18]

By analyzing the ritualization, politicization, and globalization of religion, Selka concedes the intimacy between religion, as an instrument of

Afro-Brazilian identity formation, and the struggle against the vestiges of racism in Brazil.

If Selka's study examines the connection between Afro-Brazilian identity and religiosity, Vagner Gonçalves da Silva's study "Religion and Black Cultural Identity" stresses the tensions between Roman Catholics, Afro-Brazilians, and Neopentecostals.[19] In his dense anthropological study, Silva describes the conflict among these three distinct religious groups, who nonetheless share a common Afro-Brazilian identity. Despite the differing positions on how best to agitate for political empowerment, the three religious agencies all thrive through their use of African symbols in the affirmation of Brazilian identity. Silva advances three main arguments: (1) Afro-Brazilian religions are central to the construction of Black identity; (2) Black Catholic movements appropriate aspects of Afro-Brazilian religiosity through the inculturation of theology and liturgy; and (3) Black evangelicals deny Afro-Brazilian religiosity as the central thrust for the construction of identity. Silva describes the processes through which the Brazilian government created public policies that were geared toward recognizing, protecting, preserving, and conserving the material heritage of Afro-Brazilian religions. Silva also highlights the gradual transformation of religion into a cultural heritage and how this heritage is further threatened by the religious fanaticism and intolerance of evangelicals. By their paradoxical exclusion of Africa from Brazilian culture, the Black evangelical movement deploys Black theology as a form of liberation politics without any recognition of African religious or cultural values, which are considered demonic activities. Silva notes of this tendency:

> Another alternative has been the reappropriation of symbols associated with African legacy in the Pentecostal context, but in a form that is disassociated from their relationship to the Afro-Brazilian religions. One example is the *Capoeira de Cristo*, also known as "Evangelical Capoeira" or "Gospel Capoeira," where the words contain no references to the Orishas or Catholic saints.[20]

Just as the Black evangelical movement attempts to distance itself from Africa, another movement among the devotees of Candomblé is pushing for the purity and authenticity of Afro-Brazilian religions by advancing a re-Africanization dynamic that eschews the influences of Catholicism or syncretism. Brazil may well continue to operate in this quagmire, caught between negotiating its mixed-race identity and transforming diverse Afro-Brazilian religiosities into weapons of political agitation and participation.

As much as Candomblé suffers from persecution from religious fanatics, it continues to enjoy the interest of scholars and devotees alike. Stefania Capone's seminal *Searching for Africa in Brazil* combines a complex erudition of the field of Afro-Brazilian Candomblé with a compelling ethnography. Her study attests to the premise that anthropology and Candomblé are intertwined. While Capone's study synthesizes the vast terrain of Candomblé scholarship, especially in Bahia, it also illuminates the complexity of race mixture and its bearing on religious rituals in Bahia and Rio de Janeiro, while emphasizing the challenge of debates on purity and authenticity in Afro-Brazilian Candomblé. The tripartite work, focusing on "The Metamorphoses of Exu," "Ritual Practice," and "The Construction of Tradition," also sums up recurrent controversies surrounding the shifting meanings of Exu in Candomblé worship and tradition. Capone raises a few foundational questions: (1) Why is Exu misunderstood as a diabolic character by Christian missionaries and not as a well-venerated deity of the crossroads, a divine messenger, mediator, and trickster, as he was celebrated among devotees of Candomblé? (2) Despite Exu's acceptance among Candomblé devotees, why is the same deity not accepted as an orthodox deity for initiation and possession rituals? (3) How did anthropologists, like Nina Rodrigues, Édison Carneiro, and Ruth Landes, intervene in debates on Nagô purity? In responding to these questions, Capone asserts that discourses about the purity and impurity of Candomblé houses overlap because they have been primarily advanced by Candomblé elite leaders to privilege the survival of the tradition itself amidst discourses of racial miscegenation and racial democracy. She goes on to challenge the contradictions of the marginalization of Exu despite its integration within Candomblé, especially during the re-Africanization movement of the 1970s. She ends by suggesting that devotees of Candomblé were active participants in the divisive debate of purity that accords Candomblé the status of a religion and relegates any form of religious syncretism to the realm of magic, witchcraft, and barbarity. In praise of the efforts toward purity, Capone suggests that the way forward is for syncretism to align more with the Africanizing tendencies of Candomblé Nagô: "Communication between Afro-Brazilian religions hinges on Exu because he is the only divinity present in all cult modalities. Therefore the less pure religions should look to their 'sister religions' that are closer to the true African tradition, in order to correct the mistakes of syncretism."[21] In sum, Capone exposes the contradictions of Candomblé, as both tradition and power, in the midst of hegemonic forces suppressing its vitality in an era of religious fanaticism, intolerance, and persecution. The foregoing issues about the complexities of Afro-Brazilian religious practices as manifest in the sacred and popular spheres offer an opportunity to examine how cultural production engages these contentious domains as protagonist and antagonist alike, often embodying the same ambiguities that play out in day-to-day social realities.

Overview of Chapters

The first part of this study conceptually maps Afro-Brazilian altars as the domain of the sacred, arguing that relocated religious practices are reenacted in performative, musical, and print media. Through an analysis of an interdisciplinary ensemble of works and archives, this study establishes ritual structures and strictures that are recurrent in the annual festivals, which have come to be denominated "the cycle of festivals" and that begin in June and continue until carnival in February or March. Classic studies, such as Ruth Landes's *City of Women* (1947), Mello Moraes Filho's *Festas e Tradições Populares do Brasil* (1979), and Jorge Amado's *Bahia de Todos os Santos* (1977), yield to more analytical and sociological studies about the intersection of the sacred and the profane, such as Anadelia Romo's *Brazil's Living Museum* (2010), Cheryl Sterling's *African Roots, Brazilian Rites* (2013), Scott Ickes's *African-Brazilian Culture and Regional Identity in Bahia, Brazil* (2013), and John Collins's *Revolt of the Saints* (2015). Yet, all of these studies struggle to articulate any radical alternatives to racial hierarchy, the same racial hierarchy that is embedded in cultural productions and that reinforces the stereotypes and contradictions of racial democracy.

Chapter 1, "Activating the Sacred," elaborates the historical contexts for Afro-Brazilian ritual. After this contextualization, chapter 2, "Pierre Verger and Yoruba Ritual Altars," deconstructs Verger's preservation of African religious traditions in Brazil from the viewpoint of his "colonial gaze." This chapter touches on issues such as Wole Soyinka's ownership of the plot in *Death and the King's Horseman*; Verger's wrongfully accusation of being a French "spy" in Nigeria; Soyinka's alleged dramatic rescue of Yoruba artifacts from Verger's possession in Brazil; and the critique of Verger's perceived colonial penchant in comparison with other Africana scholars of religious studies. From ritual altars to Candomblé houses, chapter 3, "Matriarchs of Candomblé: Mãe Stella de Oxóssi, Mãe Beata de Yemonjá, and Mãe Valnizia Bianch," argues that these three exemplary Candomblé priestesses serve as vital matriarchal embodiments for the preservation of knowledge in the Afro-Brazilian temples under their care. Through their social-activist agendas and creative works, these matriarchs make an impact on Candomblé and on the world beyond the confines of their immediate sacred space. By analyzing how Afro-Brazilian altars and rituals serve as evidence of the sacred, this section argues that they evidence a continued resistance to the violent instrumentalities of state persecution and an end to religious intolerance and racial inequality.

The second part, which constitutes literary manifestations of the sacred, compares several writers and their representative works. In chapter 4, Jorge Amado's *Mar Morto* (Sea of death) (1933) is compared with Vasconcelos Maia's *O Leque de Oxum* (Osun's mirror) (2006) to articulate the idea of marine power as exercised by the Yemoja and Osun divinities. Chapter 5 compares Abdias Nascimento's *Sortilégio II* (Black sorcery) (1979) and Nelson Rodrigues's *Anjo Negro* (Black angel) (1946) to tease out how Blackness is a subject of ridicule and oppression within the myth of racial democracy. Chapter 6 compares Zoran Seljan's *Três Mulheres de Xangô* (Three wives of Sango) (1978) and Dias Gomes's *O Pagador de Promessas* (Payment as pledged) (1960) to analyze how they reimagine the divinity of Sango (the deity of thunder) through the prisms of feminist solidarity and masculine revenge. Chapter 7 compares Raul Longo's *Filhos de Olorum* (God's children) (2011) with Robson Pinheiro's *Tambores de Angola* (Drums of Angola) (2004) to unveil the secrets of healing and spirituality as embodied in the rites of Candomblé. Finally, chapter 8 examines Cléo Martins and Chynae's invocative representations of Oiá and Oxóssi in *Ao Sabor de Oiá* (To the flavor of Oya) (2003) and *Encantos de Oxóssi* (Enchantments of Oxóssi) (2009) and how they express passionate encounters befitting of their characteristics. Exemplifying the complexities of magical realism, the ritualization of power, the negation of racial democracy, the recuperation of traditional powers of empowerment in the face of racial oppression, and the imperative of justice through regeneration, this entire section examines the struggle to overcome the odds inherent in racial discrimination and religious intolerance and especially the struggle to assert total being without compromising what may be considered a Black aesthetic of affirmation. In sum, the sacred in these literary manifestations is a constant reminder that Afro-Brazilian literary rituals are not ashamed to incorporate African cosmologies and sacredness into their creative endeavors toward sociopolitical liberation and self-affirmation in the New World.

The last section shifts from the literary to the performative and cultural, focusing on blocos afros (Afro-Bahian carnival groups), afoxés (Afro-religious carnival groups), and the significance of acarajé as a sacred offering turned popular and commercial food item in Brazil. In the first part, this study employs a comparative focus to analyze Afro-Brazilian performance groups. Chapter 9 compares Filhos de Gandhi (Children of Gandhi) (1949), an established afoxé, with Cortejo Afro (Afro-Brazilian procession) (1998), a contemporary and emergent bloco afro. Both groups are attached to Candomblé practices, but while the latter manifests a popular expression of spirituality-infused Carnival on the streets, an expression that is devoid of religiosity, Filhos de Gandhi is openly religious. Against this background, this study argues that more established Afro-carnival groups serve as a form of mirroring agency that brings illumination and visibility to marginalized and less visible social groups. In chapter 10, "Give Us This Day Our Daily Acarajé," this study analyzes the effects of relocation and commercialization on traditional sacred food items by comparing the traditional Yoruba bean cake, which is fried in red palm oil, to its variation in Brazil (acarajé), which traveled through the Middle Passage and subsequently served as a ritual offering to Afro-Atlantic deities, such as Exu (Deity of the crossroads), Iasān (Oya, or deity of strong winds and storms), and Xangô (Deity of thunder and fire). By comparing the two sacred food items, this study argues that acarajé has become a hybridized culinary item, one that is now available widely in Brazilian cuisine. This final section highlights cultural manifestations that ordinarily would be repressed by virtue of their connection with prohibited sacred rites. It argues that the outlet for the popularization of the sacred, which is permitted by the performative and the cultural, offers a form of negotiation through this process of hybridization.

However, the question remains: to what extent is the sacred dislocated when the popular is relocated within the popular zone? Covering critical moments of the empowerment of Blacks from the post–military dictatorship era through the end of the Lula presidency, this study examines whether hybridity solves racial tension by proposing in-depth

structural solutions that will bring about radical and permanent equality or whether it simply sweeps racial tension under the rug by giving
social agitators a carnival-like moment to temporarily escape perpetual
afflictions. When the sacred meets the profane, the negotiation of that
encounter conjures the possibility of hope for a better tomorrow. But
is it an affirmation of the transformative change that is urgently and
politically needed? One wonders whether this moment of negotiation is
transient—because the sacred is no longer persecuted like it was during
the nineteenth century—or whether it is a moment of complacency that
submits to the power of co-optation and renders change impossible or just
a dream deferred? These are some of the reflections that the present study's
triangulation of sacredness, ritualization, and hybridization quantifies and
qualifies through its critical analysis of contexts, texts, and comparative
prisms. For a lack of a better expression, it is as if hybridity brings about
an inadvertent praise of a contradiction. Ideally, Afro-Brazilians should
aspire more toward the authenticity of their Africanness than the conscious negotiation of their Brazilianness. But due to an oppressive system,
they are forced to give up their sense of affirmation and subscribe to
a convenient sense of alienation and cordial hybridity. In other words,
this book will be less a facile celebration of hybridity than a critique,
especially in the context of social equality.

Defining Concepts

Given the specific nature of the book as it relates to the intersection
of the sacred and secular, it is useful to define some recurrent concepts.
These are concepts that may not exhaust the topic per se but nonetheless
provide foundational understanding of the ideas that are explored. Sacred
rites are religious rituals, such as baptism, and special remembrance masses
for the saints, such as Christmas and Easter. These rituals also have their
secular, post-Christian celebrations, such as Réveillion and carnival. Ritualizations, meanwhile, are repetitive events that can be either sacred or
secular. The only distinction between rituals and ritualizations is whether
they qualify as "sacred" or "secular." In the context of Afro-Brazilian
cultural expressions, both terms operate intersectionally. Sacred rituals,
which are by nature ritualized, can only be distinguished by the specific
spaces in which they are enacted, such as inside or outside the parameters of the church or shrine. On rare occasions of negotiation between

the sacred and the secular, such as the radical performance of *Missa dos Quilombos* (1982) by Milton Nascimento, which indicts slavery within the sacred space of the Catholic Church, such a negotiation serves as a measure of pacification and reconciliation with Catholicism for past racial injustice and repression of African religiosity. When it comes to popular culture, these multiple dimensions of the sacred and spiritual are inseparable. Melville and Frances Herskovits have noted the tension between Candomblé devotees and the Catholic Church, arguing for the need to cultivate partnerships between American Black intelligentsia and the local press to negate the negative stereotypes associated with the Africa-derived worship. According to these scholars, the dominant classes understood the power of public festivals as a hybrid social structure geared toward controlling public opinion, discourse, and the ultimate meaning of ritualized performative acts. Popular culture was thus a crafty outlet for bottled-up frustrations by marginalized Afro-Brazilian populations.

As multiple cultures come together, there is bound to be some gradual hybridizations or negotiations of identity. For example, David T. Haberly describes the historic formation of Brazil as a negotiation between "the three sad races."[22] Hybridization in this context shares similar properties as hybridity and describes a process of identification that is neither Black nor white but both. Yet, groups fighting for a singular identity beyond the hybrid often feel fragmented, suffocated, and even negated. For example, the poor Black communities of Salvador have resisted and challenged unilateral forms of identity such as the hybrid, which they feel marginalizes the reconstruction of a Black identity that counters the myth of racial democracy (the false racial equality of Gilberto Freyre) and that creates political and economic conditions that make ancestral Africanity or Africanness impossible.[23] Of course, to survive, these groups recuperate and produce African identity through the diacritical signs of religiosity and the popularization of the sacred, such as in carnivalesque manifestations. This leads to the acceptance of an identity that is simultaneously ethnic, flexible, and plural. In a gradual process of challenging and condoning racial democracy and hybridizations, Black cultural producers insist on religious syncretism, while also leveraging for the reclamation of a kind of identity that does not totally submit to erasure but is accommodating only to the degree that total identitarian power is not usurped. In the case of Olodum, accepting whites into parades is critical to economic survival. Meanwhile, the nonacceptance of whites into Ilê Aiyê's carnival parades is an ideological statement and a form of cultural resistance. By its very politics, identity is about power dynamics and influence, especially in a culture as diverse as Brazil, which must assert a sense of control over its existing social hierarchy.

Brazilian identity is thus plagued by the following questions: Who gets to be called "Brazilian"? What benefits accrue to such individuals? What influence do they exercise, and who is marginalized and disenfranchised in the process of appropriating these benefits? Due to the brutal reality of colonization, slavery, and modernization (modernity), which brought about an influx of Europeans as industrial laborers, the formerly enslaved were marginalized in Brazilian society because they were no longer considered competitive. One consequence of such a condition is the necessity to struggle for citizenship once again, which was not effectively reassigned after the abolition of slavery in 1888. Modernity is an era of the appropriation of new economic values and a new economic order, which disenfranchised the ex-slave in favor of new immigrants—namely Europeans and the Japanese. African identity was at once a battle for self-affirmation and a claim for national belonging. In relation to modernity, Africanity or Africanness must be seen as the effort to reclaim an identity that was fragmented during the tortuous period of enslavement. But it is also a radical process of re-Africanization that began in the 1970s. This process of re-Africanization was geared toward self-affirmation, self-esteem, and a sense of humanity and pride to provide a platform for reclaiming civil rights and socioeconomic benefits. In the intersections between the sacred and the profane, Afro-Brazilian entities who were struggling for the recognition of their humanity first had to establish reverence for the Catholic Church, thereby ensuring their own cultural values by creating equivalent power dynamics between Candomblé rites and African divinities, on the one hand, and Catholic saints, on the other. This arduous but ingenious process, which John F. Collins has appropriately termed the "revolt of the saints," is a hybrid and a sign of resilience, as the marginalized groups mobilize for racial equality and social justice.

Because the most resilient Afro-Brazilian cultural productions manifest in the domain of the sacred, such as Candomblé, the sacred has been the central space of affirmation before it transitioned to blocos afros and afoxés, which support the cultural mobilization of performative rituals staged on the streets. This tripartite partnership must be seen as operating interfacially without any contradictions. Candomblé is what Rachel Harding aptly termed an "alternative space of blackness," primarily because other spaces of power and influence have been dominated by white elites. Yoruba divinities are thus revered and yet also humanized, as they represent agencies for unleashing symbolic forces that are equivalent to the dominant political structures. To not have such counter-punctual "alternative spaces" is indeed to be completely disenfranchised in body, mind, and spirit. The power to venerate African divinities translates into the power to heal, manifest, liberate, subvert, and reinvent. It is also an outlet for persisting frustrations, which urgently seek remedy after many years of deprivation and displacement. Performative rituals, whether on the sacred or secular plane, serve to renew lost energies and recuperate memories that are simultaneously traumatic and therapeutic. While these definitions do not claim to be exhaustive, they do provide some working reflections on how the popularization of the sacred is interpreted in this book.

Conclusion: Racial Democracy and Religious Syncretism

While arguments for and against racial democracy have been contentious, there is no denying that racism continues to exist in Brazil. It is no longer sufficient to symbolically celebrate the popularization of African culture in Brazil without also demanding political participation. It is imperative to create social structures that ensure the full access of all races to political power. The quest for an ideal racial democracy is like the struggle for religious tolerance, pluralism, and syncretism.[24] Unfortunately, Brazil has yet to institute equitable parity between African-derived religions, such as Candomblé, and other white-dominated religions, such as Catholicism and Pentecostalism. The pretext of religious syncretism is to claim that all religions have become fused into one and there should be no religious conflict, just as there should be no racial concern within a racial democracy. In Brazil, however, the opposite is the case. Until political and religious leadership can grant access to Afro-Brazilian participation without privileging whites and lighter-skinned individuals, the ideals of racial democracy and religious syncretism will continue to be a myth. Even with the relocation of the sacred into the popular realm, the gains are more commercial than permanently transformative. In this case, syncretism or hybridized religious culture is reduced to consumable symbols during Afro-Catholic festivals and the impact only lasts through the end of the festivities.

This book argues that the resolution of ritual structures and strictures lies in the hybridity engendered by the negotiation of the sacred
and the secular, especially for marginalized Afro-Brazilian groups who
are challenging false claims of racial democracy. By interrogating sacred
rites and the transformation of African divinities into cultural yet resilient hybrid forms—seen in the themes of the indictment of betrayal,
feminine solidarities, revenge, invocative encounters, literary rituals,
and the dualism of hybridity in carnival culture—this book highlights
performance and phenomenology as interlocking drumbeats of tradition
and change. In comparing the sacred, the literary, and the carnivalesque
via such writers and cultural entities as Jorge Amado, Vasconcelos Maia,
Abdias Nascimento, Nelson Rodrigues, Zora Seljan, Dias Gomes, Cléo
Martins, Chnae, Raul Longo, Robinson Pinheiro, Filhos de Gandhi,
Cortejo Afro, Candomblé temples, and other hybridized cultural items,
such as acarajé, this book pushes the boundaries between the sacred, the
literary, the carnivalesque, the cultural, and the performative. Through its
transformational analytical processes, this study opens new interpretative
possibilities for the hybridized resolution of contradictions, even if the
desirable access to political power for the powerless remains ephemeral,
something strongly pined for but not yet guaranteed.

Part I

Mapping the Sacred

Chapter 1

Bahia

Yoruba Diasporic Domain of Activating the Sacred

Historical Contexts

This chapter conceptualizes the potential activating vitality of the sacred within the domain of the Yoruba diaspora of Bahia, Brazil. In the history of the development of the state cultural formation in Brazil, Bahia emerges as the domain of the sacred after colonial times. Bahia is one of twenty-six states that make up Brazil, and it is situated in the eastern part of the Atlantic coast. The fourth most populous Brazilian state after São Paulo, Minas Gerais, and Rio de Janeiro, it is a dazzling gem nestled between the Atlantic Ocean and the Bay of All Saints. Bahia (*baía* or bay) was identified as such by Portuguese explorers. Bahia was the administrative and economic center point for the triangular slave trade since the Portuguese explorer, Pedro Álvares Cabral, landed at what is now Porto Seguro, on the southern coast of Bahia in 1500. Bahia was vital to the sugar economy and necessitated the importation of enslaved Africans. About 40 percent of enslaved Africans were sent to Brazil to work on sugarcane plantations. By 1549, Portugal had established the capital city of Salvador. Bahia thrived on sugar cultivation between the sixteenth and eighteenth centuries, and the city contains several historical towns dating from this era. Bahia remained under the Portuguese Crown for two years after the rest of the country became independent. In addition to Portuguese control, the Dutch also held on to Bahia for a brief period from May 1624 through April 1625. The city and surrounding area served as the administrative and religious capital of Portugal's colonies in the Americas until 1763.

Today, Salvador da Bahia is not only the historical heart of Bahia, but it is also the cultural cradle of Brazil. As the longest political and commercial center of Brazil, it served as the first great port and the first big house of activities. Salvador became the first seat of the court in 1808, as well as the center of many struggles for the independence of Brazil. Bahia was the main educational center of Brazil until the expulsion of the Jesuits following the decline of the exploration of minerals in Minas Gerais. By the end of the eighteenth century, Bahia also became the richest captaincy of the Portuguese empire. Every year on July 2, amidst processions and a carnival-like ambience, the people celebrate the Brazilian victory over the Portuguese in the War of Independence. It is usually a moment when the sacred and the profane come together, including Catholic saints as well as the Afro-Carnival groups, in celebration.

Unique in character, Bahia is visibly African by virtue of its culture and customs, especially through the influence of the Yoruba-derived religious system of Candomblé, the martial art of capoeira, African-derived music such as samba, afoxé, and axé, and the special culinary flavors typical of western Africa.[2] Salvador is the capital of the Brazilian state of Bahia. Close to the size of Texas, the state of Bahia may be said to contain the roots of the Brazilian nation. No wonder it is the birthplace of beloved Brazilian musicians like Dorival Caymmi, Gilberto Gil, Daniela Mercury, Ivete Sangalo, Carlinhos Brown, and Caetano Veloso and his sister Maria Bethânia. Bahia is also home to famed international Afro-Carnival groups like Filhos de Gandhi, Olodum, Ara Ketu, and Ilê Aiyê. Bahian geographical regions include the *mata atlântica*, or remnants of the Atlantic coast forests; the recôncavo region, radiating from the bay; the site of sugar and tobacco cultivation; and the planalto, which includes the fabled sertão region of Bahia's far interior. Brazil's second-longest river system, the São Francisco, runs from the Atlantic along the state's northern border and down into the neighboring southern state of Minas Gerais. Bahia is the main producer of cacao in Brazil and has a significant amount of mineral and petroleum deposits. The tourism industry also thrives in Bahia, given its long coastline with beautiful beaches and cultural treasures that attract many tourists. Other cities of note include Ilhéus, the birthplace of Jorge Amado, one of Brazil's major twentieth-century writers; the old island city of Itaparica, on the island of the same name in the bay; Cachoeira; Vitória da Conquista; and Lençóis, in the Chapada Diamantina region.

Overall, Bahia showcases its African influences in many areas. Whether it is in African-inspired creative clothing styles, such as agbada (Yoruba garb); dance-fight-entertainment expressive culture, such as capoeira (which originates from Angola); food that reminds one of Yoruba/African culinary tastes, such as acarajé; the baianas (ladies in hybridized Candomblé attires) offering photo opportunities to tourists in Pelourinho; festivals that venerate the deities, such as homages to Yemoja (Yoruba sea goddess); artistic works adorning commercial buildings, such as the Orixá Center, Ogunjá building, Oxumare house (among many others); and the celebration of many African divinities in a hybrid frame during Afro-Bahian carnival—all are ample testimony of the lively influence of Africa on all aspects of the Brazilian way of life.[3] Yet, is it enough to see these sacred images on the streets as a testament to the conscious admixture of the sacred and the profane, normalizing the sacred within the popular, without any sense of shock and contradiction? How exactly has the sacred been normalized and hybridized? What are the historical processes that have occasioned these transformations? From the viewpoint of ideological agitation, cultural resistance, and political change, what is the strategic collaboration between ideology and social practice when it comes to a pragmatic negotiation with the state tourist industry? Why has the domain of the sacred morphed, even dialectically, into that of the popular? Such are the questions to which this book, *Relocating the Sacred*, seeks cogent answers.

Salvador da Bahia is often referenced as the African Brazil. The capital city of Bahia, and also the former capital of Brazil through the eighteenth century, Salvador da Bahia sits on the cliffs of the All Saints' Bay, which is a beautiful sight to behold in the Northeast coastal line that covers more than four hundred square miles. After Lisbon, Salvador was considered the most significant city of the Portuguese empire during the colonial era. The primary colonial resources include sugarcane and tobacco. In addition, the flavor of Africa is all over the city, including cultural expressions such as capoeira and the Africa-derived religion of Candomblé that is often fused into carnival, not to mention the gastronomy that equally embraces culinary items from Africa, such as manioc flour, fish, spices, and palm oil. Pelourinho in the upper city and the Mercado Modelo in the lower city, which are easily accessed through the

Lacerda Elevator, are two major cultural centers that retain contemporary manifestations of a colonial structure that still maintain its sacredness by virtue of the surrounding baroque churches as well as enduring cultural events that keep the mixed aroma of the city very lively.

Colonial Foundations

One cannot fully appreciate the implications of the relocation of sacred in the popular domain without understanding the historical foundations of the Bahian state, with its economic and cultural tapestries that collectively energized the creation of a unique multicultural society. Rex Nettleford, a Caribbean scholar, once stated that any society based on festivities or celebrations alone is bound to be shallow.[4] Likewise, Ian Strahan, a Bahamian critic, argues for the interconnectedness of the plantation and paradise, as Bahia is a society founded on a plantation economy but that generates income based on tourism that is marketed to the rest of the world as "paradise." In both articulations, the critique of hedonism as opposed to rationality is meant to generate some sense of discomfort for the plight of millions, whose lives are attached to the production of pleasure at the cost of their minds and souls as they joyfully lay claim to a piece of the pie that is afforded them once a year, in the case of carnival. On the basis of this contradictory life of the oppressed, it is good to gain insights into Bahian history to better understand how the current state of intersecting divinities and festivities, as a duality of resistance and conformity, is the consequence of a coping outlet or strategy in the face of bottled-up frustrations felt by the Afro-Brazilian populations throughout the year. Aligned with a year-round veneration of Catholic saints and hybridized African deities, these ritualizations that take on new meanings for the people, the town, and the state.

The notion of the popularization of the sacred may well be a twentieth-century phenomenon because Catholicism dominated most of the colonial era when it comes to official religious worship. Anything other than Catholic was resisted and repressed, including Candomblé, capoeira, and samba. In other words, what today is considered worthy of celebration and is marketable and exploitable to tourists, was once considered taboo because it went against the sanctity of religious exclusivity. African influence was meant to be limited to slave labor and not in competition with the Portuguese value system. This was not unique to Bahia but was true in all of Brazil. The colonial history of Bahia is well integrated with that of Brazil because Bahia was the nation's first capital. Bahia is claimed to have been "discovered" with the arrival of the Portuguese in 1500, where, in Porto Seguro (southern Bahia), they celebrated the first mass in Coroa Vermelha, as led by Henrique Soares of Coimbra. The actual state of Bahia was then populated, even though it had been occupied by indigenous nations for thousands of years.

The first governor-general, Tomé de Sousa, founded the city of Salvador in 1549, which became the first capital of Brazil. The demand for slave labor brought an African population that greatly influenced the cultural formations of Bahian society. This incident would set the stage for future African influence on all aspects of Brazilian society, especially in the religious sphere. A twelve-year series of wars between Spain and the United Kingdom led to the Dutch attempt to take over the colonial sugar plantation economy, which was then still under the control of the Spanish Crown. Because Salvador was a strategic location, the Dutch sent a well-armed fleet to All Saints' Bay and defeated the Portuguese in 1625, leading the governor of the captaincy, Diogo Luís de Oliveira, to build the Fort of the Morro de São Paulo to protect Bahia against invaders. For this reason, Bahia was noted as a site of resistance in the colonial era. Despite several attempts by the Dutch and the Portuguese to gain control of Bahia, there were many social movements that resisted such efforts, such as the Tailors' Revolt of 1798 and the War of the Canudos in 1897 (fought between Republicans and the Sertanejos, as led by Antônio Conselheiro). Despite the wars, economic activities were rampant in the hinterlands, as well as on the coast of Bahia.

Bahian Sacredness

At one point, many Brazilian pop musicians have paid homage to Bahia as a sacred place of raising consciousness after a creative peregrination. For these musicians, Bahia stands as a symbol of the land of happiness. Whether it is Caetano Veloso, Gerônimo, Gilberto Gil, Maria Bethania, Carlinhos Brown, Ivete Sangalo, Margaret Menezes, or Daniela Mercury, the "Canto da Cidade" (Chant of the city) results in a certain inexplicable, transcendental, or genuine love for the city of Salvador. In "Céu da Bahia" (Bahian heavenly skies), for example, Caetano celebrates not only all the saints of Salvador but the icons of local color, such as

the memory of Mãe Menininha do Gantois (Candomblé), the culinary
palette, the breeze of the Ondina Sea, the nocturnal and romantic
moon in the works of Jorge Amado, the peace announced by the feast
of the Lord of Good End, and the warmth of the carnival procession
that ultimately makes the musical voice so passionate and appreciative
of the figurative taste of an edenic apple that Bahia represents.[5] While
Caetano celebrates the flora and fauna of Bahia as a place that makes
him feel in complete harmony with nature in all its senses, Daniela
Mercury invokes the metaphoric location of Salvador as a beautiful
zone to behold all that is beautiful and filled with Black pride. She not
only speaks for the millions who feel oppressed and marginalized, but
she also reassures them that the same location is filled with love and
should ultimately bring about the neutralization of negative forces. For
Gerônimo, meanwhile, the lyrics of "É d'Oxum" (Everyone belongs to
Oxum) reassure us that "the energy that lives in the sea / makes no
distinction of colors / and all the city belongs to Oxum."[6] Such are the
spontaneities of the Salvadorian soul that the voices of Caetano Veloso,
Daniela Mercury, and Gerônimo reverberate in their respective songs—a
testament to the vivid sacredness of the city of Salvador.

It is not by chance that yearly the tourist industry in Bahia invokes
the "cycle of festivals" that pays homage to the divinities, such as the
Festa de Iemojá (Yemoja's feast), Lavagem do Bomfim (Good End's feast),
Festa de Santa Bárbara (Santa Bárbara's feast), Festa de São João (Saint
John's feast), Festa Junina (Junine feast), Festa Natalina (Christmas feast),
Festa de Oxum (Oxum's feast), Festa de Xango (Xango's feast), and Festa
da Irmandade da Boa Morte (Sisterhood of Good Death's feast), among
others.[7] Taken as an ensemble of sacred rites, these ceremonies celebrate
divinities or Catholic saints that have been hybridized due to religious
syncretism. As such, they become moments when even profane or secular entities, such as Afro-Carnival groups (blocos afros and afoxés) and
capoeira groups, participate as a sign of solidarity for enduring statehood.
However, the sacredness goes beyond tourism; it is a process of negotiation in which the tourism industry invests in the sign of the African in
the hybridized Brazilian identity in exchange for which African-derived
cultural and religious expressions willingly participate in their alternative
visibility in a social structure that has hitherto repressed African agency
and articulation for centuries. The re-Africanization processes that over-
took Salvador in the 1970s continue to add value to the emergence of
a new order among Brazilian sacred institutions, such as Candomblé,

capoeira, and samba, among others.[8] In sum, the sacred possesses the power of transgression against any limitation that may be posed by the profane structures in which the official government operates. The official structure is strategically manipulated to dance with the sacred and vice versa. Omari-Tunkara calls this "manipulating the sacred" and theorizes the primacy of ritual and resistance without any contradiction.[9] Ironically, such negotiations between the producers of culture and blaxploiters of culture (such as the tourism agencies) ultimately benefits the owners of culture, as it is the hybridized cultural expression that is ultimately preserved for posterity.

Though a historic cultural landmark of culture and industry, Sisterhood of Good Death was originally a Catholic procession.[10] In the last four decades (1970–2010), it has been developed more as a significant sociocultural element to improve the economic infrastructure of Bahian touristic industry. This double-edged position further encourages the diversification and popularization of the sacred rite within the profane. Thus, a major regional sacred procession (primarily Catholic with ethnic incursions) suddenly becomes commercialized with the presence of musicians and performers playing to the ambience of feast and merrymaking that ultimately overtakes the event. In its full essence, the Sisterhood of Our Lady of Good Death is a relatively small Afro-Catholic religious group that was founded in the early nineteenth century and reserved for female African slaves and ex-slaves. It originally had close to two hundred women members during its peak, but that number has been reduced to about thirty members who are all over fifty years old. The festival takes place in mid-August every year, attracting devotees of Candomblé from all over Brazil as well as international tourists and researchers. The history of the religious confraternity that pays homage to the Virgin Mary also intersects with the history of enslavement of Africans in the northeastern coast of Bahia. To fulfill their exploitative economic mission, the Portuguese built many commercial towns, such as Cachoeira, which was one of the most economically prosperous towns in Bahia for more than three centuries.

Studies by IPAC (2011), Cheryl Sterling (2012), and Joanice Santos Conceição (2012) all provide compelling perspectives through which the idea of death could be celebrated, subverted, and reinvented as a form of carnivalization of the sacred.[11] Regardless of how each critic presents their arguments—how the Feast of Good Death is a community celebration, how ritual is a form of transcendentalism through which power is consolidated by Afro-Brazilians, and how, through the synergistic duality of life and death, Brazilian burial rites serve as unique spaces for female political engagement with identity—they collectively reinforce the significance of the festival as a true performance of the integration and hybridization of Catholicism and Candomblé. Like the other festivities under consideration in this book, the Sisterhood of Good Death has succeeded in fulfilling the tripartite function of preserving, reinventing, and reinterpreting African value systems, especially with regard to burial rites and the strategic communication between the living and the ancestral. Of course, with the investment of the tourist industry in the economic revitalization of Bahia, one of the unintended consequences of such a partnership is that the Sisterhood of Good Death has been compromised in its sacredness by virtue of the necessity to be open to profanization and being visibly co-opted through the media and the enthusiastic tourists who participate annually in the sacred-profane festivity.

Dialectics of the Sacred and the Profane

Mircea Eliade's The Sacred and the Profane (1987) has revolutionized the way we approach the world. For some, the world is either sacred or profane. For others, it is a mix of both. Eliade's arguments ruminate on issues of the human experience as they relate to the realities of religious rituals, space, time, nature, and memory. To be sacred is to be in alignment with godly and divine values, while to be profane is to stand in opposition to the sacred or in moral bankruptcy. Yet, such absolutism is contrary to the reality of the world, where the sacred and the profane coexist, as they both grapple with the world of regeneration, for example, as presented during the inversion moments of carnival. For example, the idea of offering sacrifices itself is marked by contradiction. If the world is perfect and essentially divine, why is there a need for atonement after the transgression of the godly? Traditional societies, such as the Yoruba, or the African world more broadly, do not make these distinctions. In the realm of the spirit, the sacred and the profane are constantly in a dancelike state—a tango perhaps—in which what is sacred can easily have its profane moments. Rituals and ceremonies are offered as a process of bloodletting, life-giving, and life-taking, and this process assumes that through bloodshed there is atonement. Pilgrims are often taken to sacred groves or spaces to offer sacrifices or bathe in sacred waters for

the sake of healing or renewal of power. In this respect, the insistence
on dichotomies and binaries is rather superfluous and rigid. The Bahian
experience offers a hybrid manipulation of the sacred and the profane
in the example of the "Bênção" event when Catholic devotees leave
the Catholic mass to begin a profane celebration one block from the
Catholic Church.[12] To illustrate the profane restructuring the ritually
sacred Bahian world, I would like to examine a few Bahian feasts, such
as Festa de Iemojá and Festa de Santa Bárbara.

Festa de Iemojá takes place in Rio Vermelho (Salvador da Bahia)
every year on February 22. The deity Yemoja is associated with gentleness,
sympathy, affection, and generosity. My first glimpse of this magnificent
festival was in 1983. Yemoja's Feast was less tourist-oriented then (as
compared to today when the media turns it into a circus) and more of
a gathering of devotees of Yemoja, who go to the riverside to present
their gifts and celebrate her.[13] From the viewpoint of religious syncretism,
this riverine orixá is the equivalent of the Virgin Mary. She originates
from the Yoruba pantheon, where her name means "yeye-omo-eja" (or
"Mother Fish"), and in the profane world she is often referred to as a
mermaid. Mostly attired in white and blue, her followers gather with
elaborate bouquets of flowers, packaged to be dropped in the sea in her
honor. Some venture further into the middle of the ocean with small
boats, and the experience could only be described as magical and riveting. Yemoja's Feast is elaborate and spectacular and takes on a whole
new meaning for the Bahian community on the festive date. The entire
community is celebrating a powerful sea mother and goddess who has
been celebrated in many Bahian songs and literature, including *Mar
Morto* (Sea of death) by Jorge Amado. Unlike in the Yorubaland, where
Yemoja has a specific location for worship, such as in Abeokuta, in Brazil,
Yemoja is among several orixás assembled in the terreiro (temple), or
Candomblé house. This means that this divinity is worshipped all over
Brazil, even if the dates vary (some states celebrate Yemoja on January
1). The contention between the Virgin Mary and Yemoja arose during
the colonial era, when the Portuguese insisted on imposing Catholicism
on the population. Since the abolition of slavery in 1888, devotees of
both Yemoja and Candomblé were able to identify similar characteristics
between the Virgin Mary and Yemoja, which led to what today is called
"religious syncretism." Gradually, the ceremonies that were once secret
and prohibited became public and popular. Today in Brazil, the Yemoja
who is venerated is no longer the "pure" Virgin Mary, even though

her image is part of the procession. Instead, it is a hybrid divinity that shares elements of Catholicism and the Yoruba belief system. Yemoja is generally believed to protect her devotees from all harm and danger, ensuring they have good fish-catching seasons and a happy family life. In sum, to pay homage to Yemoja is to appease her so that life in general becomes more livable and enjoyable.

The rituals and ceremonies for Yemoja signal all the feelings of a mini-carnival. On the festive day, the festive atmosphere along the beach is coupled with dancing and singing and the procession of the image of the Virgin Mary. The eve of the celebration is usually attended with a splash of fireworks that beautifully color the skies and announce the arrival of the festivity the following day. Offerings like Yemoja statutes, perfume, mirrors, combs, soap, and champagne are put inside miniature boats and sent off into the sea along with flowers. Some devotees simply leave their gifts on the beach, while others make altars on the beach, accompanied by singing and dancing. It is believed that if the waves carry the flowers left on the beach into the sea, Yemoja will bless the devotees with prosperity. Scholars such as Elizabeth Isichei argue that, beyond the Afro-Catholic dynamics of Yemoja in Brazil, the cultural roots of Yemoja can be difficult to trace. One variant of Yemoja, Mami Wata of the Igbos of eastern Nigeria, signals the contradictions of African divinities. The same community that venerates this divinity may also dread her, for "some devotees consider Mami Wata a Christian, and many Christians are considered a demon."[14] She concludes that Mami Wata is the result of cultural hybridity and the profanation of the sacred. Cheryl Sterling further highlights the intersectionality between the sacred and the secular, asserting that "the sacred aspects of the ritual occur in the early portion of the day, and as the day progresses the secular aspects of the celebration dominate. By nightfall, all facets of the ritual give way to carnivalesque revelry."[15] By contrast, Yemoja's Feast rallies its devotees around the beach and the sea, while for Saint Barbara's Feast, noted for its devotees dressed in red and white, devotees congregate around Pelourinho and the fire station headquarters in Baixa de Sapateiros in the lower city.

Saint Barbara's Feast takes place on December 4. The syncretic name is Santa Bárbara, while the traditional Yoruba name is Iyasan (Iansã), meaning "nine times a mother" or the "curing mother." Her characteristic personality traits include being ambitious, affectionate, mystical, temperamental, and exuberant. On the day of festivity, the procession starts in front of the church of Nossa Senhora do Rosário dos Pretos in Pelourinho, then passes through the historical center, stopping at the main fire station and the Mercado de Santa Bárbara, where free carurú (a Brazilian dish made from okra, onion, shrimp, palm oil, and toasted nuts) is enjoyed by everyone. The IPAC notebook series, especially the fifth edition dedicated to her, *Festa de Santa Bárbara* (2010), contains six articles and an introduction by Ubiratan Castro Araújo. One describes her iconographic image as a Black woman dressed in red and white, just as the daughters of the saint are dressed during sacred rites in Candomblé.[16] Two other articles, "The Cult of Saint Barbara in Bahia" by Nívea Alves dos Santos and "The Saint Barbara's Feast in Pelourinho" by Carla Bahia, offer compelling overviews of the feast. Santos suggests that it is the Saint Barbara's Feast that opens what is called the "Cycle of Festivals" in December, with its red and white colors sparkling throughout the city of Salvador: "During the whole day these colors become mixed together, animating such spaces as the Historic Center of Salvador and the Liberdade community, locations that the homage to the saint is usually more prominently observed."[17] The procession of Saint Barbara's Feast is a beautiful one to behold, and Carla Bahia describes this procession thus:

> Following the second service, thousands of people in the square return to the Chapel of Black Rosary in the hopes of joining the outing. The faith in one singular female warrior, has its origin in the historic procession and dates back to the colonial times when Yoruba deities and Catholic saints were hybridized. While some people still distinguish between the two religious figures, devotees still participate in the festivity with the mindset of honoring Iansã on the day of celebrating Santa Bárbara.[18]

This overview of the typical day of Saint Barbara's Feast provides a good context for the following analysis of O *Pagador de Promessas* (Journey to Bahia) (1987), a play by Dias Gomes that addresses the issue of religious syncretism and intolerance.

Ritual Structures and Strictures

Gomes's O *Pagador de Promessas* is a classical case study of how the sacred conflicts with the secular and how the two must be essentially hybridized. O *pagador de promessas* narrates the drama of a rural devotee, Zé do

Burro, who journeys seven kilometers while carrying an enormous cross, as promised, to the Church of Saint Barbara in Salvador. Reluctantly accompanied by his wife, Zé do Burro arrives at the church at dawn, and the couple wait for it to open. Zé's promise was made on behalf of Nicolau, Zé's donkey, from which the protagonist derives his name. As the church opens, Zé quickly explains his dilemma to the priest who not only refuses the protagonist entrance to the church to fulfill his promise but also accuses him of pretending to be Jesus based on the similarity between Zé's actions and the Via Crucis (completing the way of the cross to be crucified symbolically), as well as because Zé's promise was to Iansã and not to Santa Bárbara. With time, other characters complicate the plot by interfering with the evolving tragic action. Essentially, most of Gomes's characters are opportunists, especially the sensationalist and manipulative reporter who distorts most of the pronouncements of Zé. Beyond the local color of capoeira players and the acarajé seller-cum-baiana (Minha Tia), and beyond the side triangular "romantic" conflicts between Bonitão, Rosa, and Marli, there is an overwhelming conflict between Padre Olavo and Zé. What I read as "ritual structures and strictures" is embedded within this religious tension that Dias Gomes accentuates to call attention to religious intolerance as well as the need for religious syncretism or hybridity, as in a defining moment of disagreement between the protagonist and antagonist:

> JOE: The church in the fields didn't own an image of Santa Barbara, but the "candomblé" had this image of Iansan.

> FATHER: (*Finally exploding*) Santa Barbara is a Catholic saint! Iansan is a fetichist, African divinity! In Colonial times, slaves had to feign worshipping Catholic saints to avoid being whipped by their masters. So they boldly identified their deities with our saints. Iansan is not Santa Barbara. I tell you! You have invoked a false divinity! It was to Iansan, not to Santa Barbara that you made your promise![19]

This intense confrontation between the priest and the devotee provides a compelling demarcation between two schools of thought that should ordinarily be reconciled from the viewpoint of long-term process of hybridizations.

The Catholic Church represents its own codes of behavior that are better captured in "strictures" that have been preestablished by the Catholic faith and conventions. Padre Olavo's arguments are clear when it comes to the distinction between making a vow to Iansan (considered a "pagan" deity by the Church) and making a vow to Santa Barbara, a Catholic saint. Only the latter is accepted by Padre Olavo, as only one who makes a vow to Santa Barbara can be allowed into the Church. A ritual structure speaks to the ongoing conventions in the present in terms of shifting and adaptive structures, where religious syncretism must be given primordial consideration. The fact that Zé made his vow at a Candomblé house makes no difference to him because he considers both to be the same thing. What matters to him is fulfilling his vow, but this is not as simple for Padre Olavo. In the final analysis, faith is in the eye and mind of the beholder.

The playwright, Dias Gomes, raises the issue of free will in his "Author's Note" when he asserts: "*O Pagador de Promessas* is the story of a man who resisted compromise and was destroyed. Its central theme is that of the myth of capitalist freedom. Based on the principle of freedom of choice, the bourgeois society does not allow the individual the necessary means to exercise this freedom; thus making such liberty rather illusory."[20] The solidarity enacted by the community to help Zé fulfill his promise postmortem is considered a deliberate act of resistance, protest, and agency; yet the question remains why the protagonist must lose his life to effect change. In other words, he is compelled to be a hero (that is, a sacrificial lamb) to purge the society of its intransigence and transgression. Fulfilling a promise through death signals that nothing is facile in the community and a radical or tragic action is expected to effect change. But why must this be so? The stricture on structure ceases to be a positive posture but a negation that must be confronted with another negation to make the balance positive. Zé's transgression against the powerful Catholic Church is not self-willed but an imposition that he feels must be subverted for him to be at peace with himself. As Zé puts it frankly: "A promise is a promise. It is like business."

In his interesting study that maps urban violence in Latin America, and especially in Brazil, João Cezar de Castro Rocha amply notes how the dialectics of marginality might as well be the order of the day, from Carolina Maria de Jesus's *Quarto de Despejo* through the predicament of Zé-do-Burro in O *Pagador de Promessas*, up until the drama of Zé Pequeno

in *Cidade de Deus*.[21] Within this marginal life that the favela (slum) life
provides, where violence tries the patience of Brazilians, one can easily
appreciate why the sacred and the secular cannot possibly be separated.
To the extent that life imitates art and vice versa, much of the sanctity of
sacredness that the rural entity possesses is easily and brutally dismantled
while the individual is inevitably initiated into brutal violence to survive.
Zé is both a victim and a willing participant in this urban violence, for
he could not possibly return to the interior without fulfilling his vow. He
feels a sense of duty and honor to fulfill his promise—at any cost and by
any means. The sacred in this context is the value system that has been
truncated by the experience of hardship and poverty, only to be hardened
in the secular so that the effort to even hybridize it is equally truncated
by the reality of deprivation, such that all that can even be hoped for,
all that can be thought feasible, is the persistence and predicament of
violence. The prologue to *O Pagador de Promessas* offers a rare window
into the preponderance of evidence of ritual structure, albeit devoid of
the stricture that the Catholic Church represents:

> A scrim curtain. Beyond it, a "candomblé" terreiro," where
> Afro-Brazilian rituals are performed, in the interior of Bahia . . .
> The terreiro is a large shed or tent, festooned with paper gar-
> lands and white and red flags. To the left, a small plank utilized
> by the musicians; three "atabaque" players, one of "agogo," of
> "abge," and one of "adja." . . . In foreground, at right, is the
> "peji" a small altar with an image of "Santa Barbara" conspic-
> uously placed upon it. . . . In the rear; silhouettes of dancers
> move to the sounds of the exotic instruments, now quite low.[22]

Even in this description of the foregrounded stage, the "sacred," as in
Santa Barbara's image, comingles with the "profane" Afro-Brazilian ritual
symbols of music and performers. It is only by subjecting the racist biases
to critical analysis that what is perceived as sacred or profane becomes
all relative and problematic.

Bahia and the "Profanation" of the Sacred

The distinction made by cultural sociologists between secularization and
profanation assists us in better appreciating the dynamics of cultural syn-

thesis that many years of interactions between the strictly religious and the subliminally popular have come to be the norm in Bahia. Eduardo de la Fuente (2013) and Andreas Schneider et al. (2013) help us perform a critical literature review of select works that have been written in the last sixty years regarding how the sacred has been manipulated by the secular or the profane. In invoking the works of Emile Durkheim, Daniel Bell, and Max Weber, Fuente opens a controversial can of worms when it comes to cultural sociology. In more specific terms, the critic asserts that modern culture is neither rational nor secular but motivated by what Bell terms the "great profanation." Fuente raises a number of issues that further accentuates Bell's thesis that "all human culture has a religious or sacred quality if it is to have that quality we term cultural," namely: (1) because cultures and civilizations rise and fall, it is imperative to reject "seductive" formulations but rather embrace complex and empirically contestable sociological arguments; (2) sociology should strive to function between the sciences and the humanities; (3) all human culture should have a religious or sacred quality to have a cultural quality; (4) religion is one of the fundamental limitations to appreciating the human construction of humanity; (5) Durkheim's distinction between "sacred" and "profane" is rewarding for the argument that culture must not lose its animating spirit or become profane; and (6) Bell forecasts that human desire for transcendence may not easily be achieved despite the need for reviving moralizing, redemptive, and mythical gestures.[23]

While Bell resists the profanation of the sacred, Schneider et al. insist the "sacred" is culture specific and thus analyses of it must take into consideration cultural dynamics and identitarian variations across the globe. In the case of Bahia, the probability that the sacred will become profane is nil. Rather, the secularization of the sacred is in fact the agency that popularizes the sacred in the daily or festive life of the people. In addition, the distinction between the secular and the profane is rather superfluous, for what concerns Afro-Bahian producers of culture is more about activating demands for racial justice and equality through performative rituals than a concern for specificities of terminologies and semantics. The dialectical world of Bahian sacred and profane social encounters neutralizes those subtle differentiations, and the goal in these cultural interactions is reaching a zone of contact, dissolution, and hybridization.

Several critical and creative works offer multiple perspectives from which to glimpse the complementariness of the sacred and the profane, especially in a society where both are inseparable from an intersectional way of life. For the sake of facilitation, I have grouped the literature review into the sacred-sociological, on the one hand, and the sacred-imaginative, on the other, to distinguish from the strictly critical qua critical and the creative imagination.

By the sacred-sociological, I refer to works such as Ordep Serra's *Rumores da Festa: O Sagrado e o Profano na Bahia* (2009), Rachel Harding's *A Refuge in Thunder* (2000), Cheryl Sterling's *African Roots, Brazilian Rites* (2012), Anadelia A. Romo's *Brazil's Living Museum* (2010), and John F. Collins's *Revolt of the Saints* (2015), where the thesis of sacredness ultimately intersects with the secular or profane to produce affirmations that are at once sacred, profane, and political in different degrees and depths. Serra, for example, performs a persuasive archeology of the Afro-Catholic nature of Bahian feasts that are associated with the cycle of festivals, blocos afros, and blocos do índio, which, he argues, escaped the limited categorization of Roberto DaMatta because he does not consider the public and private nature of Bahian rituals. Harding, meanwhile, theorizes the power of Candomblé to activate religious rites as one of the alternative spaces of Blackness, where Afro-Brazilians could interact with other sacred-cultural groups, such as Catholic confraternities, dance groups, and fugitive slave communities to create a formidable entity to confront master-slave tensions. It takes the multifocal perspective of Sterling to bring into unison the disparate configurations of ritual, performance, and marginality that are embedded in carnival, Candomblé, Quilombhoje (creative imagination), and hip-hop dynamics. The invention of Bahia as Brazil's "living museum" by Romo articulates the most empowering historical and cultural analysis of multifaceted Afro-Brazil and culminates in reinventing African traditions and the politics of such a resistant positioning. Collins, meanwhile, moves the cultural to the realm of the political, and he raises cogent questions about the contradictions of Brazilian multiculturalism, racial democracy, and cultural patrimony that turns a space such as Pelourinho into a square deprived of the agency of the tormented yet absent souls who sacrificed to build it. From this perspective, the sacred as represented in the baroque churches in Pelourinho, is profanized by the many secular ceremonies and festivities held in their foreground every year.

The visually performative often obscures written ethnography due to the immediacy of the visual. It takes the written works of scholars, devotees, and travelogues to counter such tendency in academic circles.

The sacred-imaginative domain is diverse, but the sampling of a half dozen works provides a window into the world of Candomblé as it is interpreted by sociologists, anthropologists, and creative writers. The centrality of Candomblé in Bahian culture—through its abstraction in public places—serves as a strategic measure to promote respectability for a hybridized religion that American anthropologists, such as Ruth Landes, Melville Herskovitz, and Donald Pierson, coupled with their French counterparts, such as Roger Bastide and Pierre Verger, argue is an instructive reminder that, when embedded in religion, the sacred ceases to be perceived as "pagan" or "exotic." Mattijs van de Port's illuminating study, *Ecstatic Encounters* (2011), further relativizes the "cultural" in the religious sphere when she asserts: "The proliferation of Candomblé's expressive forms in the public sphere thus took off under the guise of 'Bahian popular culture,' Bahian folklore and the cultural heritage of Bahia."[24] Along these lines, studies such as Ruth Landes's *City of Women* (1947), Sousa Junior's *Na Palma da Minha Mão* (2011), Altair B. Oliveira's *Cantando para os Orixás* (2004), Simone Saueressig's *A Estrela de Iemanjá* (2009), Reginaldo Prandi's *Mitologia dos Orixás* (2001), and Pierre Verger's *Orixás* (2002 [1981]), popularize ritual strictures by facilitating access to its hitherto secretive world.

Landes aptly conceptualizes Salvador da Bahia as the "city of women" based on her own ethnographic and imaginative rendering of the city steeped in the tradition of Candomblé. Her method of allowing the knowledge producers themselves to speak of their experience as collectors, critics, and observers gives a dose of authenticity to her narrative encounters. A touching example is when two elders, Seu Manuel and Edison Carneiro, engage in an invocation of memories about African traditions that have now been transformed into Afro-Brazilian rites. What is more startling is the racist undertone that was still permissive in the 1949 context that the book was published: "Well, North Americans think in terms of race. A black man is inferior to a white man because of his race." "What about the black man's culture?" "That doesn't matter. A black man isn't supposed to have any of his own, only what he gets from whites; and that he is supposed to hide."[25] It is remarkable that these stereotypes are being recycled from the very mouths of Afro-Brazilians as a pretext to shift blame from the ethnographer. Yet, one must not miss the irony intended by local anthropologists as they subject North American racism to scrutiny in Brazil. If the method is already contested, where race alone is used to reject the validity of a people that should have included roles of cultural practices and the central role of women in the spirit possession, among others, the outcomes may well be contested as well. But Landes was a sensitive ethnographer who allowed the cultural producers to articulate their views without any sense of reservation.

The remaining studies coalesce in the praise and documentation of the orixás, with incursions into their temperaments, complexities, and individualities. Sousa Junior argues that Candomblé not only articulates Afro-Brazilian ancestrality but provides the ideal space for the development of citizenship. The themes engaged vary from the modernity of Candomblé, economy of the city, sacrifice in Afro-Brazilian religions, issues of health, case studies of Oya and Yemoja, and the leadership of women in the sacred rites as a testament that women play a central role in Candomblé. Many of the activities described embody the divine in all its manifestations. Oliveira and Saueressig's narratives, about singing for the orixás and the power of symbolism for protagonists navigating the seas to discover the secrets of Yemoja, further attest to the uplifting nature of the orixás, especially when appropriated and venerated as a source of ancestral empowerment and pride. Though written from different ethnographic and ideological perspectives, the notion of "mythology" invoked by Prando to describe the *orikis*, or the orixás, and Verger's visual iconicity, which also derives from passionate observation of sacred rites, are powerful prisms through which to document an ancestral continuum that is threatened by the passage of time and the continued intolerance and subtle persecutions that remain camouflaged in Brazilian society. Whether it is from within or from without, the celebration of Candomblé comes with a dose of sacrificial profanation as devotees are exposed to other external cultural manifestations that often dialogue with the sacred by way of musical or performative expressions, such as when devotees are simultaneously members of a capoeira academy or are members of Afro-Carnival groups. Such overlapping affiliations become mutually reinforcing such that the intersection between the sacred and the secular becomes only second nature and ultimately fulfilling.

In Bahia, no other festivity thrives better in terms of the architecture of the sacred and the profane than Afro-Bahian carnival. Sterling's study is more optimistic than mine in terms of the resolution of co-optation in the process of advancing community struggles during carnival.[26] She invokes the stakes for two of the most visible Afro-Carnival groups, Ilê Aiyê and Olodum: "This is part of the journey from empowerment to power, for that symbolic capital provides the nurturing and affirmation necessary to continue the actual struggle against an asymmetrical social and political order."[27] Yet the political strategy differs for blocos afros and afoxés in the sense that there is a difference among each organization's ideological commitment to Black struggles. Some, like Olodum, have become complacent, commercialized, and fully hybridized relative to whatever incentives they could negotiate with the state and the tourist industry. Others, like Ilê Aiyê, insist on working out such negotiations on their own terms.

Comparative studies, such as Angela Schaun's *Práticas Edu-comunicativas* (2002) and Kwame Dixon's *Afro-Politics and Civil Society in Salvador da Bahia, Brazil* (2016), debate the extent to which the Brazilian Black movement has embraced culturalism as a weapon of the strong by realizing that culture is politics, and politics is culture. While Schaun proposes an interfacial agency as a prism through which to understand the fluidity of politics and economics, she theorizes the generative and transformative nature of politics that must be incorporated within communicative channels that have the potential to develop and empower the communities.[28] On a broader scale of analysis, Kwame Dixon offers the field a somewhat missing link to Salvador da Bahia as a neglected "specialization" in its own rights. Astutely weaving the historical foundations with contemporary cultural politics that involves racial politics, education, affirmative action, and citizenship, Dixon identifies a seven-point agenda that Afro-social movements have determined to be inalienable for the racial equality mission. Of these set objectives, I find one quite engrossing: "Reposition the states' and civil society's views on racial inequality and force the state to recognize that it (racial inequality) is a legitimate political and social issue."[29] While Dixon is less concerned with the sacred and its impact on local politics, he confirms that there is a correlation between the emergence of a "new racial politics" and the mobilization of Afro-social movements that were hitherto neglected, such as the Candomblé devotees and Afro-Carnival groups. Though the carnival groups often timidly deny the connections between the sacred and the profane, the sociopolitical reality proves otherwise.

Afro-Carnival Groups and Emblematic Hybridity

Even when they do not directly articulate it, most of the Afro-Carnival groups and their memberships have some connection with Candomblé houses, including leadership positions beyond mere initiations, values that often find their way into the carnivalesque manifestations. I focus here on five of them: Filhos de Gandhi (1949), Ilê Aiyê (1974), Olodum (1979), Muzenza (1981), and Cortejo Afro (1998). Though founded at different times and motivated by different ideals, the mission of mobilizing for social change is a common commitment. Afro-Bahian carnival is the largest popular party in the world, with over one million tourists participating every year. Salvador is the capital of axé, the musical rhythm of Bahia that characterizes carnival in the state and originated in the 1950s by Dodô and Osmar. The Afoxé Filhos de Gandhi was founded by port dockers in the city on February 18, 1949. Based on the principle of nonviolence and peace as inspired by the philosophy of Mahatma Gandhi, the emphasis of the group is maintaining the Yoruba-derived Ijexá rhythm and songs accompanied by agogô (musical instrument). As the most famous afoxé of Bahia, with over ten thousand members, the group is very colorful, with white and blue necklaces that symbolize peace. Two major symbols, the goat as a symbol of life and the camel as a symbol of resistance, were introduced in 1951. Due to the respect the group gained over decades, it paved the way for the blocos afros that came decades later. Despite the respectability of the group and its nonviolent position, Filhos de Gandhi is perceived as inadvertently apolitical. When it comes to influence of sacredness, Filhos de Gandhi functions as a Candomblé house, and their songs, steeped in classic Yoruba, are considered by many as liturgic. Among the celebrities that have joined the group in procession are Gilberto Gil, Caetano Veloso, and Carlinhos Brown, among others. The group celebrated its fiftieth anniversary in 2009. Afro-Bahian carnival is best summed up by Daniela Mercury's interpretation of "Chame Gente" (Call to the people), when she praises the festivity: "Oh! Imagine this craziness of mixture / Happiness, happiness is the state we call Bahia / of All Saints, enchantments and Axé / sacred and profane / The Bahian is Carnival."[30]

Though Ilê Aiyê, Olodum, Muzenza, and Cortejo Afro are contemporaries, they do have their own peculiarities despite the shared commonality of resistance against racial discrimination. Ilê Aiyê occupies a leadership position among these groups for setting the Afrocentric and re-Africanization agenda as far back as the 1970s. Founded in 1974 by Antônio Carlos dos Santos (Vovô) and Apolônio (†) with the approval of Vovô's mother, Mãe Hilda (†), who is generally accepted by the organization as the guardian spirit of the cultural association, Ilê

Aiyê has emerged as a major player in the politics of Brazilian racial relations. Recently celebrating the fortieth anniversary of its creation, it has managed to maintain its Africanness despite pressures from the hegemonic establishment to compromise its ideal of only allowing Blacks to parade during carnival. This 100 percent Blackness attitude has generated controversy for the organization to the extent of being accused of reverse racism—thus putting it at odds with potential sponsors. Ilê Aiyê invests in the Ijexá rhythm that comes from Candomblé. In addition, since 1995, the schools (Mãe Hilda School, Erê Youth Band, Professional School) are equipped to address the needs of different students. Finally, to continue to educate the community, the group has a pedagogic extension project that publishes a series that focuses on African history and African diaspora history and culture to provide empowering information to the community.

Olodum, led by João Jorge Rodrigues, was founded in 1979 and has a more hybrid disposition because it allows whites to parade and even perform freely as part of the orchestra in the organization. With a focus on community development through education, theater, and commercialization, Olodum quickly grew to become a successful enterprise. While Ilê Aiyê does not hide its Afro-religious roots, Olodum, meanwhile, shifts its focus to the African diaspora (pan-Africa), as well as to Egypt, as a source of inspiration. The performance of celebrities like Paul Simon and Michael Jackson with Olodum lifted its stature from a local group to internationally recognized performers. The critique levied against Olodum is of its commercialization and hybridity, which Ilê Aiyê resisted until the demise of Mãe Hilda in 2015. Both Ilê Aiyê and Olodum may have had the same roots, but they have grown apart in their ideological approaches to the degree that one is visibly sacred and the other a true hybrid of racial tensions (which is not to say it is oblivious to the imperative of social justice). Just like Ilê Aiyê, Olodum also has community projects, including a youth band that performs around Pelourinho (a theater group that is now independent) and social emancipation projects.

Afro-Muzenza Group and Cortejo Afro are two of the most contemporary blocos afros. Though founded in Liberdade and Ribeira on May 5, 1981, by directors Geraldo Miranda (Geraldão) and Janílson Rodrigues (Barabbas), respectively, they are currently located in Rua das Laranjeiras, in the district of Pelourinho. Other members in the leadership of Muzenza include Munoz from São Paulo, celebrity singers such as Beto

Jamaica and Tatau, and the composer Luciano Gomes, who wrote such riveting songs as "Pharaoh" and "Swing of the Color." While the group is not as influential as perhaps more visible ones, it has consistently staged carnival with the following themes: "Twilight of Nature," "Dance of Iaô," "Kenya," "Messenger of Love," "Rastafari," and "Guerreiros of Jamaica." In 2014, the group's theme was "Reggae, Soccer and Peace." The group's first album, "Muzenza of the Reggae," was released in 1988. While the themes do not echo any sense of sacredness, the secular becomes reified as the sacred when invoked from the viewpoint of Rastafari religion. In the Afro-Bahian carnival context, samba-reggae is adopted as a double-edged musical gyration that can serve as a weapon of liberation. Afro-Muzenza Group is invested in educational projects linked with educators termed *Projeto Axé*. Cortejo Afro, meanwhile, is linked with Candomblé directly, through the mother of the founder, Alberto Pita, a Candomblé priestess of the well-established Ilê Axé Oiá, who invests in the carnival performance of Cortejo Afro in the Pirajá community. After making its carnival debut in 1999, Cortejo Afro quickly established its mission of questioning the predominance of Axé music in Salvador da Bahia, and it maintains its objective to reestablish the African identity of Bahian carnival. For example, at the 2015 Afro-Bahian carnival, Cortejo Afro focused on Oxum as a theme for its carnival. While each group shifts from one theme to the other, they consistently showcase African values and Afro-Catholic themes. As such, their hybridization marks the intersection between the sacred and the secular, not only fulfilling a crossover appeal that may not always be the intention of the blocos afros but also allowing for genuine innovation and persistence of resistant positionalities.[31]

Conclusion

The survival of African cultural values by way of hybridization processes was not an easy feat for enslaved Africans, either during slavery or after its abolition. Historical records located in Catholic orders and Afro-Catholic confraternities suggest that there were concerted efforts to eliminate the Afro-Catholic festivities themselves by ordering the creation of new strictly religious feasts to counter the popularity of the cycle of feasts among the Bahian people. The fact that several Afro-Catholic confraternities had their own buildings and headquarters was the saving grace. Festivals such as Sisterhood of Good Death, Cleansing of the Good End Church, Our Lady of Conception, and Santa Barbara may have become a thing from the past if the religious intolerance of the Catholic Church had persevered. Dias Gomes's play *O Pagador de Promessas* serves as a classic interpretation of the challenge posed by the Catholic Church against the creative efforts of the people to maintain their African-derived traditions and orixás: "Yet what Gomes misses in the interaction of the sacred and the profane lies in the intransigence of the possessive power of the sacred entity to the extent that it may refuse to let go of the possessed body."[33] In this respect, Zé emerges as the possessed body of Iansan and, until death, he cannot absolve himself of the initial contact when he seeks assistance from Santa Barbara (Iansan). Stefania Capone poses the question more astutely when she states: "How, then, can it be acceptable for a Candomblé initiate to be possessed by the spirit of a dead person, an *egun*? How can an initiate who has been ritually prepared to receive a divinity allow himself to be contaminated by the presence of death?"[33] Following the abolition of slavery, the advent of the re-Africanization process as well as the emergence of the Unified Black Movement (*movimento negro unificado* [MNU]) contributed to the resistance even if the movement took the awkward position that some of these manifestations were mere symbologies and culturalisms and needed to be more political.[34] The sacred rites meeting the secular festivals on the streets was a genial endeavor that should be celebrated and preserved for posterity. The persistent negotiation between the power of the sacred domains and the power of the culturally and politically performative seems to be the ultimate and inevitable compromise of this emblematic hybridity.

Colonial times: Afro-Catholic confraternities.

Modern times: Sacred + Secular festivals — political/cultural/economic forces = "emblematic hybridity" of Afro-Brazilian traditions in Bahia

Chapter 2

Pierre Verger and
Yoruba Ritual Altars in Brazil

Preamble

This study conducts a posthumous analysis of the contribution of Pierre Verger to Afro-Brazilian sacred legacy and its broader implications for Black Atlantic religions, especially in the context of the Yoruba-derived orisa oracular culture that Verger studied in his lifelong photographic-cum-anthropological career. Between his passionate bent for dynamic photographic ingenuity across the Pacific and the Atlantic, as well as his fateful self-discovery of the vitality of Yoruba religiosity in West Africa and South America, Pierre Verger has become something of an enigma in Brazilian artistic, medicinal, and oracular historiography. He painstaking brings together visual anthropology and African religious epistemology in a rather emblematic manner that has not been matched to date. Deploying photographic finesse as a primordial instrument of iconic cultural documentation across at least three continents (Africa, Asia, and South America), Verger's legacy fascinatingly intersects with the survival of African religions in the New World. As a student of Brazilian culture, I came to work with and got to know Pierre Verger in Brazil by chance in 1986. About the same time, Wole Soyinka had just become Nobel laureate. The possible connections between the erudite legacy of Wole Soyinka and the scientific one of Pierre Verger were not apparent to me as a young man, searching for meaning in life while living in Brazil.

49

Like Verger, I was lost between an incessant thirst for knowledge of the Yoruba world and a zeal for professional fulfillment in Brazil. Pierre Verger's ambivalent revelations to this writer, which echo a deep tone of betrayal by Soyinka, would require interviewing Wole Soyinka himself to get a balanced picture of the dramatically tense dilemma that transpired between these scholars well before the award of the Nobel Prize to Wole Soyinka in 1986. Regardless of how this contentious puzzle may be clarified and resolved, Pierre Verger's standing reputation as a photographer and renowned social anthropologist may always be mired in controversy. The most poignant of these controversies stems from Verger's challenge to the notion of "religious syncretism" in Brazil between African deities and Catholic saints. Rather, he prefers deploying the term "religious co-existence or juxtaposition"—according to him, there was never any syncretism that took place among Africans and the Portuguese, especially when it came to Candomblé or African-derived worship in Brazil. From this problematic contention alone, Verger announces himself as the ultimate oracular enigma in Brazilian cultural and visual anthropology. Meanwhile, the Verger-Soyinka controversy would be treated as a supportive aside elsewhere.

My own sojourn in Brazil during that decisive career-transition moment of the mid-1980s remains an autobiographical episode that must await the right time and medium for full disclosure. During that mysterious and uncertain season, I was simply a liminal entity who was neither sure of the future nor ready to return to an uncertain past. The past meant returning to Nigeria to continue my academic career in an environment that had been declared decadent by the financial powers of the IMF, which had just imposed austerity measures or "SFEM" (second-tier foreign exchange market) on the Nigerian economy as a trade-off for borrowing privileges with the global monetary institution. The implication meant that my dream of pursuing a doctorate in Brazil was in jeopardy. I basically had no funding; I was the metaphoric "Andrew" who had left the shores of Nigeria out of social desperation.[1] In sum, I was stuck in Brazil and desperately needed a temporary job to survive or until I got my graduate admission and funding in working order. Pierre Verger gracefully provided a position as a translator to his then-major project on Ewé (African medicine).[2] I felt quite honored and financially protected for a long while. I was not the only translator for the project. I recall several transient translators from Italy, France, and Nigeria, as well as from Brazil. Even thirty years ago, Verger had a group of research assistants working for him on multiple book projects. He paid reasonably well, as he had a grant from the French Scientific Research Council that supported all his work, but I also had the opportunity to learn a lot from him over the course of my brief stint at his research home, which was later to be revamped and named the now-famous Fundação Pierre Verger in Rio Vermelho-Salvador. This chapter deconstructs Pierre Verger's legacy in four areas that I have found pertinent to his preservation of African religious traditions but that are outside the purview of the already documented research parameters: (1) his challenge to Soyinka's authorial ownership of the historic Elesin story that became the main plot of *Death and the King's Horseman*; (2) his wrongful accusation of being a "French spy" in order to deport him from Nigeria in the 1960s; (3) the episode of Soyinka singularly returning to Brazil to rescue some of the "stolen" Yoruba artifacts that were then in Verger's possession in Brazil, which Soyinka returned to the Ile Ife museum in Nigeria after his recuperative stint; (4) and, finally, some controversies surrounding translations from Yoruba to English or Portuguese, which for this writer constitute a manifestation of Pierre Verger's colonial mentality.

Because some of these memories are more reminiscences than verified incidents, they can only be corroborated in context and not in substance, as the individuals invoked in the controversies have yet to have the opportunity to provide their own versions of Verger's narrative. Yet, in raising such an interesting can of worms, this rare view of the enigma of Pierre Verger suggests that even the best of minds have always faced their own moments of emotional trauma and weakness. The stellar triumph that scholars see today with reference to Pierre Verger's scholarly legacy also had its challenging moments. Here is a balanced tribute and a worthy critique befitting the French photographer, the Bahian initiate of Candomblé, and the phenomenal archivist-anthropologist who documented Yoruba culture well beyond the imagination of the Yoruba themselves.

Born into an affluent family in Paris on November 4, 1902, as Pierre Edouard Leopold Verger, he would later receive the initiation name of "Fatumbi" in West Africa, which means that the Yoruba oracle (Ifá) has given birth to this one. After his entire family met untimely deaths, he adopted photographic ethnography and traveled as his therapeutic pastimes, and these would define his life and career. His initiation as Babalawo, or Ifá priest, gave him unlimited access to the secrets of the Yoruba people, who are dispersed across the Black Atlantic, and especially to the secrets retained in African-derived religious and social practices that were precipitated through slavery and what Verger calls the "flux and reflux" of trade and cultural flows between Africa and the African diaspora over many centuries. After crisscrossing many nations and cultures, including China, Japan, United States, Mali, Togo, Dahomey, Nigeria, Philippines, Guatemala, Ecuador, Argentina, Peru, and Bolivia (among other countries), he finally settled in Bahia, Brazil, where he fell in love with Afro-Brazilian culture. His subsequent travels included Cuba and Haiti, as well as a return to West Africa, where he made a renewed effort to make connections between Candomblé and Ifá divination and Yoruba religious rituals; these connections would later define and redefine his scholarly production throughout his career. Based on his sustained academic productivity, he was recognized with a doctorate by Sorbonne University in 1966, became a professor at the Federal University of Bahia in 1973, and served as a visiting professor at the University of Ife in Nigeria in the mid-1970s. Verger later helped the Federal University of Bahia to create the Afro-Brazilian Museum in Salvador. Before his death in 1996, he had the vision to turn his house in Rio Vermelho into the Pierre Verger Foundation, where scholars now consult his sixty-thousand-plus photographs, negatives, as well as his most significant publications.

Comparative Approaches to Candomblé

The sacred reinvention of Africa in the Atlantic world of Brazil has served as the terrain for compelling contributions from formidable scholars from the fields of anthropology, sociology, and religious studies. Of these scholars, Roger Bastide, J. Lorand Matory, Paul Christopher Johnson, Stefania Capone, and Luis Nicolau Parés offer contrasting and contending approaches that help further clarify the place of Pierre Verger in the broader Africana religious world.[3] Bastide's focus on religious syncretism and collective memory, Matory's proposal for Nagô/Yoruba transnationalism, Johnson's invocation of the paradox of secrecy and secretism, Capone's argument for the fluidity of Afro-Brazilain religions as represented by the Brazilianization of the African Exu (or the deity of the crossroads), and Parés's Herskovitsian analytical model of African survivals—all coalesce in the vibrancy of Candomblé as a living religion in Brazil despite many centuries of persecutions, transformations, shifts, and rebrandings. To these scholarly contentions, Verger adds his own strand of "religious co-existence" between Catholicism and Candomblé, as opposed to the generalized notion of "religious syncretism," to the unfinished debate on Afro-Brazilian religion. Regardless of the strong positions, contentions, and disagreements among these scholars, culture, by its very evolving nature, is subject to change and will continue to shift to new locations. The name of "Candomblé" itself has nothing to do with Yoruba culture, sounding more like the influence of Kimbundu from Angola on the Portuguese language. The reality of Candomblé is that it was forged in Brazil through an assemblage of many ethnic religiosities from different regions of Africa, with West Africa being predominant. Given the pain of Atlantic history and the tortuous journeys across the Atlantic, the preservation of African culture and religious practices in the New World must be seen as a historical miracle. The controversies of memory, dialogue, survival, syncretism, change, continuity, and agency are inevitable elements of a shifting material culture as it passes through changes of which the scholars in contention are not oblivious.

Roger Bastide may have written his seminal work on *The African Religions of Brazil* in 1960, yet its impact is timeless. Spending close to two decades in Brazil, conducting ethnographic work, and drawing on the scholarship of Gilberto Freyre, Arthur Ramos, and Nina Rodrigues, among others (as well as on his own substantial research), Bastide takes on the challenge of describing Afro-Brazilian religion not as a simple worship but as a complex, dynamic, and organized way of life that is simultaneously secretive, "exotic," fascinating, and mysterious. His thesis on the "interpenetration of civilizations (or cultures)" coalescing in the interstices of symbolic, ritualistic, mythological, and multifaceted religious practices allows him to distinguish between Umbanda (ideology) and Candomblé (authentic yet acculturated religion), where Euro-Catholic, African, and Amerindian religious practices have blended to create an ambiguously "pure" Afro-Brazilian religion through syncretism. As fascinating as this thesis has been to scholars, it is marred by contradictions (including a "survivalist" ethos) at a time when Candomblé was persecuted by the authorities in Brazil, which reminds one of Melville Herskovits. The diversity of African ethnic groups, such as the Sudanese, the Islamicized, and the Bantu, has been reduced to one singular family or clan to fit under the patriarchal system of the big landowner, the white Portuguese entrepreneur, and the multiple ethnic groups under slavery. The elaborate analysis of such concepts as resistance, adaptation, syncretism, assimilation, and counter-acculturation, while rewarding in terms of understanding the challenges of integration or separation, nonetheless fail to account for how the Nagô (Yoruba) nation ultimately rose to become the predominant religion within Candomblé houses.[4] In other words, the interpenetration of cultures was not the key to "purity," or African predominance but was perhaps a creative ability to disguise the worship of African deities with the worship of Catholic saints and was a gesture of survival under slavery. Bastide's influence may well be more on the issue of religious syncretism and collective memory than on the quest for "purity" of religions. My take on Bastide, as an outsider/insider digesting his work, aligns with the suspicion of his "exotism" as he sought to explicate a phenomenon that was beyond his normal understanding in terms of classic religious sects. Candomblé is a living, vibrant, and active religion that survived the horrors of slavery. It is not in any way exotic. Rather, it is a way of life.

While J. Lorand Matory is no contemporary of Bastide, nor does he privilege purity like Bastide, both share a commonality when it comes to Nagô/Yoruba transnationalism and the impact of transatlantic religious, commercial, and professional networks, which solidified the Yoruba (religious) nation in the New World. Matory was taken to task by Luis Nicolau Parés for his in-depth review of *The Formation of Candomblé: Vodun History and Ritual in Brazil*, in which the Duke Don makes clear distinctions between the two scholars' schools of thought, or what he calls the "rival analytic models of Afro-Atlantic Cultural History," distinguishing between Parés's "survivals" model and his own "dialogue" approach.[5] Repudiating Parés's approach as generalizing and reductionist, Matory rather proposes what he calls "live dialogue between Africa and the Americas," thus suggesting a more complex dynamic of interactions between Africans and their descendants in the Americas, well beyond the survivalist thesis alone. Anchoring his argument on the steady decline of the Jeje nation since the end of the nineteenth century, and the steady rise of the Nagô nation of the same period, Matory emphatically affirms that "the most prestigious and imitated temples and models of religious practice in today's Candomblé are not Jeje but Nagô."[6] The painstaking efforts of Parés to establish Jeje as an antecedent of other West African groups, even when deconstructed with empirical evidence by Matory, only leads to the conclusion that Parés embraces the Herkovitsian model while Matory leans more toward the dialogic framework. The two schools of thought are complementary in their contributions to syncretism, collective memory, and dialogic imagination. Beyond his major work *Black Atlantic Religion: Tradition, Transnationalism, and Matriarchy in the Afro-Brazilian Candomblé*, and several articles, Matory argues that the Black Atlantic religion of Candomblé was steadily revised by the free African diaspora people who traveled to West Africa, thus impacting the shifting identities of religious practices. Yet one must question the validity of this exaggerated thesis in terms of the relative privilege and percentage of such travelers in comparison to the Candomblé community as a whole. For the impact to have been as significant, most of the Candomblé temples, which number in the hundreds, would have had the opportunity to travel to West Africa, which was obviously not the case. Only the elites and the privileged would have had such a unique opportunity. The strength of tradition and its preservation amid persecution is a factor that must be considered in the entire exchange about the "right" analytical model or methodology. I suggest that, to a reasonable degree, both schools of thought have something to contribute and should be read side by side, both for their enriching controversies and for their stimulating exchanges.

While Paul Christopher Johnson's *Secrets, Gossip, and Gods: The Transformation of Brazilian Candomblé* and Stefania Capone's *Searching for Africa in Brazil: Power and Traditions in Candomblé* provide contrasting perspectives on Candomblé in Bahia and São Paulo, their divergent foci on secrecy and authenticity support the claim of Pierre Verger's "colonial" gaze on Afro-Brazilian ritual altars. On the one hand, in his push to understand religion and modernity in the Americas, Johnson articulates the persistence of secrecy in Candomblé through a transition from secrecy as an authentic experience of the religion to the exigency of maintaining secrets as a way of recuperating the gradual loss of the sacred space to popular culture. On the other hand, Capone evokes the powerful image of Exu as the spiritual mediator of Umbanda and Candomblé and, hence, as a symbol of common African roots to which both scholars and worshippers tend to embrace. The central challenge for both scholars is not so much how the promises of secrecy are ultimately compromised when their works are disseminated for public consumption but also how the double-edged strategy for preserving Candomblé worship in the colonial era from assault by the Catholic Church and slavery was necessary for the "invention" of Candomblé tradition as a weapon of both resistance and liberation. The incorporation of Afro-Brazilian religious practices into Catholicism was a radical and ingenious feat by the Afro-descendant guardians of secrecy, who may have been influenced by their own secret societies in Africa. Johnson's argument that Candomblé has become a "public religion" may be limited in those parts of Brazil outside Bahia, where the tradition of secrecy is kept alive.[7] Despite the erosion of ritual secrecy by the power of popular culture, especially the cultural and social movements in Bahia, the secrecy of Afro-Brazilian ritual practices is still held in the highest esteem. While scholars often end up being initiated for the convenience of access, as well as out of a genuine passion for the rituals, the fine line between the devotee and the scholar may not only be blurred but also compromised. It is against this comparative and complex background of these approaches to Candomblé that I find the case of Pierre Verger worthy of revisitation as an oracular enigma.

Pierre Verger: An Oracular Enigma

In attributing the qualification of "an oracular enigma" to the French anthropologist, I situate Pierre Verger as an embodiment of a divine contradiction. As an initiated babalawo (Ifá priest), Verger's interest in Candomblé was more scholarly than merely participatory; as a closeted homosexual, his personal life seems obviated by his striking photographic images. These perplexing attributes may raise eyebrows in Yorubaland, which was once and is still isolated, especially during the 1960s and 1970s, when Verger spent most of his research years among venerable Yoruba religious devotees and with whom he was subsequently initiated into the oracular tradition and renamed as "Fatumbi." Yet, Verger's enigmatic catalogue is not limited to his rather enigmatic sexual orientation. It also raises cogent epistemological questions about his express and limitless access to the secrets of divination and African medicine, as most Africans are not as privileged to have knowledge of these secrets. To what does one attribute this double standard among the guardians of African culture, who would readily pass on secrets to "colonial researchers" yet would not accord such privileges to indigenous Africans? Ironically, such guardians are later "footnoted" in books as "informants" and not as authentic knowers of the ancient Yoruba oracular system. In this regard, there is the issue of the "colonial" exploitation of African indigenous knowledge systems, and scholars such as Melville Herskovits, William Bascom, Roger Bastide, and Pierre Verger, to mention just a few, may be said to be knowledge predators, even if they ended up preserving Yoruba religious culture in the diaspora, which we now recognize in the postmodern context as an invaluable service.

In the case of Verger, he was the first to document through his books and photography the many hidden ritualistic powers of Candomblé in Bahia, a privilege that is only accorded to reputable insiders and initiates. One can say there is no other way to learn about Bahia without knowing the photographic works of Verger inside and out. He represents with photography what the acclaimed Jorge Amado and Carybé evoke with literature and art, respectively. While Verger's works oscillate profoundly between the sacred and the profane, one sees the depth of professionalism and the quest for artistic perfection in his images of common people as opposed to the elites. Yet, no matter how meticulous Verger is in his scholarly work, he remains an oracular enigma because the circumstances of his acquisition of a wealth of secrets are shrouded in cultural, ethical, and intellectual mysteries. First, he had to become initiated within the Afro-Brazilian religious systems to gain his insights, even though he never practiced divination afterward. Second, his immense access also enhanced the prestige of his photographic works, which now stand as the best ethnographic collection archived by his foundation for the interest of future generations of scholars. After his arrival in Bahia, Verger served to mediate between cultures, especially between Africa and Brazil. After the arrival of Nigerian intellectuals and teachers who had come to teach Yoruba in Brazil and learn about Brazilian culture, coupled with further exchanges with Cuban intellectuals in the 1960s and 1970s, Candomblé became a site of curiosity and research focus for many enthusiasts—thus bringing about a certain internationalization and subsequent quest for re-Africanization (both sacred and profane) in Bahia during the 1970s. This dynamic cultural renaissance enhanced the work of Pierre Verger while at the same time provoking disagreements among the devotees in terms of what constitutes religious authenticity, leadership, and (in)tolerance. Given Verger's independence and his funding from the French Scientific Center, he never compromised in terms of his independence of judgment, not even when he took a controversial stance that challenged the mainstream position about religious syncretism. Regardless of his position, Verger exhibited photographic prowess and was apt to document the religious essence of living between two worlds without any contradiction.

Controversial Insights, Contested Methodologies

Verger's iconographic-ritualistic corpus is extensive, precise, compelling, and, to a certain degree, sublimely controversial. Unique in the benefits he tapped from the methodologies and discourses of previous ethnographers, such as Nina Rodrigues and Roger Bastide, as well as in the opportunity to be initiated into the Candomblé at the highest rank of a babalawo (Yoruba diviner and priest), Verger had firsthand access to rare landscapes, frenetic worships, rituals, dances, drumming, possessions, and virtually everything involved in the phenomenologies of the Afro-Brazilian religious precepts. However, this access is problematic. One wonders how many ordinary Afro-Brazilians in the 1950s were so privileged as to gain access to the secrets of Afro-Brazilian religion, especially in the African space. I suspect there would be few, if any at all, as the struggle for socioeconomic equality after the abolition of slavery in 1888 was a traumatic challenge to overcome—not to mention the financial hurdle of being able to embark on a journey of initiation in Africa.

A critical overview of Verger's works reveals a central thesis, which is really a mixture of arguments that shift or are meant to shift according to Verger's position: (1) in order to understand Candomblé and its rituals, and to draw connections, parallels, and contrasts, Candomblé must be re-contextualized in the Yoruba-specific rituals of West Africa from which it emerged; (2) photography serves as a weapon of ethnographic research that by capturing vital moments, lays the foundation for future observational analysis of the image and the memory mediated by the image; (3) Verger's general empathy and love for the people of Bahia in Brazil and Nigeria and Benin in Africa further facilitates the sacred and popular synergy between the targeted cultural personas and the gaze of the photographer; (4) on the professional and methodological level of documenting cultural history, Verger deploys a mix of impulsive, connective, and affective strategies to capture lasting images that then become permanent imprints of analysis for the photographer and future generations; (5) despite the plenitude of his photography, Verger strikes a permanent note of controversy when he insists that there is really no religious syncretism between the two belief systems, Catholicism and Candomblé, but rather a cultural and religious juxtaposition and coexistence; and (7) in a provocative accusation of Soyinka's appropriation in *Death and the King's Horseman* of a story he claims to have personally retrieved from a historian (a local Yoruba informant in Oyo town), Verger asserts that such a fraudulent use of his own research delegitimizes Soyinka's authorial claim in the play. I argue that, if this fraudulent episode was significant, then Verger would have gone public on the subject matter, not only to the immediate Brazilian local community but also globally. The fact that the polemic was only limited to the context of Soyinka's acceptance of the Nobel Prize in Literature suggests to this writer that it was a matter of unfinished business, related to another traumatic polemic about how Verger was deported from Nigeria in the 1960s.

The essential unity of Verger's works thrives on the convergences of the photographic gaze and the quest for a full understanding of the complex Yoruba religious world and its implications for the appreciation of ritual power and healing on both sides of the Atlantic. Unlike his scholarly, anthropological, and artistic predecessors, such as Manoel Querino, Nina Rodrigues, Juana Elbein dos Santos, Deoscoredes M. Dos Santos (Mestre Didi), and Roger Bastide, Verger combined Yoruba cosmogony with his passion for photography. He embodied the way of life of the orisa, and, after many years of research across the Atlantic as an outsider looking in, he finally became an insider. What then started out as an element of curiosity, adventure, and photojournalism, turned out to be a scientific endeavor with a spiritual twist, even betraying the gaze of the colonialist. The privilege Verger possessed as a white adventurer—one who happened to be sponsored by the French Scientific Research Council—also may have affected the framing of his viewpoint as an ethnographer because, in those days, Africa was only seen as "primitive" and "exotic" in the gaze of the colonial explorer. In response to Verger's critique of her book *Os Nagôs e a Morte*, Juana Elbein dos Santos accused Verger of this same arrogance. By casting a conceptual doubt on Santos's effort to construct a sophisticated theogonic system through her work on the ancestral manifestation of ritual power and the cycle of life, Verger's critique sets the stage for a distinction of scientific orientation, whether rigorously established or speculatively advanced, and for questioning each scholar's authenticity and ingenuity. But Santos's criticism is the most penetrating. Citing Verger's intransigence on the issue of religious syncretism, his insistence on religious coexistence and juxtaposition, and his further adherence to seeing the African value system as exotic and primitive, Santos argues that the French photographer-anthropologist seeks to monopolize scholarly truth for financial stability and socioeconomic privilege, both of which allowed him access to sacred terrain in the first place. For Santos, Pierre Verger only acquired the title of a babalawo for the sake of convenience and to claim credibility for his scholarly works, while never belonging to a sustained temple's membership in Bahia. In referring to this approach as "initiatic anthropology," Santos dubbed Verger as the ultimate folklorizer, whose objective was to colonize African culture, dominate it by way of an acquired knowledge system, and disseminate it as a subject of conquest that could be disseminated for commercial and political purposes. In other words, Verger was accused of deessentializing African culture and uprooting its fundamentals toward a potential manipulation of its primordial epistemological principles. While one must scrutinize the corpus of Verger's works to prove or disprove these hyperbolic accusations, I personally feel that Verger represents a colonial scholar of sorts and cannot be categorized merely as a sympathetic, disinterested outsider-observer. The Fundação Pierre Verger, which is partly self-sustaining from the proceeds of the organization, would not be there today without Verger's transformation of African culture into a raw material to be extracted and exploited for academic benefits. Though there is an advantage to the inestimable preservation that Verger rendered to scholars, it is not completely devoid of exploitative interests.

Of the diverse ethnological works by Pierre Verger, the most influential are *Trade Relations Between the Bight of Benin and Bahia, Orixás, African Legends of the Orishas, Notas Sobre o Culto aos Orixás e Voduns, Fluxo and Refluxo, Artigos,* and *Ewé*.[8] The most important biocritical works on him include Jérôme Souty's *Pierre Fatumbi Verger*, Jean-Pierre Le Bouler's *Pierre Fatumbi Verger: Um Homem Livre*, Cida Nóbrega and Regina Echeverría's *Verger: Um Retrato em Preto e Branco*, and Ângela Lühning's *Verger/Bastide: Dimensões de Uma Amizade*.[9] While each work of visual anthropology is enduring in its own right as a quest to understand community rites—even if the observer rarely believes in the spirit possession that forms the core of such a communal cosmological principle and that affirms the cyclic rite of passage between the world of the living, the ancestral world, and the unborn, as proclaimed by Wole Soyinka in *Myth, Literature, and the African World*, one cannot but marvel at the emotional distance and frigidity with which Verger approaches his ethnologist mission.[10] Conceptually and methodologically, Verger succeeds in articulating the following strategic passions of documenting history through photography and observation: (1) uniting African cultures and histories across the Black Atlantic by establishing an essential harmony; and (2) drawing transatlantic connections based on research travels in African and Afro-Bahian spaces, through which the origins of Candomblé and the passion of the practitioners become relics of spiritual continuity and resistance, even if Verger himself does not articulate this power of survival beyond a colonial gaze and conquest. Despite Verger's perceptive work on African cultural diffusion, which is echoed in the work of Melville Herskovits, he is at once a hybrid messenger of African oracular cultures as well as a problematic enigma, one who is best categorized as a Brazilian Joseph Conrad. This overview does not even include the hundreds of critical articles or the many dissertations written on Verger's visual anthropology. In providing the rich tapestry of his archival repository, the photographer-ethnographer facilitates the Atlantic crisscrossing of each subsequent anthropologist or cultural historian whose voyage turns into a renewing experience and source of limitless possibility for a scholarly narrative, regardless of the perspectives each share with or contests against Pierre Verger. The bio-bibliographical critique of Verger's world is beginning to make its way to the United States through the works of such eminent historians as Ana Lucia Araujo, whose scholarship offers a historical landscape of how Verger painstakingly portrays the religious connections between Africa and Brazil with his masterful grasp of culture, ethnography, and iconoclasm to document rare spiritual archives.[11]

Verger's extensive scholarly corpus deserves a more comprehensive critical analysis than the works of Le Bouler, Souty, Nóbrega and Echeverría, Rolim, and Lühning have sought to give because Verger's work is so diversified and multivalent. Yet a perceptive visual anthropologist would need to conduct a more rigorous analysis of technique, aesthetics, and potentially inadvertent epistemological influences that the self-taught and intuitive master may have received over the course of his career. Verger's connection to such eminent legends as Carybé, Jorge Amado, Gilberto Gil, and Juana Elbein dos Santos is ample evidence of the fact that he is held in the highest esteem. One must also wonder if there is more than meets the eye in the assessments and critiques of his universal legacy. For example, Verger humbly credits his publisher Arlete Soares for the idea of setting up a foundation: "I am enthused and in favor of this Foundation, if it can keep and preserve old materials I have collected in the course of my career. The photographs I took, which are about 60 thousand negatives, more or less, the books I put together, the papers, life around my studies, constitute a totality that can surely be of interest."[12] The richest part of the foundation are the photographs and thus must be sacredly preserved. In a study by Cynthia Garcia, the author cites Verger's statement, "Photography enables us to see what we don't have time to see, for it is fixed. What's more, it memorizes, it is memory."[13] One must understand the agency of photography to memorialize and to facilitate the recuperation of memory as documented by the camera. Due to this diversity, dividing Verger's works into categories may be the point of departure for any attempt to assess his legacy: (1) photography as a primary archival source; (2) fieldnotes as ethnography; (3) publications as the empowering reservoir of the intellectual; (4) orisa tradition across the Atlantic as a unification of the Black Atlantic religious experience; (5) scientific memorabilia, such as data on Yoruba medicine, as a recipe for oracular healing; (6) travels and encounters across the Atlantic as potential ruminations for biographical postulations; and (7) controversies with iconic personalities, including Nina Rodrigues, Carybé, Jorge Amado, Julian Elbein dos Santos, Gilberto Gil, and Wole Soyinka.

Of these potential lines of research, and beyond a cursory overview for the sake of a panoramic conceptualization, I focus on two innovative aspects: namely, the oracular orisa medicine that relates to Verger's perception of the Yoruba cosmologic vision, as well as a controversial episode between the Nigerian Nobel laureate Wole Soyinka and Pierre Verger on the issue of academic or historical ownership, a controversy that was never made public until it was shared with this writer in 1986. I call this episode the "Soyinka Saga," which, on the surface, amounts to nothing but speculation or innuendo, given the circumstance of its revelation. These provocative issues amount to an effort to expand the legacy, critique, and even defense of Pierre Verger when one considers the sheer power of his legacy for posterity in Black Atlantic religious studies. While he was not qualified to be a visual anthropologist in the 1940s through 1950s, when he worked as a freelance photographer for global magazines he was already an apt practitioner of what is today known as the field of visual anthropology. What do we owe to Verger's precision and sympathetic eye behind the camera and to the vision that accompanies his moments of revelation, which ultimately become his legacy for the rest of the world? Before Verger, the Afro-Brazilian religion of Candomblé was barely visible. It was persecuted just like capoeira and samba. Locked up in the interior for its own safety, it had to escape the constant assaults of the police, who were, at the time, censoring any form of subversive performance deemed an assault on the Catholic faith and defending Catholicism against heresy and frenetic spiritual possession.

Whether such efforts by Verger were considered innovative or folkloric is immaterial. The fact is that there are now today sixty-five thousand negatives that capture for posterity a Black Atlantic religion in the safe ambience of scientific preservation and analysis. This fact is indeed a victory for religious tolerance, even if Verger himself has been accused of religious intolerance against religious syncretism.

Verger's *Orixás*, now a classic sought after by scholars all over the world, was probably derived from his *Dieux d'Afrique*, which was based on comparative contents. As a startling illustration and critical examination of the Yoruba pantheon, *Orixás* provides rare insights into the otherwise secretive rituals of Yoruba deities over the centuries. Whether called orisas, orixás, or orishas, they retain the characteristics of the historic and humanized heroes and heroines of Yoruba society, who once lived as individuals, later became deified through their tragic flaws or excesses, and have since been worshiped as heroes of Mother Nature as they unleash their protective and destructive forces, depending on necessity, provocation, or invocation. *Orixás* systematically brings to light the following: introduction, initiation, and ceremonies, as well as specific deities, such as Exu, Ogum, Oxóssi, Ossain, Oramiyan, Orunmila, Xangô, Yansan, Oxum, Iemanjá, Oxum, Omolu, Nana Buruku, and Obatala (Orixalá). Verger painstakingly ensures to highlight their characteristics and controversies as they leave their African context to become hybridized and reborn in Brazil. Verger's startling black-and-white images, numbering in the hundreds, invoke the overwhelming emergence of the Yoruba world and its consequent New World formation. Where the two cultures collide, especially in the Bahia-Africa dynamics, through Yoruba influences, and transformational re-Africanization processes, the deities produce lasting cultural archetypes, such as Oxum, Xangô, Iemanjá, and Oxalá, among many others. Beyond this panorama of representative deities, Verger articulates his position that, instead of religious syncretism, there was more of a religious coexistence between not-so-well-understood exteriorities of the Catholic faith and African "fetishes," which practitioners wanted to see as part of the same category even though both were "perfectly distinct."[14]

If we consider Verger's *Orixás* to be disrespectful of African religion and deities, he compensated these views with works such as *African Legends of the Orishas* and *Lendas Africanas dos Orixás*, both of which were illustrated by Carybé, an Afro-Argentinian turned Afro-Brazilian artist. Arlete Soares, in her prefaces to these two collections, pays homage to the value of Yoruba oral tradition, while also privileging the originality of the babalawo, through whose mouth some of these tales are heard for the first time. She writes, "Fatumbi gathered and patiently annotated all of these tales, which are based on the narratives of African diviners. It should be recalled, however, that the legends presented here are just a tiny fraction of the vast universe of stories that a *babalawo* must memorize during the course of apprenticeship. All are direct and spontaneous testimonials to the richness of Yoruba culture, which has had such a strong impact on the culture of Bahia."[15] Verger's efforts to introduce Candomblé to both Brazilian and American worlds was no small feat. In addition to sharing a wealth of information about the rituals and traditions of West African cosmological belief systems, Verger's experiences transformed the seemingly naïve scholar-photographer from a mere dispassionate observer to a savvy intellect whose prejudices were counterbalanced by a scientific approach to the preservation and annotation of the many photographic, ritualistic, and medicinal works, which have now become part of the cultural heritage of humanity. With the Pierre Verger Foundation, established in 1988, the once-itinerant French photographer can rest well, as the many memorabilia he left behind can supplement the living memory of Afro-Brazilian religious and iconographic legacies and will stand the test of time. Though the underlining value of Verger's works is largely documentary and archival, his meticulous intellectual and analytical rigor shifts the discourse from mere collection to that of ethnography—thus transforming his archives into viable visual anthropology, with a self-sustaining power of agency for future generations of scholars.

When it comes to the sophistication of ideas and intellectual growth in Verger's magisterial oeuvre, I consider *Ewe: The Use of Plants in Yoruba Society* and *Trade Relations Between the Bight of Benin and Bahia* as his ultimate legacies, even beyond the panoramic *Orixas* series. While *Trade Relations* may have initiated his more profound sociological inquiry into the transatlantic trade, *Ewe* traverses the terrain of the oracular, where the secrets of divination and medicine combine to unleash havoc and healing, depending on the intentions of the perpetrator, who is not defined in the recipes. These recipes are clearly prescribed in careful and scientifically potent declamations that come in degrees of ofo, afose, afogbohun, awise, epe, majele, oogun, ase, ashe, and aseje. Among the many medicinal potions are ones that can heal, help a woman get pregnant, permanently alter someone's destiny, and even send someone on a proverbial journey of no return. Let me return to the controversial methodological issue: how was

Pierre Verger, an expatriate scholar in Nigeria, able to effortlessly access and obtain these vital competencies in traditional medicine practices, while more seasoned indigenous enthusiasts have not been allowed the same access based on the requirement of "initiation" or "non-initiation"? Today, Verger is the sole author and owner of a wealth of information about Yoruba medicine. The Pierre Verger Foundation is the sole beneficiary and maintains the research center, which is open to scholars—a worthy endeavor. Though this rich reservoir of oracular and medicinal knowledge was secured and collected through research privilege, I find it problematic that it was never allowed into the hands of the original Yoruba knowledge keepers, who were barely footnoted and cannot receive any royalties for their knowledge. If photography was deployed to extract a lasting memory for future generations, the same device may also be used to correct this ethnography and is now vital to negotiating the links between ethnology and respect for human patrimony.

In a study that questions the deployment of the use of the camera in anthropology, João Martinho Braga de Mendonça engages issues such as ethics, institutionalization, archives, and teaching in order to challenge the work of Margaret Mead.[16] Suggesting that Mead's past work provokes ethical and political questions, such as the way Mead dressed up like the natives while in the field, Mendonça questions the absolute necessity (or not) of the camera, as well as the necessity of other "time, kinesthetic, tactual, olfactory, and gustatory recording devices" that anthropologists use to capture the totality of an archive to assess human behavior.[17] This critique of the anthropological works of Margaret Mead sounds an extreme note of warning regarding the potential invalidation of scientific objectivity, especially when artistic and literary expressions collude in the broader anthropological prism, which is both facilitated by the camera as well as by observation notes that help in the classification and categorization of analytical conclusions. A visual anthropologist is indeed in a quagmire if he or she is unable to deploy modern methods to recuperate vital information from the location of study.

Whether photography is described as an art of taking notes in the field, as an evocative technique, as kinesics, as a teaching device, or as a form of synergetic interaction between the anthropologist and the photographer, Pierre Verger's work is pioneering in the context of a rather secretive ritual experience and the absence of data on it. Yet, the referential contexts that the photographs reveal, such as the location, people, and occasion, as well as the noted dialogues and performances, become part and parcel of the visual anthropological process of analysis. Verger's photographs can be compared to analyze the changes that took place while the photographs were being taken. In sum, striking a balance between the anthropologist and the photographer is not really a bad method because such a scholarly partnership can bring about a more dependable archival result for the research process and the communication of research findings. Rosane Andrade further clarifies the identitarian element of photography, especially when the researcher is faced with limited methods: "We look at photographs in order to recuperate the past in the present. We take photographs to appropriate an object that is likely to disappear. There is certain magic involved when we immortalize people and time in photos. For the urban tribes, photographs are the proof of their existence, identity, and history."[18] When photography is seen as a two-pronged weapon—deployed to uncover rare sociological and historical insights but also tempered with the moral dignity of the native subjects being studied—a visual anthropologist may ultimately be frustrated by the professional exigencies of data collection, as well as the realistic models of successful fieldwork. Thus, ideas about methods and hypotheses are conditioned by the shifting individual peculiarities and subjectivities of the researcher in relation to the unpredictable nature of the ethnographic locale. Verger is indeed no stranger to this insight, but he seems to have paid less attention to the political agency of the natives at the price of securing his data by any means necessary.

A further close examination of Verger's significant intellectual corpus dating from the 1950s through the 1990s reveals a golden jubilee of Black Atlantic visual anthropology, especially if we factor in the works by others that included his photographs and which were geared toward tourism, daily living, architecture, nature, and popular festivals in places he had visited worldwide.[19] Verger's *Dieux d'Afrique: Culte des Orishas et Vodouns à l'ancienne Côte des Esclaves en Afrique et à Bahia, la Baie de Tous les Saints au Brésil* documents a ten-year, crisscrossing research odyssey in West Africa and Bahia at the insistence of the French scholar Théodore Monod and the French Scientific Research Center (IFAN), who had invited Verger to embark on this cutting-edge work. Through an elaborate tapestry depicting the many Yoruba deities along the coast of West Africa and their corresponding agents in Brazil, Verger establishes himself as a pioneering Brazilian visual anthropologist without equal. Verger's exploration of religiosity in Africa and Brazil has had an incredible impact on researchers all over the world. Similarly,

Indiens pas morts is a tripartite effort to document rare images and is focused on Peru, Bolivia, and Ecuador. The rare photographs are taken by the trio Pierre Verger, Robert Frank, and Werner Bishof. The editor Delpire realizes their painstaking artistic efforts by presenting their visual anthropology, which now constitutes perhaps the first experimentation in visual anthropology in the Pacific.

Four other compelling works—namely *Notes sur le culte des Orisá et Vodun à Bahia, la Baie de tous les Saints, au Brésil et à l'ancienne Côte des Esclaves en Afrique*; *Retratos da Bahia, 1946 a 1952*; *Orixás: Deus iorubas na África e no Novo Mundo*; and *Pierre Verger, Le Messager/The Go-Between: Photographies 1932–1962*—constitute a mix of extensive research and autobiography not entirely disconnected from the main emphasis of his career-long investment in photography.[20] Verger's progressive analysis facilitates a sense of rigor, as his books relate to each other in a synergetic, even symmetric manner. While *Notes* serves as an incisive reservoir of liturgic power by registering the sacred chants and orikis (praise songs) of the Yoruba pantheon, *Retratos da Bahia* excavates the world of Bahia through classic images of splendorous architecture, the inner and external beauties of the Candomblé worship grounds, the Model Market in the lower city, the popular feasts that constitute the opium of the people, as well as the bay itself—documenting one of the most enchanting spaces of Black Brazil.[21] Beyond these representative works is *Orixás: Deus iorubas na África e no Novo Mundo*, which is the most lavishly illustrated of Verger's black-and-white photographs. Similar to *Dieux d'Afrique* in its fascinating selection of Yoruba deities and their resonances in Bahia, it records over 250 photos that are accompanied by analytical texts that bring insightful illumination to the curiosity of the reader.[22] One is at a loss for how to qualify these major works beyond praising their documentary value, the rigor of Verger's analysis, and the overall consistency of data, despite the controversy of extracting this mosaic from its sacred source with neither a sense of violation nor retributive justice. Collected in conjunction with Jean-Louis Pivin and Pascal Saint-Léon, the main corpus of Verger in his prime closes with a photographic autobiography, *Le Messager/The Go-Between*, but the issues and contexts in this autobiography are not exclusive to the photographer. If one could call Verger's work an archival harvest of sorts, its significance surely transcends the photographer and his status and curiosity as a traveler. It is in this sense that "oracular" seems to sum up the enigma that Verger's visual anthropology encompasses.

Every scholar must define what he or she considers to be the ultimate part of Verger's legacy. By my own account, and beyond the spectacular celebration of such titles as *Orixás* and *Retratos da Bahia*, I find two major works—*Fluxo e Refluxo* and *Ewé: The Use of Plants in Yoruba Society*—as those works by Verger that are most deserving of revisitation and reevaluation. After over thirty years of studying Africa and Brazil to uncover not just the legacy of slavery but also the defining religious relics that kept the two cultures alive, work that still generates controversies of religious intolerance, Verger was ready to make the scholarly statement that became his doctoral thesis in African studies at the Sorbonne: *Flux et reflux de la traite des nègres entre le golfe de Bénin et Bahia de Todos os Santos du dix-septième au dix-neuvième siècle*. The value of this text is not so much the documentary and multivalent perspectives that Verger advances to conceptualize the Yoruba world but rather the innovative visual anthropology that presents images of performative rituals of the deities that were heretofore unseen. Striking in their visual depictions of blood, decapitated heads of animals, and humans drinking blood, these photographs suggest a certain exoticism and exorcism of the bloodletting ritual, which is performed for the recuperation of the vital energy that is released from the expiring body of the sacrificed animal. Despite the curiosity these images create in the minds of subsequent researchers, access was acquired at the expense of the producing culture's privacy. It is doubtful that the ritual performers willingly allowed the documentation. I suspect that there was monetary or material exchange, through which Pierre Verger gained unfettered access to such elaborate secret initiations. This is rather common in Africa and Brazil, as anyone with a camera is suspected of being "foreign" (a tourist), someone who has come to get to know the people and their traditions. Yet, Verger is no ordinary foreigner. He is indeed a researcher who has studied many cultures and, based on his source location in Bahia, knows the value of the deities to the ex-slaves in Bahia, having gone to Africa to corroborate their origins and validities. My question remains: what did the ritual performers gain in return? Verger has the negatives, the books, and the copyrights; the natives barely have footnotes. As humans, they have been turned into research objects for gainful purposes.

African medicine is an entirely different subject entirely. Because I was involved with the translation of his work *Ewe: The Use of Plants in Yoruba Society* from the original Yoruba notes (which were directly recorded from Ifá divinatory masters or babalawos), I had my emotional reservations even doing the work—though I needed the money he was paying me to survive in Brazil for almost two years. One must then confront the moral question of my own expediency as one of the translators alongside Verger's objective to get the complex work out for posterity. Considered a work that was the culmination of more than twenty years of research—collecting plants, noting their healing potencies and the necessary enchantments (coupled with the sacred offerings) that accompany their applications—I was emotionally grieved that, as a Yoruba individual, I was not allowed to gain access to these secrets in my own country without being initiated. Initiation is not easy, and Verger had his basically "sold" to him. Initiation to Ifá divination may require no less than seven years of apprenticeship. Though Verger went back and forth between West Africa and Brazil, he never spent seven years with diviners, nor did he acquire the typical knowledge of medicinal power and rituals beyond what he acquired for collection and documentation purposes. The work is unquestionably seminal, but his means of collecting data is what I find fraudulent. My methodological contention notwithstanding, credit must be given to Verger for organizing the book in a scientifically accessible manner, with a list of over two thousand plants that are used in Yoruba traditional medicine, along with their prescriptions and enchanting formulae, through which the power of healing is invoked and materialized. Some of these prescriptive incantations are then highlighted in a glossary that contains their scientific names as well as pictorial images for easy identification. One can only marvel at Verger's rigor in his approach to this classic compendium of African medicine, which transcends much of the value attached to the visual anthropology that the dynamic world forged by photography and cultural interpretation engenders.

Taking the barren woman as a case study of a malady that requires resolution or healing, Verger's *Ewe* represents a depth of knowledge of medicinal remedies that is so profound that one can visually accompany the processes of the redemption of the womb, purification, the creation and insertion of a new fetus, protection and retention of the fetus, as well as the strength or ease of delivery. These multifaceted processes for securing a pregnancy from conception to birth speaks to the wealth of Yoruba knowledge on childbearing, which must not be lost. Though Verger has documented these processes, and it may well be advantageous to return his commercialized "book of secrets" to the Yoruba medicinal practitioners as a recycled guide, a lot must have been lost

during translation. Most of the incantations are from the Ifá divination
system (oracle) and, through translation into English or Portuguese,
the translator must have made some convenient adjustments that are
predicated upon the level of competence of said translator. Also, the
translation from orality to writing is a zone of ambiguity that many try
to avoid because it is filled with enchanting invocations that are not
translatable, except by the rare, educated diviner, and because they are
also accompanied by musical performance. A translator steeped in Ifá
worship would translate differently than a non-Ifá adherent. As a result,
when the traditional healer evokes verse 27 of the Ogbe turupon, which
is the ritual activator of pregnancy, he is indeed inviting the forces of
impregnation that are present in or invoked upon the incantated and
ritually processed medicinal leaf to visit the barren woman and make
her pregnant. The incantation goes thus:

> Ewe gbomopon / Eku omo ati iyo /A o gun un. /A o se pelu
> eku emo. / Ao fi iyo ati epo pupa si i. /A o pe ofo re, / ki
> obinrin je e ni ojo kinni ti o ba ri alejo (osu) re. / Ogbe sure
> ponmo / Obe posese ponmo / Ojo kewa ti a ba ri emo ni aa
> ri omo re / Eje ti lamorin yii ri oyun ni ki o fi se / Omo ni
> ko o fi bi / Gbomopon ki i fi ehin sile l'aiponmo.

> (Leaf of dyschoriste perrottetth, / one guinea-pig and salt /
> Grind the leaves, cook them with the guinea-pig in salt and
> palm oil. / Recite the incantation. / The woman should eat
> this on the first day of menstruation. / Ogbe, hurry to carry a
> child on your back/ Ogbe, run quickly to carry a child / On
> the tenth day after seeing Emo, we always see his children /
> Having finished menstruation, so-and-so will conceive / She
> should deliver a child successfully / The gbomopon leaf never
> leaves its back free without carrying a child on it.)[23]

This divination and application to the barren woman articulate the power
of Yoruba divinatory principles, as it reiterates the ability of indigenous
knowledge to provide a cure for what would ordinarily be a condition,
such as fibrous conditions that lead to barrenness that may require some
form of surgery. Yet Verger's colonial foray into the Yoruba world takes
more credit than it gives back to the same world and its diviners, who
perform millennial curative feats that would take modern cultures cen-

turies to develop. Such a complex culture, which can divine the cause of barrenness, as well as prescribe specific incantations to correct the deficiency, deserves respect. Only an acknowledgment of the wisdom of the Yoruba diviners and their application of medicinal plants cum oral incantations could redress this imbalance.

In her own incisive study of the phenomenon of the icon in Bahian Candomblé, Lisa Earl Castillo calls into question Verger's projects as his main contribution to visual anthropology.[24] Castillo is critical of Verger's violation of the sacred zone, through which self-serving technical observers not only document religious history through the gaze of photography but also celebrate their own professional accomplishments. Castillo may not have intended to confront anthropological methodologies in ritual studies, but, in tone and tenor, she creates a dialogic tension in her interpretation of the dilemma of photographic representation as it affects Candomblé practices in the nineteenth century and beyond. Castillo boldly rejects the idea of self-representation, while also suggesting that these were nothing short of "scientific racism," which was prevalent at the time. Successfully mapping an extensive ethnographic terrain, where she invokes previous tangential studies on the subject matter, she describes the contributions of Nina Rodrigues, Ruth Landes, Juan Elbein dos Santos, Susan Sontag, Roland Barthes, and Pierre Verger, among others.[25] The deployment of photography was once a sacred act for collecting the memories of rituals because the images were recorded by members of the Candomblé family who were seen to be safe guardians and not the usual external intruders, who were often transient and foreign elements and who, in some instances, also contributed to the assessment of what is "authentic" Candomblé by virtue of their own socialization in the terreiros (temples) and its material, cultural, and sacred aspects. But, to what extent is Pierre Verger a Candomblé family member, and what qualifies him to be such if his ulterior motives fell somewhere between documenting and disseminating the ethnographic findings he was meticulously gathering? One could argue either way. First, Verger may not have started out as an exploitative ethnographer, but the circumstances, including the fact that the French Scientific Research Council had placed this responsibility in his hands by basically funding his work, were such that he could not give up. Second, the fame and fortune that accompanied the gathering of precious religious data must be balanced against their status as a permanent reservoir of cultural treasures—and, especially, against the matter of their future, visionary legacy.

The Soyinka Saga

Beyond criticism of the colonial exploitation in Verger's gaze as a visual anthropologist, as a scholar, and as a Candomblé initiate, I invoke the example of barrenness in the cosmic vision of Verger's *Ewe: The Use of Plants in Yoruba Society*. I do this to protest his colonial foray in the translation project, for it was one of the aspects of those translations that I did for Verger that permanently traumatized me as a Yoruba in 1986. Though grateful for the opportunity, I also realize, in retrospect, that it was as if I were complicit in translating Yoruba secrets to the rest of the world without giving adequate credit to the diviners whose knowledge was diminished. Meanwhile the knowledge of the collector was given undue preeminence. Beyond these productive and problematic ruminations on the select works of Pierre Verger, I also take issue with a few episodes of controversy that evoked the name of the Nobel laureate of literature in 1986, even though the details and verities of this controversy dwell outside of my comprehension. I was working with Verger at that time, and it was evident that the news of this award troubled him greatly. He went on to cite three incidents that made Soyinka undeserving of the recognition. I could not be more startled. As a Nigerian myself, I felt that the recognition that was not given to the Yoruba diviners in the Verger project I was struggling to translate was nonetheless being given to a contemporary writer whose works also evoke Yoruba virtues and values. That was consolation enough for me, but it was not sufficient for Verger. In *Death and the King's Horseman*, Soyinka conceptualizes "The Fourth Stage" as the space where the worlds of the living, the ancestral, and the unborn intersect, the space where the essences of the three worlds come together.[26] Ironically, it was this same seminal book that was part of Pierre Verger's accusation of "fraud." Verger's contentions were not interrelated but somehow dealt with his sense of victimization at the hands of Wole Soyinka. He alleged that: (1) Soyinka was not the original owner of the horseman's (Elesin) story; as a matter of act, he (Verger) was the one to whom an Oyo diviner-historian had told the story, and Soyinka had stolen the story from him without giving him any credit after he had recounted the story to the playwright upon returning from Oyo. Verger further alleged that (2) Soyinka singlehandedly spearheaded the campaign to deport him from Nigeria by accusing him of being a "French Spy" in the late 1960s, while he was a visiting professor in Nigeria. Finally, (3) when Soyinka paid him a courtesy visit in Salvador-Bahia, Verger soon realized that it was a mercenary operation after Soyinka made away with many Yoruba royal head masks belonging to Verger.[27] It was a frustrating time indeed to be working for Verger, and I could neither sufficiently console him nor adequately understand the totality of the saga that was unfolding before me. I could not understand if I was a victim of history or a witness to an invaluable moment worthy of critical analysis.

Starting with Soyinka's *Death and the King's Horseman*, the playwright never once denied that ownership of the main story belongs to foundational Yoruba history. The puzzling claim by Verger that he owned the "story" as a visiting professor who had happened to have been told by a Yoruba diviner continues to baffle the imagination. As a Yoruba myself, I see no reason to even attempt to corroborate the story by inviting Soyinka to defend his use of the material that belongs to his people. Once again, Verger's colonial foray and sense of entitlement on an encroached territory seems to be raising its ugly head. Ironically, if Verger had taken time to read the "author's note" to the play, all his apprehensions would probably have been tranquilized. Closing Soyinka's note to *Death and the King's Horseman*, the playwright taunts the reader: "The Colonial Factor is an incident, a catalytic incident merely. The confrontation in the play is largely metaphysical, contained in the human vehicle which is Elesin and the universe of the Yoruba mind—the world of the living, the dead and the unborn, and the numinous passage which links all: transition. *Death and the King's Horseman* can be fully realized only through an evocation of music from the abyss of transition."[28] Beyond the historical, which Soyinka also rejects as inconsequential to his play, the colonial factor is equally dismissed as merely incidental, although one can argue that Soyinka cannot really divorce himself from the grounding of historical context, given the crisis of ideology between colonial administration and natives, who contest colonial violence and seek independence through some form of resistance and struggle. Verger's claim is that the plot of the story in *Death and the King's Horseman* would amount to plagiarism in today's parlance. Yet the playwright does not need to announce his act of borrowing, even of the historical, because, as a creative writer, he already possesses poetic license to create. One wonders if Verger's claim was provoked by some genuine resentment against Soyinka because Verger also charged the playwright with having committed some other unorthodox, unforgivable, and possibly mean-spirited acts, which had to be challenged during that moment of the "celebration of the Nobel" in 1986. Regardless of the pain that Verger felt and his claim that he should have been given credit by Soyinka for the story of Elesin, which Verger shared with him, poetic license seems to have worked against Verger in this matter.

In introducing the Norton critical edition of *Death and the King's Horseman*, Simon Gikandi was quick to note the complexity of the work, as well as Soyinka's efforts to go against the grain of the previous generation's obsession with history. This constancy placed Soyinka's work at odds, or at the very least in some controversial rapport, with the majority of his contemporary critics:

> But *Death and the King's Horseman* represents a significant departure for Soyinka in its concerns with a specific historical episode, an event that took place in Oyo, western Nigeria, in 1946 . . . Soyinka had asserted that one of the limitations in African writing after decolonization was its obsession with the past. Did *Death and the King's Horseman* represent a reversal of Soyinka's earlier doubts about the writer's obsession with history? Can *Death and the King's Horseman* be considered a historical play? For many critics, Soyinka's use of historical account as the basis for the dramatic conflict in *Death and the King's Horseman* is deceptive.[29]

If Soyinka was never interested in portraying the exact episode of ritual suicide in 1946, one wonders why Verger would continue to obsess over the "borrowing" (or stealing) of this episode without acknowledgment, as if Verger were the don of African history who had to be consulted for the right to use national (Nigerian) cultural heritage. Soyinka also borrowed from previous playwrights, and Duro Ladipo's *Oba Waja* (Three Yoruba plays) served as a source of inspiration for Soyinka, more than the actual ritual episode of 1956, in which Soyinka was least interested.[30] Regardless of how one reads Verger's response to the news of Soyinka winning the Nobel Prize in literature, the underlining motivation was more rage than rationality, and he was responding to the many conflicting episodes in which both were embroiled over the years.

The next issue was Soyinka's accusation that Verger was a "French Spy" while he was a visiting professor in Nigeria, an accusation that made the Frenchman immediately eligible for deportation back to France. Because the details of that political situation are not available to this writer, the question raised for the curious mind is the motive behind such a political machination. What exactly was Verger doing that qualified him as a "spy"? What secrets was he collecting from the Yoruba diviners that were deemed to be beyond the limits of public knowledge and that could be perceived as an assault on national treasure, the same way that museum artifacts would be treated? Did Verger have any license to freely record and obtain cultural secrets from the national guardians of Nigerian cultural heritage and scientific history? These are questions that Verger was unable to answer, and Soyinka did not oblige to incriminate himself by admitting being part of a sting operation that got Verger deported. Again, there is no corroborating the claim beyond the fact that we know that Verger was indeed deported from Nigeria. While such an episode must have been traumatic for Verger—with consequential humiliation and potential loss of data and dignity, especially if there was no iota of evidence that Verger was indeed a French spy—it indicates the extent to which human beings could go to defend their core values. If for the sake of argument Verger was perceived to be an imposter who was collecting secretive and sensitive cultural data from diviners by taking advantage of their knowledge system and not compensating them, then it is not inconceivable that a group of professors could gang up to stop that exploitative process. Perhaps, in that context, a schemed deportation could have transpired mischievously.

The last episode of a leveled charge against Soyinka followed a dramatic visit by Soyinka to Verger's home in Rio Vermelho, Salvador. It was reported that when Verger stepped out of his office to the kitchen to offer Soyinka a cup of coffee as his guest, by the time Verger returned with the cup, Soyinka had disappeared with a few Ife heads (artifacts), which were later confirmed by the Nigerian newspapers to have been returned to the Ife Museum in Ile-Ife, Nigeria. One can only wish for more sagacious events to heighten the controversies in the life of Verger with respect to Wole Soyinka. If Verger were still alive, he probably would have more to say about these events—and so would Soyinka. While Soyinka is still alive, he has remained quite isolated, and it is even rumored that he has no email account through which one could communicate with him. As a matter of fact, Soyinka has publicly threatened to tear up his green card and return to Nigeria if Trump were ever to become the president of the United States—and, to his credit, he did just that. As a result, it is quite difficult to corroborate the innuendos and controversies. Perhaps it is a case best left for Soyinka's own *The Lion and the Jewel*.[31]

Conclusion

By virtue of its multidimensionality and interdisciplinarity, the Verger project fascinates scholars and general enthusiasts alike but often leaves them puzzled about the legacy of visual anthropology and its impact on the legacy of the indigenous people of Africa and the collateral survivors of the African diaspora. While the issues brought to bear here range from the gaze of the photographer to questions about methodologies in the field, one cannot help but pose the lasting question: who owns the cultural heritage of the people studied by anthropologists and who should have the authority to benefit from the permanent income generated by the estate of the visual anthropologist? The answer is not simple. In the case of the Pierre Verger Foundation, we know that there is not just the foundation to contend with but also the gallery. It takes a lot of financial funding and reinvestment to maintain the legacy and keep breaking even. Even if there is some indirect governmental contribution (the foundation enjoys nontaxable status), its role as Brazilian cultural agency transcends Pierre Verger, who is now long gone. Yet, the controversy remains that, from the Black Atlantic visual and religious perspective, can the legacy of Verger be divorced from the exploitation of the people he studied? New perspectives shed light on Verger's sojourn in Nigeria, as well as the "authenticity" and "sacredness" of his work in spite of his colonial methods, coupled with his place alongside such eminent global thinkers as Nina Rodrigues, Roger Bastide, Carybé, Juan Elbein dos Santos, Wole Soyinka, Jorge Amado, and Gilberto Gil, and these new perspectives only add value to the idea of Vergerism, which deviates from his eminence. The specific controversies surrounding Wole Soyinka's Nobel Prize, including what Verger considered to be an oversight in Soyinka's acknowledgment of his sources, as well as his undue maltreatment by Soyinka in both Nigeria and Brazil, are such episodes that should not be promoted except as an academic exercise in curiosity. Regardless of the truth—if there is anything such as the "truth" in the academy—one would want to elicit more transparency around Verger's claim, beyond the heat of the moment after the bestowal of the Nobel Prize. The issue here is more about cultural heritage and goes beyond the Nobel. Of course, in 1986, Soyinka was the first African to receive the honor, and it was not unusual for a renowned and disgruntled scholar such as Pierre Verger to take advantage of the major euphoria surrounding Wole Soyinka's definitive eminence and to vent his frustration at his own feeling of being slighted for whatever reason—whether real or invented. Candomblé religion remains a vital force of continuity, renovation, and tradition in Brazil and, in its empowering status of resistance against historical African subjugation under slavery, should be viewed beyond its apparent *exotica* and studied more as a living ritual practice and a way of life, just like any other world religion.

Exhaustive; often repetitive, analysis of Pierre Verger's work in Brazil. Details PVF and Afolabi's own personal + professional relationship with it.

Chapter 3

Matriarchs of Candomblé

Mãe Stella de Oxóssi, Mãe Beata de Yemonjá, and Mãe Valnizia Bianch

Mãe Stella de Oxóssi, Mãe Beata de Yemonjá, and Mãe Valnizia Bianch are venerated priestesses, political matriarchs, and cultural intellects of the Candomblé sacred houses of Ilê Axé Opô Afonja, Ilê Omijuarô, and Terreiro Pilão do Cobre, respectively. Each embodies age-old wisdom that is derived from many decades of apprenticeship, political leadership, and social activism in the administration of Afro-Brazilian temples, or terreiros. Typical of African oral storytelling tradition, their writing, including *Osóòsi: O Caçador de Alegrias* (Osóòsi: Hunter of joys), *Caroço de Dendê* (Seed of palm oil), and *Reflexões: Escritas de Mãe Valnizia Bianch* (Reflections: Writings of Mãe Valnizia Bianch), is steeped in Afro-Brazilian moralistic stories of wisdom, heroism, history, preservation, counsel, healing, courage, and power, especially the core virtues of the three major divinities that the authors consider their guiding spirits: Oxóssi, Yemonjá, and Oxalá. Warfare and maternal strength are women's requisite qualities, and they must not only fight to protect their children but also nourish them with the subtleties of wisdom to cope with the adversities of life. Likewise, Oxalá, the supreme deity, not only protects all his devotees and children but also serves as a divine patriarch who reassures everyone of peace and continuity of life as mediated through his maternal underbelly in the personality of Yemonjá.

These three priestesses' representative works have become valuable resources for the larger community of devotees and researchers, and they express the vitality of African traditions, which are gradually being forgotten against the erosion of oral tradition and that must be passed on from generation to generation. This chapter seeks to unravel these living museums of sacred tradition amidst a corrosive modernity and how these works constitute the personal mythologies of the three matriarchs in question. It analyzes how their narratives intersect with both their own historical trajectories and their political legacies of many decades spent resisting religious persecution. While their stories transcend the Brazilian space and historical timeframe, they form a reservoir for reconstituting traditional religious practices, especially when faced with the challenges of religious syncretism, fanaticism, and intolerance. Drawing on a number of historical and anthropological works that provide context for appreciating these stories—such as J. Lorand Matory's *Black Atlantic Religion*, Ruth Landes's *The City of Women*, Maria Hita's *A Casa das Mulheres*, and Mestre Didi's *História de Um Terreiro Nagô*—this chapter argues that the Candomblé priestesses serve as vital matriarchal fortresses in the Afro-Brazilian temples for the sustenance of knowledge and growth. They resist the violent instrumentalities of the state while demanding racial equality, an end to religious intolerance, and respect for Afro-Brazilian religions. Through their social activism, these women have expanded the global impact of Candomblé beyond the confines of their immediate Brazilian sacred spaces.

(En)Gendering Candomblé

To better appreciate the significance of the sacred and how it has relocated into popular culture, one must also understand the history of Candomblé. Rachel Harding rightly describes the institution as a "refuge in thunder," a refuge through which music, dance, and even cryptic silences take on new meanings and where "suffering people reorient themselves and their environment to an alternative experience" and as a source of political power.[1] In other words, the invocations of the deities through ritual dance, the cultivation of the power of healing through community transformation, and empowerment through symbolic leadership style—all these culminated in the establishment of a cultural movement that resisted slavery. Especially in the nineteenth century, Candomblé was an identity formation that countered the subjugation and oppression of slavery. As an Afro-Brazilian religion, Candomblé was created during slavery as a religion in which different ethnic groups from Africa, namely the Yoruba, Fon, and Bantu, came together to practice Africa-derived religion. When Africans were forced to convert, and it was not safe to openly practice African traditional religion without fear of reprisals from the enslaver, it was also mixed with Catholicism to mask its Africanness. The word *Candomblé* translates to the veneration of selected deities (orixás) through dance and music, and it was assumed by the enslavers that the rituals and ceremonies would involve vital energies, frenetic dances, and spirit possessions. Hence, these manifestations were too powerful for the enslavers, who suspected that the enslaved could turn such an event into an opportunity for rebellion. Therefore, gatherings were persecuted until the enslaved Africans were able to devise a strategy to conceal their Candomblé religious practices by pretending to worship Catholic saints while actually venerating African deities with similar sacred symbols and characteristics. This was a strategic process of religious "mixing" that later became known as "religious syncretism." Despite persistent persecutions that lasted through the 1970s, when the law requiring police permission before holding religious ceremonies was abolished, Candomblé still remains persecuted by Christian fundamentalists, such as the Pentecostals, who see African religious practices as diabolical forms of worship. At the same time, a more radical Candomblé movement, known as "anti-syncretism," has been created to counter religious syncretism.[2] It subscribes to the belief that there is no reason to mask African deities under Catholic saints anymore and that authenticity and purity of African religions should be the way forward. This movement, along with the quest for Afro-Brazilian identity through a re-Africanization process that took place across Brazil in the 1970s, opened the gateway for the relocation of the sacred into the realm of popular culture across Brazil.

While some Candomblé temples are urban, most are still very rural, as Edison Carneiro argues in *Candomblés da Bahia*. Rural settings allow them to be far away from the colonial and police persecutions that only subsided in the era of President Vargas in the 1970s, when devotees could finally gather freely for their spiritual events without needing police permission.[3] The advantage of the rural setting was not only the serenity of an ideal, thick forest, graced by natural plants and protective trees, but also the ambience, which allows general ritual sacrifices (ebo) to be conducted in the open without fear of concerned outsiders, onlookers, or fanatical persecutors. As Candomblé houses compete for prominence

amidst the declining status of traditional religions in modernity due to
Brazil's allegiance to European values and Catholicism, older leaders
of temples often feel the need to present their houses as "pure" and
"authentic" and to present themselves as guardians of African cultural
heritage and religious traditions. It was in this context of purification
that Iyalorixás (priestesses) took prominence within Candomblé. Luis
Nicolau Parés argues that the claim to authenticity may well be more
closely associated with a historical figure than with actual knowledge
of Yoruba traditions. Regarding what he calls the "Nagôization process
within Candomblé," Parés contends that "Candomblé experts indeed
have a critical sense for differentiating what they judge 'certo' (authentic,
true) from what they label 'errado,' 'deturpado,' or 'misturado' (wrong,
modified, mixed)."[4] Through this Nagôization process, African religion's
survival in Brazil has been remarkably influenced by Yoruba mythology,
regardless of its ethnic origins. Except for the Bantu, or Angolan and
Congolese, which had minimal influence, the Ewes, or Jêjês, have been
completely syncretized with the Nagô/Yoruba belief system. Despite the
continued persecutions of Candomblé temples by Pentecostals and evangelicals, the Afro-syncretic Candomblé communities remain resistant to
attacks of religious intolerance.

In his own analysis of Candomblé practices in nineteenth-century
Bahia through the prisms of priests, followers, and clients, João Reis
argues that the final authoritative work on Candomblé studies in Bahia
has yet to be written. While crediting the efforts of such scholars as Nina
Rodrigues (on Ilê Iya Nassô), Pierre Verger (on Ilê Axé Opo Afonja),
Vivaldo da Costa da Lima (on Ilê Axé Iya Nassô and Alaketo), Rachel
Harding, Dale Graden, Renato da Silveira, and Jocélio Telles, among
others, he relates his own systematic archival research in which he highlights the biases of noninitiates (who had no scholarly interest in the
subject), "outsiders, writers, reporters and white and mestizo officials who
unfortunately produced the manuscripts and printed documents available
to the historians" and who often failed to ask historical questions of the
informants they interviewed.[5] Reis identifies potential sources, such as
police records and newspaper articles, as well as fictional works, such
as O Feiticeiro (The sorcerer) by Xavier Marques, and ethnographical
works by Raymundo Nina Rodrigues. Drawing specifically from articles
in the newspaper O Alabama (1864–1871), Reis reaches the following
conclusions: (1) there is more information about the characteristics of
Candomblé participants during the second half of the nineteenth century

than the previous period, which is why he focuses on the latter period; (2) different ethnic groups and nations (e.g., Yoruba, Fon-Ewe, Hausa, Angola) all became known as "Africans" due to the predominance of the Yoruba nation (Nagôs in Bahia), which was treated as equivalent to "Africa"; (3) though the writers of the newspaper articles consulted in O Alabama were not initiated into Candomblé and were prone to condemn, persecute, and malign the religion, there is still much that can be gleaned from their records; (4) and despite the fact that of the eighty-one Candomblé leaders studied, fifty were men and thirty-one were women, this is no indication of gender bias because there were greater numbers of women among the initiates and the clientele of Candomblé, which led to the formation of a very strong female leadership in the twentieth century; (5) there is abiding evidence to suggest that in the second half of the nineteenth century, Africans, mulattoes, and a few whites were integrated in the Candomblé ritual structure; (6) women became dominant figures in Candomblé leadership because they were initiated in greater numbers than men; and (7) the history of Candomblé in nineteenth-century Bahia is connected to the creolization and racial hybridization that became a survival strategy for the religious practice. While Reis's historical survey of Candomblé in nineteenth-century Bahia provides a critical optic for the rise of interest in the study of Candomblé, it also stresses the emergence of women in the leadership of Afro-Brazilian temples in the twentieth century.

In their edited volume Presença do Axé (Presence of power), which echoes similar efforts by the Bahian government in the last two decades to map the Candomblé temples, Denise Rosalem da Fonseca and Sônia Maria Giacomini turn their attention to the temples in Rio de Janeiro.[6] Sponsored by the Special Secretary for the Promotion of Racial Equality (SEPPIR) between 2008 and 2010, and constituting an introduction, seven chapters by collaborative scholars, as well as a preface by Mãe Beata de Yemonjá herself, the work has had a lasting impact on curious scholars. Initiated at the insistence of Mãe Beata de Yemonjá, to whom the book is dedicated, it sets out to perform a systematic cartography of Rio de Janeiro's Candomblé houses. Far from being an exhaustive project, it sets out to map, as much as possible, Rio de Janeiro's Candomblé terreiros. Of the 847 houses visited, located in 30 of the 92 municipalities, at least two-thirds of the communities located in the favelas were left out for logistical reasons. Four main issues can be discerned from the compelling work: (1) the persistent invasion of Afro-Brazilian sacred spaces by neo-Pentecostal fanatics; (2) the silencing of the ritual performance voice of the temples; (3) physical persecution, verbal intimidation, and violent domination of the sacred spaces by agents of religious intolerance; and (4) the striking realization that the aggressors are usually men while those attacked are usually women. In addition to protesting racial and religious discrimination, the book appeals to the Brazilian government to intervene more decisively to prevent violence and resist efforts by neo-Pentecostal agents who continue to invade Afro-Brazilian spaces without respect for the mysteries and secrets of the institution. In their conclusions, the editors appeal to the Brazilian government to further assist the religious conglomerations to guarantee their security and protection, given their vulnerability and poverty: "In other words, by virtue of the State's own omission, we continue to allege that Afro-Brazilian devotees constitute a human group that finds themselves in a vulnerable situation. . . . From this standpoint, there is a sense of urgency to develop public policies that allow for the construction of specific Afro-Brazilian agendas in the advancement of socio-environmental sustainability of Candomblé worshippers."[7] Although the book does not focus on the significance of the Iyalorixás of Rio de Janeiro, it is remarkable that the study itself was inspired by Mãe Beata de Yemonjá.

Serving as an emblematically rigorous study of the notion of a Candomblé "house" (casa) led by matriarchs, Maria Hita's A Casa das Mulheres n'Outro Terreiro (Women's house in another temple) focuses on two such Iyalorixás, namely Dialunda and Dona Cida, who control the Candomblé temples in Amaralina, Salvador da Bahia. The ethnographic study interrogates issues of matriarchy, matrifocality, identity, blood family relations through "house" membership (brotherhood or sisterhood), belonging, struggles against poverty, and domestic violence as they affect the complex social conditions, labor market, and survival of the devotees within this complex and intense social structure. The matriarch embodies the symbolic power of the grandmother of all, whether in religious or family relations terms. Following a conceptual chapter that analyzes family lineage and relations within the "house," the remaining chapters creatively address the urban contexts of Amaralina in relation to the families and to real poverty, violence, and black women's leadership within the household. Although the study focuses less on the religious social structure and more on the matriarchal structure, it nonetheless gives some insight into how matriarchal family structures operate. In her Reflexões, Mãe Valnizia Bianch offers some insights into the psychology of leadership within Candomblé beyond the expectations of hierarchy, respect, veneration of the orixás, festivities, initiations, sacrifices, and healing rituals, all of which constitute some of the social rhythms within Candomblé.[8] She states: "Candomblé is an example of a welcoming, caring religion without prejudices; and I speak based on my experience of 29 years at the Terreiro do Cobre. . . . One of the greatest challenges for a leader is knowing how to lead within and around one's community, using psychology as a resource."[9] In addition to their leadership, women have been the foundational roots for the formation and sustenance of Afro-Brazilian identity over many centuries of struggle.

When it comes to how women and select priestesses have come to be dominant in Candomblé, studies vary in their critical positions and biased convictions about this strategic institutionalization and historical trajectory, which does not negate the contributions of priests in the emergence of Candomblé nor in its continuity in the twentieth century. These scholars include Ruth Landes, who, in her controversial *The City of Women*, details her ethnographic encounters with Candomblé priestesses and their cult ceremonies in the 1930s; J. Lorand Matory, who in *Black African Religion* and in "Gendered Agendas," challenges the claims of Landes and Genevieve Dempsey to argue for the importance of female enfranchisement and gender equality within the broader commitment of Candomblé to the dignity of marginalized Afro-Brazilian communities; and a host of Brazilian feminist scholars, such as Daniela Cordovil, Jean Santos and Elaine Antunes, and Élida Regina Silva de Lima, who, through the prism of spiritualist gender relations, further complicate the tensions among scholars about who exactly has the legitimate preeminence in Candomblé leadership. When these positions are sensitively analyzed, one reaches the conclusion that a more balanced perspective, one capable of appreciating the power dynamics of social and gender hierarchy within Candomblé, would derive from mixed methods, including theology, archival research, and ritual observations.[10]

Mãe Stella de Oxóssi and Happiness Motif in O Caçador de Alegrias

Toward the end of my second sojourn in Brazil in the 1980s, I had the opportunity to have my palms read by the chief priestess of the Ilê Axé Opo Afonja. It was July 1986, and I found myself faced with a big decision to either return to Nigeria or remain in Brazil after an explor-atory research trip to pursue my graduate studies. Known then simply as "Mãe Stella," she looked at me sternly in the face after looking at my palms and said: "You still have two big journeys ahead of you." I was not sure whether it was the return or exploration of other parts of the world beyond Brazil—but I knew I had to prepare myself for another life journey. By the following year, at about the same time she interpreted the oracular reading of my palms, I was on my way to the United States to pursue my doctoral studies. Our paths would cross again about twelve years later, when she was visiting New Orleans for Jazz Fest.

Mãe Stella de Oxóssi was born "Maria Stella de Azevedo Santos" on May 2, 1925, and she joined the ancestors on December 27, 2018. She died of a stroke in Santo Antônio when she was ninety-three years old. Though she trained as a public health nurse and worked in the Bahian community for thirty years, she was even more passionate about training in the way of the orixá that she had been born into. In 1976, she became the fifth Iyalorixá (chief priestess) of the Ilê Axé Opô Afonjá, which was founded by Mãe Aninha (Eugênia Anna Santos [1869–1938]). She was known for her writing on the beliefs and practices of Candomblé, which were intended for the general public and not for practitioners. Not only was she well known in the local and national community by political and spiritual movers, but she also left her imprint on many creative, educa-tional, and ethnographical works, culminating in her induction into the Bahian Academy of Letters in 2013. She occupied seat 33, which used to be occupied by the renowned Castro Alves and by Ubiratan Castro Araújo. Mãe Stella's creative and critical works include *Odu Adajo/Ofun: Coleção de Destinos* (Divine secrets: Collection of destinies), *Meu Tempo é Agora* (My time is now), and *Ososi: O Caçador de Alegrias* (Hunter of joys), among others. Before the culminating honor of the Academy of Letters, she was also awarded two honorary doctorates by the Federal University of Bahia and State University of Bahia, in 2005 and 2009 respectively, as well as with honors and commendations by the Bahian Government and the Ministry of Culture. In the media, her contributions to the promotion of cultural dissemination were acknowledged with a citation of commendation by the O Estado de São Paulo. Mãe Stella was succeeded at the Ilê Axé Opo Afonja by Mãe Ana de Xango (Ana Verônica Bispo dos Santos), who is fifty-three years old and has been initiated into Candomblé for twenty years.[11]

Though she was initiated by Mãe Senhora (1890–1967) on September 12, 1939, she did not stop learning and immersing herself in Afro-Brazilian rites and rituals to better prepare for the leadership responsibilities that were ahead of her. She also visited sacred sites in Nigeria, such as the Osun Grove in 1981. In addition to encouraging others to emulate such a connection with Africa by embarking on cultural and spiritual journeys, she started writing articles and books on Candomblé traditions that have been passed on orally by her predecessors. Some of her legacies include a museum and a school. She was also adamant about the purity of Candomblé, and she fought against religious syncretism and for removing Catholic images from Candomblé altars. By 1991, she had fought for and achieved the recognition of Ilê Axé Opô Afonjá by the National Institute of Historic and Artistic Heritage (IPHAN).[12] When she suffered a stroke in 2017, she moved to the city of Nazaré das Farinhas in the interior of Bahia and later died in Santo Antônio de Jesus on December 27, 2018. With the wealth of her legacy remaining, her death is just a process of transition and not a total separation from those who appreciate her contributions. On the one hand, *Meu Tempo é Agora* serves as a template for invaluable precepts and shared cultural values, which serve as foundational for the organization of a Candomblé temple, both as a physical space and as a space of ritual and ceremony. Organizing a Candomblé temple also constitutes the cycle of festivities and the spiritual way of life of all the devotees. On the other hand, *Ososi: O Caçador de Alegrias* reveals many of the mysteries of Oxóssi, the divinity-protector, who is a hunter, a warrior, and a negotiator of both the earthly and otherworldly realms that enrich her subconscious.[13] By stressing the trilogy of Exu-Ogun-Oxóssi as deities of the crossroads, justice, and the path, Mãe Stella reminds us of the humanity of the hunting profession, which is related to the survival of the human race. Finally, in *Odu Adajo: Coleção de Destinos* (Divine secrets: Collection of destinies), Mãe Stella shares wisdom from Yoruba Ifá divinatory principles as they shape human destiny. Some of these tales of the deities were previously serialized in a column "Opinião" in the Bahian newspaper *A Tarde*, through which she communicated with the Bahian community. The ultimate homage to Mãe Stella is put together in a volume edited by Cléo Martins and Raul Lody, *Faraimará: O Caçador Traz Alegria*, which was to celebrate the sixty years of her Candomblé initiation. Divided into two main parts, "Patrimony and Culture" and "Memory and Tradition," the twenty essays celebrate the legacy of Afro-Brazilian religious rites. Of Mãe Stella, Jaime Sodré writes, "A new cycle is inaugurated in the brightness of a new star, Mãe Stella is a cyclic history; her time is indeed now and forever."[14] After twenty years, this brilliant statement is as relevant today as it was when Mãe Stella was still alive. It represents the glowing stature of her life, even in death.

Constructed as a creative and spiritual work of reflections on Candomblé traditions, with a special emphasis on the Oxóssi deity, *Ososi: O Caçador de Alegrias* shares the characteristics and temperament of Oxóssi with curious readers while also highlighting some of the ceremonies that connect this hunting deity with the rest of the Afro-Brazilian temple as a religious society.[15] In five traditional stories that are intertwined with personal reflections, the priestess-storyteller makes the stories accessible despite their air of mystery and magic and simultaneously explicates the myths and histories of sacred creation, as well as their connections with the profane world in which we live. In other words, there is no separating the sacred from the profane. Mãe Stella writes how she felt compelled, at the urging of her children, to write a book of memories. Using her memories of her interactions with past elders from whom she learned a lot about African myths and legends, she writes about her own orixá, Oxóssi. The narrative moves from theorizing symbology, mythology, and humanity as they relate to African deities (especially Oxóssi), to connecting these to the earth, femininity, and the cycle of life, and even to funeral rites where the dead is honored through a rite of passage called asese, a two-pronged process of paying homage to the departed as well as consoling the living. In his foreword to the work, entitled "The Purest Symbol," Ubiratan Castro de Araújo, the former president of Fundação Pedro Calmón, highlights Mãe Stella's passion for the mystical world through which Afro-Brazilian religiosity gains its own legitimate expression without subscribing to reductionist folklorization or syncretism. As Araújo puts it very candidly, she insists on respect and dignity for Candomblé: "Black religiosity is a sincere and respectable expression of the faith of a people; and this is what Mãe Stella is committed to doing in this publication—and she obviously achieves her objective with a very rare felicity."[16] Mãe Stella confirms this high praise when she identifies her orixá as the ultimate determinant of her destiny, as well as the decoder of the mysteries of the world. She asserts: "I feel intimately connected to my orixá; I am him and he is me."[17] This powerful, symbolic, yet spiritual connection runs through the entire narrative, as Mãe Stella educates the world about the intricate connections between the divinities and humanity.

Once Mãe Stella establishes her focus on Oxóssi, she goes on to theorize the symbiotic relationship between myths, symbols, nature, and humanity as she invokes cultural and religious theorists such as Carl Jung, Elíade, and Joseph Campbell, placing them in conversation with African mythology, where their ideas on the earth, symbols, the sacred and the profane, and mythology coalesce into an intricate communication between nature and humanity: "Everything our religion professes originates from nature. Our dogmas were not dictated by a distant God, but are learnt through man-divinity interaction with nature. Our deities indeed deploy this interaction as a form of communication with us."[18] Mãe Stella argues persuasively that we comprehend the supernatural through the power of symbols. Drawing on the example of initiation in Candomblé, she further contends that the initiate goes through a rite of passage that involves a process of purification, sacredness, orientation, and apprenticeship to be in harmony with self and the divinity. In so doing, the son or daughter of the saint will recognize his or her own individuality in the spiritual father or mother. Because mythology is not logical, its repetition through songs and dances in Candomblé rites, rituals, and ceremonies allows for the preservation of tradition and ancestry within Afro-Brazilian religion. Expanding the limits of symbols, the priestess elaborates on the connection between the earth and the woman as interchangeable entities when it comes to creation myths. The earth is also the woman who, through the power of creation, carries a fetus to term the same way a grain is planted in the earth to spring into life. Creation myths involve Orisanla (Supreme being), Oduduwa (Yoruba god of creation), and Iyami Agba (Feminine divinity); the latter is endowed with the ability to procreate through the menstruation cycle, thus participating in the creative process. To illustrate the connection between myth and history, the priestess recounts the story of Oxóssi and the funeral rite (asese) made for this hunting deity when he passed away. Three morals are decipherable from this story: (1) the funeral rite is meant to prepare the dead to become an ancestor; (2) the funeral rite also consoles the living while also counseling them to live with dignity because they will be the next to become ancestors; (3) with this understanding, the dead not only become ancestors by joining the Orixá pantheon but also leave behind a "soul" to advise the living during their transition. Thus, the funeral rite is not a melancholic occasion but a mixed blessing, which is pregnant with nostalgia and hope.

It should be noted, continues Mãe Stella, that to speak of a mythological universe is to tell the story of the beginning of the world, that is, a time when phenomena, even after being lived and experienced, could be properly explained. Through this prehumanity period, which is celebrated through itan (histories), orin (songs of praise), adura (prayers), oriki (ritualistic praises), and ritualistic symbolism, we come close to the meaning of the mysterious orixá world. The veneration of the divinities is thus a way to preserve their rites and authenticity over the centuries. Despite interethnic wars, during which one tribe may become an oppressor of another by imposing their cultural values, African religious belief systems were kept alive through the process of assimilation. As a result, these cultural interpenetrations led to some mythical intermarrying, such as Sango with Osumare, Yemoja with Osala, Nana with Osala, Osun with Sango, Osun with Osoosi, Osun with Ogun, and Oya with Sango. At times, these deities are presented as interdependent family relatives. For example, Ogun is presented as the brother of Osoosi, Logunede as the son of Osoosi and Osun, Erinle as the son of Osun and Osoosi, Osun as the daughter of Yemoja, and Osoosi or Erinle as the sons of Yemoja (in other instances, they are her lovers). Osoosi and Osanyin were known as inseparable friends, and Oya was known as the adopted daughter of Osoosi. There are so many other complex relationships. In African mythology, it is possible also for deities from different ethnic groups to become vital protagonists of the same mythological saga. To illustrate one of these relationships, Mãe Stella narrates the story of how Osoosi was betrayed by the friendship of Osanyin, who took advantage of his drunkenness to cover him with honey. Though Ogun helped him to get over the situation by providing him with medicinal remedies, Osoosi hated honey so much afterward that he no longer wanted anything to do with it. Many other stories arrive at the same moral conclusion that it is important to obey the advice or instructions given by the deities because disobedience often leads to punishment and loss of freedom.

To better understand religious concepts in Candomblé, one must also be mindful of the relation between myth and history as counterparts in the formation of human values, especially in antiquity. While Mãe Stella calls this period of Yoruba history a "primitive community,"

it is not intended to be an aberration but an acceptance of the value system inherent in that period of human civilization. In other words, what appears "primitive" to the modern world has its internal dynamics and logic. The way of life of our great ancestors, while apparently "primitive," has all the intelligence to live in harmony with nature. As hunters and gatherers, our African ancestors were able to make use of the skin of the animals they killed for clothes, bones for instruments of war and for domestic use, as well as meat for sustenance. While Osoosi is considered the great hunter (tobi ode), Ogun the leader of the paths (Asiwaju/Oluona), Omolu as the black hunter (ode dudu/orisa ode), these epithets suggest that at one time most of the other deities were also associated with some form of hunting, as each deity must protect itself and survive in an animal kingdom in which human beings have to pretend to be animals (to dress up as animals) to catch their prey. Mãe Stella goes as far as to suggest that such deities as Orisanla, Osun, Ewa, Oba, and Oranmiyan have all been associated with the hunting tradition at one point or another. Given the proximity of humans with animals, it goes without saying that some checks and balances (taboos) had to be put in place to prevent humans from consuming animals that were deemed totems (ancestral spirit animals of the family). With the honorific title of king of Ketu, Osoosi is forbidden, for example, from consuming the head of a cow (ori malu), as well as honey (oyin). Oranmiyan, the youngest son of Oduduwa, who not only ruled over Ile Ife but was also the king of Benin and the first Alafin of Oyo, is also esteemed as a great hunter in Yoruba history. Mãe Stella draws on the story "Honey, Once Again" to illustrate how strict the hunter deity is with his children, especially when it comes to taboos. It is forbidden for family members within the same orixá/Candomblé house to be lovers because they are "children" of the same father or mother. However, one day an initiate fell in love with a daughter of the saint. The news went wild and the Iyalorixá found out, calling both to swear in the house of Osoosi that they were not lovers. They did and both became miserable until death. The moral of the story is not to contravene what is stipulated as taboo.

Beyond recounting the story of Osoosi, Mãe Stella takes advantage of this case study to disseminate some pertinent ritual events that are open to noninitiates and invited guests. Drawing on the mythological personality of the Xamã or Ajẹ (animal god or totem god), Mãe Stella invokes the indestructible and eternal spirit of this being who is not subject to the laws of nature. Well versed in the ritual chants and dances of Candomblé, the hunter deity can resurrect the spirits of animals who may have died during hunting ventures. For this reason, the singing and dancing during Candomblé rites are considered sacred. During a ritual performance that is called Xirê, the myths are reenacted for all the divinities. In the case of Osoosi, the characteristics of hunting are the use of the bow and arrow. There are many stages to this ritual dance: (1) Agabi is the stage when Osoosi prepares for hunting, during which he takes steps to protect himself with bow and arrow when confronted with any danger; (2) Jika expresses Osoosi's royalty through his mounting of a horse; and (3) Agere is the action of mounting the horse. The ritual performance is not meant to simulate the actual hunting but is none-theless symbolic, as what is hunted during the ritual dance are negative energies, such as sadness, anguish, deception, and sickness. The degree of intensity will be proportional to the energy of each participant in the audience. At some point, the hunter deity will leave the sacred space and go out to the exterior three times while singing this song: "Wara wara tafa loni / Wara wara tafa Ode" (Come and release your arrow today / Come and release your arrow, spirit hunter).[19] When Osoosi is quantified in the context of his core values, his bow and arrow signify a quest for perfection. As Mãe Stella succinctly characterizes the hunting act: "Reaching a target evokes the achievement of an objective, a quick, almost instantaneous realization, which makes it a symbol of thought that leads to light and the creative organ. The hunter's arrow owes the security of its trajectory and the strength of its impact to the courage of the launcher and this means that hitting the target is the ultimate spiritual perfection."[20] By closing the narrative with a detailed descrip-tion of a feast to Osoosi, Mãe Stella confirms the title of the book as an homage to the "hunter who bring happiness" through ritual offerings that are best captured in a hymn dedicated to this deity: "We, making the sacrifice, Illustrious Lord / Illumination-filled hunter / Lord of the earth, *orisa* that consumes the meat / Receive with your two hands the animal."[21] Through her illumination of the ambience, decorations, joyful singing, and ritual sequences of dances, Mãe Stella has left a credible legacy for future generations. *Ososi: O Caçador de Alegrias* is not just a personal celebration for Mãe Stella—it is a creative tribute, one that documents the aesthetic, religious, artistic, and political values of the hunter deity in Candomblé studies.

Mãe Beata de Yemonjá:
Mythmaking and Sacred Wisdom in *Caroço de Dendê*

As with her many contemporaries who left Bahia for Rio de Janeiro to further propagate the teachings of Candomblé, Mãe Beata de Yemonjá is a nationally renowned Iyalorixá. Born "Beatriz Moreira Costa" in Cachoeira de Paraguaçu, in the Recôncavo Baiano, in 1931, to the parents Maria do Carmo and Oscar Moreira, Mãe Beata moved to Salvador in the 1950s to live with her aunt and husband, the babalorixá Anísio Agra Pereira, or Anísio de Logunede. After studying with Pai Logunede, she was mentored by Mãe Olga do Alaketu, who initiated her in 1985 to the Yemonjá deity in the terreiro Ilê Maroiá Lájié in Salvador. To cope with patriarchal ideas and her own matrifocal consciousness, she tried out new creative and liberating outlets through Black theater. She also married Apolinário Costa, her only boyfriend, with whom she had four children: Ivete, Maria das Dores, Adailton, and Aderbal. Unfortunately, for no known reasons, Mãe Beata divorced her husband in 1969 and moved to Rio de Janeiro in search of better opportunities. Taking on all kinds of menial jobs to raise her children, Mãe Beata, against all odds, worked as an alternative on Rede Globo TV programs, including participating in the telenovela "Verão Vermelho" (Red summer). Her legacies include founding in 1987 the Candomblé temple Ilê Omiojuarô and serving as the President of CRIOULA, a Black women's organization and NGO in Rio de Janeiro that is famed for fighting sexism, racism, and violence. She received many honors and awards in her lifetime, including being featured in Nova Iguaçu carnival through the Garras do Tigre (Guts of the Tiger Samba school) in Rio de Janeiro in 2014 and being decorated with the Tiradentes Medal in 2017. Mãe Beata joined her ancestors on May 27, 2017, from an undisclosed illness. Of paramount importance to her legacy is her masterpiece of sacred wisdom, *Caroço de Dendê.*

Though the criticism on Mãe Beata's works is not as robust as that on Mãe Stella, it is significant enough to warrant a biocritical study by Harold Costa, *Mãe Beata de Yemonjá: Gui, Cidadã, Guerreira.* In addition to a few articles on her creative work, the temple she presided over for thirty years is documented in Marcos Serra's *30 Anos do Ilê Omiojuarô: Ancestralidade, Educação, Arte e Ativismo nas Redes de Mãe Beata de Iyemonjá.*[22] Both of these works attest to Mãe Beata's contributions to the larger dignity of Afro-Brazilian religious culture. Her poignant

statements on religion—"I belong to a religion whose time is defined
by ancestrality. A fruit is only harvested when it becomes ripe. The
leaf falls off at exactly the right time"—confirms her respect for ancęs-
trality, which also extends to the principles of democracy.[23] Throughout
her lifetime, Mãe Beata was invested in the reclamation of racial and
religious equality for Afro-Brazilians, as well as in religious activism for
respect for Afro-Brazilian religious practices. Despite the Brazilian government's claim of promoting the inclusion of Afro-Brazilian population
into the mainstream Brazilian democratic processes, the reality is that,
since the 1990s, Candomblé temples have experienced constant attacks
from Pentecostal churches, who consider Candomblé to be a diabolic
religious practice. As a result, the practitioners have become more active
in defense of their faith, even organizing a march in 2009 (Caminhada
Nacional) to demand government efforts to include them in the political
participation process. As Elina Hartikainen points out, "If Mãe Beata
presented a quintessential example of speaking well, at the November
2009 event, no other practitioner could match her experience in the
religious register."[24] Mãe Beata's mission was to preserve Afro-Brazilian
religious heritage through orixá worship, and she demanded that it must
be respected and protected, and there should be no need to be ashamed
of it under any circumstance, for it represents the forces of nature and
Afro-Brazilian ancestral legacy. Beyond highlighting her involvement 'in
the Unified Black Movement (MNU) and the Candomblé cult, Harold
Costa's *Mãe Beata de Yemonjá* provides a more intimate biography that
captures her many qualities as a religious leader, social activist, and poet.
Her resilience is well captured in one of her poems, in which she affirms
her Black womanhood: "Once again I say I am strong, I am a warrior,
/ I do not run away from the struggle. I will have to die this way."[25]
While Mãe Stella advocated the return to traditional social hierarchies
as a way to recuperate the social glue that emphasized respect for elders,
Mãe Beata embodies a resolute warrior with defined political goals.

When it comes to her ability to harmonize her roles as a community
leader, Candomblé temple's priestess and writer Mãe Beata is a strategic
coordinator of the many tasks that demand her attention. The strength
comes from no other domain than the spiritual. In this sense. a cursory
assessment of her Ilê Omiojuarô terreiro is indispensable. In *30 Anos do
Ilê Omiojuarô* (Thirty years of Omiojuarô temple), Marcos Serra, a professor, actor, and insider of the same temple, provides us with stimulating
insights on ancestrality, education, art, and activism. He emphasizes two

major projects that represent the intersections of spirituality, Afro-Brazilian identity, and political empowerment in the temple: *OriRe* (Good head/ destiny) and *A Cor da Cultura* (The color of culture). By developing and maintaining ritual and cultural activities, such as sacred obligations to the divinities, the feast of the Aiagbás, Black theater, basic education, computer literacy, and Afro-Brazilian culinary tradition, among others, Mãe Beata transformed a spiritual setting into a pragmatic educational and community center. Marcos Serra underscores the overlapping responsibilities of Ilê Omiojuarô as a community organization when he affirms that "talking about education for ethnic racial relations, Afro-Brazilian cosmogonies, and educational networks in the candomblé houses, confirms that this culture that was systematically excluded from school life for centuries due to racism, always remembered in a picturesque and folklorized way, how to survive together with its main heritage in our everyday lives."[26] The revival of the oral African poetic tradition is only one of many aspects of the African cultural legacy that Mãe Beata has creatively and painstakingly preserved in *Caroço de Dendê*.

What Mãe Beata's *Caroço de Dendê* offers readers is quite different from what Mãe Stella offered. In it, her life is laid bare for the reader as an extraordinary Afro-Brazilian woman who struggled to make something of her humanity against all odds. She was an initiate in Candomblé who rose to become a spiritual leader and a poet who sings about being an Afro-Brazilian woman warrior, about Chico Mendes, about her daughter Maria de Oxum, and about Zumbi dos Palmares, among others. Containing over forty short stories, with an introduction and a preface by Vânia Cardoso and Zeca Ligeiro, respectively, *Caroço de Dendê* is a rare cultural document that reminds one of Mestre Didi's *Contos Crioulos da Bahia* and other African tales that contain a deep moral sense and great wisdom. Inspired by the African oral tradition, where knowledge is passed on from generation to generation and preserved by the experiences of slaves, Mãe Beata becomes an elder-storyteller and passes on to her children the wisdom of her ancestors. The topics of the stories in *Caroço de Dendê* range from ancestral mythologies, community costumes, histories of various divinities, ancestral characters or heroes (and heroines), fables, proverbs, symbols, religious phenomena, fantasies, allegories, and supernatural events, all of which are meant to serve as profound reflections to assist humanity to live by high moral standards. Each story seeks to answer a question at the end: what is the moral? This means the stories have a didactic function; they are meant to convey a moral. While most of the stories are informed by the reality of the Candomblé tradition, they are also relevant for day-to-day living, as a guide to the perfect way of life, contentment, and happiness. In other words, mythmaking collides with wisdom to bring out the best in humanity. According to Vânia Cardoso, memory is deployed in the stories as "a retelling and a recreation of mythical daily traditions of the Candomblé temple."[27] Zeca Ligeiro considers the stories to be an "African cultural legacy that was forged in Brazilian land; hence, constitutes a sum total of heterogenic and harmonious stories that were recollected and reinvented by Mãe Beata."[28] Meanwhile, Júlio Braga notes that "the author's stories, legends, and morals, are craftily woven into autobiographical pieces that are not meant to be revealed as such since they have an impact beyond the immediate reality of the storyteller."[29] These critical positions are limited because they could also recognize the significance of the female voices in the stories, which are largely dominant in the ritual dynamics of Candomblé traditions.

Caroço de Dendê adopts a multifocal approach, an approach that appears in the thematic preoccupations of the stories, to fully achieve its aims. These aims may be summed up as: (1) to establish the African oral poetic as the millennial reservoir through which sacred wisdom is preserved for future generations; (2) to draw from stories that Mãe Beata herself heard from elders and to invent new ones from personal experience to maintain the continuity of sacred traditions within the Candomblé temple; (3) to make a case for the African oral tradition as a viable repository of knowledge that can stand side by side with Western knowledge systems through efforts to universalize the moral significance of African short stories; (4) to make the stories appropriate for both children and adults by allowing for the intervention of the supernatural, the magical, the marvelous, fantasies, and allegories, thereby treating the stories as a double form of entertainment, both for escaping harsh realities and for leaving readers with a moral; (5) to establish herself not only as a storyteller but also as a priestess who has mastered the art of passing on sacred knowledge to present and future generations by personalizing some of the stories, such as the ones dedicated to her mother Mãe do Carmo and her daughter Maria do Oxum; (6) to put in written form a comprehensive code of conduct for her devotees as well as for ordinary people who want to learn from African sacred knowledge on diverse themes, which range from issues of madness (punishment for transgressing tradition or advice), the value of humility, reward for good character and conduct, veneration of the Great Mothers for their protection, appreciation and respect for the power of nature by not violating their space, and encouragement for the weak in the society. Of the forty-three stories, at least one-third of them are focused on women as protagonists, heroines, or villains. Though the stories cover many aspects of human life, I have chosen to focus on stories where female protagonists are privileged to highlight the significance of women in Candomblé.

Through the interactions of human characters with supernatural beings, readers learn to revere sacred entities and traditions. For the most part, these stories teach a moral lesson by presenting protagonists who transgress traditions and are consequently punished. The title story "Caroço de Dendê" (Palm oil seed) is a paradox because it reveals sacred wisdom that should ordinarily be kept secret within the Candomblé tradition. The story narrates how Olorum, the Supreme God, had arrogated to the palm seed with four eye pointers (symbolic of the dotted 'eyes' on a typical palm nut seed that is used during divination, for example) the responsibility to see the whole world and keep its secrets, while he endowed the palm seed with three eye pointers no such responsibility. To cause confusion, Exu, the deity of the crossroads, wanted to cause a rift between the two seeds, so Exu approached the three-eyed seed to reveal its secrets to him. Instead of subscribing to Exu, it rejected the wiles of the diabolic spirit through a wise paradoxical question: "How could I? If I only have three eyes and not four like my brother, to whom Olorum gave this power?"[30] After failing at his own gimmick to cause a rift among the two brothers, Exu quickly and mysteriously disappeared. While the moral of the story is aptly loyalty to one's brother, it also teaches one not to allow a third party to cause unwarranted and irreparable havoc in a cohesive community or family. The fact that Mãe Beata chooses this story as the main title suggests that readers are privileged to enjoy rare insight from sacred wisdom, which should ordinarily be shared only among the few initiated entities of Candomblé. Because the title story, in which a trusted character does not betray the other for selfish gains, deviates from the norm of transgression and punishment, it shows Mãe Beata's graciousness and her bountiful heart. Rather than restrict this rare Afro-Brazilian folk knowledge to the domain of the temple, Mãe Beata chooses instead to educate the larger Brazilian community.

On a more conceptual level, "Caroço de Dendê" falls within the dynamics of the Yoruba trickster, with its twists, turns, and ambiguities. The didactic effect of the trickster figure is to force the reader to be suspicious of its every move, as it intends to deceive and outsmart its opponent. As Ropo Sekoni and Henry Louis Gates Jr. appropriately advance in *Folks Poetics* and *The Signifying Monkey*, respectively, Exu is the master of antithesis and of critical interpretation. Thus, Exu must be read carefully to understand how he manipulates his victims. Fortunately, in "Caroço de Dendê," the antagonist does not fall into Exu's trap. In the twelve stories I analyze, Exu is the central deity who operates among the major protagonists and characters and compels them to submit to their tragic flaws, such as the flaw of disrespect in the stories "Samba in the House of Exu," "Daughter Who Becomes Dumb," "Queen Mother and Lizard Prince," and "Woman Who Knew Too Much." Beyond the intervention of the Exu figure, most of the stories feature the themes of madness and the triumph of good over evil, both as comic relief and as castigation, and these themes appear in "Samba in the House of Exu," "Cleaner's Skirt," "Cursed Riches," "Ekodide Feather," and "Oyá Seju." The remaining paradigmatic stories depict the transgression of tradition, a transgression that reflects a number of flaws. For example, (1) in "Ancestral Mother," because she abandoned a newborn, a woman is charged to return to the world of the living to raise her child to adolescence; (2) in "Ayná," a woman's promiscuity results in her giving birth to ugly bastards; (3) in "Aramaçá" (Rare fish), the contravention of the taboo of not eating fish as an initiate of Yemonjá turns into magical realism; and (4) in "Ayná," the betrayal of secrets is crudely punished with a human defect. In their divergent challenges and confounding resolutions, the stories reveal profound thoughts about the many ambiguous manifestations of African spirituality, mystification, and morality.

In the story that closes *Caroco de Dendê*, "Story Dedicated to my Mother Carmo," which was dedicated to the writer's mother, Mãe Beata does not pretend to share a work of fiction but rather shares elements of her own autobiography. The story recounts the life of her mother who loved to eat fish and always wanted to have children. Once she became pregnant, everyone was happy for her and kept asking her in solidarity if she was carrying twins. This was because she had lost five sets of twins during pregnancy. In a sense, it was a way of celebrating with her, as she had already given birth to twenty-five children. Mãe Beata also recalls the memory of a well-respected woman called Tia Afalá who was the midwife of the plantation. The most striking part of the story is the detailed account of her birth:

Table 3.1. Structural Grid of Core Stories from *Caroço de Dendê*

Story	Character	Transgression	Punishment	Moral
Samba in the House of Exu	Sambista (woman)	Lack of respect for tradition	Madness	Be wise and respect elders
Cleaner's Skirt	Otaciana	False promise of a festivity skirt	Madness	Never trick an orixá
Cursed Riches	Plantation owner	Killed witness to buried riches	Loss of riches to the oppressed	Good always thrives over evil
Ancestral Mother	Iya Mi	Death after delivery of baby	Returned to raise child as a bird	Never abandon a newborn baby
Ekodide feather	Poor girl, evil father	Father wishes to sell daughter	Oxum provides a rich bride	Never berate a deity's daughter
Queen Mother & Lizard Prince	Proud sister, humble sister	Pride, berating ugly sister	Humble sister marries Prince	Be humble!
Woman who knew too much	All Knowing Woman	Woman claims invite to event	Mother shamed at the event	Only God knows everything
Daughter who becomes dumb	Juvita, Wayward daughter	Shames mother via blasphemy	Dumbness	Never disrespect authority
Ayná	Ayná, her absent husband	Ayná sleeps with other men, including king and hunter	Bastards born ugly; husband sends wife away	Only the mother knows the child's paternity
Oyá Seju	Oyá Seju and Idjebi	Father oppresses daughter	Daughter takes responsibility	Never rush to judgment
Rare fish type (Aramaçá)	Yemonjá's daughter	Eats forbidden *moqueca* (fish stew)	Shock as cooked fish come alive	Never eat a deity's taboo
Iyá Inâ	Iyá Inâ	Betrayal of secrets	Potion fills her mouth with fire	Never betray secrets

One day, Mãe Carmo felt like eating fish. She grabbed the fishhook and went fishing in the river which ran through the plantation. As she was fishing, her baby water broke in her stomach. She came out of the river, and as she was crossing the street, I was born, right there. A little girl. They called Auntie Afalá, who took both my mother and I home, in order to cut the umbilical cord. Auntie realized that the little girl was strong, but still had a soft head. The old midwife then stated:

—Look, I will put some leaves on the head of this child. She is the daughter of Exu and Yemonjá.[31]

After seven days, the leaves were removed from her head, and the midwife recommended her initiation right away. The narrator completes the story with a sense of pride: "Today, I am an initiated daughter of an Orixá and an activist for my religion and my race. My name: Beata de Yemonjá."[32] Though she may have heard other stories from other elders of Candomblé, which were passed down from generation to generation (only to be reinvented by her), she chose to dedicate this one, her most authentic, to her mother. When the entire collection is viewed in the light of her social and religious activism, it is a lasting testament to her political agency.

Mãe Valnizia Bianch: Reconstructing Memories and Histories in *Reflexões*

Rachel Harding, author of *A Refuge in Thunder*, not only recuperated a religious legacy by documenting and translating the essays of Mãe Valnizia Bianch, but she also helped to put the Terreiro Pilão de Cobre (Copper Pestle Temple) on the map. Located in Engenho Velho da Federação, Salvador da Bahia, Terreiro Pilão de Cobre is one of the oldest Candomblé temples in Salvador, and is a contemporary of such famed sacred shrines as Casa Branca do Engenho Velho and Casa de Oxumarê. Terreiro do Cobre's history originates from Barroquinha in 1889, where, like Terreiro do Gantóis of Mãe Menininha, women leaders or Ialorixás were at the helm of affairs in Candomblé, and their temples were characterized by the worship of the three nations of Ketu, Jeje, and Bantu. Flaviana Maria da Conceição Bianchi, who wrote *Reflexões* and is the current Iyalorixá of the Terreiro Pilão de Cobre, is the granddaughter of the founder of the temple, Mother Valnizia de Airá. As an insider of the Candomblé community of Terreiro Pilão de Cobre and an elder initiate (egbomi) for over twenty years, Rachel Harding offers the curious enthusiast a vivid window into the world of religious community rites, struggles, and concrete achievements against incredible challenges. The semiautobiography of Mãe Valnizia Bianch reflects on the Yoruba cycle of life, cultural and religious festivities, family, hopes, iconic homages to warrior women in her life, such as her mother Telinha de Yemonjá, and the Yemonjá deity, the environment and the vitality of healing, her father Ayrá, the magic of words, the importance of respect and religion, as well as the place of leadership in Candomblé. As broadly diverse as these issues are, Mãe Valnizia Bianch succeeds in synthesizing them through the wealth of her experience and wisdom, which emanates from the cogent examples that run through her recollections and memories. One clear commonality among the narratives of Mãe Valnizia Bianch, Mãe Stella de Oxóssi, and Mãe Beata de Yemonjá may well be that all are unassuming and dynamic in the way they share their wisdom. Rachel Harding describes Mãe Valnizia Bianch's wisdom as "wisdom imbedded in ancestral strength," through which she communicates "wide compassion and the sharp discernment of people not easily impressed by the material trapping of power."[33] What I find quite remarkable in the collection of essays is the fact they were originally published in a monthly column in the A Tarde newspaper between December 2014 and August 2016. Beyond its documentary value as a reservoir of wisdom and African ancestrality in Brazil, the collection also serves as a rich source for the popularization of the sacred in light of religious fanaticism and intolerance following the recent neo-Pentecostal assaults on Candomblé. As a sample of how the author's columns often leave the reader with closing words of wisdom and advice, let me share a typical occasion, when she unveils her deity as Oxalá (Supreme deity) while signing off from her column: "The world needs human beings to be more humane, so that our children and grandchildren, all children, may have a better future . . . May Oxalá place his alá (luminously white garb) to brighten the hearts and minds of our leaders, to better our country's situation."[34] I find this style of writing to be quite compassionate, popular, alluring, and quite accessible to all races, religions, and sexual orientations.

In the many chapters that make up her collected writings, Mãe Valnizia Bianch focuses on celebrations, festivities, cultural values, religious rites, and homages to her parents and to Oxalá. She focuses on these because they are some of the most profound essences of Candomblé as an integrated or hybridized religion, and the Iyalorixá dialogues with the broader Bahian religious communities and Brazilian audience with cogent specificity. Among its many functions, including striking a unifying chord, the writings of Mãe Valnizia Bianch deploy religion as a political form of social activism and agency by bringing the reader's attention to many social injustices: racial discrimination, poverty, violence, religious intolerance, lack of education and opportunities for Blacks, and an overall sense of despair, deprivation, and inequality. Drawing on how religious entities participate in popular culture and invest in the education of children, she calls attention to how a religious organization can become active and transformative in the community. Tying together the importance of religion and leadership, the author invokes the violence faced by children and how a leader must adapt her psychology to best address the situation. In her own words: "We feel powerless in the face of the reality our city and our neighborhoods, not knowing if our children will make it to school as they risk being hit by a stray bullet."[35] She argues that it is not enough that children face such risks and that marginalized and persecuted religious organizations must protect their children; they must also address the distorted images of Candomblé on social media by neo-Pentecostal evangelicals who are bent on destroying Afro-Brazilian religious expressions and identity. Teaching her community through personal example, the author shares moments of struggle for Candomblé and how many terreiros face the battle for the survival and continuity of their Africa-derived traditions. Inspired by the energy of her ancestors and parents, she is determined to share the sacred stories of her past, as if in "a conversation, during a reading or walk contemplating the sea, important dates, or when sensitivity is the vector that directs the writing."[36] Rachel Harding's translator notes go beyond the definition of Candomblé as a "religion of radically inclusive community of extraordinary care and of rootedness," and she draws parallels between what she experienced in Brazil and what she experienced in the United States by relating her memories of her mother and other female relatives. She passionately articulates the significance of the collection of essays when she asserts: "I saw in Mãe Val's essays, many connections between the lives of Afro-Brazilians and those of their cousins living elsewhere in the diaspora. I felt I was seeing and understanding new layers of experience inside the communities of urban Salvador that I have come to love. . . . My hope is that this collection of essays serves to strengthen the bridge between one side of the Afro-Atlantic world and another."[37] The many didactic levels of the collection make it appropriate for new devotees, as well as for general readers who are curious not just about Afro-Brazilian religious practices, faith, and spirituality but also about how this entity has survived and passed on its traditions despite many centuries of persecution. Through syncretism and the popularization of the sacred, the ancestral devotees were able to mask African deities by pretending to worship Catholic saints as a form of syncretic survival. One of the author's many epiphanic moments comes alive when she talks about how healing comes in many forms: "In one form or another, believing or cultivating spirituality is important for human beings . . . the important thing is to believe in the sacred, as that is what helps us to heal ourselves . . . anyone who works to heal others also heals herself/himself."[38] The richness of the collection makes it challenging to synthesize as it touches on virtually every social issue—from the personal and communal to the religious and spiritual.

Other aspects worth mentioning are those sublime moments when hardship takes on a new meaning for the author as she tries to communicate the aesthetic of poverty and survival. When the author talks about Christmas and family, she remembers "the spicy, aromatic smell of the leaves mixed with the scent of the seasons' fruits: pineapple, mango, watermelon and umbu." In addition, she captures the pain of poverty when some children cannot hope to get anything from Santa Claus: "When I was a child, Papa Noel almost never passed my window. Sadly, the commemoration of Christ's birth brings happiness for some and sadness for others, especially for less privileged children who don't understand why Papa Noel doesn't leave presents at their windows."[39] The author talks about her great-grandmother, Telinha of Iemanjá, who loved to run to the Terreiro de Jesus (Pelourinho) during carnival, to watch Filhos de Gandhi, an Afoxé carnival group that dressed in white. Interestingly, it was this great-grandmother who raised her and who guided her as she assumed leadership of the temple. Striking also is her long list of the great warrior women whom she celebrates: Mãe Tatá of the Casa Branca Candomblé temple, Iya Nitinha de Oxum, Mãe Stella de Oxóssi, Lélia Gonzáles, Vilma Reis, Yeda Pessoa de Castro, Makota Valdina Pinto, Alaíde do Feijão, Ana Célia da Silva, Olga Mettig, Irmã Dulce, Ana Alice Costa, and Lídice da Mata. While she laments how times have changed and vital lessons of life are being lost as children no longer appreciate the value of asking elders for forgiveness during the Holy Week, she also insists that mothers should be celebrated every day. In fact, she sees herself as the spiritual mother of hundreds of people, all of whom she considers her grandchildren, as if they were biologically her own. In addition, she begs for the protection of the environment and for celebrating the June festivals without environmental or human destruction. She remembers Auntie Cutu, whose memory leaves her with much happiness. Of all the festivities celebrated, it is that of the Ibejis (twins) on which she elaborates most. She describes the occasion of the Ibeji Rope, where candies and fruits are hung as treats. After singing, everyone jumps to grab a few of the treats while the traditional caruru is served to the delight of everyone. Overall, though fragmented and synthesized, her narrative captures the multidimensional perspective of Candomblé as a way of life and as it intersects with daily rituals and political agitation for racial equality, inclusion, and empowerment.

Conclusion: Mãe Stella, Mãe Beata, and Mãe Valnizia Compared

Afro-Brazilian mythology evolved through slavery and survived through many decades of persecutions by the Brazilian hegemonic state, by the police, and by fanatical neo-Pentecostalists who consider Candomblé to be satanic. Deploying mythical stories, Mãe Stella, Mãe Beata, and Mãe Valnizia use their creative works to preserve the history and mythology of Candomblé. While what used to be sacred oral tradition is now documented as written culture, it nonetheless preserves its core Afro-Brazilian cultural values by expanding its reach, from the educated to the uneducated, and by archiving that wisdom for future generations. *Ososi: O Caçador de Alegrias* and *Caroço de Dendê* expose the intertwined significance of the Orixás by explicating their characteristics through the lens of mythological narratives. Through the application of wisdom, memory, strength, and power, these exemplary women of orixá share with the reader the symbolic qualities of their personal divinities, including Oxóssi, Yemanjá, and Oxalá. In so doing, we get a rare window into the sacred world of hunting, the agonies of the world, and the expansiveness of the world as protected by the gracious mother of all Yemonjá, as well as her spiritual patriarchal partner Oxalá, the "immortal king of all things white."[40] Despite their separation from Africa, these three writer-priestesses take us on a journey to Africa through exemplary protagonists, personal reflection, and semiautobiography. While Mãe Stella and Mãe Beata have now joined their ancestors, in their visionary commitment, along with Mãe Valnizia, they have left the living with a part of themselves, passing on the tradition to generations yet unborn. In addition to preserving Afro-Brazilian mythologies, the three matriarchs also relocate the sacred into popular culture, as the narratives are now available for all generations to appreciate into the future. Through individual reminiscences, reflections on leadership qualities that preserve age-old traditions, and representations of the supernatural, they give the sublime and the magical, which are associated with femininity and religiosity, realist manifestations and profound new meanings.

Part II
The Sacred in Literary Manifestations

Chapter 4

Jorge Amado and Vasconcelos Maia

The Sea/River as Iemojá/Oxum's Domain

With its myriad mysteries, rituals, and popular festivals, Bahia is that part of the Brazilian cultural tapestry that never ceases to fascinate insiders and outsiders from all walks of life. During the feast of cleansing of the Good End Church, the enchanting images of the baianas beautify the ambience, and the appetizing aroma of acarajé being sold by baianas on street corners provokes the palate of tourists and locals alike. The blocos afros adorn Afro-Bahian carnival with their colorful costumes and music, and capoeira players reenact a striking and historical tradition of resistance for many generations. Bahia reimagines the idea of an Africa that has been hybridized even when resistance persists. In the same vein of creating an alternative cultural expression are the novelists Jorge Amado and Vasconcelos Maia, whose novels *Mar Morto* (1936) (Sea of death) and *O Leque de Oxum* (1960) (Oxum's mirror) involve encounters at sea. In the former, a love triangle between Iemanjá, Guma, and Lívia exemplifies the tension between the worldly and the otherworldly. In the latter, deities manifesting destructive forces through their human vehicles dramatize the tension between the virtues of the deities and their counterpoints. While the power of literary re-creation offers documentary value for Candomblé rituals, which are otherwise less visible to the average Brazilian, these creative works further facilitate the reader's encounter with the intersection of ancestrality, love, and hybridity. Through a critical reading of the primary characteristics of Iemanjá and Oxum, as embodied in the characters Lívia and Matilde,

among others, this chapter argues that the ancestral serves as the medium
for the preservation of African culture through strategic hybridizations
and reverse rites of passage.

In the domain of Atlantic feminine deities and water spirits in
Brazil, there is an interesting hierarchical physical location of the three
main goddesses. Identified in syncretic terms as the Virgin Mary, they
are as follows: Iemanjá lives in the middle of the ocean, Oxum lives on
the surface of the waters, and Nanã dwells in the depths of the ocean.
This chapter focuses primarily on Iemanjá and Oxum, who share the
caprices of female vanities, voluptuousness, sensuality, fertility, beauty,
and potential for destructive energies. As the ultimate embodiments of
feminine principles and aquatic symbols, Iemanjá and Oxum constitute
the archetypal female as manifest in their many renditions in the Brazilian syncretic religion of Candomblé. As primordial supernatural life
forces that are manifest in the creation, the existence, and the survival
of life that their abode of the seas and rivers appropriately represent, they
are the sources of life without which living itself ceases to be possible.
Bahia is the ideal location for what is termed the "cycle of festivities,"
including those for Iemanjá and Oxum. The annual Iemanjá festival that
takes place in early December and January in Rio Vermelho reenacts the
meshing of the sacred with the profane, as Mircea Eliade theorizes in *The
Sacred and the Profane* (1987). The commonality of both deities resides in
their association of the feminine with the aquatic, especially as it relates
to water as the source of life. Water becomes the archetypal symbol of
human existence—human blood, menstrual blood, amniotic fluid, sexual
arousal fluid, and water from elements of nature—and embodies both
the protective and destructive forces of life. In other words, the water
that sustains life is also that which causes death, such as in catastrophic
natural disasters like hurricanes.

Jorge Amado and Vasconcelos Maia: Complimentary Contemporaries

Though a few decades apart in age, Jorge Amado and Vasconcelos Maia
share a commonality when it comes to their penchant for modernism
and hybridity, and neither received the best critical response in their
early years. Amado, due to his affiliation with the Brazilian Communist Party (PCB: Partido Comunista Brasileiro), was ostracized by the

government, while Maia was learning to shift his "white" writing to Black-hybrid writing through linguistic crealization and self-immersion in Afro-Brazilian culture. Both writers were invested in Afro-Brazilian religion and were frequent attendees and honorary guests at the Ilê Axé Opô Afonjá. In their shift from bourgeois writing to writing about the Afro-Brazilian experience, devoid of racial stereotypes and prejudices, they became spokespersons for Black people and their oppressive conditions. Amado had been an established novelist since the 1930s, while Maia was a short-story and novella writer who would eventually gain recognition after World War II through the *Caderno da Bahia* group. Maia's creative corpus includes *Contos da Bahia* (1951), *O cavalo e a rosa* (1955), *Primeiro mistério* (1961), and *Histórias da gente baiana* (1964). In *O Leque de Oxum* (1961), racial tensions are highlighted and resolved mystically. Maia deploys the oral tradition and elements of magical realism to complicate interracial relations to expose the urgency and futility of racial discrimination. When compared to Amado, Maia seems to do a better job with the psychological development of his characters, even though he is less visible than Amado. Since their passage to the beyond in the 1980s, Maia seems to be gradually gaining attention as a formidable writer, one to be reckoned with alongside Jorge Amado, one of the greatest Latin American writers of all time.

Conceptualizing Atlantic Feminine Divinities

Afro-Brazilian culture integrates the religious forces with those of expressive popular culture forms as found in music, carnival, and other festivities in which specific deities are venerated. In Salvador da Bahia especially, Iemanjá and Oxum are visible around the city—in the house constructed for and dedicated to Iemanjá in Rio Vermelho and in the songs dedicated to these favorite female deities. They constitute reservoirs of cultural and religious memories, and the characteristics of these deities are further propagated and popularized in the mouths of the people, such as the song "É d'Oxum" by Gal Costa, sung by Gerônimo:

> Nessa cidade todo mundo é d'Oxum / Homem, menino, menina, mulher / Toda cidade irradia magia / Presente na água doce / Presente n'água salgada / E toda cidade brilha Presente na água doce / Presente n'água salgada / E toda

cidade brilha / Seja tenente ou filho de pescador / Ou impor-
tante desembargador / Se der presente é tudo uma coisa só /
A força que mora n'água / Não faz distinção de cor / E toda
cidade é d'Oxum.

(In this town everybody belongs to Oxum / Man, boy, girl,
woman /The whole town irradiates magic / Present in sweet
waters / Present in salt water / And the whole town shines
/ Be it a lieutenant or a fisherman's child / or an important
chief judge / The gifts they bring mean all and the same thing
/ The strength that lives in the water / Does not distinguish
between skin colors / And the whole town belongs to Oxum.)

The rest of the song includes Yoruba-sounding words that have been
corrupted over the years of religious adaptation and preservation in Brazil.
The incorporation of Yoruba expressions speaks to the gratitude shown
to Oxum. As the singer insists on pleasurably "navigating" the waves of
the sea, it is as if he is conjuring the spirit of the Oxum deity herself to
join him in a ritualized dance that appeals to both the sacred and the
profane alike. Both divinities, by their riverine spiritual characteristics,
are the domain of fertility and multiplicity.

Whenever African deities travel across the Atlantic, even during the
Middle Passage, they are participating in the dispersal and preservation of
the African past. Despite the horrors of slavery, our ancestors somehow
crafted a path of survival, even if it meant feigning ignorance about the
catalogue of oppression that accompanied that horrendous act of injustice
against humanity. Of the many deities that made the journey along with
millions of African captives, a few deities resonate all over the diaspora,
namely Xango, Iemanjá, Ogum, Oxum, Esu, and Oxossi. Of these, the
female divinities, Iemanjá and Oxum, often find a privileged place among
devotees due to their connection with the sea and river. In other words,
the fluidity of their aquatic nature takes their characteristics beyond
elements of nature to more esoteric levels of cosmologic proportions.
They are often intertwined, even in the Catholic faith or in syncretic
religions, where they are seen as Ladies of Conception or the Virgin
Mary. With their embodiment of maternity and motherhood, they occupy
many spheres of fertility, procreation, protection, and nutrition, as well
as the feeling of fury amid calmness, especially when provoked by other
invisible or terrestrial forces. The two texts under consideration in this

chapter imbue Iemanjá and Oxum with some of the same characteristics. As a result, our focus will be on these two and their interactions with the lives of the characters with whom they engage.

Iemanjá, whose color is often white and blue, is regarded as the "mother of all," as she can control the heads of every being in the world. As queen of the sea, one of her *orikis* (praise names) goes like this: "Immense Mother / Intense Hand that the world embraces / Hand of the Sea, owner of the world / Iemanjá's Hand / Mother of the world."[2] From these qualities, we can deduce that Iemanjá dominates natural phenomena, while she is also in leadership circles among the Aje society. Her symbol is a fish she holds in her hand like a scepter. In the edited volume *Yemoja* (2013), Solimar Otero and Toyin Falola focus on the gender and sexuality of this deity. Meanwhile, J. Lorand Matory in *Black Atlantic Religion* (2005) privileges purist Candomblé circles more than the syncretic ones, even though the essential unity of the function of each deity is unquestionable. This syncretism often graduates from the sacred to the secular, as in the Feast of Yemoja described by Cheryl Sterling: "By early evening, all offerings are concluded and the street, stretching for a kilometer on either side of the Casa de Iemanjá, appears like a mini-carnival."[3] This is a clear indication that the sea goddess is involved in all the affairs of men and women, regardless of where they find themselves. Due to the different cycles of festivities in Salvador, it is uncommon to have disparaging dismissals of the deities, who are quite visible all over Bahia. In his focused study *Iemanjá: A Grande Mãe Africana do Brasil* (2002), Antonio Vallado covers the trajectory of the divinity from Africa to Brazil through the different initiation rites that are part of the Brazilian cultural way of life. Pierre Verger, in *Notas sobre o Culto dos Orixás* (2002), provides us with another oriki that articulates the uniting force of Iemanjá: "Forcefully, Iemanjá / Leaves the river like a rainbow / The woman with humid breasts / She remains calm even when upset with someone / She takes his friends by the hand / With sweetness, she joins them together around her."[4] This harmonious virtue complements other attributes of maternal protection as she positions herself as mother of all. Yet, one must not dismiss her volatile potential, such as the jealous competition in *Mar Morto* between her and Lívia for Guma, where it is only through Guma's death at sea that Iemanjá fulfills her wish. *Mar Morto* is a classic Amadian novel, and the title refers to those human bodies that do not return to the land. In death, Iemonjá has craftily become their mother under the sea.

Oxum, on the other hand, shares some attributes with Iemanjá. She is as a maternal figure, though her symbol is the mirror she carries in her hand and her colors are gold and yellow. Lydia Cabrera (2002) and Joseph M. Murphy and Mei-Mei Sanford (2001) address the vitality of Oxum in different ways. Cabrera compares Iemanjá and Oxum in the Afro-Cuban pantheon; beyond the shared attributes of fertility, beauty, power, and protectiveness, Cabrera also argues that both deities occasionally have warrior or masculine tendencies due to their strength and ferociousness when provoked.[5] Drawing from his own artistic research, Rowland Abiodun postulates that "visual representations of female *orisa* like *Osun* have influenced Yoruba aesthetic considerations and artistic processes far more than scholars have acknowledged."[6] In this sense, the Osun deity influences the religious and the artistic spheres in Africa as well as in the diaspora to the extent that the commonality remains a constant and should be celebrated. This is the same conclusion reached by Mircea Eliade in *The Sacred and the Profane* when she establishes the inextricable connection between the zone of religiosity and the collateral zone of the popularization of sacred culture, where the sacred is at the service of the profane and vice versa. What is most curious about both deities is the quality of transgression and castigation. In *Mar Morto*, Iemanjá seems to have an unspoken rule that Guma is not to marry Lívia. In going against this rule, Guma becomes vulnerable and ends up a victim of the storm that is controlled by Iemanjá. Thus, he becomes the victim of the consolatory aphorism that "*it is sweet to die at sea.*" In the same vein, in *O Leque de Oxum*, Matilde is forbidden to marry Undset, and she pays the ultimate sacrifice with her life. Conceptually, these Afro-Atlantic feminine deities are ambivalent characters who embody the duality of degeneration and regeneration. In a sense, their wards may well be at their mercy because they can choose to be benevolent or malevolent, depending on whether or not they get their way. It is a matter of destiny, yes, but it is also a matter of power and ruthless jealousy.

Amado's *Mar Morto* (1936) (Sea of Death)

Mar Morto recounts the life stories of Bahian sailors who live by the dockside. By weaving stories of their daily lives of hardship and love with the supremacy of the sea goddess, Iemanjá, Amado brings to life a rare glimpse of how the sea challenges sailors in their quest for survival. Such is the fate of Guma and Lívia as they find themselves in a love triangle with Iemanjá. Their narratives amply demonstrate how the sea is interwoven in the life of the sailors: in other words, the countless storms they risk as a daily ritual, the smugglers they confront at sea, and the sustaining power of romantic love conspire to authenticate their lives as extraordinary and as human. Amado's creative works often privilege Candomblé by associating the literary with the sacred through profound portrayals of the relationship between characters and the Afro-Brazilian religion. Through compelling dialogues between religion and literature in works such as *Jubiabá* (1935) (Jubiabá), *Mar Morto* (1936) (Sea of death), *Capitães da Areia* (1937) (Captains of the sand), *Gabriela, Cravo e Canela* (1958) (Gabriela, clove and cinnamon), *Pastores da Noite* (1964) (Pastors of the night), *Compadre de Ogum* (1964) (Ogun's companion), *Dona Flor e Seus Dois Maridos* (1966) (Dona Flor and her two husbands), *Tenda dos Milagres* (1969) (Tent of miracles), *Teresa Batista* (1972) (Tereza Batista), and *Sumiço da Santa* (1988) (Disappearance of the saint), Amado captures the Yoruba oral tradition and the Afro-Brazilian storytelling imaginary. My choice of *Mar Morto* privileges the forceful manifestation of the sea goddess, Iemanjá, in one of Jorge Amado's most mythological works.

The context of Amado's writing of *Mar Morto* is instructive. In 1936, the year of publication of the novel, Amado was imprisoned for two months in Rio de Janeiro on the charges that he was a communist and supported the abortive military coup against the Vargas regime. It was a time when being a communist was seen as subversive and reprehensible. Upon release, he was approached by a British publisher in Brazil, José Olympio, to write a new novel. Though he had started writing *Mar Morto* in Salvador da Bahia, he completed it in Rio de Janeiro. The novel was honored by the Graça Aranha award from the Brazilian Academy of Letters the same year it was published. As the most poetical and lyrical of his novels, *Mar Morto* has been acclaimed as the novel about the "secrets of the sea": "a mystery that even old sailors don't understand."[7] In terms of the plot structure, the novel is primarily a story of love between Lívia and Guma. The story includes characters like the female goddess Iemonjá; black Rufino and his biracial lover Esmeralda; Old Francisco, Guma's uncle who works on nets; and the saucy Rosa Palmeirão, among others. As a paradigmatic text of African ancestrality, which is both hybridized and preserved in Brazil to the extent that it has helped assimilate African mythology into mainstream Brazilian literature,

Amado's novel succeeds in popularizing African traditional religiosity by elevating it to the same level of Greco-Roman mythology and originality. Given the importance of orixás in Brazilian culture, Amado was adept in recognizing the significance of African culture in Brazilian national consciousness and translated such strong influences into popular culture through literature. In sum, Amado has set in motion the popularization of cultural syncretism between Eurocentrism and Afrocentrism by appropriating African mythologies at a time they were not yet fashionable.

In its tripartite plot structure, Mar Morto brings together the mythology of Iemanjá as Mistress of the Seas and of Sailors, the Flying Packet, and the Sea of Death to tell a lyrical story of love. Guma and Lívia are tied together by a series of events that culminate in a moment of heroism on the part of the sea, the female deity herself. Beginning in media res and written in the third person using colloquial language, Mar Morto deploys flashback techniques to tell the story of Lívia as she awaits the return of Guma, her spouse, from his tempestuous fishing adventures at sea. It was then after this opening episode that the omniscient narrator begins the story by simply following a logical timeline, with very little psychological development of characters. In fact, the flat characterization is reminiscent of stereotypical images. The landscape transcends Salvador and extends to other neighboring Bahian cities, such as Itaparica, Cachoeira, Maragogipe, Santo Amaro, and the Bahian basin, as well as Rio de Janeiro. Indeed, Mar Morto presents many complex internal structures and associations, and the many levels are worth exploring to gain a fuller understanding of the symbolic and literal interactions between characters, spaces, entities, paradigms, allegories, and identities. These complexities are unified through mythologies that define the world of the sacred as it interacts with the profane in a cosmological tension and resolution that leads the characters to better express their own individualities and connectivity with the world of Iemanjá and the nurturing space of Candomblé.

On the level of characterization, several characters overlap when paired with others based on the defining manifestations of their "push–pull qualities." Underlying these characterizations is a deeper sociopolitical consciousness of the recuperation of African mythologies that have been silenced in Brazilian culture. Amado seeks to recuperate the myths and exclusionary values that emanate from the violent legacy of slavery, which obfuscated them over time and cultural space. In this symbolic gesture is a protest against social injustices and oppressions that have kept Afro-Brazilians behind the veil of visibility and from participating in the larger sphere of Brazilian identity. In rewriting the Brazilian nation, Amado creates a historical moment by shifting the power dynamics to favor the marginalized culture of Afro-descendant populations despite their gradual assimilation and race mixing. As a result, several arche-typal relationships emerge within the novel, which may be perceived as metaphors for the Brazilian nation: Iemanjá-Orungã, Lívia-Iemanjá, Guma-Xangô, Esmeralda-Iansã, Rosa Palmeirão–Iansã, Rufino-Ogum, Iansã-Iemanjá, and D. Dulce-Dr. Rodrigo, among other binary or com-plementary relations. Of these relations, the Lívia-Guma-Iemanjá love triangle is the most compelling within the plot structure, as it gives an air of magical realism to the whole plot of tension, transgression, tragedy, and regeneration—as if the characters in question are conditioned by an intertwined fate or destiny.

Such a destiny is what Patrícia Trindade Nakagame (2016) argues is outlined by Amado in the very beginning of the novel as a permanent apprehension of the sea by Lívia as it relates to the constant absence of her husband from home:

> *Mar Morto* se inicia com uma cena de tempestade, anunciada como "falsa noite," que chega antes da hora, impondo a escuridão e o perigo. Está antecipada neste capítulo a impre-visibilidade que marca todo o livro em questão, definindo a vida dos homens do mar, que não podem saber das mudanças do tempo e, assim, arriscam-se diariamente em seus barcos. A natureza arrebatadora pode, assim, revolucionar a vida dos marinheiros sendo uma ameaça constante a eles. O medo torna-se rotina, de tal modo que pescadores e familiares se esforçam por habituar-se ao inesperado, sabendo que a morte, a finitude e a dor podem estar presentes em uma noite como aquela.[8]

> (*Mar Morto* begins with a storm scene, announced as a "false night," that arrives at dawn imposing darkness and danger. It is predetermined in this scene the unpredictability that marks the whole book in question, defining the life of the sailors, who cannot know the changes of time and thus risk their lives daily on their boats. The sweeping nature can suddenly transform the lives of the sailors, which are in constant danger. Fear

becomes routine, so that fishermen and their families strive
to get used to the unexpected, knowing that death, finitude,
and pain may be present on a night like that.)

This constant fear of death will serve as the organizing motif throughout the novel, as Iemanjá, the forceful sea goddess, remains in constant
conflict with Lívia.

Iemanjá-Orungã dynamics are better appreciated in the mythical
relationship between mother and daughter, because in the narrative
of *Mar Morto*, one gave birth to the other. Meanwhile, Lívia-Iemanjá
embodies the sister-in-law/motherhood tension, as if Iemanjá is indeed in
amorous competition with Lívia and would rather have Guma for herself
under the sea. However, Guma is not such an easy target because he is
a warrior figure associated with Xangô. The Esmeralda-Iansã duality is
manifest in descriptions of Rufino's mistress, who would later lose Rufino
to the wiles of the sea, as a "pretty, busty mulatto girl, with rolling hips,
a good chunk of womanhood."[9] The Rosa Palmeirão–Iansã dynamic also
shares the stormy and warrior-like characteristics, as Rosa embodies the
"qualities" of Iemanjá (as mother-lover) in addition to those of Iansã.
When Rosa falls in love with Guma and wants to have his child, Guma
finds himself sleeping in her arms while she sings: "*Sleep, sleep, little baby,*
/ Bogeyman's on his way."[10] This song invokes the jealousy and wrath of
Iemanjá, who is the only one who can be mother and lover at the same
time. The Rufino-Ogum duality embodies some of the same qualities as
Guma and, in fact, the two are best friends. Here is a case of a passing
love triangle that involves Rufino, Guma, and Esmeralda. Once Rufino
meets Esmeralda, he cannot resist her enchantment, and he chooses to
live close to Guma, Esmeralda's occasional lover. Rufino ends up making
love to his best friend's mistress, while his real wife, Lívia, is sick and
asleep in the next house. Rufino ultimately kills Esmeralda in a jealous
rage and later commits suicide at sea. It is as if he goes to sea to meet
with Iemanjá to absolve himself of his sins. Meanwhile, the relationship
between Dona Dulce and Dr. Rodrigo embodies the notion of the "new
man" as conceived in socialist parlance. In fact, Dr. Rodrigo may well
be seen as the alter ego of Jorge Amado, given his subtle socialist ideals.
Yet, all of these extra-conjugal affairs do not imply that the Afro-Brazilian
family is completely destroyed. Indeed, the relationship between Maria
Clara and Master Manuel embodies the stabilization of the Afro-Brazilian
family as evidenced by their long-standing marriage and happiness.

The love triangle between Lívia, Guma, and Iemanjá offers a deeper reflection about the intricately intertwined and inseparable worlds of the sacred and the profane. From the religious perspective, Iemanjá comes into a love relationship to lay claim to her power to affect both characters as a spiritual being. Through the prism of Guma, she is able to control worldly affairs because he must set out to sea to conduct his daily professional rituals. At sea, Iemanjá is there either to protect him, love him, or cause him havoc if he refuses to pay homage to her as the sea goddess. Ultimately, Guma belongs to Iemanjá in life and death. The life of the sailor, by nature, is inextricably intertwined with that of the sea. From the Yoruba cosmological principle of a regenerative life cycle that incorporates the world of the living, the dead, and the unborn, the death of Guma triggers his unification with Iemanjá, his mother and lover under the sea. While Guma is still alive, Lívia worries if he will ever return to her. Thus, in addition to other women competing for Guma's love, Lívia is also in competition with the goddess Iemanjá. Even though the sea goddess lives under the water, she occasionally reveals herself to those on earth by appearing in her divine elegance and voluptuousness, as when old Francisco observes her on the docks in a scene that ends the book: " 'Look! Look! It's Janaína.' They looked and saw. . . . She saw a strong woman who was fighting on. The fight was a miracle. . . . On the waterfront the sailors saw Iemanjá, she of the five names . . . it was the second time he had seen her."[11] Such close encounters between the sea goddess and the dock dwellers reinforce her expansive mythology, as she demonstrates her power over the sea and over the earth. Guma must love Iemanjá to protect his profession as a sailor who needs protection from the tragedies at sea. At the same time, he must balance his degree of loyalty to Lívia with that of Iemanjá to survive in both worlds.[12]

In the lives of sailors, the sea is a force to be reckoned with and a zone of life and death. The novel opens and closes with the sea's ability to wreak havoc on the lives of the sailors on the waterfront of Salvador da Bahia. Its centrality is unquestionable because the same sea that brings life and the livelihood of fishing can also take it. The characters in *Mar Morto*, portrayed as "victims of economic and historic forces beyond their control," speak compellingly about Afro-Brazilian religions and their impact on the lives of devotees.[13] Amado himself describes these devotees as "the men and women who brought from the depths of slavery, on their shoulders, such beauty that they have rescued and

preserved for us."[14] In other words, the mythology of Iemanjá strikes a
chord in the survival of Africans in Brazilian culture. The novel sums
up the plot structure by providing an author's epilogue, from which I
extract just the highlights:

> Now I should like to tell the dockside tales of Bahia . . . Ieman-
> já's people have much to tell. Come listen to these stories and
> these songs. Come hear the story of Guma and Lívia, which
> is the story of life and love on the sea . . . Even when that
> man loves these stories and these songs and attends the rites
> of Dona Janaína, even then he doesn't know all the secrets
> of the sea. For the sea is a mystery that even old sailors don't
> understand.[15]

The humble statement serves as Amado's caveat to the reader that the
mysteries of the sea cannot possibly be deciphered by the writer alone,
despite his forays into Afro-Brazilian religious circles. It takes the knowledge of the sailors themselves to tell their own stories. Because the sea
takes center stage in the drama of the lovers and sailors, Iemonjá, the
goddess of the sea, turns out to be the heroine despite herself. Despite
the many characters, poor and rich, struggling and aspiring, constantly
on the move between the land and the sea, some of whom lose their
lives at sea or choose to commit suicide, the sea remains constant and
untouched. This implies that the destiny of men and women is subject
to that of the sea but not vice versa.

Beyond the sea and the tempests, other characters participate
in the drama of conflicts, as sailors, fishermen, vagabonds, prostitutes,
and children of the saints (filhos e filhas-de-santo) all face unspoken
tragedies or challenges. The sea is held in high esteem as it instructs
the people of its superhuman powers when compared to the fragility
of man. Thus, Lívia lives with a permanent fear of losing Guma to
the sea as she contemplates the song from a distance that reinforces
that fear of the unknown, "It's sweet to die in the sea": "She's weeping,
she's afraid. She, too, is afraid of that day when her man might stay at
the bottom of the sea and never come back. When he would go with
Iemanjá, mistress of the sea, mother of waters, sailing off to other lands
and seas."[16] Despite the protagonists' ambivalence about the sea, they
also see it as a friend and a source of their livelihood and existence. As
mother and wife, Iemanjá carries her transatlantic expansiveness from

Africa to the New World, and she is known by five names according to the inclinations of her admirers or devotees. Thus, she is: (1) Iemanjá, mistress of the docks, lady of the seas and waters; (2) Dona Janaína, as seen by the canoemen; (3) Inâe, as seen by the blacks who dance for her; (4) Princess of Aiocá, by those who see her as a queen of mysterious lands; and (5) Maria, considered a pretty and venerated name. The narrator pays homage to her when he describes her qualities: "She dominates those seas, she adores the moon she comes to see on cloudless nights, she loves black people's music. Every year the feast of Iemanjá is celebrated by the Dike and at Monte Serrat. Then they call her by all of her five names, give her all her titles, bear her gifts, sing for her."[17] To complete the adoration and homage, Iemanjá is called upon to come out of the sea to feast with the people during the Iemanjá feast every February 2: "Iemanjá come . . . / Come from out of the sea . . . / Siren of the sea, rise up today . . . / Siren of the sea who wants to play."[18] The special homage to the sea goddess is incomplete without the narrator's acknowledgment that, in addition to the fear of the wrath of Iemanjá when the sailors are still alive, she is mother and wife to them. But, when they die at sea, they become like children, desiring her body for their posthumous amorous desires.

As an enchanting, paradigmatic prose poem about the hardships of sailors on the waterfront of Salvador da Bahia, *Mar Morto* describes, as the title suggests, the sea as that which has the potential to suffocate the life out of its dwellers and interactors and as that which brings about sustenance of life, adventures, and hope. This is not a conventional love story with highly developed characters; rather, the sea is also a protagonist. Characters are often described with flat or even stereotypical images—from the adept sailors, lovers, religious devotees, prostitutes, and heroes—but this is in service of protesting the social oppression that has been conditioned by many centuries of slavery. Amado assures the reader that he is simply retelling the story as he has been told by the courageous sailors themselves, who are in populist contention against the exploitative atrocities of the ruling elites. To give the story a local color, Amado interlaces the stories of the sailors with some popular songs and anecdotes that echo "string stories" (*ABCs or Cordel*). Old sailors, like Jeremaias or Francisco, recount memories of past glories, exploits, and hardships because they are now too old to sail—but, still, they embody the memories of such Brazilian heroes as Besouro, Lucas da Feira, Zumbi dos Palmares, and Lampião, among others.

How else can the sea be described by Jorge Amado? The narrator sees it as a womb and as a trap. It is a location of endless conflict and spatial hierarchies, where antagonistic tensions in the name of survival play out and where transgressions and punishments betray the reality of a city divided by the haves and have-nots. Land and sea are separated by the same social dichotomy that organizes the lives of those who live by the sea and outside of it; those in the upper city and those in the lower city; those who occupy the feminine space of domestic work and hope for the return of their loved ones at sea and those who occupy the masculine space that separates the street from the home; those who are free and those who are enslaved. As a result, most of the events are unpredictable, and oftentimes the sailors and their wives or lovers live in a world of fantasy and dashed hopes, as in the story that sums up Guma's life:

> A black man is singing today too. He says that sea people's wives have a terrible lot. Old Francisco smiles. He buried his wife, the doctor said it was her heart. She died suddenly one night when he came back in a storm. She threw herself into his arms and he noticed that she wasn't throbbing anymore and she was dead. She'd died from the joy of seeing him come back, the doctor said it was her heart. The one who stayed behind that night was Federico, Guma's father. A body no one found because he'd died to save Francisco, and that's why he went off with Iemanjá to other beautiful lands. It was his brother and his wife in one single night. Then he reared Guma on his sloop, at sea, so he wouldn't be afraid.[19]

When seen as the deterministic principle that decides the lives of the sailors and their loved ones, the sea combines sadness and joy, violence and sweetness, tragedy and comedy, agonies and pleasantries, hopes and disappointments, freedom and bondage. Forgetting and mourning their sorrows in songs and alcoholic drinks, the sailors must get used to the lyrics of the aphorism-song that says, "*It's sweet to die at sea.*" However, this sweetness is more of a consolation or spiritual rationalization than reality. Indeed, it is sad to die at sea and for loved ones to never return to the land, as is the case of Guma who loses his father to the sea, is raised by Francisco, and eventually also loses his life to the sea.

The last chapter of the novel, appropriately entitled "Sea of Death," encompasses the tragic dramas of Lívia and Guma as they navigate the struggle between life and death that defines most of the characters, including the sailors, their wives, and their mistresses. This duality is a constant in the lives of all the waterfront dwellers. To stay alive, the husbands must set out to sea to fish amidst storms with the risk of never coming back. Likewise, the wives agonize for hours and days, praying and hoping for their loved ones' return. It is a strange tension between nature at sea and the affairs of men and women on land. The sea, after all, is a sacred territory all its own, to which the unprepared seek refuge of survival only to be betrayed by the death that eventually knocks at their doors. Instead of adventure, the ensnared characters are confronted by the wiles of the sea, to which they are condemned, and by the destiny that awaits each sailor. They are trained to be detached from the city and from the land, and so the destiny of each sailor is intertwined with that of the sea—it is a destiny of no return. Despite their efforts to assist these men and women of the waterfront, to improve their lives as social agents by teaching their children, Dona Dulce and Dr. Rodrigo could not have any transformative change in their lives even after moving to live with them. While these committed teachers may be the alter egos of Amado, their efforts against the imminent destiny of the sea are in vain. Characters such as Guma, Lívia, Rosa Palmeirão, Bagé, and Besouro, among others, all metaphorically and symbolically end up in the abyss of Iemanjá's kingdom of death.

While it is customary for most of Amado's novels to be adapted into films, *Mar Morto* never benefitted from this noble gesture. Instead, *Porto dos Milagres* (2001) (Port of miracles) captures some of the episodes of the novel as translated into a soap opera that aired from February 5 to September 29, 2001. The soap opera was based on two works of Amado: *Mar Morto* (1936) and *A Descoberta da América pelos Turcos* (1992). Instead of a simple story of love between Guma and Lívia, the soap opera contains a far more complex plot involving many more characters and spaces. In *Porto dos Milagres*, Félix Guerrero, who has plotted a coup, and his wife Adma are on the run from the police in Spain. They receive a prophecy from a gypsy that Félix would cross the sea to become a king. Both Félix and Adma return to the coast of Bahia, Brazil, specifically the city of Porto dos Milagres, where the richest man, Bartolomeu Guerrero, Félix's twin brother, lives. Adma poisons Bartolomeu; Félix inherits his fortune and becomes king. Soon Adma orders the death of Arlete, a prostitute who had just given birth to a baby fathered by Bartolomeu. Heeding the orders, Eribert, Adma's foreman, kills Arlete, but as fate would have it, nature saves the baby, which drifted to the boat of Frederico, a fisherman, whose wife, Eulália, had given birth to a stillborn. Frederico consoles himself with the found baby, who he sees as his own son sent to him by Iemanjá. This is how Guma, the adopted son of Frederico, becomes a legitimate heir to the wealthiest man in Porto dos Milagres. Lívia, the niece of Augusta Eugênia Proença de Asuncion, emerges as an inheritor of a huge fortune from the past. Rosa Palmeirão also emerges as an ex-prisoner who returns to Porto dos Milagres to discover the whereabouts of her niece, Arlete, the prostitute who had been missing for many years. Rosa soon gets involved with Félix, unaware that he was involved in the death of Arlete. Guma emerges as a revered fisherman in the community, and Lívia becomes the girlfriend of Alexandre, son of both Félix and Adma. Lívia falls in love with Guma, Félix's political enemy, yet Félix does not realize that Guma is his nephew. He simply holds on to power as prophesied by the gypsy. Though the plot is far more complex, the reemergence of Guma, Lívia, and Rosa makes for an interesting reenactment of the power of the sea in the lives of Brazilians.

Though *Porto dos Milagres* differs significantly from the plot of *Mar Morto*, one cannot miss the theme of destiny, as Iemanjá and the sea bring Guma to Bartolomeu. The fact that Guma and Lívia mysteriously come together as lovers in this soap opera is also a testament to the extent to which both have become assimilated into Brazilian mythology. An interview with Amado confirms the centrality of Iemanjá and the sea in *Mar Morto*:

> A.R: For me there are two books for which there is a special coloration. *Mar Morto* and *Seara Vermelha*.
>
> J.A.: Mar Morto is a book about the sea . . . It is in *Mar Morto* that the sea is a dominant novelistic space, even predominant. Things happen there, it is about the life of man of the sea. It is a singular case-study.[20]

Amado is precise about the specificity of the role of Guma in *Mar Morto* as an embodiment of the collective consciousness of the fishermen from Salvador. At the same time, the cinematic adaptation in *Porto dos Milagres* further expands this perspective by embracing the exclusive interpretive quality of Guma as an embodiment of the maritime utopia overseen by Iemanjá, a water goddess and an orixá who takes men to the kingdom of love and fulfillment.[21] By rejecting a political alliance with Félix Guerreiro in exchange for a political post, Guma thus ensures that he does not fall into political corruption by selling out his people. Both texts enjoy the cultural hybridity proposed by Amado without betraying the tensions of class struggle, which puts the dominant group against the working class. The more Iemanjá ceases to be an exclusive deity for the poor and becomes a deity for all Brazilians, the more she embodies the fluidity that hybridity engenders and the more she brings many races and cultures into a conversation that would be otherwise impossible without cultural synthesis. As mother and protector of all her children, Iemanjá has the capacity to share her qualities with all the races under her expansive transnational territory. While the whole book focuses more on the triangle among Lívia, Guma, and Iemanjá, Amado does not miss the opportunity to make his own position about miscegenation clear with the mulatta Esmeralda, who would rather have an affair with white Guma than be faithful to black Rufino:

> "All you have to do is ask Rufino."
>
> "Him? I don't want any black man's child. What I need is a child by someone whiter than me, to make the blood line better."[22]

This act of calculating desperation on the part of Esmeralda is ample proof that even destiny is not permissible when it comes to social mobility through racial engineering or race mixture. That seems to be a proven thesis of Amado's creative corpus.

Maia's O *Leque de Oxum* (1960) (Oxum's Mirror)

Though Carlos Vasconcelos Maia was not as prolific as Amado, his admiration for the celebrated Brazilian writer is exemplified in the dedication of *O Leque de Oxum* to both Mestre Didi (Deoscoredes Maximiliano dos Santos) and Amado. Mestre Didi is more of a sculptural artist than a writer—though he did record several Yoruba tales under the collection

Contos Crioulos da Bahia (2004). What unites all three cultural producers may well be their association with Candomblé rites in Bahia and the centrality of ancestrality in their work. Born in Santa Inês, Bahia, on March 20, 1923 (deceased in 1988), Maia left a considerable amount of anthologized short stories and collections, but his significant legacy remains the novella *O Leque de Oxum* ([1961] 2006). Following Amado, he also tells the stories of Bahian people and the panoramic search for Bahian identity as it manifests in the streets: the tiers of stairs, lush hills, trenches, ghettos, churches, bars, castles, waterfronts, capoeira players, fishermen, prostitutes, and devotees of Bahia of All the Saints. The more prominent landscape of his works resides in the Candomblé temples, where he invokes the African divinities well before they became a cultural constant and agency for even Jorge Amado. In his introduction, Maia suggests that "with the publication of *O Leque de Oxum*, the author hopes that the work would contribute to the dissemination of the beauty, fascination, and finesse that are preserved in the best Bahian Candomblé temples and also call attention to the splendor the religion offers potential fictional writers."[23] This is a worthwhile aspiration, but it is important to note how it not only recognizes the validity of Afro-Brazilian cultural expression but also expands its impact within the Brazilian literary canon.

The ancestral turn that constitutes for Maia a legitimate concern for the second phase of Brazilian modernism must be understood not simply as a regionalist phenomenon but also as an endowed moment with a transformative political agenda to demarginalize Afro-Brazilian cultural expressions. In ritualizing and celebrating the ancestral, Maia goes beyond collecting the characteristics or historicizing the origins and transformation of Afro-Brazilian divinities in Brazil, as Pierre Verger did in his highly acclaimed works (e.g., *Orixás*). Maia pushes the limits by fictionalizing the roles of different members of Candomblé, who participate in the entire world of spirit possession and ritual. In other words, the cosmogonical world of Candomblé is translated into the world that Latin American writers have come to associate with magical realism. By invoking "Oxum" (River goddess) and her attribute "Leque" (Mirror) in the title of the novella *O Leque de Oxum*, Maia sums up the essential images that define the deity in name and iconicity. Set in the era of the temperamental and jealous King Xangô of Oyo, the main plot revolves around an impossible love between a Swedish man, Undset, and the beautiful priestess Matilde, who had been dedicated to Xangô in Ponta de Areia (Itaparica), the noted island in Bahia where devotees annually celebrate ancestrality in the egungun masquerades.

After twenty years of absence, the narrator returns to the Mãe Senhora Candomblé temple in Engenho Velho de Brotas in Salvador. He takes the reader on a fascinating journey across the worlds of the ancestral eguns, a frenetic and energetic celebration during which the musical instruments of *atabaques* and *agogôs* produce a supernatural concert that ushers the ancestors back into the land of the living. Once the offering to Exu (Deity of the crossroads) is initiated, the baba eguns are spiritually invited, as over fifty women, all dressed in white, do an elegant dance. It is an all-night festivity that keeps all involved energized and possessed. It is during these frenetic moments that Undset meets Matilde. He falls in love, and all he can think of is passionate sex. Undset cannot control himself, and, like most men who just meet a woman they love, Undset convinces Matilde to go to Itaparica with him. They travel across the ocean from Salvador. He was completely overwhelmed by Iyalorixá Matilde, who had been expecting him because an Ifa diviner had revealed to her that their destinies were linked. In the closing magical-realist scene, Matilde disappears through a well to the astonishment of the lover. Only in the morning can he see all that was left of Matilde: the Oxum mirror, a symbol of her authenticity.

Through *O Leque de Oxum*, Maia brings to life the mystical world of Oxum by associating her with a story of love and ancestrality. In a narrative twist, the reality of whiteness embracing Blackness serves as a discourse of hybridity, because both cultures come together to create what will now be a legacy that both cultures willingly accept. The praise of alterity here transforms the perspective of the white outsider, who, though in love, is made to appreciate Matilde beyond just the passion they share. Rather, by disappearing during a ritual dance, it is as if Matilde and her relics reenact the story of Oya in relation to Xango in Yoruba cosmology. The mirror left in place of Matilde symbolizes what must now be used to venerate her legacy and memory. Instead of Undset processing Afro-Brazilian rites as "backward" and "diabolic," he serves the role of a nonracist admirer who gains rich insights into the knowledgeable world of Candomblé. The titular text itself is followed by five other "crônicas" (chronicles), including "Axexê" and "Uma Festa no Alaketu."[24] The introductory section of *O Leque de Oxum* serves as a general background to the life and times of Maia and his involvement with Candomblé rites. One finds, for example, that the author participated in the group *Caderno*

da Bahia (1948–51), which is credited as an important instrument for
the launching of regionalism-modernism (1930s) in Bahia. In addition
to his creative and editorial leadership, Maia published short stories and
chronicles in books, journals, and reputable national and international
magazines (side by side with canonical writers, such as Mário de Andrade,
Graciliano Ramos, and Guimarães Rosa). Yet most of his works remain
out of print and unknown by the wider public, which makes his works
seem marginal. Regardless of his lack of circulation among major players
at the time, he is today considered a worthy inclusion in the canonical
literature of Bahia. Like Pierre Verger, who was also Ojuoba (a revered
honorific title in the Candomblé of Ilê Axé Opo Afonja), Maia occupied this position until death and used his knowledge of the temple to
create fictional characters, such as Iyalorixá Matilde, who represents
the priestess he knew in Opo Afonja. Maia was not limited to Salvador
when it comes to immersing himself in Afro-Brazilian religion. He was
also a frequent member at the Ilê Aboula in Itaparica, where he gained
insight into the mysteries of the baba eguns that defined his profound
novella, O Leque de Oxum.

Divided into three parts, including an introduction, O Leque de
Oxum portrays the life and death of Matilde, a Candomblé priestess who
finds love in the eye of a foreigner. She subsequently decides through
ritual self-sacrifice to become an ancestor after the rites of egungun. Some
fundamental questions about what prompts Matilde to disappear, beyond
the simple issue of love, remain: (1) What motivates the rapture of a
Candomblé priestess, one who leaves both lover and temple behind, and
the implication of her disappearance in a sacred setting? (2) How does
one interpret the romantic encounter between Undset and Matilde in the
first place, being mindful that it is an encounter between European and
African value systems? (3) What are the larger implications for cultural
hybridity if no children were birthed in the relationship? (4) Why was
Itaparica the choice for their romantic escapade and not somewhere else
in the city of Salvador? The answers to these curiosities may come from
one of the African tales collected by Pierre Verger, which accounts for
how both Oxum and Olokum became different waters:

> Ifa replied:
> You, Oxum, must go to a certain place
> And in this place, you will be well received.
> Other rivers will follow you.

None will surpass you,
wherever you are present.

Oxum assembled all rivers.
And the rivers all followed her.
When they got to the lakeshore (*osa*),
the rivers covered her completely.
When they left the lake,
they completely covered the sea (*okum*).[25]

While the context here is more of a competition between the female goddesses about who is the true queen of the waters and who is not, the tale basically explains the prescriptions given by the Ifa oracle. However, the more fundamental cosmological question of the rationale for being transformed into aquatic entities from supernatural beings remains. The mystical qualities of Oxum offer even deeper meanings. Yoruba cosmology defines her as the "Orisa Osun who controls rivers and sweet waters" for a reason. Indeed, her waters speak to the menstrual, nutritional, and birthing properties that qualify her as "Yeye" (or "mother"). In this configuration of motherhood, the transformation in the context of the ancestral feast defies the imagination because Undset and Matilde have yet to have children. Yet Matilde's community role as agent of fertility and procreation outweighs her own personal interests. She is at once the giver and the protector of lives with which she associates. The relic of the mirror may also be interpreted as a religious insignia to be used in her memory and worship as well as the symbol of her beauty and immortality.

As a personality that justifies her self-sacrifice through the lens of "motherhood," Oxum comes with several attributes that define the totality of her being. Drawing from Yoruba cosmology, Diedre Badejo identifies some of these qualities: "Yeye, the Good Mother, is a tapestry: (1) kinetic spiritual energy, (2) warrior-woman, (3) giver and sustainer of life, and (4) a beautiful, wealthy woman, indeed. . . . As an *orisa* of power and fertility, Osun's iconography envisions the womb as a powerful matrix nurturing myriad possibilities."[26] In the context of O Leque de Oxum, her womb is the well she leaves after her disappearance, a well from which humanity can forever drink. But her mirror is an even more iconic symbol of power, as she feels her devotees need to behold her to bless and venerate her. Though the two distinct divinities, Oxum and Iemanjá, often overlap in their syncretic rendition as diverse "Our Ladies of Conception" or Virgin Mary, both are archetypes of maternity in Brazilian popular culture. By focusing on the amorous relationship between Udset, a European in love with the Iyalorixá Matilde, Maia takes his passion for the recognition of Candomblé in literature and culture to another level. Indeed, until recently, Afro-Brazilian cosmogony has not always been positively portrayed in Brazilian literature. Rather, it is represented as fetish, satanic, barbaric, and diabolic. Maia takes this negative representation head-on by introducing explicit characteristics of orixás, their rituals, symbologies, dances, and meanings.

When considered in the light of the amorous relationship between a white man and a Black priestess, the case of O Leque de Oxum is even more compelling. In a sense, Maia allows the narrative to serve as a rite of passage for the outsider Undset, suspected to be the fictionalized representation of Pierre Verger, and the priestess Matilde, the fictionalized version of Mãe Senhora Oxum Muiwá of the Opo Afonja temple. The initiation structure may be captured in the following sequence: (1) outsider descends into a "heart of darkness" along with his inherent stereotypes and biases; (2) he falls in love with a native and leadership personality of the temple (Oxum); (3) he is introduced to the rites and ceremonies of the devotees and begins to participate, thus discarding his previous racist discourses; (4) he witnesses the descent of the ancestors (baba eguns), but discovers his lover has also been raptured in the process of the enchanting ceremony; (5) by the time he wakes up from his slumber, his lover is nowhere to be found because she has become a fountain of water, or a deity; and (6) all that is left is her mirror, her symbol as an orixá (Oxum). Because Maia is not an outsider to Candomblé, his "Introduction" disabuses the mind of the naïve reader about his qualifications to focus on the importance of Candomblé. It also provides a panoramic view of the differences between African traditional religion and the syncretic type in Brazil that was conditioned by the interaction of African, Amerindian, and Catholic elements. Maia explicates the Afro-Brazilian religion at two levels: orixás (deities) and eguns (ancestors). The divinities deal with the forces of nature while ancestors deal with elements of societal structure. Beyond the love between Undset and Matilde, there is another spiritual dimension to the story. Matilde belongs to Oxum, the same way Xangô sees Oxum as his ancestral wife. For falling in love with Undset, Matilde runs the risk of being punished for not heeding the messages of the Ifa oracle, who warned she must not engage in any terrestrial relationship. Once Matilde, who embodies Oxum, gets entangled in a terrestrial amorous relationship, she transgresses the harmony of the cosmos and must be punished for her transgression. As Ívia Alves notes, "In this struggle of life, the deities are stronger and take the transgressor away through death. Death is no longer seen here as a sudden interruption, but a passage into 'another dimension.'"[27]

The themes of death and separation and death and rebirth (reincarnation) are constants in the works of Maia, especially in O Leque de Oxum, where the furious Xangô comes down to take Matilde to live with him as an Oxum reincarnate in Orun (the other world). Matilde knows all along that her destiny is linked with that of Undset; as a result, she knows that the consequence for such a forbidden love is that she will probably die young or too soon. But she cannot help herself due to her love for Undset:

> She had been waiting for him. Her destiny, from the day she was born, has been connected to his, Ifa would never mislead. She also knew that she was not going to have a long life if she followed him in love. That Xangô would snuff life out of her if she went with him. But she also knew—and this is what her heart was telling her—that no force, human or supernatural, would stop her from being with him.[28]

Whether it is a matter of destiny or an act of disobedience, Matilde's death is cast for her. Undset not only chooses to live in Salvador, but he brings her numerous gifts every morning, including flowers, sweets, incense, fish, a woolen dress, jewelry, perfumes, and words of love. He attends all the initiation ceremonies of the deities—from Xangô to Oxalá—and gradually starts assimilating the language of musical instruments and their significance, a substantial change from his previous outlook on the "pagan" rites. Undset also starts to feel the weight of the burden of Matilde, and, together, they decide to face the jealousies of Xangô in good faith. No longer able to wait, Undset proposes marriage to Matilde—against the warnings of the Ifa oracle—but he does not pull her away from her cycle of obligations to Oxum. Yet, Xangô cannot accept the sacrifices. All he wants is Matilde without any sacrifices. Despite these challenges, both Undset and Matilde decide to continue their love and marriage.

Three years after their marriage, they participate in the Feast of Oxum. Everything is ready for the festivity in Brotas. In the meantime, they are staying on the island of Itaparica. Both have a profound sleep but do not hear the waves of the beach reaching the house. When Undset wakes up, Matilde is nowhere to be found:

> I got up suddenly, went towards the windows, and back to the bed, I realized Matilde had disappeared. . . . I called her. There was no answer. I looked all over the house for her. I could not find her. Her disappearance was bizarre: there was no *egungun* festivals then. I even ran to the beach . . . Matilde was not at the beach.
>
> Matilde! I shouted as loud as I could . . .
>
> Matilde! Matilde!—I screamed incessantly . . .
>
> Stuck to the ground, I located Matilde's image by the well, her image unlike that of the living. It was as if I was in a trance. . . . Only in the morning did I find something, cold and golden on the stone; Oxun's mirror.

In this symbolic closing scene, Maia intensifies the drama of Matilde and Undset by ridiculing the outcome of their transgression against the warnings of Ifa. Both realize that their destinies are tied to each other, the same way Matilde is tied to Xangô and Undset to the Candomblé communities of Bahia. With the death of Matilde and her reincarnation in the other world, Undset faces his own destiny and joins the society of the baba eguns. Though a European who had come to Bahia in search of adventure, he ends up immersing himself in the culture of the community and becomes one of their spokespersons without any racist disposition. In O *Leque de Xango*, Maia has constructed an epic that succeeds in educating both the indigenous devotees and the amorous outsider about the power of the Afro-Brazilian religion, which deserves respect, inclusion, and preservation in Brazilian canonical literature.

Comparative Analysis and Conclusion

The movement to include Afro-Brazilian experience in mainstream Brazilian discourse has been a long struggle that has taken more than a century. Since the abolition of slavery in 1888, Afro-Brazilians have articulated the desire to be recognized as human beings in different media and movements. The efforts for inclusion have called for a shift from treating Afro-Brazilians as objects to being seen as subjects. As subjects of their own destiny, Afro-Brazilians must be in control of the discourse and not treated as outsiders. Yet, religion remains a bone of contention. Due to religious syncretism, the tendency is to see Afro-Brazilian religions as acceptable only if they are processed through the lens of syncretism with Catholicism. In so doing, it is more fashionable to treat issues of trance and spirit possession as negatives and as transgressive, even dia-bolic acts. Since the advent of regionalism, writers like Jorge Amado and Vasconcelos Maia have taken the position that creative works that explicitly pay homage to Candomblé rituals and ceremonies should be a legitimate part of Afro-Brazilian literature.

Against this backdrop, this chapter has sought to compare the love triangles in Jorge Amado's *Mar Morto* and Vasconceles Maia's *O Leque de Oxum*. Both share themes of transgression against the norms of nature: the unspoken taboo that devotees of Iemanjá and Oxum, respectively, should not have matrimonial bonds on the land (physical abode) because they can easily suffer the consequences of being raptured by the divinities through physical death and spiritual regeneration into another realm. Such are the experiences of Lívia and Guma, whose lives are bound by the spirit of the sea goddess (who sees Lívia as competi-tion when it comes to her love for Guma), as well as of Matilde and Undset, who are under the spell of Xango, who wants Matilde (Oxum goddess) for himself. The two texts share fascinating parallels in the sense that they depict how love is truncated by the powerful deities Iemanjá and Xangô. Iemanjá feels Guma is beholden to her because only she can protect him as a sailor and fisherman who sets out every morning in search of fish. The same deity that protects him from storms and tragedies at sea can also decide to cause havoc and permanently regain him through a shipwreck. Likewise, Matilde transgresses the warning not to marry Undset, the European outsider, but is too much in love with him to heed the warning. Ultimately, they are married and Oxum comes to rescue her from the hands of the stranger-lover, who in turn is initiated as a baba egun in the Candomblé community. Both texts celebrate Afro-Brazilian mythologies and traditions against an alienating modernity and marginalization.

Chapter 5

Abdias Nascimento and Nelson Rodrigues

The Fallen Angel as Betrayal of Blackness

This chapter examines the consequences of rejecting one's Black racial heritage while embracing white otherness and how this desire is symptomatic of Black sexual curiosity and transient pleasure. The two antagonistic forces operating in this paradigm of self-negation are conditioned by the "whitening" ideal. On the one hand, the Black male protagonist desires the white woman as the ideal of racial superiority that temporarily fulfills the "humanity" of the Black man. She also provides hope for the progenitors as inheritors of a better life in a racist society where racial hierarchy then places the miscegenated fruit in a higher ranking. On the other hand, the white female antagonist seeks the Black male body for pleasure while deliberately exterminating the mixed-race offspring as a "forbidden angel" that must be silenced as a stigma of "contamination" of the white race. The Black protagonist is indeed in a quagmire of sorts because he is not able to have free will and negate whiteness when such a decision often leads to struggle, poverty, and death. Rather, he chooses to embrace whiteness as a strategic measure for shameful inclusion in a problematic "racial democracy." Such complex conditioning causes the protagonist to pay a huge price for rejecting his racial heritage. This plot is the thrust of the dramas in *Sortilégio II* (1979) and *Anjo Negro* (1946), with their respective protagonists Emanuel and Ismael. Likewise, the antagonistic positioning of Margarida and Virgínia (respectively) equally translates the contradictions of miscegenation because both white female characters insist on aborting the "forbidden angels." Through desire, seduction, and power, the Black protagonists become tools of sexual manipulation in the

135

hands of white women when they are accused of "rape." They are then punished through rejection—first by the same white women and then by their own self-rejection of their race. The psychological consequences are immeasurable, for the betrayal of Blackness plays out at many levels as a form of unintended symbolic castration and self-hatred. Abdias Nascimento and Nelson Rodrigues perform a profound questioning of "racial democracy" by subjecting this contradictory thesis to scrutiny through the many layers of the playwrights' complex characters.

Depending on how individuals self-identify, racial demographics in Brazil reveal that it is quantitatively a multiracial country, with the second-largest "Black" population in the world after Nigeria.[2] As much as the data persuasively support this neglected Black presence with the myth of racial democracy, the status quo of white minority rule and a disfranchised Black majority continues to be the norm. Through rituals and performances of hybridity, Brazil masks the complexity of racial tension by emphasizing the rationality of multiculturalism as the ideal norm, while blaming those who subscribe to racial oppression as enemies of progress who are deliberately working against the peaceful negotiations of race and racism. The irony remains that the ritualization of racial democracy is indeed not the intention of the perpetuators of racism; rather, it is a historical outcome of many centuries of strategic masking and survival by Afro-Brazilian descendants, who elected to avoid racial oppression and potential erasure of their Africanness. Such domains of strategic negotiation include religion and culture—two zones of inextricable hybrid performativity as religiosity, music, and culture blend with popular expressions. In the mix of these ritual performances, miscegenation seems to be the in-between, pivotal space that Gilberto Freyre (1933), Homi Bhabha (1994), and Carl Degler (1986) deem inescapable and a disservice to the impoverished and marginalized populations.[3]

Sortilégio II by Abdias Nascimento and *Anjo Negro* by Nelson Rodrigues are two classical works by eminent Brazilian playwrights, which present the world in a complex imagination where Blackness is betrayed in the process of performing a problematic racial democracy. I conceive of "mixed race extermination" as the offspring of black and white partnerships whenever they end up not actually embracing the ideals of racial democracy but instead destroy it as a matter of contradiction (with incestuous implications). The strength of this ironic twist is what makes this comparative study compelling and worthy of critical exploration. It is equally noteworthy that the two dramatic texts were actually anthologized in *Dramas para Negros, Prólogo para Brancos* (1961), a monumental dramatic work that represents the mission, vision, and accomplishment of the Black Experimental Theater of the 1950s, as spearheaded by Nascimento.[4]

Racial democracy often fails to make its own case for a nonracialized society. In *Racism in a Racial Democracy* (1998), France Twine locates the contradictions of the Vasalian community she studied in Rio de Janeiro in the 1990s when she reaches the following troubling conclusion: "In contrast to what I expected there was a pattern of resistance to interracial marriage among Euro-Brazilians of all socioeconomic positions. Euro-Brazilians resisted *mestiçagem* by actively discouraging family members from establishing families with Vasalians of predominant or salient African ancestry."[5] On the basis of this ethnographic finding, it stands to reason that the larger population suffers from the same whitening mentality, as social conditioning compels the lower classes to aspire to social mobility through race mixture. The resistance to mixing is indicative of a desire to maintain white supremacy, as opposed to the official idea of Black erasure through miscegenation. If the one-drop rule in the United States imposed institutional racism, then the Brazilian race-mixture experiment promoted a nonracial discourse that was premised on a fallacious sense of an all-inclusive nation devoid of racism. Even within Brazil, the schools of thought on racial democracy differ widely. There are those like Gilberto Freyre who believe that social inequalities in Brazil are the aftermath of class and capital accumulation and not necessarily of race. Yet there are those who differ, such as Twine, Nascimento, and Christen Smith, who lay the blame at the altar of racial violence and genocide. Christen Smith, in her seminal work *Afro-Paradise*, argues that most Brazilians perform "rituals of racial tolerance," that is, attempts to create a "new racial democracy" as a form of Afro-nationalism that taps into social welfare programs to minimize social inequalities.[6] Unfortunately, these affirmative action-type efforts only scratch the surface of redressing structural racial discrimination that remains untouched. Brazil has functioned as a testing ground for the comparative understanding of the American experience of racism. Seen as a model for racial integration, the reality is that the Brazilian counterpoint to American racism is different because racial harmony seems apparent but is not easily decipherable due to the many shades of color that exist as a result of race mixing.

Responding to Frank Tannenbaum's thesis in *Slave and Citizen* (1947) claiming that slavery was not justified by the institution of slavery, Carl

Degler in *Neither Black nor White* (1986) rejects Brazil's claim of a "racial democracy." Rather, he posits that "the key that unlocks the puzzle of the differences in race relations in Brazil and the United States is the mulatto escape hatch."[7] In other words, Afro-Brazilians were not treated with any sense of dignity while the mulatto was treated as an icon of social mobility—even though, in the United States, mulattoes were classified as Black due to the one-drop rule. Drawing upon oral sources and archival materials, Kim Butler in *Freedoms Given, Freedoms Won: Afro-Brazilians in Post-Abolition São Paulo and Salvador* (1998) compares two cities with minority and majority Black populations, respectively. She concludes that segregation and social stratification contributed to the disenfranchisement of postabolition Black communities despite the lack of official statistical records, which sought to obliterate any reference to racial disparities. The three categories she identifies as integrationists, alternative integrationists, and separatists indicate that some prefer the assimilationist model while others wanted to stay Black and proud. While wealthy whites enjoyed their exclusive privileges, Black activists insisted on creating their own Black communities and ethnic solidarity to gain some form of symbolic political power. Embracing mythic racial democracy meant that Afro-Brazilians were trapped within the lower-class strata, and the denial of racism in fact reinforced racial discrimination and social inequality. Though Brazil is gradually coming to terms with the existence of racism of Brazil, the actual measure to confront its violence and propose solutions is still lacking. For this very reason, the performative works of Nascimento and Rodrigues creatively expose the issues so that readers can draw their own conclusions. In other words, this chapter problematizes racial democracy by exposing its contradictions in the world of the protagonists, who suffer the loss of the "black angels" who are supposed to be the ideal offspring of the miscegenation experiment.

Sortilégio II and the Fallen Black Angel

Drawing upon the creative tensions of assimilation and re-Africanization, in *Sortilégio II* Nascimento subjects the protagonist Emanuel to a ritualistically chaotic world to address the complexities of racial relations in Brazil. The notion of the "fallen black angel" serves a functional duality: (1) embodying Emanuel himself as he goes through performative and self-exorcizing rites of passage; and (2) embodying the offspring of both Emanuel and Margarida that the latter mysteriously kills due to the shame of Black stigma and fear of Black progeny. Such a context creates a tension that must be seen as deliberate and yet symptomatic of a larger problematic society when it comes to its denial of racism and the burden that carries. The drama of Emanuel is also the drama that befalls his "black angels" or children—deemed not "human" enough to be loved and cared for by an interracial couple because they are essentially not white enough. In other words, they are not white but Black—and, thus, being mixed race is not truly a racial option but a problematic escape. From the very beginning of the play, the life of Emanuel is haunted by police brutality, even though he has assimilated into Brazilian culture by studying medicine in Europe and acquiring the hallmarks of civilization and finesse. Alas! He remains a classical case study of Blackness and the victim of racism in a so-called racial democratic political dispensation.

Sortilégio II (1979), though an even more mystified version of Sortilegio (1959), in which Black women are given more challenging, spiritually fulfilling, and leadership roles, was written in the context of Nascimento's leadership role in the Black Experimental Theater (Teatro Experimental do Negro [TEN]). In Black Experimental Theater, Nascimento sought to challenge the racist views prevalent in Brazil that kept Afro-Brazilians invisible, marginalized, and disenfranchised. Sortilégio II is essentially a moral fable, one that is written in the context of a Black theatrical tradition that embodies Black culture and themes without sacrificing any artistic finesse. Emanuel is a Black attorney who rejects his culture and religion in exchange for social mobility in a racist society. Though he loves Black Ifigênia, he chooses to marry Margarida, a white woman, for social mobility. Tragically, Emanuel psychologically suffers from Margarida's illicit affairs with other men and kills her. Emanuel suddenly becomes a fugitive, as the long arm of the law demands he answer for the murder of a white woman. He ends up in an Afro-Brazilian religious temple (Candomblé) where he is tragically murdered by Ifigênia in a crime of passion. In his search for total freedom, physically and psychologically, Emanuel finds himself launched into cosmic chaos, as he struggles to resolve the contradictions within him as well as within Brazilian society in terms of racial relations. Once he loses his cool, he can no longer maintain the equilibrium of the "black angel" that he used to be; instead, he must contend with his rites of passage. Nascimento devises some stylistic strategies, such as mystery, puns, figurative language, and the dubiousness of action and reality, to enrich the play with a symbiosis between liturgic dramaturgy and real-life drama. To facilitate this ambivalence, the director introduces a chorus that counters individualistic readings, in that Emanuel ceases to be an individual and becomes a socially implicated being. Through this air of social tragedy, Emanuel assumes the place of a hero who is punished by the gods—not for the original crime against Margarida but for the sacred crime of wanting to whiten himself. Despite this "punishment," which resonates as a rite of passage to exorcise himself from his fatal desires of whiteness, he exclaims at the end of the play: "I killed Margarida. I am a free black man!"[8]

In "A Ritual Choreography: The Orishas' Steps in *Sortilégio*," Leda Martins complicates the ritual drama, arguing that through Nascimento's play, Black Brazilian culture can be better understood as multidimensional, deploying signifiers and conceptual strategies that involve "duplicity, theatricality and intersection."[9] Beyond exposing the virtues of TEN and the invisibility of Black characters that Nascimento seeks to redress, Martins suggests that Emanuel was not actually punished for his transgression through his ritual act to rid himself of the traits of his assimilation and alienation but voluntarily submitted to Exu, the deity of the crossroad, mediation, and transformation of character. One must not take lightly the power of the gods to unleash retributive justice on a transgressor. However, in the case of Emanuel, he is ambivalent because he unconsciously kills Margarida out of rage, and this act sets off a series of traumatic actions in him as he realizes Margarida does not truly love him but only desires his black skin. In this sense, Exu may be playing the role of reconciling inner conflicts within Emanuel. He is not only running from the law after killing a white lover, but he is also desperately in search of the meaning of his life and his true identity. As a matter of fact, Martins sees in the approximation of Exu with Emanuel an alter ego of sorts: "In the structure of *Sortilégio*, Emanuel becomes a double of Exu, a spectral image of the Orisha through which an experience of fragmentation is transformed into an experience of movement and completeness, reentering an otherness until then pulverized by the blows of the ideological system of the false Brazilian racial democracy."[10] Emanuel may have entered the zone of ambiguity and ambivalence to defragment himself toward a new beginning; yet, it will take more than Exu to endow him with the virtues of ruptures, intersections, and convergences. Emanuel's will to rid himself of all the vestiges of racial fragmentation is crucial. Nascimento transforms Emanuel's shifting status as a protagonist—from omosonu (the lost child) to omowale (the returnee child). The fallen black angel rises again like the phoenix to celebrate his Blackness and wholeness. The distortion of Black values that first led Emanuel to reject his Black culture must be challenged. In the negation of the Brazilian falsity of racial democracy lies the point of departure for Emanuel's relocation into the new orbit of African rehumanization. By rejecting the fixed religiosity of the Catholic faith, Nascimento in *Sortilégio II* privileges the triad (the worlds of the living, the dead, and the unborn) that Wole Soyinka theorizes in *Myth, Literature, and the African World*.[11] In other words, ritual drama transforms the protagonist's agency better than the structural codes of behavior imposed by the dominant power.

Without articulating it, Nascimento finds a nexus between the sacred and the popular by integrating racial complexities within a setting that would ordinarily have been suspect or strange, such as the enactment of equal rights between the oppressed and the oppressors. Beyond the radical rejection of the whitening ideal through Emanuel's renewal within Afro-Brazilian religion, the play appeals to the celebration of the sacred acts of Candomblé by privileging the daughters of the saint (filhas-de-santo) and the priestess (Iyalorixá) who function like the chorus in a Greek tragedy. Perhaps Nascimento's thesis is multilayered or, to a certain degree, even experimental. Afro-Brazilian religion is not usually seen on a day-to-day basis, except during certain annual festivities such as the Festa de Iemanjá (Iemanjá feast). Thus, the idea of staging the sacred world of Candomblé in the 1950s is revolutionary. In addition, the function is not just to challenge the invisibility of Afro-Brazilian culture but to engage biased minds of the positive aspects that Africa-derived religions bring to Brazilian culture. In the context of the play itself, the presence of Afro-Brazilian religion negates the air of repression and persecution with which it was associated in the nineteenth century, when police raids of terreiros (Afro-Brazilian religious temples) were very rampant. Nascimento exemplifies the power of the sacred when he assembles the chorus (filhas-de-santo) to set the stage for Emanuel's arrival to begin his ritual dealienation:

FILHA DE SANTO II: Emanuel won't be long . . .

FILHA DE SANTO I (correcting her): Watch your tongue!
Doctor Emanuel, *Esquire*.

FILHA DE SANTO III (ironic): Esquire to his white woman. Not to me.

FILHA DE SANTO II (conciliatory): There is a black woman in the story too: Ifigênia. Don't forget.

FILHA DE SANTO III (polemical): She hated being black.

FILHA DE SANTO II: But they gave her a saint's name: Ifigênia. The name of a dark saint.

FILHA DE SANTO III (vehement): Black. A black saint. No one escapes his color.

FILHA DE SANTO I (lyrical): She wanted to be white . . . white inside . . . at least on the inside . . .

FILHA DE SANTO III (violent): No one chooses his color. The color of your skin is no shirt you can change whenever you want to. (Impassioned.) Race is fate . . . it's destiny![12]

Here is a well-crafted rendering of critical commentaries as they affect the love triangle between Emanuel, Ifigênia, and Margarida. The chorus focuses on the drama of Ifigênia, who hated being Black. Both Black Emanuel and Black Ifigênia suffer from racial neuroses, which suggests that both these Black protagonists hate their natural color and desire to be white or to whiten themselves. The daughters of the saint scold Ifigênia for her low self-esteem and lack of pride in her Blackness. As a moralistic episode in a broader fable of racial equality, instead of a legacy of slavery and its attendant dehumanization, Nascimento taps into the Afro-Brazilian historical past to document memories of Africa in its transformative glory, turning characters such as Emanuel into Afro-Brazilian heroes.

While Emanuel undergoes transformative rites of passage for the betterment of the collective Afro-Brazilian race, it is rather far-fetched to draw parallels between this Abdisian character (Emanuel) and Rodriguian character (Ismael), as manifest in Black Angel (Anjo Negro). Yet, Nelson Rodrigues puts it rather convincingly: "Black Ismael—the hero—is beautiful, sensitive and intelligent. However, this catalogue of qualities is not exhaustive. If he were perfect, we might fall into an inverse exaggeration and portray a black man as false as the other. Ismael is equally capable of evil, dark passions, violence, and hate. But, in the matters of love or cruelty, he is, and will always be a man with dramatic dignity, not a naughty boy."[13] Rodrigues highlights certain compelling virtues about Abdias Nascimento that unite him with those of Ismael. Though faithfully married to white American Elisa Larkin, Nascimento did not exhibit the same tensions and apprehensions of Ismael and Emanuel. Rather, as a public intellectual, scholar, and activist, Nascimento exuded all the passions of a revolutionary who used his energy to ensure the dignity of all Afro-Brazilians. Rodrigues insists on dedicating the play *Black Angel* to Nascimento, which is more of a salutary gesture than an attempt to draw intrinsic parallels and influences. Even if we argue that Emanuel or Ismael may well be the alter egos of Abdias Nascimento, this is more of a creative pretext for attaining a political resonance and legitimacy in the characters portrayed. One quick example of the grandiosity of Nascimento is the fact that he did away with *do* from his name, a symbolic action that implicated how he got rid of the association of his person with a sense of inferiority in the context of the naming of slaves as if they were property belonging to "white slave masters." In his preface to his recent work on Abdias Nascimento, Femi Ojo-Ade aptly explains: "By a simple stroke of genius, Nascimento rejected slave status and declared his humanity as an absolute. His decision to delete the simple but significant word, *do*, from his name is an act of affirmation and confirmation of human dignity and identity as everyone's right, not the privilege of a minority of masters."[14] In sum, no matter how one tries to equate the ingenuity of Nascimento to any personality living or dead, when it comes to absolute investment in the dignity of his people, Nascimento is, indeed, larger than life itself.

From the foregoing transnational dimension of Abdias Nascimento emerges, simultaneously, his Pan-African consciousness. José Martins (1993), Sandra Richards (1995), and Femi Ojo-Ade (2014) add a conceptual framework to what Elisa Nascimento (2007) has cogently theorized as "building Afro-Brazilian identity on stage."[15] Each critic, in their search for the "soul" of Nascimento, extensively and incisively celebrates this magnanimous man of the moment by drawing connections between his radicalism within Brazil and the persistent struggles for the dignity and mental freedom of all Afro-Brazilians. One cannot possibly discuss *Sortilégio II* and the Black Experimental Theater without situating both works and movements in the consciousness of a South American, North American, European, and Negritudist man—Nascimento was truly a global citizen. While Martins invokes the Caliban-Ariel dynamics of Nascimento's response to racial discrimination in Brazil, Richards deploys the Exu paradigm as the "vehicle for shattering social norms" in the midst of contradictory identities. Elisa Nascimento uncovers the "camouflaged form of racism," and Ojo-Ade celebrates the ingenuity of a Brazilian man for all seasons. As a selective quadripartite synthesis of a monumental work, they all offer myriad perspectives from which to continue to digest how, in a single character, Afro-Brazilian heroes like Nascimento and Zumbi dos Palmares are invoked. The playwright's legacy—and that of *Sortilégio II*—transcends our understanding of the work itself but reaches that explosive and controversial FESTAC-77 moment when Nascimento was barred (or excluded) by the Brazilian government from participating in the Pan-African event in Lagos, Nigeria. Some of the works that emerged from that context, such as *Mixture or Massacre?* (1989) and *Sitiado em Lagos* (1981), remain the most authoritative accounts of Nascimento's positions against racial democracy in Brazil. A more political theory of Nascimento lies in what he conceives as Quilombismo—a social theory that envisions a Brazilian government that includes all Brazilians but without the racial prejudices that characterize the falsehood of racial democracy. Without question, *Sortilégio II* will remain a Brazilian masterpiece for all times.

At the core of José Martins's article "Blackness and Imagined Community of Afro-Brazilians in Literature," lies three interrelated questions—that are also anchored on a singular one: "Am I a black man?"[16] For Martins, this central identitarian question leads to others because the response to that question is indeed a prelude to a perpetual "nostalgic search for African paternity" that is being conducted by the protagonist Emanuel in *Sortilégio II*, following W. E. B. Du Bois (1986) and Cornel West (1993).[17] What unites these paradigmatic questions is their personification of Negritude and the Caliban metaphor. In other words, the process of consciousness raising that Emanuel went through resulted in a new attitude toward appreciating Afro-Brazilian cultural values in their positive totality. Invoking Roberto Retamar's *Caliban and Other Essays* (*Caliban e Outros Ensaios*), Martins argues that by adapting the attitude of the Shakespearean Caliban to the Latin American world in opposition to the Ariel model, Retamar has succeeded in crafting the revolutionary agency of Caliban for Latin America.[18] When applied to the drama of Emanuel in *Sortilégio II*, one can reach a number of conclusions: (1) the protagonist affirms his Afro-Brazilian identity at the end of his ritual drama; (2) the protagonist extols Afro-Brazilian cultural values in general especially when it comes to dignity, Africa-derived religiosity, and self-esteem; (3) the protagonist finds synergy between Afro-Brazilian religious practices (orixás) and ancestral mysticism that translate the vital force within him as a resource he deploys to counter any hegemonic assault on his Afro-Brazilian way of life; (4) the protagonist questions his assimilationist past by advancing a more Afrocentric worldview; and (5) the protagonist not only sees his culture as a vital influence on Brazilian national culture, he insists that his total de-alienation is nonnegotiable, hence the intensity of the moment he rejects assimilation and restores his Black lineage for posterity:

> FILHA DE SANTO I: Oh black Emanuel, your time has come!
>
> FILHA DE SANTO II: Your time of pain and passion.
>
> FILHA DE SANTO III: Your time of liberation.
>
> EMANUEL: Take this trash. With these lies and others you make black people lower their heads. You crush what pride they have. . . . And they are tamed. Castrated . . . Margarida was quite convinced I was fascinated by her whiteness! As a woman, you never meant anything to me . . . I couldn't have loved a creature that carried the mark of all that had debased me, humiliated me, mocked me . . . rejected me. I wanted a son with a deep black face. . . . Steel fists, to smash the white world's hypocrisy.[19]

Soon after this ritual drama, Emanuel regains his true freedom and, as the playwright intends it, returns to the world as a new Zumbi—a symbol of strength and heroism. The protagonist enjoys a deified status after completing his rites of passage from innocence to experience. In addition, Emanuel seems to justify Margarida's death as a necessary ritual sacrifice so that she could also be reborn into a new, redemptive value system. The cycle is complete, and regeneration is in motion so that the entire community can heal and transform its agency into one that detests racial discrimination and promotes equality for the unborn as propagated by

the triad (the worlds of the living, the dead, and the unborn) of Wole
Soyinka in *Myth, Literature and the African World.*

Drawing upon complex Yoruba divinatory worldview, Yoruba
mythology, and the semiotics of performance to analyze two plays, *The
Story of Oxalá* (1958) and *Sortilege* (Black mystery) (1958) by Zora Seljan
and Nascimento, respectively, Sandra Richards attempts to unveil the
ideological opposites in the discourse of racial democracy. On the one
hand, Richards critiques Seljan's interpretation of the Oxalá story that
unconsciously favors the replication of Brazilian racist hegemony. On
the other hand, Richards aligns with Nascimento's manipulation of the
contradictory identities of Magarida and Emanuel, as immersed within
the rituals of Candomblé. Through this complexity, Nascimento, while
challenging racial democracy, ends up in a contradiction in the sense
that, for Richards, "the cast members seem to be light-skinned" as if
the mixed-race person is the acceptable norm and Black a deviation
to that norm.[20] While Richards appreciates the deployment of Yoruba
mythology in the enactment of the drama and liberation of Emanuel
through a ritual performance, she is not as persuaded that Nascimento
did the same for Margarida and Ifigênia. In other words, she takes issue
with the fact that the reconstruction of the identities of the female
characters did not guarantee them equal liberatory powers in the play
and that this construction inadvertently puts women in less progressive
roles and capacities. She goes on to theorize quite convincingly the
presence of misogyny in Nascimento's works and the need to be attentive
to the subtleties of cultural contexts, codes, and meanings in the overall
production of the compared dramatic texts:

> the use of Yoruba culture destabilizes the fixity of a dramatic
> text beyond what would be presumed in Western dramaturgy:
> Under certain performative conditions determined in part by
> a spectator response, the transformative power of axê operates
> so as to multiply perspectives, complicate the possibility of
> interpretation, and evoke a (near) double reality which par-
> allels that of the social order. . . . As the keeper of axê and
> orixá who presides over the hermeneutics of divination, as
> the generative sign of contradiction, chance, and change.[21]

Richards's critical engagement reveals that while such dramas produced
to challenge domination may have a stake in the agency of transfor-

mation, they must also be mindful of the potential fragmentation and ambivalence of their resistant disposition to social order so as not to replicate that same order in the process of negating the status quo. The critical balance in Richards's article is rewarding, for it signals indeed that Afro-Brazilian theater has come of age beyond the critical surveys that used to be the main response to dramatic works. The fallen black angel, as Richards warns, needs not be singular, so that the redemption readily provided to the male protagonist is also made available to female characters.

If the comparative prism that Richards uses is beneficial for a better understanding of Emanuel's protagonism in comparison to the "Jesus" figure invoked by Seljan's Oxalá, Elisa L. Nascimento's *The Sorcery of Color* (2003) performs an incisive social history of Afro-Brazilians through a critical reading of Black social movements and the works of Abdias Nascimento and the Black Experimental Theater. While the whole book is highly sophisticated and informative, my focus lies with her specific reading of Nascimento's masterpiece *Sortilégio* as a piece of identity construction for all Afro-Brazilians. What is striking in this study is Nascimento's ability to combine racial and gender inequalities in a book that boldly attacks the hegemonic silence that has kept Afro-Brazilians under oppressive control. In a twofold paradigmatic exegesis, Nascimento establishes the African concept of axé as the binding vital force that maintains continuum in the African diaspora to later analyze the moral and psychological tensions suffered by Emanuel due to his color and race. Through such extended suffering, the conflicts of living in a racist society as a Black man is put in relief, as what the critic considers the "vicissitudes of being black in a Western society."[22] The many forces working against Emanuel in a racist society do not allow him to fulfill himself as a citizen. Even in his love life, cultural life, social life, and religious life, Emanuel is being manipulated by forces beyond his control. Nascimento goes beyond locating the existential forces against Emanuel to also critique why female subjects such as Margarida and Ifigênia are portrayed as "prostitutes," even though they both serve as the social anchors through which racism is played out. She surmises that "sexuality, indeed, is at the heart of racism."[23] Richards does not let Abdias Nascimento off the hook so easily. First, she insists that even though Ifigênia acts as an agent for Emanuel's redemption, she ends up not participating fully in it, if at all. She argues further that both Black Emanuel and Ifigênia are deprived of overcoming "the impasse created by the dominion of whiteness because they have not overcome it together."[24] Nascimento believes that camouflaged versions of racism are conjured up by the sorcery of color, and, to counter it, Black social movements must return to African cultural roots to challenge that construction with a more spiritual weapon that has political undertones, even if they are not explicitly articulated. It is thus a rewarding experience to note in Femi Ojo-Ade's *Home and Exile, Abdias Nascimento, African Brazilian Thinker and Pan African Visionary* that Nascimento's return visit to Ile-Ife (Nigeria) in 2007 to receive the covetous honorary doctoral degree was a "wonderful homecoming."[25] One can only take away the following from Nascimento's argument: collective liberation is more desirable than individual.

Anjo Negro and the Mixed-Race Angels Betrayed

Of Rodrigues's major dramatic works, *Anjo Negro* is perhaps the most daring in its quest for transformative change by addressing radical racial problematics. In this three-act tragedy, Rodrigues exposes more tensions than he can probably resolve—from drawing interesting parallels with classical tragedies, such as Sophocles's *Oedipus Rex*, to dramatizing the ambiguities of whiteness and Blackness that derive from alternative models challenging "racial democracy"; to representing degenerate incestuous relations between family members, violent rape, and exploitative confinement; and to enriching the complexity of the plot structure through the symbologies of Blackness and blindness. While Rodrigues may not have set out to openly draw parallels with Greek tragedy, there are subtle yet conscious echoes, structures, and influences to warrant such a claim. A quick example is the adoption of the chorus model, in which Rodrigues deploys eight black women sitting in a round wailing about the death of the third offspring of Virgínia and Ismael. The racial question is quite obviously addressed, but there are also attempts at mythmaking, spiritualizing, and moralizing—such that when faced with the abundance of evidence about racial discrimination and even Black self-hate, the notion of racial democracy is directly deconstructed, if not completely reduced to a fallacy, given its contradictions. Character names (e.g., Elias, Ismael, Ana Maria, and Elijah) have a biblical ring, which raises the question of whether Rodrigues consciously created these characters for some symbolic effect. Ismael embodies the Oedipal complex in the sense that he has carnal knowledge of his stepdaughter before murdering her and, thereafter, backing himself into a corner due to self-hate. By desiring Virgínia's love and whiteness, he rejects his own Blackness, such that all his conflicts evolve from this psychological conflict and dilemma. Both characters are victims of the burden of racial discrimination and its denial. In the final analysis, Ismael is betrayed by his lack of self-esteem and black dignity.

Anjo Negro deconstructs the Greek mythological model by complicating the plot in which Black Ismael and white Virgínia remain in a problematic relationship, even after the death of their third offspring. (The reader learns that their three children have been conceived in rape and subsequently killed by Virgínia for being Black.) Later, the reader also learns that Elias, Ismael's stepbrother, has been sexually seduced by Virginia—leading to Ismael's rage and desire for revenge and culminating in his murder of Elias with the help of Virgínia. The pathetic seduction continues as Ismael seduces his own mixed-race daughter, Ana Maria, who was born of sexual relations with Virgínia. To prevent Ana Maria from knowing that Ismael, her father, is Black, he blinds her. Ultimately, Ismael and Virgínia accept their interracial relationship. Yet, Virgínia locks up Ana Maria to die in a glass mausoleum. Yet is the validity of racial democracy radically negated when Virgínia and Ismael exterminate the mixed-race Ana Maria? Is the claim of racial democracy itself a myth? The predicament of Ana Maria raises a number of questions toward the rejection of the miscegenation thesis: (1) Is leaving Ana Maria on a permanent "death bed" a sign of the hopelessly terminal condition for racial democracy in Brazil? (2) What is the symbolic meaning of the glass mausoleum—is it a burial for the living dead? (3) Why did Virgínia and Ismael not kill Ana Maria like the other three "Black" children? (4) Were the first three exterminated children a source of melancholy for the couple? and (5) What is the significance of incest in the drama of Ismael, and how is it related to the series of woes based on his own prejudice against his own race?

To answer the foregoing pertinent questions, we must invoke Katherine McKittrick's Demonic Grounds (2006), where she outlines how diasporic locations are defined by a legacy of violence that inversely obliges female subjects to counter forces of domination. The setting of Anjo Negero draws on this trope of being located within a demonic structure. The main characters—feminine or otherwise—are all condemned to acts of destruction and self-destruction on a "demonic ground." Alluding to Marlene Philip's notion of Black femininity as a series of racial-sexual "uneven geographies and resistances" that are the result of perpetual bodily history, McKittrick argues that "the scale of the body, for black women, is both illustrative of public racial-sexual disavowal and a location of politicization."[26] Rodrigues's *Anjo Negro* is indeed a political statement on how the human body is not only exploited and manipulated for personal gain but also a candid reflection of how the same body is rejected, soon enough, against the grain of moral code. Ana Maria's blinding and death, while radically against the miscegenation thesis, debunks the claim of a racial paradise because reality must be distorted to give Ana Maria the idea that her father, Ismael, is white just like all men in Brazil. The mausoleum serves as a symbol of her insularity from the truth of the rest of the white world. It's also a kind of an open museum, where the fictitiousness of racial democracy could be rejected by making Ana Maria believe that Ismael is the only white man in the world (given her own blindness). Virgínia and Ismael spare the life of Ana Maria initially because she was conceived in love as the white or "mixed-race" exceptionalism that both so desired as an interracial couple—despite the fact that Ana Maria is in fact the offspring of Elias and Virgínia. For Virgínia, however, these children are considered Black and not white—even if they are of mixed-race parentage. Indeed, the three children Virgínia drowns are violently eliminated because they are Black, and the couple would rather have white children—an impossibility. In the final analysis, Ismael's self-hate regarding his skin color is the ultimate trigger for his self-destruction and for the destruction of others because all that he wants to embrace is whiteness. He even kills Ana Maria once he discovers that she is the offspring of Virgínia and Elias.

As radical as Rodrigues's *Anjo Negro* may be, a subtext persists that could not have been openly staged in the play but that is nonetheless suggested by the very actions or nonactions of the protagonist, Ismael. He must go through a rite of passage and self-exorcism to showcase to the rest of the world the tragic effects of denying one's racial heritage. The love-hate relationship between Virgínia and Ismael speaks to the contradictions of the social theory that Brazil upholds in the form of the fictitious ideal of racial democracy. This myth is foundational because it highlights the violence of Brazilian social and ethnic formation that continues to be negated. The interracial couple advances many ambiguous actions to justify their belief in an oppressive system, but ultimately the tragedy of their lives, coupled with its absurdity, points in one direction. Only through tragedy can this hypocritical theory of Brazil be addressed and redressed because a historical past of slavery cannot hold Brazil in perpetual ransom if change is desired. The logic of miscegenation is turned on its head to challenge its fallacies and to postulate the dead-end of a racist society. Ismael is faced with a disturbing dilemma: he is unable to hide his confusion, the same way he is unable to overcome the contradictions of his destiny as a Black man forced on him in a racist society that expects him to desire whiteness as a "diploma of acceptance" even after acquiring all the hallmarks of social mobility, such as his education and status as a successful medical doctor. And yet he is treated like a second-class citizen. Unable to be proud of his Blackness, Ismael becomes a ticking time bomb. Ismael is unable to produce a white offspring because he is Black, and Elias's betrayal means an enraged Ismael must eliminate the offspring. Ismael may destroy what he wants to build because, in his conviction, he would rather fail in the process of taking his destiny in his own hands than lament how he allows himself to be cuckolded by a stepbrother who sleeps with his wife. In revenge, Ismael kills whomever he percieves as responsible for his melancholy. Unfortunately, Ismael ends up a tragic hero: all the privileges to which he aspires—social status, riches, whiteness, prestige, and even a white woman—do not fulfill his dreams.

From a religious perspective, the intertwined themes of racism, rape, and incest are all the same sins of the human mind in the sense that they have been diabolically projected from the manipulative altar of destiny. It is the responsibility of Ismael to resist and denounce all the efforts to change his purpose in life. In writing or staging a bold work such as *Anjo Negro*, Rodrigues questions prevalent contemporary representations of the Afro-Brazilian man as a stereotypical vagabond or street hustler. Ismael challenges this negative representation, and, as a self-assured and bold character, the protagonist falls into a conflict that can only be resolved by opting for whiteness. Rodrigues transforms Ismael into an ethical man of dignity who may be entangled in mythical and political tensions but is nevertheless so courageous that despite his resentments he resists the stigma of being seen as a trickster or any predetermined stereotypical role and feels a sense of pride in his accomplishments in a society that rejects him as a Black man. Ultimately, he betrays his race, his family, his children, and his entire world by submitting to the pressures of adopting whiteness. By accepting the dominant oppressive conditioning that renders him barely accepted in the white world, he demonstrates a lack of any modicum of control or self-esteem.

The catalogue of absurdities that led to the violent acts against everyone around Ismael is ample indication that Rodrigues sets out to critique the social inequalities and hypocrisies of racial democracy, as well as confidently assert that there is indeed racism in Brazil. Whether it is the three infanticides, the blindings and murders of Elias and Ana Maria, or Virgínia's hallucinations that Ismael is raping her each time they are intimate—all speak to the urgency of the racial dilemma that needs addressing. As Fred Clark notes in *Impermanent Structures* (1991), to better appreciate the dramatic text, it must be processed at many levels due to its complexity:

> Rather than a simple presentation and condemnation of racial prejudice, Nelson uses the issue to bring into question basic human values and emotions, and ties these to the ambiguities of perceptions of reality and illusion in human existence and experience. The text in other words, should be read on two levels or from two different but quite interrelated perspectives: first as a treatment of the black man in a white society, and how he attempts to resolve this problem, to create his own reality and identity through illusion (or fiction); and second, as a text in which the plot parallels the creative process itself—i.e., as a text that reflects its own construction by reflecting the process of fiction as it creates the realities of the text.[27]

I concur with Clark that these two levels of reading an "unpleasant theater," as coined by Rodrigues, help the reader to decipher the obsessive tendency in Nelson Rodrigues to want to intensify opposition between reality and illusion through shock.[28] This delineation reveals that we are dealing, on many dramatic stages, with a complex world of constant struggles that seeks to decipher meaning based on the many layers of signs that define our world. As a matter of fact, Ismael's actions are symptomatic of a protagonist who is limited in his choices but who cannot afford to be static or surrender to the oppressive racist society that wants him to fail. While failure is not an option for an educated and intelligent middle-class character such as Ismael, there are other societal forces beyond his control. His body, while resisting the reality of his historical past, constantly reminds him that he has yet to overcome the stigmas of slavery.

To further accentuate the dramatic intensity of *Anjo Negro*, the playwright suggests that Ismael cannot have it both ways—he can either meet all the expectations of the racist society or feel acceptance—but not both. Instead, through painstaking efforts, he conquers major adversity by becoming a successful physician, which translates as prestige in a racist society; yet by being frustratingly violent and cruel to everyone around him, including keeping his wife a prisoner, he ends up enacting a self-fulfilling prophecy of estrangement that makes him ashamed of his Blackness. This obviously is the last straw; it is his tragic flaw. After doing all that was required to overcome the adversity associated with his Blackness, he is still not accepted as a Black man and is traumatized by the experience. He is compelled to aspire taciturnly to an elusive whiteness. Acceptance of one's identity is everything; otherwise, one will suffer a psychological crisis of consciousness. The chorus of ten Black women sitting in a semicircle (as in Greek theater) plays a significant role in the play by placing a curse on whoever denies their identity. Because the entire play is framed around issues of racism, rape, and incest, it is logical to make the main characters accountable for their actions. Divided into three acts, the foreground hardly seeks to be realistic. Rather, in the first act, a wooden box full of clothes is placed on the first floor where the ten Black women are seated. There are two beds on the second floor, though one is damaged. On the first floor, Ismael, considered the Black angel, wears a well-ironed white suit with matching shoes. On the second floor, dressed in black, Virgínia mourns. It is remarkable that the house has no roof: "The house has no roof so the night might invade it and possess its inhabitants. In the background, tall walls which grow along with the black men's solitude."[29] These brief details about the setting of Ismael's house offer the reader an intimate insight into the simplicity of the household but the complexity of the forces operating within it that we will get to know. It is important to introduce us to the ten Black women that function as the chorus because they constitute an alter ego of sorts for the playwright. They not only devalue the virtues of the whites and promote those of the Blacks, but they also ensure that the one who transgresses Blackness is expressly punished or cursed. Overall, one gets a sense that the setting is highly restrictive. Only Ismael, the black angel, controls every movement around the house. Whites are not allowed to even come close. When it comes to the pending curse, the play seems to suggest that Ismael is doomed for denying his racial heritage at the convenient expense of desiring the white race.

A thesis play of sorts, *Anjo Negro* embodies the plot structure of violence that is mediated by misplaced passionate encounters that are at best calculating and at worst deeply disturbing and mean-spirited, especially when human emotions and lives are involved. The characters act violently toward one another and are simultaneously implicated in the violence they mete out to others in the name of reciprocal vengeance. Yet, underlining these tensions are traces of hidden love in hate and hidden hate in love—to the degree that love becomes relative and shifting. Take the case of Ismael: he commits many serious errors of judgment in love due to the disparity between his individual and collective consciousness. For him, the love he gives Brazil is not reciprocated by Brazil. He needs to prove that once he has a sound education, he can easily benefit from the assimilation model and privileges promised by Brazilian racial democracy. Instead, he suffers the pain of seeing his mixed children killed one after the other because his wife does not accept Black children. His gravest error still is to kill his own daughter. Ismael's internal conflicts seem irreparable, but the perpetrators of racism do so without any sense of accountability. They do not feel they are committing any egregious error because it is a matter of common knowledge that Brazil is racist. Though Ismael is judged as an individual who fails to dignify his own Blackness and who succumbs to the social pressure of embracing whiteness that does not fulfill him either, his stoic attitude is engendered by a context that must also be considered. The thesis, though open to many possibilities, may be reduced to a desperate cry for help. His deliberate rebelliousness departs from dialogue to the more sinister agency of direct violence and violation, which calls attention to the urgency of his situation. When the catalogue of violence is revisited, Elias and Ana Maria did not have to die; the three mixed-race children did not deserve to be drowned by Virgínia; and the overall senseless violence did not remedy the erroneous claims of racial democracy.

The fundamental puzzle for the reader or audience is the question Rodrigues poses through the voice of Elias: "What makes one reject one's color?" The play gets to a point in its dramatic development when all the characters' veils and masks come down. In the case of Ismael, the decision is made that he would become "white" as a strategy of survival. He is meticulous in his objectives and accomplishments. Consequently, he rejects his own Black mother, whom he blamed for the stigma of color he carries to his disadvantage in Brazilian society. He dresses in an impeccable white suit all the time—a symbolic gesture of his assimilation into white society. As a counterpoint, Virgínia also seeks her own moment of perfect revenge by having a white baby after she had killed all the fruits of the union between herself and Ismael. Ana Maria, the white daughter of Ismael, emerges as a complex character; however, her real father is Elias. Ismael's revenge, blinding Ana Maria using acid and killing Elias, is symptomatic of the level of degradation that racial democracy brings to virtually every character of *Anjo Negro*. The closing of the play raises some issues for resolution: the mausoleum has no special power to protect Ana Maria from the knowledge of her father, even though her blindness is meant to be an enhancing factor of her complete ignorance. Ismael lives with Ana Maria, who believes that all men, like Ismael, are white. Virgínia soon loses her mind, even as she notices the incestuous relation between Ismael and Ana Maria. Without closure, Ismael and Virgínia continue to have Black children who are killed. Only one question remains for Ismael: of what logical significance is this surrealistic attitude of Virgínia if not blatant racism? Racial democracy first destroys the individual conscience before launching an irreversible social assault on the collective imagination.

Of the many contending constraints of the cobweb of mythical racial democracy, Elias's epistemological question about negating one's color lends itself to a psychoanalytical answer. Unbearable socio-psychological conditioning can easily trigger a reaction in a human being that forces such a person to either be ashamed, frustrated, or subconsciously reject his or her racial heritage as a coping mechanism. Such realities are contradictory and repressed because the victim of such a troubled state of mind has lost all sense of rationality or conviction that things could be otherwise. What stares such a character in the face is the need for an elusive balance and relative justification. Ismael's world is antagonistic within itself. His white spouse, Virgínia, consciously kills her Black offspring because she is prejudiced. Yet she is in love with a Black man—quite a contradictory circumstance. Ismael condones Virgínia's crimes because they are bound by an illusory love and because they both desire and embrace whiteness. Both are clearly against race mixture. Ismael's success in a white hegemonic world is incomplete if all he can show for it are his professional accomplishments. His Black skin continues to be a hindrance to his complete acceptance in a racist society. By participating indifferently or indirectly in the murder of his own children, Ismael may be renouncing his paternity, hence absolving himself of any guilt or responsibility for their extermination. The question remains: had the children been white, would Ismael's response to the killings of the mixed-race children have been different? What specific ideological statement could Rodrigues be making about racial democracy in relation to Brazilian racism? Valdemar Junior captures this implied Brazilian contradiction in the forbidden Black racial heritage when he argues, "Em *Anjo negro*, Nelson Rodrigues assume sem rodeios o estágio avançado da degenerescência que atinge a sociedade brasileira, quando Ismael insere-se na família em crise para aprofundar ainda mais o fosso em que essa se encontra" (In *Anjo Negro*, Nelson Rodrigues directly recognizes the advanced stage of the degeneration that has befallen Brazil, when Ismael integrates himself within a family in crisis in order to get to the crux of the matter).[30]

Speaking of social degeneration, when it comes to the influence of Gilberto Freyre on the theater of Nelson Rodrigues, one need not go too far to arrive at the same conclusion reached by Henrique Buarque de Gusmão, when he asserts that within the tragic corpus of Rodriguian works, "It is possible to affirm that . . . a series of other questions are appropriated by Nelson Rodrigues: expression of a given political culture in which the patterns of behavior of characters are focused on personal relations at the expense of collective and institutional conventions; the constant presence of violence as a form of regulation of social life, the presence of a series of excesses, whether of violence, shame, passion, and authority—all of the elements deemed necessary for the manifestation of the tragic situations proposed by Nelson."[31] Yet it is through the insights of Freud (1925, 1895) and Lacan (1985) that we finally gain a richer understanding of the underlying quagmires that plague Ismael. In "The Negatives" (1925), Freud suggests that the only measure for a character to acknowledge the consciousness of repression of trauma is to establish a distinction between denial and refusal. Ismael is a Black character who is socially, culturally, and intellectually marginalized. Freud (1895) further notes that in such a context this unbearable condition places the burden of threatening factual reality on the victim, who, for Lacan (1985), is traumatized by the triggering factor of neurosis that can lead to silence or outright rage.[32] Ultimately, because of his neurosis, Ismael denies his Black children, accepts an incestuous white child in the person of Ana Maria as legitimate, and simultaneously exterminates both the daughter and the proxy white progenitor. Because trauma is also sexualized, the resultant death drive after each sexual act with the previously exterminated three "black angels" signifies the reality of a perpetual cycle of abuse, cruelty, and violence—which ultimately leads Ismael to come to terms with his own self-imposed castration.

Comparative Analysis

Emanuel and Ismael are complex racial protagonists who are morally and psychologically traumatized. As they struggle to overcome the untold obstacles a racist society has mounted against them, they perform rituals of transgression and redemption, even as they violate conventional rules and are violated by forces beyond their control. They come to terms with what René Girard calls "the sacrificial crisis," which implies that the process will necessitate certain deliberate misunderstandings so that the audience or spectators at no certain moment can conclude with certitude the vitality of the sacrificial act.[33] In the case of Emanuel, his sacrificial crisis occurs when he kills Margarida and realizes that he has transgressed and must flee for his life. Regardless of the justification for killing their mixed-race children, he is a fallen Black angel and must redeem himself through a ritual drama involving total surrender to African rites of passage. Ismael is even more complex in his encounter with his sacrificial crisis. He discovers, rather too late in the play, that his stepbrother, Elias, is the father of Ana Maria—whom Ismael has blinded to ensure that she never sees him as a Black man but as a white man who is desirable in a racist society. Elias chooses to blind both Elias and Ana Maria, but the revelation of Ana Maria's paternity heightens his crisis, so he murders both. Virgínia is a catalyst of Ismael's sacrificial crisis. Both Virgínia (*Anjo Negro*) and Margarida (*Sortilégio*) are privileged white women who distort the destinies of the two protagonists, Emanuel and Ismael. By "longing for the taboo," in the words of Julee Tate, both Emanuel and Ismael become victims of prohibitive interracial love.[34] Yet, by the same token, this is a contradiction. Racial democracy suggests that race-mixture forges the best in the two races, but the fact that both protagonists are destroyed for doing just that heightens the sacrificial misunderstanding. Both are heroes and villains, for they are sacrificed at the altar of miscegenation and redeemed at the altar of African mythological and cultural values. While women are portrayed rather stereotypically as "prostitutes," their portrayals are balanced by the power of feminine deities, such as Oxum and Iemanjá. Emanuel and Ismael are symptomatic of the retributive justice and warrior-like characteristics of Ogum and Xangô, respectively.

In the final analysis, through sacrificial rites, both protagonists participate in the symbolic extermination of miscegenation while opening the
possibilities for renewal through sacrificial offering to the gods.

Chapter 6

Zora Seljan and Dias Gomes

Sacred Feminine Solidarities and Sango's Revenge

Cosmologies, mythologies, and mythmaking are some of the myriad ways through which human beings explain the world around them. From prehistoric times to the present, how we interact with the defining elements of nature and dignifying deities for the mysterious roles they play in our lives are part of our annual or daily rituals and ceremonies for renewal. We deify as well as humanize the divinities. It is a constant cyclic process of comingling with the living, the ancestral, and the yet to be born. When it comes to an exemplary deity we engage in this chapter, despite his characteristic volatility, Xangô is revered as a multivalent possessor of such accolades as deity, royalty, and pragmatist. Continuing the conceptual trajectory of relocating the sacred from the sacred groves and temples to multimedia and popular outlets, this chapter examines Zora Seljan's dramatic interpretation of this enigmatic divinity from the multivalent perspectives of his equally powerful "wives," namely, Oxum, Iansan, and Obá. While Seljan's tripartite play *Três Mulheres de Xangô* (Three wives of Sango) pays homage to the qualities of Xangô, it also highlights his many weaknesses as a temperamental character who often regrets his uncontrollable actions. As a comparative lens to Seljan's play, this chapter also turns to Dias Gomes's *O Pagador de Promessas* (Payment as pledged), which provides a critical narrative against religious intolerance by subjecting the Catholic Church and its representatives to ridicule for their tendency to see Afro-Brazilian religion as perpetuating satanic rituals while treating Catholic rites as devout and divine.

159

Both Zora Seljan (1918–2006) and Dias Gomes (1922–1999) deploy Xangô rage as part of their vehement protests against all forms of racial discrimination and religious intolerance. By comparing these texts, this chapter revisits the issue of religious tension despite "syncre-tism" to better assess the extent to which Brazil has come of age from the era of religious persecution that dates back from the colonial era. The works maintain a consistency in their perception of religion as an agency of violence and of potential harmony when properly channeled toward achieving cosmic balance amidst terrestrial disharmony and contentions. A gendered perspective will also be used to compare the differences between the playwrights' representative works. Even in West Africa, where versions of Xangô's myth and reality abound as manifest in the edited volume *Sango in Africa and the African Diaspora* (2009), a response to religious intolerance as in the case of Brazil is still quite rare. Thus, the unique opportunity to compare these perspectives of praise of Xangô and the critique of the Catholic Church is a viable invitation for dialogue between the devotees on both sides of the sacred spectrum.

Ritual Dynamics, Axé, and Setting

The pattern of resurrection of the sacred in popular spaces, including but not limited to street altars and print and social media, echoes an interesting phenomenon in Brazilian cultural production in recent times, especially in Bahia. The challenge for the cultural critic is how to explicate the dynamism of the process because culture is not static and exists in the function of other intertwining dynamics, such as actions, violations, provocations, invocations, and memories. In *Locating the Sacred* (2014), Claudia Moser and Cecilia Feldman suggest that the sacred must be located through many channels and protocols, of which the "interrelationship between ritual and setting" must simultaneously engage the matter and *topos* of ritual without dissociating it from its practice and sociocultural context.[1] Candomblé or Afro-Brazilian religion is the Brazilian equivalent of the site of vital force that is reminiscent of the Yoruba pantheon.[2] When properly provoked and invoked, these deities are activated to execute the properties they are associated with by design, so that Xangô, deity of thunder and lightning, may be sum-moned to wreak electrical havoc on an adversary who has deliberately done evil. These deities may be either temperamental or cool; hence, the male ones are often associated with hotness while the female ones are linked to coolness. They are also liminal, as in the case of Yemoja, who is deemed Mother-Fish and can lure unsuspecting fishermen to their deaths at sea so that they can ultimately join her under the ocean.[3] In any case, the destiny of both the living and ancestral worlds are unified in the deities. The manifestation of the sacred in popular culture comes in various forms, but we are concerned here with Iansan, the deity of whirlwinds and the common denominator between the two central plays under analysis.

The defining characteristics in the Africa-derived syncretic religious manifestation that is today known as Candomblé took roots in Salvador da Bahia at the beginning of the nineteenth century. Candomblé developed through a creolization process that combined African traditional religious beliefs of formerly enslaved Africans in Brazil with the Catholic faith, especially between 1549 and 1888, when Candomblé soon transformed itself into a location of resistance, where African mythologies and rituals were kept alive through performative rituals. The devotees of this religion often become possessed while singing, dancing, and making ritual sacrifices. When it comes to the vitality of the religion, Roger Bastide, a renowned scholar of Afro-Brazilian religions, has been credited for the "invention" of Candomblé in terms of his involvement with the ritual practice. Arguing that the sum of the two religions cannot possibly produce an exclusive synthesis but one that is equally subject to the relics of the two even after religious syncretism, Bastide concludes: "There is juxtaposition, overlapping, shifting emphases, temporary watertight compartments. Against some commonly held views of syncretism, people are quite capable of adhering simultaneous to diverse, heterogeneous beliefs. It is true that Candomblé recreates something of Africa. The large public hall where the daughters and sons of the gods dance is a reproduction of the village square."[4] In other words, every worshipper is aware of the complex codes and anomalous settings that shift from the African setting to the terreiro and then to the Catholic space. The same deity operating as Ogun in Africa, now becomes an orixá in Brazil, manifesting its character as a Christian saint. In this tripartite embodiment of sameness and difference, rituals are intricately conditioned by their settings and vice versa to produce a sustained process of ritualization and naming that the rituals engender.

With their highly percussive drumming, ritualistic ceremonies of the Afro-Brazilian religion have steadily influenced the Brazilian "musicscape," including samba and bossa nova.[5] Unifying the many ethnic groups that were forcibly removed to work as slaves in Brazil, Candomblé activates ritualistic practice as a preservative gesture of the ancestral cult of memory. Similarly, axé, the life force full of magical power, controls all that transpires in the lives of those who submit to it for protection and blessing. The leaders of such sacred locations are the iyalorixás and babalorixás. In order to appease the orixás, the Yoruba-derived nagô music is deployed through instruments such as atabaques (drums), xequerês (gourds covered with a net of beads to produce a rattling effect and common in West Africa), agogô (gong bell), and agidavis (drumsticks)—thus creating a complex syncopated matrix of liturgical melodies that are geared to summon and imitate the orixás. Even when the dancing and singing cease, the atabaques and agogô bells continue to produce a rhythmic flow for the subsequent ritual enactments.

From the sacred location of the Candomblé, the music produced by devotees often finds its way into the secularized and popular space. Over time, what is supposedly "sacred" has suddenly become popular. Most of these efforts at popularizing the sacred are led by the afoxé groups, carnival-type fraternal organizations that model themselves after the irmandades, Catholic lay sisterhood-brotherhood groups that formed in Salvador in the seventeenth century to preserve African cultural traditions. The sacred has now become truly secularized. It is no longer unusual for afoxé groups or even blocos afros to congregate in popular spaces to celebrate such festivities as Festa de Yemanjá, Festa de Santa Bárbara, or Lavagem do Bonfim. Afoxé groups were initially ostracized for using sacred music, but since the rebranding of Filhos de Gandhi (Sons of Gandhi) as a major Afro-Brazilian organization, the stigma has waned. Indeed, afoxé groups may have declined due to the military dictatorship, but Gilberto Gil revolutionized Candomblé music by infusing afoxé ideology into popular music once he became a regular member of Filhos de Gandhi. Two of his more renowned DVDs are *Refavela* (1977), specifically the song "Patuscada de Gandhi" (Revelry of Filhos de Gandhi), where Gil adds a spiritual quality by calling to many of the orixás. Since participating at the FESTAC 1977 in Nigeria, Gilberto Gil was inspired to keep infusing music with Candomblé Ijexa rhythm. Beyond the popular space, both Candomblé location and carnival settings in Brazil negotiate the blurring of the boundaries that exist between the sacred and the popular. Against this complex background of locating the sacred, relocating it, and ultimately, appropriating it for creative and political empowerment, I proceed to analyze Seljan's *Três Mulheres de Xangô* (Three women of Xangô) with special emphasis on Iansan, or Santa Barbara, as conceptualized in the making of the "Woman of Xangô."

Zora Seljan's "Iansan: Mulher de Xangô"

"Iansan: Mulher de Xangô" is an integrative part of the trilogy, *Três Mulheres de Xangô*, in which three of Xango's wives manifest abiding characteristics of power and domination against their husband, who is far more subdued than what legend tells us. Though the three women, Oxum (deity of beauty and fecundity), Iansan (deity of whirlwind and storms), and Obá (deity of the stormy rivers) exude different characteristics, they also share some commonalities. Iansan, the central focus of the play under analysis, is a fierce female warrior. She is the doyenne of the marketplace and keeps watch over the gates of the cemetery. She is the ultimate force of change in nature and in life. In a powerful preface to Zora Seljan's *The Story of Oxalá*, Antônio Olinto, a renowned Brazilian cultural critic, educates the reader about the proximity of Brazil and Africa. Fifty million years ago, the two continents were like the extension of each other, and "the shores and beaches of Bahia, North Rio Grande and Ceará were joined to the lands of Lagos, Badagry, Porto Novo and Lomé."[6] Given this spirit of rapprochement between African cultural traditions and Brazil's vitality in cultural mixing as a matter of survival and preservation, it took the adaptive temperament of Zora Seljan to produce unique Afro-dramas about the specific Yoruba experience in Brazil. Olinto pronounces Seljan's artistic production as "mythological theatre," writing that her characters are gods and goddesses with the same demeanor on stage as when they are ritualized in the shrines.[7] Seljan captures Afro-Brazilian language, myths, beliefs, hopes, disappointments, and the spirit of resilience to survive the brutalities of enslavement.

Born on December 7, 1918, in the city of Ouro Preto in Minas Gerais, the daughter of a Croatian father, an engineer named Lessa Seljan, and a mineira mother, a teacher named Aracy Lessa Seljan, Zora Seljan was interested in journalism and literary studies. She moved to Belo Horizonte, where she completed high school and mingled with writers, such as Fernando Sabino, Paulo Mendes Campos, Otto Lara Resende, and Ruben Braga (whom she married). They lived in Rio de Janeiro and São Paulo and had one child. She was influenced by communist ideas of friends, such as Jorge Amado, Graciliano Ramos, and Candido Portinari. She visited the Soviet Union as well as other Iron Curtain countries during the Cold War era. She met several African leaders, and, influenced by the positive cultural renaissance from her travels, she returned to Brazil, particularly Bahia, where she studied African rituals and the African diaspora. It was in this context that she met her second husband, Antônio Olinto. In 1958, she moved with Olinto to Nigeria, where he was an ambassador. Upon her return to Brazil, she founded Conjunto Folclórico Oxumaré and was inducted as a leader at the Ilê Axé Opo Afonjá in Salvador. Her dramatic production was clearly significant for the appreciation of Yoruba culture in Brazil. Seljan's works include: *Festa do Bonfim; História de Oxalá; Iemanjá e Suas Lendas; Iemanjá: Mãe dos Orixás; Exu, Cavaleiro da Encruzilhada; Oxum Abalo, Iansan: Mulher de Xangô,* and *A Orelha de Obá;* and *Os Negrinhos: O Negrinho do Pastoreio, Negrinha de Iemanjá,* and *Negrinhos das Folhas.*

Seljan's dramas are generally invested in Yoruba mythology that includes the orixás and their bearing on sacred entities, elements of nature, and their manifestation in the daily affairs of men and women. A mythological theater, in the sense invoked by Antônio Olinto or mythologist Joseph Campbell, suggests that all societies perform rituals and ceremonies with a sense of duty to receive pleasure and power—such as glorifying victories, heroes, supernatural powers, and the deities.[8] These rituals often come in dramas that depict the cycle of life and the primacy of the afterlife. Others include festival dramas geared toward honoring deities such as Dionysus and Apollo. While tragedies resonate well with our modern society, they also furnish opportune ways to make sense of the quest for life's meaning, as well as the complex personalities of the deities. In the specific case of Seljan, the place of cultural hybridity in a space laden with deep Yoruba thought systems must be a challenging one because "the framing of Seljan's text supports Bastide's contention about the contraction of spatial distance rather than a total identification of one belief system over another."[9] In other words, Seljan's work must remain faithful to Yoruba mythologies and Brazilian miscegenation, while at the same time subject to the exigencies of modern theater by way of impacting the person through the power of ritual.

Through the prism of Xangô and his three Yoruba mythological wives, Seljan crafts an Afro-Latin American world (more lucidly, a Yoruba diaspora) in which Yoruba orixás manifest their inherent powers while remaining sensitive to the complexities of other abiding environmental spiritual forces, such as the advent of Islam and colonialism. In this process of what Ali Mazrui has termed "triple heritage," Seljan takes advantage of the sophistication of the Yoruba world while putting other religious or theatrical influences into conversation.[10] Miscegenation was not a matter of convenience but of necessity as Portuguese colonials in Brazil satisfied their sexual urges with the natives. Through a creative strategy of religious syncretism, enslaved Africans were able to preserve their African rituals and ceremonies, which culminate in the creation of Candomblé, a formidable Afro-Brazilian religion that pays homage to the Yoruba deities or orixás while serving as a locus of resistance for all forms of cultural contamination and social oppression. In his insightful study "Xangô and Other Yoruba Deities in the Plays of Zora Seljan," Robert Lima observes that enslaved Africans survived the shock of slavery through "preservation of . . . deeply-rooted indigenous oral lore by the slaves themselves."[11] From Africa to the Caribbean and the Americas, Yoruba deities have remained preserved and hierarchized, and in the temples they are invoked by the faithful despite their long separation from Africa and the violence they suffered at the hands of slave owners while masking their precious cultural and religious value systems out fear of repression. Seljan is in the good company of African (and African diaspora) writers who have sought to document how cultural producers have painstakingly preserved Yoruba rituals through various agencies of initiation, rites of passage, and the popularization of the sacred.

Seljan's *Três Mulheres de Xangô* privileges the power of women to interfere in the affairs of nature and of men. Iansan, Oxum, and Obá are three strong mythological Yoruba women who were believed to have all married Xangô at one point in their lives. Much has also been said and written about Xangô, who is often spoken of in the same breath as these phenomenal women. We know he was king of Oyo and was married to Oya, and he also was believed to have committed suicide in Koso ("did not hang"), a literal naming of the negation of suicide as if denying it occurred. Generally speaking, suicide is taboo in Yoruba culture, especially for a king. In mythological representation, duality is a constant, just as we witness in Greek culture. Every individual, including Xangô, embodies in his collective consciousness the representation of at least two women. In the case of Xangô, the prominent ones were Iansan and Oxum. Iansan is combative; she is the deity of winds and tempests; and she is one who carries a sword in hand while riding on a horse as she identifies with her own symbolic representation. Oxum, meanwhile, is vain, superficial, and fertile. Xangô is quite jealous, loves women, is full of himself, but has a moral sense of justice. When Xangô is in love, he demands total loyalty, is wary of death, and hates conflicts in his kingdom. Yet, Xangô's women are not ordinary in stature; they are often portrayed as being at least as powerful as Xangô—hence their curious propensity to transgress, provoke, cause intrigues, and even protect as they deem fit. Of the three magical women, Iansan and Oxum are Xangô's favorites, so it is no wonder that they fight for his attention. Xangô never gives up on any of his wives despite their eccentricities. Iansan is the ultimate feminist: she is always by Xangô's side, protecting him by sending rays of lightning to whoever wants to do him harm or destroy their love. She assumes such accolades of being a fighter and warrior, and she is as domineering and jealous as Xangô, with whom she enjoys living in permanent conflict. Meanwhile, Oxum is the peacemaker. Fertile, sweet, domestic, talkative, and superficial—she is quite befitting as a wife. She accepts for her offering aphrodisiacs, such as honey and eggs, which give her sexual energy. With life being a series of conflicts and resolutions, Iansan and Oxum encompass the life of Xangô to ensure that he remains in a perpetual mode of indecision. Likewise, the alternating characteristics of Iansan and Oxum could also be embodied in one single woman.

The centrality of the orixás to Brazilian drama is not unique to Seljan. Playwrights such as Vinicius de Moraes, Abdias Nascimento (and the Teatro Experimental do Negro group as a whole), Antonio Callado, Dias Gomes, Chico Buarque, Jorge de Lima, Jorge Andrade, and Joel Rufino dos Santos also put orixás at the center of Brazilian drama. Among the younger generation, one could also mention Cuti, Miriam Alves, and Axévier, among others. Seljan's entire dramatic corpus investigates the relationship of the orixás with the world of man or of interdeity conflictual dramas. For example, *Historia de Oxalá* deals with the coexistence of a Yoruba deity Oxalá and the corresponding Catholic saint Senhor do Bonfim. Illustrated by Carybé, *Três Mulheres de Xangô* is prefaced by an introductory chapter with details about stage directions as well as clarifications about characters, dances, music, and scenic actions. The precision was such that Seljan even specified the connection of the characters with Greek tragedy: "My characters are deities who manifest themselves through dance / . . . / May the Orixás give them same vitality of the Olympian Gods."[12] In *Três Mulheres de*

Xangô, the playwright brings together plays such as "Oxum Abalô"; "Iansan, Mulher de Xangô"; and "A Orelha de Obá"—all of which require creative energy, folkloric culture, musical sensibility, and artistic choreography in order to be staged. Tales of Oxum told in the play are part and parcel of the rich Yoruba tradition from Candomblé and not to be confused with "macumba" in Rio de Janeiro. The themes range from (1) oracular warnings to divert mishap; (2) facing the consequences like destiny when one does not heed warnings; (3) the creation myth and the role of Obatala in the creation of human beings and other creatures; (4) Oxum Abalo and the story of the Yoruba Goddess of Beauty; (5) Oxum's plot to free herself of the insatiable Xangô by setting up her younger sister, Iansan, with him; (6) the enmity between Muçurumins and Xangô; (7) the risk that orixás will be terminated if the state of conflict remains perpetual; (8) Iansan's unleashing of destructive energy based on her feeling of defamation by the council of the orixás; (9) the reuniting of Iansan and Xangô; (10) the story of Iansan and Xangô after the advent of Islam; and (11) the intertwined narratives of Xangô, Oxum, and Iansan. If there is any commonality in the stories, it lies in the transcendence of Yoruba mythology over and above national and individual levels. By helping propagate the stories of the orixás to the world, Seljan indeed serves the function of the griotte, recounting tales, embellishing them, and maintaining moral standards. Seljan may have preserved orixás for posterity, but in so doing she shared with us the functional artistic model for Yoruba mythological playwriting.

The Significance of Xangô's Wife Iansan

The power of Candomblé resides in the sacred and its ability to reach equilibrium and harmony based on the natural elements of the universe. Each orixá appropriates its ancestral history by approximating its attributes of dance, music, and performance. A sacred model in communion with the divinity fills itself to the brim at the altar of sacrifice. Seljan's empowering approach does not limit itself to simply representing the sacred rituals of the Candomblé but also to ensuring that, in the process of relocating it to the cultural manifestation, the unconscious and mythical art becomes one through religious awakening. Reginaldo Prandi appropriately notes, "The Orixás have defined characteristics that are archetypal in the stages of human life, such as birth, growth, sexual activities, diseases, and death."[13] Given Zora Seljan's mission to ensure a synergistic transposition of the sacred into the profane, even if that means entertainment or stage production, her dramaturgy has never remained the same, and the vivaciousness of the Yoruba in the ritual performance is essential. How then does Iansan, an embodiment of contradictions and complementarity, translate the virtue of being Xangô's wife? She does so by qualifying her own being, which the whirlwinds and tempest translate as a potentially stormy agency. Iansan embodies that agency that defines her as a seeker of children: "Oya could not have children / But she had nine, / After sacrificing a lamb. / Thus out of respect, / For her request to be answered /Iansan, mother of nine children, / Never again ate lamb."[14] Iansan's temperament is stormy and that gives her a competitive edge over more cooling or female orixás. The intrigue that often defines the character of Iansan is manipulative and therapeutic. She must be volatile to be seen as an equal partner to Xangô, but she can also be harmonious enough to appear nonthreatening to have her way with her rival, Oxum. She is ultimately savvy and strategic, keeping Xangô for herself against the will of Oxum and Obá, the other wives.

Seljan's "Iansan: Mulher de Xangô" documents the synergy between Xangô, the God of Thunder, and Iansan, the Goddess of the Wind, when both unite as a formidable force of social justice and protection for humanity. Before the play on Iansan, Seljan had presented the reader with "Oxum Abalô," an homage to the Goddess of Beauty, who had been welcomed into the world of indigenous Indian spirits, who dances in front of her mirror to exhibit her prowess and vitality. The narrative anchors its message on the rivalry between Oxum and Iansan. To further intensify the intrigues, Oxum sets up Xangô to be ensnared by Iansan. They get close and cozy—leading to jealousy from Oxum. Other deities get involved, and what started as a mere intrigue among jealous wives ends up becoming a conflict among the orixás. Thus, the supernatural world commingles with the natural order of things, as ancestral spirits and living spirits celebrate their interdependence. The story of "Iansan: Mulher de Xangô" thus takes off after Iansan assumes the leadership of Xangô's household. If the importance of African cultural heritage is anything to go by, Seljan advises a potential director to put emphasis on the overall credibility of the moral story of African descendants: "It is important to have respect and enthusiasm for African cultural heritage; separating fetish cults, gross grafts, selecting the positive, legendary and grandiose aspects. Examine the Xangô's double-edged axe for example, not only as a piece of wood, but the origin of fire, symbol of thunder."[15] This admonition prompts Iansan to shout at the end of the play, lamenting how the deities have deceived her:

> IANSAN (*stepping down the stairs and walking towards the 2nd floor*)—I was defeated for taking the counsel of the Orixás, but I must have my way. Ah Xangô, my husband! You did not support me! You are running away from me! You do not want to listen to me! I am struggling with an open heart since I am neither afraid of your power nor do you intimidate me. Come and get Martin-Fisherman, if you are able to! (*Screaming*) Xangô! Xangô! Iansan challenges you in heaven and on earth![16]

Though conciliatory and unpretentious, Iansan simply pleads with Xangô without giving up her own power. Her voice is lucid, precise, and direct. The cathartic moment reveals a sense of fragmentation that must be undone to return Iansan to wholeness. Though she feels betrayed and abandoned, she is completely resolved to challenge the status quo. Iansan is a powerful woman whose destiny is not in any mortal man's hands: only in her own. Her story in relation to Xangô's shows interdependence and a stoic attitude when faced with life's challenges. Stormy as she is temperamental, Iansan is able to harmonize her world by first dealing with her own self, reaching out to the antagonist and reassuring the powerful man of the household that his time is up. Iansan, after all, is an independent woman. That is her essence.

Following the three-act model, each of the three plays that constitute the trilogy deploys Oxum as a logical personification of the feminine because she embodies fecundity. Oxum is portrayed as: (1) the maintaining fountain of fertility; (2) the exalter of women who menstruate; (3) the feminine power of pride; (4) the power of procreation; (5) the embodiment of beauty, grace, and elegance; and (6) the abundance in everything. After feeling abandoned once by a hunter deity, Oxossi, she makes a deal with Exu, who makes available the king Xangô for her consolation and happiness:

> OXUM: Don't be funny, Exu. Do you need anything?

> EXU: I had some idea.

Oxum: Which one is that?

Exu: Oxóssi and you need to learn a lesson.

Oxum: You have spoken well; but what can I say?

Exu: Did he not go searching for a lamb?

Oxum: Yes, he did.

Exu: If you want, I can prepare the flock for a longer journey.

Oxum: And what do I gain?

Exu: Thus Xangô will visit you. . . . Only you will have the honor of the feast. People will say you as a great queen; that your house is magnificent; and that Oxóssi is just a savage.[17]

The drama between Iansan and Oxum is cleverly inserted into the "change and continuity" trajectory of the three women of Xangô. Through mythology and archetyping, the third play, "A Orelha de Obá," brings together the three women once again by focusing on Obá, Xangô's wife, who cuts off her own ear. The play then develops around different people who are accused of being part of the violent act to annoy Xangô or the dramatic ploy of just being the culprit. Xangô assists his wife by using a balm that helps the ear to grow back. The episodes of accusations and counter-accusations intensify the drama. By ritualizing the affairs of the deities, Zora Seljan invites the audience to witness the human dimension of the divinities. Iansan, Oxum, and Obá are female entities with whom Xangô finds himself entangled in passionate love and with whom he must negotiate varied emotions to have matrimonial bliss. By humanizing the deities right before our very mesmerized eyes as spectators, Seljan craftily unites the world of the supernatural and the natural.

Dias Gomes's O *Pagador de Promessas*
(Payment as Pledged)

Both Dias Gomes and Zora Seljan were Brazilian playwrights with different degrees of visibility, complexity, radicalism, and fame. Contemporaries when it comes to the deployment of orixás in their plays as a statement against religious intolerance as well as the preservation of Candomblé in ritual performance, the two are united in a social vision that popularizes the sacred. Seljan started her career as a newspaper critic for *O Globo*, *O Dia*, and *Diretrizes*. She also created the Orixás Theater and wrote pieces such as *The Three Women of Xangô*, *Iansã, the Warrior*, *The Waters of Oxalá*, and *Exu, Knight of the Crossroads*. She was married to the writer Antônio Olinto and previously to Rubem Braga. She graduated with a degree in economics from the University of São Paulo and trained as an essayist in the United States at Columbia University in 1965. At the University of Lagos (Nigeria), where she resided for two years, Zora Seljan was a reader of Portuguese and Brazilian literature. Seljan also founded the *Conjunto Folclórico Oxumaré* in Brazil. As a journalist, Seljan wrote about various literary, economic, and political issues. She was the first South American journalist to visit Russia and other Soviet countries. After this trip, she wrote "And I Saw the Popular Democracies," an essay published in 1951. From the writings of her father, the Croatian ethnographer Stevo Seljan, she gleaned material to write articles on Italy's invasion of Abyssinia. After the war, her husband went on a cultural mission to Nigeria, and Zora began research on African customs, culture, and arts, using the theater to convey her findings. Meanwhile, Dias Gomes was a Brazilian playwright known for his controversial subject matter. He was born in Salvador da Bahia and started writing plays at the age of fifteen. Later in his career, he wrote soap operas, and he wrote the first Black soap opera on Brazilian television, and it still has the highest rating of all time. He was also a writer for numerous Brazilian TV shows, miniseries, and a few movies. *O Pagador de Promessas* (Payment as pledged), based on his play of the same title, was the first Brazilian movie to be nominated for an Oscar, and the only South American film to ever win the Golden Palm at the Cannes Film Festival. In 1950, he married Brazilian telenovelist Janet Clair, whom he was married to for thirty-three years and had three children. She died in 1983, and six years later he married Bernadeth Lyzio. With Lyzio he had two daughters, Mayra Dias Gomes, a writer, and Luana Dias Gomes, a student of economics at Stanford University. He died in a car accident in São Paulo in 1999.

In mapping the intersection of theology, religion, and popular culture, Elaine Graham (2007) conjectures that "popular culture is serving to mediate understandings of the nature of religious belief and practice."[18] In the case of the drama of Zé-do-Burro in *Payment as Pledged*, what remains puzzling is the impossibility of this protagonist to transcend the limits of religious belief. This is how he finds out, rather late and in death, that what is considered a sacred space is indeed an altar that does not negotiate alternatives or compromises. His simple promise to pay back the gesture of Santa Barbara (or Iansan) makes no difference to him from the viewpoint of religious syncretism but will make a huge difference for the Catholic Church. Healing his donkey mysteriously turns tragic, and while struggling to bring a big cross inside the church and pay his pledge, he is accused of mixing Christian symbols with rituals of Candomblé. When mediated by the contributions of Mircea Eliade in *The Sacred and the Profane*, the resolution (or lack thereof) of the dilemma of Zé-do-Burro questions how the spaces (sacred or popular) are blurred in a hybrid (yet intolerant) society, where to be devout may not necessarily mean to be completely in service to the precepts of traditional Candomblé. Dias Gomes, however, indicts a society that is full of religious hypocrisy when a simple gesture of paying promise turns inadvertently deadly for the protagonist. The intersection of theology, religion, and popular culture is the divide between orthodox clericalism and the popular culture that translates the meaning of culture itself because it is produced by the people and for the people. Zé-do-Burro must forever wonder why a simple pledge to a deity could turn so deadly.

Dias Gomes is world renowned. He made a name for himself early in life and started producing works that garnered a lot of interest at the age of fifteen. Known as a master of many genres, especially in North American theatrical circles, he has crisscrossed theater, television, radio, cinema, and literature. His dramatic productions can be divided into two phases. The first phase includes works he produced as a teenager that did not get much critical attention. Gomes's second phase coincides with his maturity and contains his most representative plays, such as *O Pagador de Promessas* (1960), which was adapted into a film that won the Golden Palm at the Cannes Film Festival. The plot deals with the singular story of Zé-do-Burro, a rural dweller who has come to the city of Salvador to pay his pledge to Iansan/Santa Bárbara, the savior of his donkey, Nicolau. He travels twenty-one miles to fulfill this promise at Santa Barbara's church. The promise could have been easily fulfilled, if not for the obstacles encountered by Zé-do-Burro.

Typical of Greek tragedy, the conflict that ensues in the plot leads to a tragic end. As Anatol Rosenfeld notes in *O Mito e o herói no Moderno Teatro Brasileiro* (1996), the play is similar to Greek tragedy because of its (1) development of a conflict, (2) tragic ending, and (3) rigor of unity of action and time as Aristotle defines it in *Arte Poética* (2007). Aristotle further argues that tragedy is not about imitation of people but about imitating actions of life toward a tragic flaw.[19] In *O Pagador de Promessas*, Zé-do-Burro moves from innocent happiness to suddenly being tragically flawed: he does not surrender his conviction to the intransigence of the church as represented by Reverend Olavo. Zé-do-Burro's error is that he makes his pledge at a Candomblé temple and not at a rural church. Not only is he blinded in his logic, but he will not compromise his own position within the church, which was by virtue of power politics the only solution left for him. Amid the chaos in the city, he feels lonely, desperate, and helpless. In the play, one witnesses the solidarity of the people (such as the capoeira group) who, after his death, place his body on the cross and force it into the church to fulfill his promise—an act that is transgressive and defiant. The simplistic Zé-do-Burro does not understand the complex metropolis nor does the city understand Zé-do-Burro. In other words, Gomes reenacts the tragic dimension of the antihero, placing him in conflict with the city and its dislocative energy. As Rosenfeld puts it, the catalogue of Zé-do-Burro's alienating actions is overwhelming; his troubling extremism and tragic flaw are equally disturbing.

For Rosenfeld, "We have a rare case of a pure tragedy, whose hero, with dignity, sustains it consistently, despite the humoristic beginning in which his maladjustment becomes laughable based on cultural structures of the city."[20] As a matter of fact, the protagonist belongs to another world, a primitive one to be precise, where rituals are the very essence of life. However, from the viewpoint of the church, why was Zé-do-Burro forbidden from entering the sacred space to pay his pledge? He had made his promise in what the church considered a diabolic space, an Iansan shrine. The tragic confrontation between Zé-do-Burro and Padre Olavo speaks to how both entities perceive transgression and resolution. Even the Bishop, who had the power to forgive heresy, could not convince Zé-do-Burro to make another promise and reject the "diabolic" one. For Zé-do-Burro, it did not matter, for a "promise is a promise," and he was committed to depositing his cross on the altar of the Santa Barbara Church.

The Cross as a Sacred Space

O Pagador de Promessas recounts the saga of Zé-do-Burro, who travels to the Santa Barbara Church in Salvador to pay a pledge. Part of his pledge

is to carry a cross like the one Jesus carried. He also divides his property
with the poor. In essence, he becomes an activist for social justice. He is
even confused with the new messiah for his act of piety. The church feels
threatened that it might lose its power if another individual competes for
religious prominence. In other words, the reverend sees in Zé-do-Burro
someone who is keen on profaning the Catholic faith. As the guardian
of the sacred temple, Reverend Olavo feels that he must close the doors
of the church to Zé-do-Burro. However, the conflict of the play could
have been resolved if Zé-do-Burro had heeded the advice of Rosa:

> Rosa: But you have already paid your pledge. You have carried
> a wooden cross to the Santa Barbara Church. There you have
> the Santa Barbara Church. There you have the cross. Done.
> Now let us get going.

> Zé: But this is not Saint Barbara Church. The church is that
> one in the inner door.[21]

Quite faithful to his pledge, Zé-do-Burro does not allow any form of
distraction to detract from his objective. Though tired and hungry, he
does not see himself in a position to negotiate anything but to fulfill his
pledge. For Zé-do-Burro, the sacred space is not at the entrance but in
the inner chambers of the church—specifically, the altar of the Santa
Barbara Church.

To appreciate the archaic mindset of Zé-do-Burro and the notion
of the sacred in the promise, Mircea Eliade offers a theoretical model.
For the sacred being, there is always a sacred space that must be seen
as strong, significant, and vivid, but there are nonsacred spaces that
are nonstructural, inconsistent, and even amorphous. From the tension
between the sacred and the profane, we have the idea of a space. While,
for a man who lives in a world devoid of sacrality, such a space is conceived in its totality, homogeneity, neutrality, and purity of all religious
prepositions, for one who believes in the nonhomogeneity of space,
the sacred space is filled with values that elevate the religious man.
The essence of the sacred is lived by the believer, with the sentiment
of primordial experience, and is homologous to the foundation of the
world. It is strong and significant. Eliade proposes the term "hierophany," which means the manifestation of the sacred. The term implies
something of the sacred that reveals. By hierophany, the sacred is only

known, and, by being known, it is revealed. It breaks the homogeneity of space, while revealing an absolute reality. According to Eliade, the manifestation of the sacred can occur with any object that gains sacred importance by the symbolism it acquires. At manifestations of the sacred there are mysterious acts that are ontologically related to the founding of the world. This reality does not belong to our world and can only be linked to faith by faith. Only through the mystery of the sacred can we understand its message. Hence, hierophany is linked to belief. Being a manifestation of faith, outside the religious sphere, every hierophanic sign is emptied of value.

The image of Santa Barbara reveals the presence and intercession of the Virgin Mary in the lives of those who have faith and believe in the power of the saints. In the Christian imaginary, Mary symbolizes sacrifice and gift. Mary is the supreme mother, the one who endured everything in the name of God and on behalf of Christ, the Savior of mankind. It represents the power to be without sin, for being a virgin, she conceived the son of God. The Holy Virgin Mary is one, and she is multiple; she is the intercessor of humanity with God the Father and His Son Jesus Christ, present in all the saints of Christian hagiography. However, for those who do not believe in these religious symbols, the image of a saint, photograph, or any other form of representation is exactly what it presents: a photo in the form of an image, which can ultimately be seen as an adornment for the decoration of an environment. To live the sacred, the religious man must ritually mark the sacred space. Based on the conception of the nonhomogeneity of space, man needs to establish the "fixed point," or the sacred concentration and the central axis of any future orientation. This is the reason why temples are needed. Mircea Eliade uses the term "center of the world" to account for the symbolism of the center. The concept of symbolism of the center is approached in the work of Mircea Eliade, particularly in the study that the historian of religions makes of the sacred and profane in archaic and modern societies. This is notably evident in the works *Myth of the Eternal Return* (1985) and *The Sacred and the Profane* (1992). In his study of religions, Eliade analyzes the role of sacred space in the life of traditional societies, regardless of the particular aspect of this space: holy place, cultural house, city, and "world." The symbolism of the world center signals religious behavior in relation to the space in which a religious man lives. Because it is a sacred space, which is given by a hierophany or ritual—and not a profane, homogeneous space—these spaces are loaded with power. Sacred power means at the same time reality, perennialism, and effectiveness. Therefore, it is necessary that Zé transpose the threshold of the church to be at peace with Santa Barbara.

In the archaic thought of Zé, the church is inside the door; therefore, the threshold is the threshold of passage from the profane to the sacred: "I promised to carry the cross into the church, I have to take it. I walked twenty miles. I will not soil the saint because of a half a meter." In the play, half a meter separates the square from the church, and that's where Zé remains because he is not authorized to fulfill his promise within the church. Asked by Father Olavo about the feat, the humble Zé-do-Burro explains the origin of the promise with the simplicity of the countryman who is not yet corrupted by the wickedness of the city. After explaining the promise, there is a change in the priest's attitude as he concludes that the promise had been exaggerated and pretentious. In fact, Zé had tried everything to save his donkey, Nicholas: he called a doctor, administered medicines, patted cow dung on the wound, and asked the Black healer Zeferino to pray for the donkey. None of this managed to save the animal. Finally, tired and desperate, he came to a solution: take the donkey to the terreiro de Maria de Iansã. There, the Mother of Santo says that Iansã, owner of the rays and thunderstorms, wounded Nicholas, and Zé had to make her a promise. It has to be a good promise because Iansan, who struck Nicholas with lightning, will not allow for any nonsense:

> Zé: And I remembered then that Iansã is Santa Barbara and I promised Nicolau that if he got well, I would carry a wooden cross to her church, on the day of her feast, a cross as heavy as that of Christ.[22]

Zé also promises to divide the land with the poor farmers. His promises are based on the donkey feeling better. After Nicholas is cured, Zé fulfills his promise. First, he divides a part of his land between the poor farmers, and then he goes to Salvador to deposit the cross at the altar of Santa Barbara. The altar symbolizes the sacred place of thanksgiving.

Zé does not differentiate the sacred and the profane when he goes to a Candomblé terreiro and makes a promise to Iansã while invoking Santa Barbara. After all, he believes in the sacredness of spaces destined for the faithful. In this way, the space of the terreiro embodies the same sacredness as the church. However, he does not consider the environment surrounding the church to be sacred. The façade of the church outside does not signify the church nor does it carry the symbolism of the church within. Even within the church, the sacred place is the altar, where he intends to deposit the cross. From this comes the dramatic tension:

> Zé: (In desperation) But Father . . . I promised to take the cross to the high altar! I have to keep my promise!

> Father: Then do it in a church. Or anywhere, except in a den of witchcraft.[23]

We have, besides religious intolerance, the revelation of the power of the sacred. Zé does not accept any agreement that deflects the course of the promise for fear of divine punishment. He fears the sacred forces, believing in the power of grace in proportion to the power of punishment. The healing power of the donkey could turn into the wrath of the saint in the deviance of action:

> Zé: No, this miracle business, you have to be honest. If you wrap the saint, you lose credit. Again, the saint looks, consults his settlements there and says:—Ah, you are Zé-do-Burro, the one who has already passed my leg! And now come make me new promise. Well, go make a promise to the devil that you carry him, you poor dead man! And there is more: saint is as good as a *gringo*, if he betrays one person, all the others know.[24]

The man's simple language in the explanation points to the relation of fear established between him and his belief. We believe that this fear is responsible for the belief and maintenance of the power of the sacred. This fear of being punished appears in other parts of the play, revealing a man fearful of staying out of reality, that is, out of the sacred. Zé fears divine wrath. Religion is then conceived as a terrible power that bestows and punishes. According to Eliade (1992), sacred space elevates the religious man to a medium distinct from that in which his existence takes place. In the temple, man binds himself to the divine, providing a break with the profane. In this way, the church is part of a different space from the street where it sits. In the play, the complicating element is the space in which the promise is sourced. The church does not accept mixing temples of the cult to deities unfamiliar to the Christian hagiographia.

For the priest, Zé serves two masters: God and the Devil. He goes on to insist that a "pagan" ritual that begins in a Candomblé temple cannot have its end within the Catholic Church: "FATHER: (Exploding) It is not Santa Barbara. Santa Barbara is a Catholic saint. You went to a fetish ritual. You invoked a false divinity and it was to her that you promised this sacrifice!"[25]

In the third and final act, Zé is seated on the steps of the church. Feeling helpless in the face of the situation, he realizes there is no way to place the cross on the altar of Santa Barbara. In the same spot where the cross sits, a capoeira group forms. Two berimbau players, a tambourine and a reco-reco, sit on a bench and the "comrades" form a circle, at the center of which squats Master Coca and Manoelzinho Sua-Mãe. The berimbaus cry, and Rosa, overcome by curiosity, approaches the group. It is at that moment that Iansã and Santa Barbara meet, bridging the terreiro and the church. The simple people who identify with Zé-do-Burro sing and play capoeira. The rituals of Candomblé shuffle the meaning of the sacred and the profane. After the dance, My Aunt serves the caruru, being careful to give the first dish to Santa Barbara, that is to Iansã. At the end of the play, we find Zé-do-Burro, knife in hand and retreating toward the church. The priest comes behind and bangs his arm, causing the knife to fall into the middle of the square. Zé-do-Burro runs, and the cops take advantage and fall on him, dominating him. The capoeiristas fall on the policemen to defend Zé-do-Burro, who disappears in the human wave. There's a shot, and the crowd disperses like a stampede of cattle. Zé-do-Burro is shown in the middle of the square with his hands on his belly. He takes another step toward the church and falls dead. The Father lowers his head and returns to the top of the stairs. Master Coca consults his companions, and everyone understands his intention and nods. Master Coca bows before Zé-do-Burro, holding him by the arms, and the other capoeira's come to help load the body. They place him on the cross, on his back, with his arms outstretched like a crucified man. They carry him like this and advance to the church. Rosa follows them. Intimidated, the Father and the Sacristan retreat; the beatas that accompany the priest run away, and the capoeiristas enter the church with the cross and the body of Zé-do-Burro. Galego, Dedé, and Rosa close the procession. Only My Aunt stays on the scene. A tremendous thunderstorm crashes over the square. My Aunt shrieks, frightened, and touches the ground and her forehead with her fingertips: "I will go to my mother!" Finally, the cross reaches its destination.

As we just discussed, the outcome of the play brings together the sacred and the profane. Zé on the cross is carried by the people of the terreiro. Stretched on the cross, he represents the figure of Jesus Christ, who was crucified and who gave his life to save mankind. Both are overcome by intolerance; they die, but they do not give up on their steadfastness regarding the faith that binds them. Both Zé and Christ are defeated heroes. They serve as models of conduct for our actions, for enclosing values such as dignity, honesty, and decency. The message of Dias Gomes's play goes far beyond questions involving religious syn-cretism. It signals the need for respect for the human being at the core of his essence. Therefore, the action of the capoeiristas in the outcome of the play is not understood here in terms of a sacred place or profane place in the destiny of Zé-do-Burro's cross but only as an attitude of respect for the belief of the protagonist. Thus, both the cross and its owner proceed to the sacred place and are consumed sacrificially in the act of posthumously paying the promise.

Recuperating the Axé[26]

In the course of this chapter, a number of ideas have come forth in relation to the qualification of agencies derived from Yoruba cosmologies, such as those that activate the vital energy that the deities emanate as they function to protect or even revenge transgression by their devotees. At the heart of this activation is the term "axé," which is deployed loosely to mean life force or spiritual energy that every being possesses to crown a supplication or bring a wish to fruition. Axé already belongs to the sacred space in Candomblé, where its authority and legitimacy stem from the original foundation of the temple. To recuperate axé is to recover it from oblivion even if the dislocation is temporary. By analyzing the select works of Zora Seljan and Dias Gomes, this study has reached a series of conclusions: (1) whether a playwright is appropriating a temperamental or a cool deity in their dramatic invention, the duality of cosmological power always functions as a tool for creativity and analytics; (2) the variety of orixás explored in the works of Seljan and Gomes share something in common: they focus on Iansan, as well as other female deities like Oxum and Obá; (3) the manifestation of the full power of each deity can be affected by the context of activation, whether sacred or otherwise; (4) the sacred and the profane can temporarily be blurred during hybrid and transitional events, such as the manifestation of the carnivalesque; and (5) axé is recuperated from its temporary dislocation in creative engagements and relocated back to its origins, such as in the dynamic setting of the Candomblé ritual.

The specific analytical framework of the tensions between Iansan, Oxum, and Obá, in relation to their husband Xangô, allows the audience to better appreciate the humanness of the deities and feel more at ease with their actions. The axé that could have been lost over many generations of persecutions, violence, and aggression against Candomblé now finds itself revitalized in such works as *Três Mulheres de Xangô* and *O Pagador de Promessas*. While Seljan succeeds in heightening the conflicts between the female orixás to the degree that they reveal their humanity, Gomes takes a different route by exposing the corruption of the capitalist society, which exploits religion while also empowering the media to distort the reality of a devout rural dweller. By complicating the attitude of the reverend in relation to what constitutes a "sacred pledge" and a "satanic pledge," Gomes is at once declaring a social conscience that indicts the corruption of the state as well as that of the clergy. As axé is recuperated from these creative tensions through the actions and nonactions of the characters, it is relocated to the solemn ambience of significant proportions. As the vitality of axé continues to manifest in religious, social, economic, touristic, and political movements, one can only visualize a time when there will be less concern about distinguishing between the sacred and the profane than ensuring their interdependencies, such as we have in axé music, which is currently one of the most globalized phenomena in Brazilian cultural history.

Chapter 7

Raul Longo and Robson Pinheiro

Afro-Brazilian Deities in Literary Rituals

This chapter analyzes the convergences of two devotees of Umbanda and Candomblé and their experiences of creative spiritual freedom and sacred therapeutic outlet. The texts under consideration in this chapter, *Tambores de Angola* (Drums of Angola) by Robson Pinheiro and *Filhos de Olorum* (God's children) by Raul Longo, celebrate the many African spirit-deities that made Bahia their home after crossing the Atlantic. Pinheiro has written over a dozen works on the subject of spiritism and even has a press and consultancy firm (Casa dos Espíritos [House of spirits]). Meanwhile, in his reminisces on his life in Bahia in the 1970s, Longo is passionate about the survival of the orixás in that cultural-spiritual landscape. One text is a profound encounter with ancient knowledge as the author seeks therapeutic healing from the spiritual forces of Umbanda, as mediated by a spirit medium the protagonist acknowledges as Ângelo Inácio. The other is a collection of "stories and chants" from Candomblé ceremonies. For both narrative voices, curiosities and necessities translate into more profound spiritual discoveries about the mysteries and magic of invisible forces that affect the affairs of the mundane and the terrestrial from a sacred zone of supernatural revelations and manifestations. Through these literary rituals, the narratives document religious secrets that continue to face unwarranted persecution in Brazil due to religious intolerance.

181

Theorizing Sacred Ritualizations

As a scholar of religion and psychology, Owe Wikstrom does not exaggerate when he argues that "liturgy is, from a historical viewpoint of the ritual center, the socially supported and architectonically accompanied symbolic world within which Christian religious experience has emerged and through which people could/can (?) find an answer to their life questions."[1] This idea of a "symbolic" world offers a myriad of perspectives to understand the creative text outside its sacred space but still locked within liturgy by virtue of the binding spirit of enactment and memory. Moreover, Durkheim, who might have been left out of the debate on the sacred and the profane, has something to articulate on the ambiguity of the sacred. For Durkheim, the "sacred is far from being synonymous to the divine."[2] Beyond the Durkheim-Eliade controversy, the sacred also has many variations that cannot be conflated into one. In fact, there are day-to-day forms of sacredness that do not qualify, for example, as sacred liturgy but are routine practices that ritualize the sacred in the popular frame. An interesting dimension of the sacred lies in the liturgical chant or sacred music that distinguishes itself from the mundane song. Father Mark Daniel Kirby defines liturgical chant as that which "insofar as it springs from the 'proletarian, communitarian and quotidian' enactment of the liturgy, is in dissociable from sacred song."[3] This is a powerful reflection in the sense that the criterion for liturgy is that it must come from the grassroots or "from the people" and cannot be imposed from the top down. The divine, after all, is an extension of nature or its embodiment, and nature is the manifestation of the divine in the process of planting and harvesting, for example. It is the rhythm of life. Kirby goes a little deeper as he gestures toward the chant that is imbued with emotion and power:

> It is only natural that the worship of God is to be expressed in song. Inasmuch as the Christian by his baptism is a "transformed" being, so his praise of God in the worship of the Church should reflect this transformation. His praise cannot be reduced to the "language of this world," stripped of all balance, rhythm, and harmony. The word of God and man's response to it certainly is not just the reflection of an "ordinary" conversation. Rather it is a word charged with emotion and filled with the power of the Holy Spirit. As

soon as the word becomes identified with the contents of its
message, it calls for order (rhythm) and *melos* (arrangement
of pitch), i.e., a musical form. In this way, the perfect word,
the fully developed word, most always has the nature of song.[4]

A chant then, like a divine song of praise, has a melody to it; it is the
uplifting of the spirit in honor of a greater spirit deemed to have been
faithful, bountiful, and benevolent.

One wonders how Candomblé and Umbanda could be processed
as agencies of liturgical chants under these contesting and even complementary understandings of the sacred-divine. Yet, these Afro-Brazilian
rites are far from being limited to the sacred, for the nature of hybrid
cultures indicates that anything remotely "authentic" has been negotiated
away by the currents of time, space, and the migration of values. This
is not necessarily true, and some relics of Africanity are retained despite
the overwhelming imposition of race mixture and negotiation of shifting
identities in Brazil. Mattijs van de Port, in *Ecstatic Encounters* (2011),
perceptively notes, "The great majority of anthropological studies on
Candomblé tell you to study the cult as an Afro-Brazilian formation.
Candomblé's cosmology, rituals and aesthetics are to be seen through
the prism of their 'Africanness.' Clearly, there is by no means a unified
understanding as to what this 'Africanness' means, and whether it ought
to be understood as 'root,' 'origin,' 'survival,' 'resistance,' 'invention,' 'continuation,' 'core,' 'display,' or 'memory.' Yet virtually all studies position
Candomblé in this particular framework."[5] While Port is concerned that
what constitutes the definition of Africanness is relatively subjective,
the fact that the Afro-Brazilian community insists on its relevance as a
counter-measure against the vestiges of slavery and cultural dispossession
is ample proof that the struggle to assert identity remains a rift that
most of the formerly enslaved have yet to overcome. Social movements,
such as blocos afros and afoxés, transform the many layers of identity
formation into an expression of resistance against racial discrimination.

One of the measures deployed today by Black social movements
to counter the whitening ideal Brazil adopted in the colonial era is to
draw specific inspirations from Afro-Brazilian history. Examples include
Afro-Carnival groups and famous musicians who promote Afro-Brazilian
dance and percussion and mimic the African American civil rights
movement as a source of inspiration. In addition to Gilberto Gil singing in Portuguese about Jamaica and various Bob Marley songs, such as

"No Woman, No Cry," and Caetano Veloso singing "Soy Louco Por ti América" (Crazy about you America), Afro-Brazilians play the music of Fela Kuti. Other efforts include rallying around Angela Davis, a radical feminist voice in America, to protest police violence against women and children in Brazil. The claim of a "racial democracy" does not mean racism is extinct. On the contrary, racism is prevalent though masked by subtle layers of pigmentation due to many centuries of race mixture. Despite the abolition of slavery in 1888, Brazil has continued subtle forms of discrimination, even though it never legislated segregation. The active promotion of interracial marriages created a mixed-race population that many hoped would make the whole nation coexist without race. With this conflation of races, it was difficult for different oppressed racial groups to form coalitions and fight racial discrimination, such as what happened in the United States. These efforts of race mixture were ultimately superficial because they did not cogently counter the racial divide. It turns out that spirituality was the more empowering zone of resistance, as Rachel Harding appropriately argues in *A Refuge in Thunder: Alternative Spaces of Blackness* (2000). "Ilê Axês," as most devotees refer to Candomblé houses, have shifted from being the space of the original Kandombele (place of prayer, festivity, and music in the Kimbundu language) to the space of ritual practices that have been retained by former West African and Central African slaves, which then shifted to an assemblage of epistemologies, rituals, worldviews, and visual art forms. Ilê Axês are places where deities are enshrined for veneration and recuperation of cultural and historical memories. While the sacred ritualizations that are interpreted by Robson Pinheiro and Raul Longo will vary due to their allegiance to different religious denominations, Umbanda and Candomblé respectively, the commonality of veneration of the deities remains a constant in their work.

Robson Pinheiro:
Tambores de Angola (Drums of Angola)

Tambores de Angola (1998) creatively contextualizes and theorizes the Brazilian theology of Umbanda. It was authored by Spirit Angelo Inácio but revealed psycho-graphically to the Spirit Medium Robson Pinheiro, who offers a beautiful vision of the Umbanda faith. In showing the difference between Umbanda and spiritism, *Tambores de Angola* articulates the function of some of the faith's entities through the experience of the young man, Erasmino, who was obssessed with a spirit from Umbralinas (the coastal zones). This is a rich book in structure and beauty when considered as a primer for initial contact with Umbanda. Before giving any details, the book reveals to the reader the narration of a medium, who tells about a personal paranormal experience when he was in a coma following an operation. A few days after his traumatic ordeal at the hospital, he is sought out to author the book *Tambores de Angola*. Erasmino, the protagonist, suffers from serious obsession with demonic entities. His mother comes to the rescue, and in her desperation to find a solution to the issues her son is dealing with, she takes him to an Umbanda Center that she herself barely knows. It is in this section that the origin and fundamental rituals are explained, with special emphasis placed on the spirits of old Black slaves who died in slavery (pretos velhos).[6] Through a focused treatment, the spiritual group discovers the source of the spiritual attack on the young man Erasmino. It turns out that it has to do with a "building" that was possessed and occupied by some spirits who are resolute with vengeance and are thus possessing people. A plan is thus hatched by the spiritual team to destroy the "building." With the assistance of Exu, Pretos Velhos, and many other spiritual entities, all of whom are controlled by Grandma Catarina, the team succeeds in destroying the evil spirits and sending many of them to the goodness path.

As Erasmino gains consciousness and begins to feel better, he reluctantly continues with the treatment while retaining some biases against Umbanda due to his lack of familiarity with the faith. At this juncture, a spirit friend explains the work of Allan Kardec, a doctrinarian spirit, as well as other precepts of Umbanda. Erasmino then joins the Kardecist Center, where, over time he familiarizes himself with the works of Allan Kardec. It is during these treatment sessions, geared toward the suffering entities, that a spirit narrates its persecution, hate, and wish for vengeance against a man who had committed so many atrocities during slavery, abandoning him in total misery, stealing his wife from him, and sexually abusing his daughters. These atrocities are all an aside to the larger atrocity of the slave trade. The treatment group of spirits working with Erasmino pleads and tries to persuade the suffering spirit, who is adamantly on the path of vengeance but to no avail. It was only after many treatment sessions that the spirit is successfully liberated without incident. Erasmino is subsequently interrogated about his own past, and

he seems no longer interested in vengeance after finding out rather sur-
prisingly that the man who had done him so much evil was none other
than himself in a past reincarnation! The book ends with teachings on
the fundamental moral principles of Umbanda. While Pinheiro has produced a remarkable piece of creative work that is intertwined with the
principles of Umbanda, one cannot but raise the question on the limits of
artistic production and ideological investment. In the natural or symbolic
order of things, Erasmino the protagonist, the other fictional characters,
the members of the treatment team, the spirit, the spirit medium, and
a host of other loyalists implicated in the Umbanda faith, may well
have collectively produced a doctrine through the pretext of narrating a
mimetic story. The spirit double of Robson Pinheiro and Ângelo Inácio
is fascinating and yet questionable. Dogmatically, one may be tempted to
respect the precepts of Umbanda, but a reader must also subject authorial
intentions to critique. What or who endows the two spirits in question
with the power to divine, perform therapies, and see the paranormal? Is
this process teachable? How long does it take, and what are the cogent
manifestations thereafter? How much of the methodology is measurable
and how much is speculative? By narrating an emotional and obsessive
story, Ângelo Inácio projects onto the reader the existence of a marvelous exchange between the spiritism centers, the Candomblé houses, and
the Umbandist centers. For a detached critic, the entire narration is at
best an imaginative fantasy, as demonstrated by the consolation provided
Madam Niquita who brings her son Erasmino for treatment:

> God be praised, me daughter! God be praised! You been
> come to old black woman him shrine for help, but old black
> woman see more for ya heart. Me see mother him heart as me
> be long time ago! You dey suffer for ya beloved son. But me
> daughter, no worry. Trust ya God, we Great Papa, and with
> time, all thing go better. We go work with Erasmino; and we
> get ya friends them, and old black woman, to help as well.[7]

Beyond just promissory words from the old Black woman, there is no
quantifiable scientific evidence that Erasmino will be healed by mere
speculative consolation given by his mother. There may be some spiritual act of faith, but other than that, Erasmino's fate is as dicey as the
desperation of his mother. All they can hope for is healing without any
concrete evidential manifestation.

As provocative, foundational, and controversial as the works of Pinheiro are, their inner depths reveal a certain radicalism that challenges the mainstream ideologies propagated by the Brazilian Federation of Spiritists (FEB), which are primarily based on the works of Jean-Baptiste Roustaing, Bezerra de Menezes, and Chico Xavier. One then wonders what the main difference is between Pinheiro and these others if they still share the common principles articulated by Kardec? Pinheiro can be seen indeed as an integrationist and inclusionist, such that the people who deal with many psychological and emotional ailments can begin to get treatment without any concern about expensive hospital bills. To better appreciate the contributions of Pinheiro and better appreciate his legacy, it behooves this critic to perform a comprehensive bibliographic mapping of the Umbanda epistemology. At this juncture, a few questions are appropriate to understand the commonality in Umbanda: (1) Can there be any reconciliation between Kardecist spiritism and Umbanda à la Pinheiro? (2) How has Pinheiro appropriated, in the Foucauldian sense of "discourse production," to legitimize his own "new discourse"? (3) What impact do Allan Kardec and Chico Xavier have on Pinheiro's epistemology? (4) What has the methodology of psychography contributed to Umbanda? (5) How has the creation of his own press (casa dos espíritos) influenced his sense of creative freedom and productivity? In answering these questions, we can begin to formulate a theory for the totality of the worldview and legacy of Robson Pinheiro.

Spiritism as a doctrine started in France in 1857 with the launching of O Livro de Espíritos by Kardec, who was deemed a "great intellectual integrity" that was minimally "affected by fantasies and little inclined to the fights of imagination." He is responsible for the elaboration of a doctrine that can be understood as an "observatory in time in which people realized, through approaching pertinent questions of life such as death, sickness, religion, love, family, and finally, the sciences, the latter under the impact of great changes."[8] Kardec may have attributed the authorship of his works to "higher spirits," while he himself served as an intermediary; however, it is not enough to lend credibility to Kardec's articulations of spiritual forces because we are dealing with facts and not shifting speculations. Kardec deployed the methodology of Universal Control of Spiritist Teachings (CUEE), which was based on the use of consensual multiple mediums on the same subject matter. For Iracilda Gonçalves, only through psychographic communication can spiritism produce and disseminate its own doctrinal principles—seen as a collective "game of truths," with the goal to "demarcate the place of religiosity in the midst of other truths which have unity of mediums as its basic principle."[9] In this sense, Pinheiro appropriates the doctrines of Umbanda while adhering simultaneously to the Kardacist concepts.

Beyond influences and initiation to spiritism, Pinheiro hails from Minas Gerais, and he recollects how he grew up a poor child, playing with the children of the cosmopolitan favela of life. Despite early contact with spiritism, he became evangelical; ironically, on the day he was supposed to be ordained, he was visited by two spirits that he called "demons." Pinheiro notes that the spirits communicated through him and left a note on the church's floor that read: "Your training in this religion ends today."[10] Pinheiro later converts to spiritism. He shares something with Chico Xavier, who also converted from Catholicism to spiritism. He seems to have elaborated his functioning model as an amalgam of Umbandist principles and that of Karden, although Umbandists disagree with this hybrid formulation. This subtle disagreement is well articulated in *Tambores de Angola* when, in a psychography credited to Ângelo Inácio, Euzália (ou Vovó Catarina), the spirit in charge of curing Eurasmino, warns that the spirit must be quite suspicious of "familiar spirits," especially regarding those of our "workers who manifest as *caboclos* (Brazilian of mixed white and Indian or Indian and black ancestry) ou *preto velhos* (spirits of Black slaves who died as slaves)."[11] The warning of Vovó Catarina is attributed to the thinking that both religions can "work together with the same goal in mind, which, ultimately, is the moral upliftment of our souls."[12] Pinheiro is critical of those who arrogate the term "spirit" to themselves as if they have the exclusive dominion over spiritism. And this is the crux of Pinheiro's controversy: the imperative of inclusion of others in what is supposed to be an exclusive and privileged terrain of power. Pinheiro argues, for example, that the use of bombonjiro in Umbanda is only a variant of pombagira (female consort of Exu, agent of the crossroads) in Candomblé. Pinheiro's critique goes to the foundational heart of the creation of Umbanda, in which there is a rift in belief systems caused by the spirit known as "Caboclo das Sete Encruzilhadas" (Mixed-race Brazilian of Seven Crossroads).[13] The Caboclo das Sete Encruzilhadas goes against Kardec's doctrines. As far as Pinheiro is concerned, what matters is not so much who has the power to speak in the name of spiritism but rather who has the power to seek to embrace loyalty to Kardec and Chico Xavier and their positive contributions to Umbanda.

If Pinheiro has produced a corpus of a "new spiritism," one must examine closely what the import of *Tambores de Angola* is to this new wave. Since its publication in 1998, and based on its sales records of about two hundred million copies (it is now in its thirty-third edition), there is no question that *Tambores de Angola* is a turning point in the construction of a unique spiritist cosmology that stabilizes and unifies the precepts of Umbanda with the spiritist theories of Kardec. The fact that the entire book was written in a trancelike state that lasted six hours when the psychographer was hospitalized while recovering from a coma is indeed noteworthy. The trance was an energizing phenomenon that explains how the medium was able to release his entire consciousness and body to a spiritual being, thus acquiring extra-normal capacities that are not possible in ordinary life. Here are excerpts of Pinheiro's memories of his encounter with the guardian spirit during the moment of writing:

> I approached the computer as told. However, in order not to see what will be written, I was to maintain the zoom reduced. . . . The presence of the spirits was extremely pleasant. Once the writing process was completed, I amplified the zoom and I found a name I had never seen before. Ângelo Inácio. Who was this fellow?—I inquired mentally. Could he [have] been an obsessionist? Perhaps that should be my next question, following the logic of fantasies that concern modern spiritists: obsession and animism. I return to the beginning of the text and a very strong title: Drums of Angola.[14]

The coinage of psychography as the writing process in which a spirit and a medium are working together to create a discursive enlightenment lends credence to the ability of the mind to cede to a higher force and activate dormant spiritual energies to bring a new spirit-story alive.

The narrative takes the reader on a journey with the main character Erasmino, whose health goes from bad to worse due to the daily frustrations that get the best of him, including his job as a city worker, his alcohol abuse, and his obsession with women. Pinheiro qualifies this state of the degenerative protagonist as that of "fascination" or spiritual perplexity, and it is during this state that he starts hearing voices and having persistent migraines. He is eventually treated at an Umbanda Center by a medium spiritist named Mother Odete. The narrative goes on to reveal the mythic origin of Umbanda and the interconnections and differences among Umbanda centers. Even though the novel addresses the issue of Umbandist rituals and their spirit guides (caboclos and pretos-velhos), Umbandist circles are very critical of the work. Pinheiro responds to the criticism: "The affront came through the media. The institutions where we performed our work were disqualified by a certain newspaper in Minas Gerais, which was linked with the Umbandist movement."[15] Most of the criticism levied against the book was based on the critics' suspicions that the book is an attempt to codify or conceptualize the entire Afro-Brazilian religion. This attack made Pinheiro distance himself from the more orthodox spiritist movement. This predicament, however, had its dividends: it opened the floodgates for others to come to know the works of Pinheiro. Indeed, *Tambores de Angola* became a turning point in the emergence of a new spiritism beyond the three types of obsession highlighted by the teachings of Kardec (simple obsession, fascination, and subjugation). Pinheiro suggests that the only cure for this type of "complex obsession" would require specific treatments, such as apometria and antigoecia.

The criticisms levied against Pinheiro notwithstanding, his legacy remains in the continued success of his written work, as well as the missions and visions highlighted by his institute. After reading some of his works, especially *Tambores de Angola*, one is awakened by getting to know more about his philosophy because it allies with day-to-day values and the grassroots. The institute states that in terms of a mission they "provide cutting-edge knowledge, research that addresses science and spirituality and work for the implantation of a new conscience, in the formation of free thinkers, independent of ideas, attitudes and free from pseudo-doctrinal mental boxing."[16] And in terms of "goals," the institute intends to "provide free online training courses and promote the specialization of people around the world in matters involving science and spirituality, in an approach devoid of prejudice and the inculcation of conscience."[17] In tandem with the vicissitudes of the innovative exponent of a new spiritism, *Tambores de Angola* serves as a perfect primer for appreciating the postmodernist posture of dealing and coping with religion and with a quest for understanding the dimensions of the paranormal. The ability to extend communication beyond the mundane to the realm of the spirit world need not be a capacity found in the living dead but also in normal beings who have cultivated the ability to transcend physical limitations by subscribing to outer-body experiences that are teachable and learnable. While Pinheiro took in revelations from spirits, Raul Longo would deploy cultural memories to revisit Bahia and activate the orixás and their characteristics in a rather fascinating literary interpretation.

Filhos de Olorum:
From Religion to Ambivalent Ritualizations

Mestre Didi, Pierre Verger, Jorge Amado, Zora Seljan, and Juana Elbein Santos have all written about the Afro-Brazilian experience and Candomblé. Some like Jorge Amado have even fictionalized it extensively. To this illustrious group of preservationists of African religious tradition in Brazil comes Raul Longo, who has created a totally new genre that mixes what the subtitle calls the "stories and chants" of Candomblé to recuperate memories for the devotion of someone who has left and returned with nostalgia. Thus, the author alerts the reader in his introduction: "In the name of its deities, which embraced me with love and affection of its people, I try here once again, to ask the reader some understanding in waiting till the end of each story, and hope that the next one is even better and successful as presented to me by my nostalgic day-to-day Bahia."[18] The twenty-one stories that make up this collection vary in their concern with the orixás and their logic. The title itself is provocative: if the orixás are the "children of God," what then are the devotees and initiates? In Yoruba mythology, the king is regarded as second in command to the gods. In other words, the authority of the king is next in rank to that of the deities. Raul Longo also notes in the editorial, "I wrote this book when I lived in the Bahian capital. It was a period I lived with the great masters of Afro-Brazilian culture. From the globally renowned to the common people on the streets and peripheries, forests and shanty towns, beaches and in the field. I recorded these intimacies about the deities and through the Orixás, I created photographic characters of my literary perception. I speak of men, women, old ones, and children, through their archetypes and meanings."[19]

The work of Raul Longo opens a new vista in the codification of sacred rituals through ambivalent profane reconstruction and creative acumen.[20] Unlike the descriptive, documentary, and sensual works by Jorge Amado, Longo's Filhos de Olorum (Children of God) is indeed a celebration of recognition for Candomblé, which ceases to be a censored religion and becomes a cultural reality that is seeking acceptance and approval through a creative process in which the craft of ingenuity announces the depth of ancestrality without having to justify its own significance in a racialized social hegemony. This unorthodox approach to divulgating a restricted or controversial subject serves a multivalent purpose. It shifts the discourse from purely religious reference to a complex terrain of struggle for the appropriation of Afro-Brazilian cultural heritage with rich and endless possibilities for the creative imagination. The reinvention of Africa in Brazil has always come at a price: millions of Afro-Brazilians share the legacy of slavery and the immeasurable sacrifices made to maintain African religions and cultures in the Black Atlantic as an instrument of resistance. In the specific case of Brazil, the survival of African cultures took a more aggressive and assimilationist approach, in which the European hegemonic culture imposed on the Afro-Brazilian people created a need to remain in the shadows by negotiating their patrimony. The compromise was not intended to be an equal partnership but more akin to subordination to the precepts of Catholicism, purity, and power. By contrast, Candomblé was simultaneously persecuted by the police in the colonial era and vilified as satanic and diabolic. However, what was once isolated, hidden, and persecuted is now venerated and popular as the sacred grooves into the spectacular domain of the profane. As was the case for Zé-do-Burro in *Payment as Pledged*, a capoeira group helps the deceased Zé by mounting him on a cross and carrying him into the church by force to fulfill his promise.

Candomblé used to be a terrain of struggle, which Rachel Harding in *A Refuge in Thunder* appropriately deems an "alternative space of blackness."[21] Not only are Afro-Brazilian religions influencing Afro-Brazilian musicians, artists, and performers, but devotees of Candomblé and Umbanda are also feeling emboldened to demand concessions and negotiations with the same state authorities that persecuted their parents and ancestors. Afro-Brazilian Candomblé practitioners now feel they should be able to say they are Catholics or members of the Candomblé faith without any fear of persecution or reprisal. Three decades ago, after the end of the military dictatorship, Afro-Brazilian activist groups went as far as to demand that Afro-Brazilian culture be relocated to the center of Brazilian popular and festive manifestation as opposed to the traditional religious sphere. Instead of having religious festivals in remote locations in the interior or in basements, Afro-Brazilian festivities are now conducted in the open as part of normal popular rites, performances, and celebrations. Despite this exciting moment, the surge in evangelical Christianity in Brazil also raises another challenge for Candomblé or Umbanda, as a quarter of Brazilians self-identify as evangelical while only a fraction identifies as Afro-Brazilian religious worshippers. The intolerance and prejudice continue, as evangelical groups attack Afro-Brazilian shrines for no rational reason while some evangelical churches label Candomblé shrines as zones of devil worship. As the next step in the demand for religious freedom, legally binding marriages are now being officiated by Candomblé priests. Such strides in turning against the challenges of religious persecution and fanaticism are meant to ensure that Afro-Brazilian religions keep their place among other mainstream religions in Brazil.

It is against this complex historical background that *Filhos de Olorum* must be critically appreciated and assessed. Comprising twenty-one "stories and chants," an introduction, and a glossary, this fictional compendium of the most representative orixás documents the life of Afro-Brazilians as they work with Black social movements in the 1970s. The cohesive collection is a nostalgic reminder of a positive time in Afro-Brazilian history when agitations for racial equality and consciousness raising reached a peak. Regardless of the continued challenges facing Afro-Brazilians, Raul Longo hopes for a time when "at the end of each story, that the next one be better just like nostalgic day-to-day Bahia."[22] The author appreciates the energy of participating in developing the African presence in Bahia while at the same time protesting poverty through the celebration of African values in the midst of samba and mulatas and through the critical lens of religious intolerance and white hypocrisy. Deploying orikis (invocative poems) as a point of entry to the knowledge of African deities, Longo performs a literary ritual by reinterpreting the characteristics of the orixás without becoming redundant. He humanizes them to the degree that their worshippers can see their own intersectionality and commonality with the orixás. Catherine Bell in *Ritual Theory, Ritual Practice* (2009) articulates that ritual is "a 'window' on the cultural dynamics by which people make and remake their worlds."[23] In other words, Raul Longo appropriates what Bell considers "the Ritual Body," as a measure to penetrate the many possessed bodies through which ritual is reenacted.[24] Each orixá performs the agonies of the body by "undermining the framework 'disembodied' objectivism that has constituted the dominant model used in the humanities and social sciences."[25] Layered on the historic fixtures and textures of the act of signification and resignification, the different identitarian episodes seek to share the capacity of the writer to deviate from the norm once in a while, recalibrate essential invocations, and still retain memorable meanings despite these creative manipulations of the sacred. These "children" of God are not just referential paradigms for the stories, but they also embody the fruits of divinity to the degree that these children are orixás in their own rights who seek immense redemptive capacities from their daily routines and escapades.

There is no other compelling moment to engage ritual if not that moment of critical analysis of how it impacts the "body structure" of literary texts and the "body politics," beyond its immediate application as a symbolic social act. The correspondence between the acts propagated by a fictional text and the theoretical implications within the social milieu that nourished its emergence is an important one. A literary construction is not effectuated in a vacuum. In the cosmic order of things, that which is symbolic is metonymic of the rest of the social reality. As a result, a story about Xangô automatically carries all his attributes as king, warrior, and religious leader. Such attributes relocate the deity into a realm of ritual and the sacred. Ritual, however, is more complex than it is perceived to be in different societies. As the ritualizations of religion morph from the sacred into the profane, the zones of ambiguities and ambivalences remain unresolved and complex. If ritual signals a symbolic zone of activation of meaning, then ritual can always be separated from religion, because ritual deals with structural rhythms while religion is the actual base of faith and cosmology. As far as its relevance to the present discussion, the current debate between scholars of religious traditions and ritual theory is neither here nor there.

On the one hand, scholars of religion disregard the contributions of ritual theory because they believe religious traditions need to be theorized on their own terms and not by theories imposed on them by social scientists. Yet can meaning and representation determine defining questions for religious traditions and not actual ritual performances? In responding to this interrogation, Clifford Geertz, in his provocative book *Myth, Symbol, and Culture* (1974) offers the anthropological approach as the primary point of departure for the paradigm shift in the analysis of ritual in religious traditions. For Geertz, the essence of religion stems from ritual because "the world as lived and the world as imagined, [are] fused under the agency of a single set of symbolic forms." In this Geertzian proposal, culture is considered a text. On the other hand, recent approaches to ritual theory question the validity of studying rituals as strictly religious phenomena that are imbued with meaning. Frits Staal (1993) suggests that there are no symbolic meanings going through the minds of religious performers, and ritual performers are only concerned with the proper execution of rules that are engaged in performing ritual. Understanding every ritual action as completely self-absorbed and self-contained, Staal defines ritual as a pure activity, in which the faultless execution of rules is all that matters. What the performer *does* matters, not what he or she thinks, believes, or says. Even if one does not entirely agree with Staal's thesis, the main point of subsuming the analysis of ritual action under the study of religion is problematic and inappropriate, especially without first having analyzed the ritual actions themselves. Until cultural and religious scholars cease deploying linguistic concepts for the analysis of ritual actions, it will be challenging to move beyond the duality of form and meaning, thought and action. Instead of scholars being preoccupied by form and meaning, they should engage the internal complexities of ritual actions to access their import as a series of constructions of social relations. Raul Longo deliberately challenges these polarities by working on the fringes of alternatives and intersectionalities.

Filhos de Olorum offers an excellent case study in the analysis of Afro-Brazilian religiosity by a writer exposed to the rituals through cultural immersion but who is now more of an interpreter than a ritual participant. By keeping a critical distance between the devotion and its cultural symbolization, Raul Longo escapes what could have challenged the literariness and aesthetic finesse of the text if it had been written as propagandist literature. Thus, the first story, "Xirieê Ri" (We were once children), or the praise name of Obá, must be seen as a conscious manifestation of the subconscious, even as the story pays homage to Obá, one of Xangô's three wives, by telling of her unreciprocated love for Xangô, the deity of thunder. The story is not limited to the "Obá body" but is an extension of it that constitutes the reinvention of rich Afro-Brazilian reality. The story has a structure that encompasses the following: (1) the origins of Afro-Brazilian people; (2) the advent of slavery and its stark realities as captured Africans traverse the Atlantic; and (3) the struggle for and attainment of independence through resistance and flight. The title of the story not only gives a few clues, but it also reinforces the fact that all God's children have riveting stories to tell. The reference to the fact that "we" were once children (Xirieê Ri), means that while the present struggle calls for a new vision and strategy, the struggles of the past must not be minimized even if they seem less than proactive or even reactive for any reason. As "Children of God," the collective celebrates the totality of courage necessitated by the many centuries of oppression to stay alive to tell the story. Obá's story is actually subtext for the entire narrative, which is about the Afro-Brazilian struggle and experience. What then is the significance of Obá? In Yoruba mythology, Xangô is more iconic and relevant to the celebration of the Pantheon than the three wives because their own stories are told in relation to Xangô and not as independently celebrated deities. That the writer singles out Obá and not others, such as Oxum and Nana, also implies that Obá may have been the "favorite," even if Xangô did not express this clearly. In mythology, Oxum was often considered the favorite and had a stake in the undoing of Obá by giving her bad advice on how to win the heart of Xangô.

The first phrase of the story indicates recognition of a location or a place of origin: "We come from other backlands."[27] This symbolic reference to Africa or to the Northeastern region of Bahia is an invocation of nostalgia, which is not necessarily a romantic "return" but a formulation of constructive jubilation in the midst of oppression. The reference to Africa is indeed a form of nostalgic return as a coping mechanism because Africa still provided solace and consolation for the untold injustices suffered in the hands of the colonial oppressors. The use of "other" backlands means Africa shares some of the characteristics of Bahian tropical climes and is seen as an extension of Bahia and vice versa. The first movement captures many stunning images: (1) an acknowledgment of coming from an arid and poor community in the aftermath of slavery; (2) Oba as a powerful deity who teaches forgiveness and fortitude; (3) an overview of the hardships of slavery and how, due to disobedience to the counsel of Obá, the Afro-descendants were sold into slavery, while their brothers and sisters were sold to other lands as well; (4) a utopian desire to conquer Brazil as Afro-Brazilians revel in their historic pain and oppression, with a wishful quest for revenge. By focusing strictly on one central character and making other concerns secondary, Longo complicates what could have been a linear plot structure. By replacing it with a story-within-a-story approach, Longo uses this structure to celebrate the grander vision of the dignity of all Afro-Brazilians. The writer, however, signals in the prefatory note the feeling of assuming a multipartite responsibility in writing the stories: patriotism, cultural agency, and the necessity to challenge hypocritical moral judgments. These motifs for writing clearly seal the intentionality for the writer's mission to transcend a personal mythology and incorporates the collective will and political empowerment to honor his people.

The second movement in the construction of the story is equally compelling. It defines the apogee era of Afro-Brazilian struggle and the postabolition politics of liberation (especially from 1888 to 1988). The story does not start with the struggle but with the original colonial contact with Europe: men who resembled the "color of the Moon" or "color of the skies" brutalized Afro-Brazilians despite their hospitality and generosity toward the European colonizer.[28] While the atrocities against Afro-Brazilians were numerous, the writer celebrates resilience and invokes the spirit of heroism for the ancestors who lost their lives in the process of enslavement and resistance:

> We survived and here we are. We were separated and divided by the big country of whites. We saw our brothers being sent to the plantations in South and North America. Others were sent to the mines or to the backland farms. But we were never alone . . . There was always a current holding us and whips sounding on our backs.[29]

In this succinct elaboration of pain lies the imperative of hope. Even if Obá was a pretext, she does not feature as a central character. Rather, Africa, Bahia, and Afro-Brazilians are the central characters. By shifting the perspective from the individual to the collective, Longo asserts the power of numbers: for the individual can play a heroic role through sacrifices while the collective may also play a similar role and yet survive. What begins as homage to the warrior spirit of Obá ends up being a critique of social oppression. The story favors not the individual achievement but the social vision of the collective consciousness.

The third and last movement closes the protest to the "body Obá" as it goes through a rite of passage and as information is withheld. The reader awaits a moment when Obá might intervene in her own feeling of injustice but to no avail. Instead, all the challenges invoked seem to emanate from the plight of Afro-Brazilians. This is a moment of flight in search of freedom. It is the "quilombo" moment of maroon settlement and the readiness to fight for freedom. Obá in no way participates or is given any voice in this process. Given that the theme is unreciprocated love of Obá toward Xangó, a curious mind wonders if the analogy is established here between the collective will of the people to be free and the intransigent position of the oppressor. It also stands within reason for a neglected Obá to be likened to Afro-Brazilians who have been abandoned by the colonizers and enslavers. Regardless of who the central character is, what matters here is the unflinching resolve for freedom and the collective will to resist oppression. To have moved the narrative from the sacred plane to a literary ritual or festival indicates that through creative imagination, the sacred can also play in the frontiers of myth, history, ritual, and politics. As the story ends, the narrator invokes the spirit of Obá, warrior mother and wife of Xangô, to come to the rescue of her children who have chosen to honor her. "Ossa-osi," the deity sitting on the left hand of Xangô and who continues to protect her children as long as they dutifully venerate and call upon her:

> This is all we have left, in these margins of our Obá river, which they call Saint Francis; to teach our children to sing, calling upon our Mother. One day, she will hear our call and come out of the sea. She will pardon us for not heeding her advice and will fight on our side. Then we would conquer Bahia and it will become our new Guiné. We shall conquer Brazil and it will become our Africa.[30]

The association of Guiné with Bahia, and Brazil with Africa, is intended to be a Pan-African call to consciousness, such that African values are created and preserved right in the heart of Brazil, even though Europeans had no plans for African culture to survive. A curious reader cannot help but ask: why does Obá appear as a passive character who takes no bold action? The central plot of her unreciprocated love for Xangô is only recounted by the narrator and not articulated by her own voice. This inequality in gender relations may be subtle but must be addressed as problematic. Because Obá is the intended protagonist of the story, one wonders how the collective Afro-Brazilian experience ends up taking over this privileged role. Obá may well be a metonymic representation of the ideals of the Afro-Brazilian diaspora as it cultivates a global space for the negotiation of identities and transgression of local oppression. Yet, Obá is equally positioned as the antinomy of Xangô. Where Xangô is the patriarchal oppressor, Obá is deemed the counter-agency of Xangô's hegemony. She expands her "territory" by protecting her devotees as opposed to focusing on the disparaged experience activated by Xangô, who does not reciprocate her love.

Filhos de Olorum, through the sheer creative intelligence of the author, hides the craft of Candomblé's religious belief system. It shares morals about daily living and not necessarily about the ritual action itself. Instead of sharing the knowledge of Candomblé by taking the reader to the zone of worship, Raul Longo chooses to save the reader such emotively overpowering details by problematizing the plight of Obá and turning her character from that of a victim (as disparaged by Xangô) to that of an independent heroine who is now honored and will continue to be honored by her children. For the sake of recognizing the juxtaposition between creative freedom and religion-infused narrative, let us revisit the legend of Obá and Xangô in the Yoruba pantheon. Obá, the name of an African river, is also associated with fresh water, but she can also revolt and become wild and dangerous. She is the companion of Bará, an orixá of the front (guardian of the crossroads pathway) and a warrior who comes alive with the invocation of the razor and machete. In one of the most popular legends of African religions, it is said that Obá and Oxum are Xangô's wives, and each has an assigned week to care for their husband. Whatever Oxum does, Obá copies. Oxum cannot imitate the cooking recipes of Obá, a blessing because she could use this power to overcome Xangô. One day Oxum decides to end the imitation and invites Obá to her house, where she receives her with cloth tied around her head, up to the level of her ears. Oxum prepares a broth for Xangô and tells Obá that she has put Xangô's ears in the food, which is a lie (she has added mushrooms). When Xangô arrives, he eats all the food. When Obá sees this situation, she runs home and begins to prepare the broth, following Oxum's directions, except that Obá really cuts off Xangô's ears. When Xangô eats the food, he grows sick and spits out everything. The war continues between Oxum and Obá, but now it is much more serious. Xangô cannot handle the conflicts and debates and decides to kill both Oxum and Obá, who run to the bush and turn into rivers. Today, this location is known as the meeting point of the Oxum and Obá rivers. The legend also notes that, when Obá is dancing, she always covers her ears as a measure to protect them from Xangô's wrath. In comparing the story and the legend, the literary genius of Raul Longo comes alive, as he creatively dismantles the myth and replaces it with political power. Obá is no longer the passive archetype in Yoruba mythology but a powerful heroine in her own right.

As the daughter of Yemanja (Mother Goddess), Obá, is a revered sacred-popular-political personality who is one of Xangô's three wives,

alongside Oya and Oxum. There is an air of rivalry among the three
wives to provide an heir for Xangô because he is responsible for the
continuity of the kingdom of Oyo. Obá occupies this favored position
as the first wife and her children are in line to be heirs to Xangô's
kingdom. Ironically, Xangô loves Oxum the most because she is the
one who knows the secret to his palatal satisfaction. When asked why
Xangô loves Oxum so much, she reluctantly tells a bogus story that she
always adds her own ear to the food she cooks as part of the ingredients.
Obá is so full of joy that she cuts her entire ear off to seek the love of
Xangô. While eating, Xangô sees the big ear and is filled with rage. He
immediately accuses Obá of trying to poison him and bans her from the
kingdom. Obá cries so much that her sobs turn into a river, her namesake.
The River Obá also intersects with the Osun River, and the point of
encounter always generates turbulence, an ample indication of the persistent rivalry between the two wives. Though a slightly varied version
of the previously mentioned Obá myth and legend, it is an instructive
reminder that these oral stories authenticate the main versions because
the plot structure remains essentially the same. One returns to the same
question: why were the legends, myths, and folklore less interesting to
Raul Longo? For some genial reason, the writer took critical distance very
seriously and ended up with a masterpiece when it comes to a collection
of Candomblé stories in *Filhos de Olorum*.

A more traditionally acceptable form of Afro-Brazilian religion
when compared to Umbanda and Caboclos, Candomblé may be generally characterized as the zone of axé in Afro-Brazilian cultural studies.
Based on the worship of African deities, the orixás, Candomblé syncretizes these enabling and empowering spirits with the saints of popular
Catholicism, Native American spirits (Caboclos), and other possessing
spirits, such as sailors and prostitutes, trickster figures, gypsies, and old
slaves. The typical Candomblé group is more formally organized and has
a hierarchical structure with a focal point of a shrine or temple that
serves as the mediating source of vital energy. Each temple is headed
by a spirit-medium, known as a Pai-de-Santo (Father in sainthood) or
Mãe-de-Santo (Mother in sainthood), and these spirit-mediums in Candomblé are mostly women. Each Candomblé group tends to represent a
particular African ethnic group or nação (nation). Given how established
Candomblé is, it is quite curious why Raul Longo would depart from
the religious precepts of Candomblé to create a narrative world where
characters are normalized and not deified as such. The remaining twenty

stories, whose titles are part of the praise names (oriki) of the religious personalities (deities), share some of the dynamics of the first and are exemplary points of entry into the world of Afro-Brazilian cultural and political experience. Some of the stories include: "Salubá!," which honors Nana; "Eparrei!," which is the salutation in honor of Iansan; "Ogunhiê" an homage to Ogum; "Ode" a salutation to Iemanjá; "Laroiê" a reference to Exu; "Kawo Kabiesile" the veneration of Xangô; "Atoto" the veneration of Obaluaye; "Ora ye ye o!" a praise to Oxum; and "Aroboboi" the name of praise for Oxumare.[31] Despite this fascinating assemblage of orixás in a single pioneering literary volume, Longo skillfully does not subscribe to any ideological impositions emanating from Candomblé. Rather, *Filhos de Olorum* is a compelling work of art in its own meritorious right and will set an inspirational standard for aspiring writers to come.

Even when Longo's efforts are "ambivalent" or syncretic, there is a sense in which such a qualification renders the freedom to create within a stifling process. The artistic must always be in service of ideology and not vice versa; art for art's sake has its place, but it is not always warranted in the context of revolutionary consciousness that the resistance against Brazilian hegemonic oppression demands. Moreover, while the concept of syncretism has been rejected by some scholars, the affirmation that Candomblé represents a "pure" form of African spirituality derived from the Yoruba is now debatable, even though it is yet to be disproven as the vital source of many trans-diaspora religions. Candomblé thus reflects a continuation of Yoruba religious beliefs and practices in their "crystal purity," and it continues to be perceived as "purely African." Of course, this view remains challenged by recent scholars. The importance of the concept of syncretism is emphasized as a zone of convergence and of juxtaposition with other religious cultures. In this argument, while syncretism is difficult to justify as a paradigmatic concept, it is still a useful tool to explicate what happens when two cultures collide.[32] Yet, various scholars have indicated in their ethnographic studies that the beliefs and rituals of Afro-Brazilian cults in such cities as Recife (Candomblé–Xangô) and São Luis (Tambor de Mina) are indeed syncretic. While all of Longo's stories can be categorized as "syncretic," the eighth story in the collection, dedicated to Iemanjá, is even more syncretic than the others.

Entitled "Odê!," an invocation for Yemoja (Iemanjá), Mother of Fish (or Mother Queen), this Atlantic goddess, the "mother of all," is the source of all waters. She hails from the rivers of western Africa, such as the River Ogun. She is motherly, protective, and cares deeply for all her children, comforting them and cleansing them in moments of tragedy or melancholy. She is said to be able to cure infertility in women. Like the sea in a storm, she is destructive and violent.

Iemanjá was originally brought to the New World with the African diaspora, and she is now worshipped in many cultures. In Brazilian Candomblé, where she is known as Yemanjá or Iemanjá, she is the Sea Mother who brings fish to the fishermen and is represented by the crescent moon. As Yemanjá of Brazil, she protects boats traveling on the sea and grants safe passage to all her devotees who venerate her with gifts on the Feast of Yemanjá, which is held annually on February 2. By and large, the many quotable excerpts and passages reveal a master at his craft: poetic, incisive, provocative, invocative, digressive, detailed, metaphoric, and pragmatic. The writer's use of language reminds one of expressionist and symbolist modes of expression. Not much is left to the postmodernist imagination, for the concern is for the grassroots, and Longo echoes the patois of the people when he chooses to privilege their parlance by introducing choruses intermittently in the stories. Another peculiar style is the interjection of Candomblé songs and chants, which become interludes or refrains as the stories progress. "Odê!" is structured into three parts: (1) setting up the praise of Iemanjá and her importance in the pantheon; (2) a narrative about the daughter of Iemanjá questioning her mother about the dark lake and the white sands; and (3) a reflection on Iemanjá's jealous attitudes on her special day when gifts are given to her (from soap and combs to flowers) as tributes to the Queen Mother's global appeal and iconicity of beauty. While it serves as a tribute to Iemanjá, like the opening story of Obá, the story does not invoke her until it does so indirectly at the end. Instead, the central protagonists are a mother and daughter who are having a conversation about the significance of Iemanjá.

Regardless of the approach adopted in reading the ambivalent stories in Filhos de Olorum, the traditional ritualistic vision, the sociological-anthropological incursion, or the postmodernist–cultural dynamics approach, Afro-Brazilian religions leave their indelible mark on all spheres of life, even despite controversies and resistances to hegemonic forces that are determined to distort the value of the recuperative historic memory that Candomblé embodies. Whether it is in literature, theater, cinema, television, fine arts, or popular music, without talking about carnival and their electrifying schools of samba, gastronomically diverse culinary tradition, and, above all, its special way of seeing the world after many centuries of race and culture mixture, Candomblé invests these sacred-profane manifestations with the necessary presence in the formation of national culture, well beyond the confines of the religious sphere.[33] Through visibility, social prestige, and respect, Candomblé has attracted even highly skilled whites who are now fully involved in the faith despite how, in its beginning, it was exclusively invented for Afro-Brazilians. The increasing presence of whites with elevated incomes and advanced educational achievements in Candomblé is only surpassed by the Spiritists or Umbandistas. Despite the advent of Umbanda in the 1960s through the 1980s, it was Pentecostalism that complicated the mix in the 1990s. Today, only 3 percent of Brazilians identify with Afro-Brazilian religious culture. While literary criticism can announce the death of the author or deconstruct the social context that nourished the literary and cultural production, the stories in *Filhos de Olorum* are flexible enough to be celebrated as documents of the orixás. These stories even deconstruct them by adding a profane dimension that allows readers to see the complexity of the sacred when faced with a social reality in which the devotees celebrate their orixás as they see fit. It is imperative for the sacred not to be blind to socioeconomic realities. In doing so, the faithful are only promised a better life in the aftermath: not in the here and now, where they need racial equality, religious tolerance, gender equality, labor relations, and equal pay (not to mention access to basic educational, medical, social, political, and financial security). After all, the conscious manifestation of the subconscious is all about state of mind.

Candomblé and Umbanda:
Comparing *Filhos de Olorum* and *Tambores de Angola*

These model Afro-Brazilian religions share a commonality of historical marginality given that they are forms of expression that have been persecuted for many centuries. As a result, there is limited research information on them when compared to the more centralized religions such as Catholicism and the evangelical movement. The controversy regarding what constitutes ritual and religion is a false distinction when it comes to the more serious issue of solving immediate social problems. The transatlantic slave trade forcibly brought millions of Africans to the Americas as slaves. The enslaved, in turn, also brought their religions, deities, and belief systems. To survive, these once-clandestine groups had to subject themselves to a process of miscegenation with European Christianity, as well as with indigenous belief systems and other African religiosities, creating what today is known as religious syncretism. Though marginalized and impoverished, Candomblé and Umbanda provide solace for millions of devotees who are mostly Black and brown and who connect with these belief systems as a form of spiritual solidarity, consolation, and psychological fulfillment. Given the association of these religious sects with trance, spirit possession, and animal sacrifice, they are also quick to be negatively stereotyped as activating "black magic" or diabolic practices. The general conclusion is often that these religions are "primitive" and "backward," in the sense that black magic can never replace the "Catholic Church." While evolutionists were busy discrediting Candomblé as a viable religion, Umbanda emerged as a more acceptable alternative, as the founders sought a religion for urban, middle-class elites, one that could possibly cater to the interests of the Brazilian nation. From the colonial era through the present, Afro-Brazilian religiosity has evolved from a repressed sect to a syncretic religion that struggles to maintain the African values in the face of the hegemonic forces of assimilation.[34] As a result, Afro-Brazilian religions have deployed Candomblé as a form of African reinvention. Beyond this constant struggle with syncretism and re-Africanization processes, which feature in the works of Jorge Amado, Caribé, Dorival Caymmi, Caetano Veloso, and Maria Bethânia, Umbanda adds a new challenge as it claims to aspire to a more encompassing national religion that incidentally has been supported by artists such as Clara Nunes, Milton Nascimento, and Martinho da Vila. Despite their divergences, the two texts under comparative critical analysis, *Filhos de Olorum* and *Tambores de Angola*, present conceptual issues that cannot be simplified by their differing ideological and religious orientations alone.

On the one hand, *Filhos de Olorum* reenacts a postmodernist approach to the appreciation of Candomblé. The stories are not meant to be a direct interpretation of the characteristics of the orixás; rather they are free, even complex elaborations of associations and dissociations that help align them to their humanity and extra-humanity as they challenge and contrast the values predetermined for them in the realm of racialized social order and transdiasporic folklorizations. The two case studies deployed in this chapter seek to deconstruct the traditional images of Obá and Oxum, respectively, while empowering the Afro-Brazilian people as in control of their own destinies. The deities are no longer the central forces of agency; instead, the stories elevate the centrality of the human in the negotiation of significance and meaning. *Tambores de Angola*, on the other hand, is far more complex. Aside from not obeying the genre principle of "prose narration," its reflexive narrative exposes the reader to the power of spiritism as it affects the transfigured protagonist who became a medium after suffering what should have been a cardiac arrest. The activation of power (axé) resonates as through spirit forces, and the recuperative medium narrates activities that he and only he could have witnessed. In form and content, both seek to share with the reader the most esoteric and pragmatic dimensions of human life.

Both texts are quite different in context and social reality, but the cultural criticism deployed may invite an alternative mode of seeing Afro-Brazilian religiosities—not as contradictory and competing essences but as complementary resonances of the same Africanized roots during global chaos and errant brutalities. The discourse of the children of God in *Filhos de Olorum* and that of the spirit medium in *Tambores de Angola* may well be a call to solidarity at a time when meaning itself is devoid of signification, when what is sign and what is illusion depends on the background and orientation of the articulator. In an era of hybrid and ambiguous enunciation, when what is articulated may well be the opposite of what is intended, when the language of articulation is conflated to suit the many voices being assumed and negotiated with, the truth becomes nonexistent. At best, a deity or a spirit medium occupies a realm of agency that helps effect transformation in the lives of troubled human spirits.

Chapter 8

Cléo Martins and Chynae

Oiá and Oxossi in Invocations and Encounters

Drawing upon the multidimensional agencies of Oya and Osossi as river (preying) and forest (hunting) personalities, the narratives of Cléo Martins and Chynae, preserved in *Ao Sabor de Oiá* (In the Style of Oya) and *Encantos de Oxossi* (Enchantments of Oxóssi), respectively, explore individual experiences mixed with characteristics of deities that propel the actions of the protagonists in question. Written as mementos and memories that intersect with profound influences of imposing divinities in the lives of the narrators, the texts describe how the virulence of Oya's winds are calmed by the tranquil forests of Oxóssi. Both texts share intimate invocations and poetics of intertwined intensities that are better understood as homages and reflections by two dedicated authors who register aspects of their lives as they are determined by sacred precepts. Through an analysis of these intimate encounters between the profane and the sacred, the reader gains refreshing insight into the world of Candomblé as dignified by the verities of the mundane, which are inseparable from the celestial or spiritual. African diaspora cosmologies are enriching in their intersections with gendered dualities and peculiarities of female divinities, especially when it comes to the predominance of women in Candomblé. And yet, the reality is that women in leadership positions are less recognized than men as they affect public visibility and social policies. The approximation of Oya and Òṣóòsi in this chapter is only incidental and not meant to indicate any inherent comparison that forges a paradigmatic alliance. At best, the quest for spiritual harmony in

Yoruba cosmology often necessitates the notion of unity within opposing or dichotomous forces, such as when female and masculine energies collide. The tension thus produced between the opposing forces results in a natural harmonious essence. When it comes to female power, as has been the subject of many studies in the anthropology of women in Candomblé, it is evident that despite their involvement with visible social causes, women are not duly recognized as often as men. In addition to engaging the specificities of each deity in question, through the respective works under analysis, this chapter argues that the power of Odu, the feminine divinity, serves as a point of entry into empowering female and male deities as they manifest their principles of violent cosmic winds and the contemplation of the beautiful, respectively. Ultimately, in the overlapping terrain of invocations and revelations, the deities tangoing with the power of Odu receive the divine blessings in relation to their own identitarian quests that are, at worst, hidden and, at best, discovered. Through the deconstruction of the hybridized textures of cosmological representations, Yoruba identity spurs forth as a permanent quest in the naming of an African diasporic culture.

Conceptualizing *Odù's* Multifaceted Identity

In its most basic usage, the word Odù, like most Yoruba words, is ripe with multivalent meanings.[1] In Ifá divination, the term is all encompassing. Odu refers to a deity, the mythic wife of Orunmila, and it is also the term used to invoke signs that are revealed during the act of divination. The multifaceted nature of Odu empowers it to manifest as secrecy in all its dimensions. The interlocking power that stretches from the Yoruba world, across the Atlantic, and into the inner sancta of diaspora reverberating through divination, must be seen as the endless spectrum through which the world is perceived and processed. Nothing happens that has not been foretold and foreseen; nothing is foretold that cannot be circumvented and redirected, provided destiny is fulfilled without destroying the primordial openness of ritual action and infinite possibilities. Such is the dynamism of the forces of nature that are framed within cosmological phenomena. Much of what is reality is an illusion, and illusion itself is just a matter of one's frame of mind. When the attributes of Oya and Ọṣọọsi are localized within the oracular force of divination, the tempestuous forces of the wind conspire with the healing virtues of the forest to provide a conceptual possibility in the elusive identity of Odu.[2] We are part and parcel of what the other is in form and in content, and our interconnectedness is a positive commonality we share as beings with witnessing capacities. The alliance between Odu (knowledge of secrets) and Igbo Odu or Igbodu (forest or womb of secrets) exemplifies the power of extradimensional planes for the initiation of secrets that are required of all Yoruba diviners (babalawos) of the Ifá oracular system.

Ifá is both a religion and a system of divination in which the verses of the literary corpus are known as the Odu Ifá or Ifa thought system. Orunmila is identified as the Grand Priest—that is, the one who revealed divinity and prophecy to the world. In this ancient knowledge system, there are a total of 256 Odus, with each having its own character, personality, and attributes. Each Odu is a complex creature, with its own assigned number of paths to find meaning in life. The Odu is like a signatory and photographic memory that records while simultaneously revealing everything that has ever happened, is currently happening, and that will happen in the future regarding the person for which consultation is being sought. In other words, Odu has the final say on all matters. During consultation, divination sets out to discover the Odu of a person at a given time. Odu stipulates the path of such a person, the specific details of their circumstance, and what can be done to improve their situation. Consultation will recount the Odu of the person by describing the possible paths of the person's life and what to do to avert crisis by offering sacrifice (ebo) or to conduct ritualistic and purification acts. When a person is initiated as a priest or babalawo, the person is said to be born with an Odu. Such a person is then accompanied by that Odu for their entire life and guides their path forever.

Beyond the identities of Odu as deity, wife, and oracular repository, Odu invokes the predicament of divinatory power that is endowed on a locale where the initiation of those new to Ifá is conducted. Igbodu is one such extradimensional zone of supernatural proportions that defies human understanding. Through sheer wisdom of the Yoruba ancestors and priests, they have been able to identify this mysterious zone and many others as locations of extreme power. Our ancient ancestors were not only adept at locating these zones of worship and authority, but they also had a habit of locating them and building either stone temples or pyramids on these locations as a way of accessing the multiple divine blessings passed down from one dimension to another and from generation to generation. As many initiates recount, the experience of encountering Igbodu or the physical manifestation of an extradimensional zone can be profoundly overwhelming, mystical, and regenerating. Anyone who can pass through the initiation process and exit Igbodu still intact can surely manipulate the physical dimensions of the world. Through invocations, supplications, and rituals, the initiate is schooled in spiritual discipline and responsibility—that is, toward attaining the ultimate good character.

Yoruba society used to be matrilinear. In this historical context, Odu manifests herself as a female divinity who has come to the visible kingdom (Earth) with Ọbatálá (Òrìṣànlá, Ọbarìṣà) and Ògún. Òlódùmarè (God) had sent them to create Earth. Ọbàtálá had the power of creation while Ògún had that of technology and war. Odu returned to Òlódùmarè before leaving the invisible kingdom and asked Òlódùmarè about her power. Òlódùmarè responds:

> You will be Ìyá wọn (The Mother of all).
> Mother for all eternity, you will support the world.
> You will be the mother of all men.
> They should warn you, Odu, of all the things you intend to do.
> The man alone cannot do anything in the absence of women.
> He gives you the power of Ẹyẹlé the bird.
> He gives you the gourd of Ẹyẹlé, the guardian bird (this is the igbà of Odu).[3]

Òlódùmarè asks Odu how she will use the power, and she says she will kill anyone who refuses to listen to her. Children who plead with her (to give knowledge to them) will be rewarded with money; however, if people become impertinent with her, she will take it back. He warns her not to abuse this power. She says that as long as people do not challenge her authority, she is going to give them blessings; however, if they do challenge her powers, she will kill them. Yet when she gets a little arrogant and abuses her power, then the command over that power is transferred to men. The power of magic continues with the power of women.

What does this have to do with the women who seek the ìgbà of Odu? She ends up marrying Ọrúnmìlà (in some versions it is Ọbàtálá), and he must promise her that none of his wives can look at her. Thus, the women are not allowed to look at the ìgbà of Odu (it is clarified that the author is speaking of ìgbà Odù, or the inside of the Igbòdù, the sacred site where the Babalawo are initiated). The ìgbà of Odu is the most powerful object in the Yoruba religion. Women may become Ifá diviners and belong to the cult of Ifá with the same status as men, but they cannot look at the igbà of Odu, giving men the power over it in the cult of Ifá, for women cannot manipulate the Ikin. But, it is still female power, which is qualitatively better than male power. In practical terms, this puts the control of the cult of Ọrúnmìlà in the hands of men.

The story of Odu is found in Odù Ìrẹtẹ Ogbè:

You step on the brush.
I walk the brush.
We threw the brush on the floor together.
Ifá was consulted for Odu by these Áwo.
They said, Odu goes from Heaven to Earth.
When she gets to earth.
They said Odu, this is your beginning.
Olódùmarè gave her a bird.
She took this bird with her to Earth.
Aragamago is the name that Òlódùmarè gave this bird.
Aragamago is the name of that bird transported by Odu.
He said:
You Odu, any venture on which you send this bird, it will
    do.
He said:
Any place that pleases you to send this bird, it will go.
He said:
Whether it is to do evil or good.
He said:
Whatever he pleases tell him to do, he will do.
Odu brought this bird to earth.
Odu said no one else will be able to look at her.
She said she should not be looked at.
If any enemy of Odu looks at her, she will blind their eyes.
With the power of this bird, it will blind their eyes.
If the pairs of your enemies look into the gourd of this bird.
This bird Aragamago, will break their eyes.
She used this bird this way.
She used it until she reached the house of Ọrúnmìlà.
Ọrúnmìlà went to consult his Áwo.

The oracle stated that if we teach intelligence to someone,
     their intelligence will be intelligible.
If we teach stupidity to someone, their stupidity will be
     obviated.
The Babalawo of Ọrúnmìlà's house consulted Ifá to learn
     the day when he would take Odu as his wife. In this
     way Ọrúnmìlà would take Odu as his wife.

The Awo of Ọrúnmìlà said:
Hmmmnnnn.
They said you intend to take Odu as your wife.
The power will be in your hands.
They said that because of this Ọrúnmìlà power should
     make an offering to the Earth.
In the interest of all its people.
They said that, so that this power, she will not kill and eat
     it.
Ọrúnmìlà made the offering.
When Ọrúnmìlà made the offering, they consulted Ifá for
     him.
Ọrúnmìlà held the offering outside.
On Odu's arrival, she found the offer on the street.
Hee!
Who made this offering to the earth?
There is!
Èṣù says:
Ọrúnmìlà made this offering to the land.
Because he wants to marry you.
Odu said, not bad.
All the things that Odu performed behind it, these will be
     the bad things.
Told him to eat.
Odu opened the gourd of Aragamago, his bird, on the ground.
She told him to eat.
Odu entered the house.
When she entered the house, Odu called Ọrúnmìlà.
She said: Ọrúnmìlà, I arrived.
She said, her powers are numerous.
She said she did not want them to fight.

She said she did not want to fight with Ọrúnmìlà.
She said that even if someone asked for her help, she
   asked for his help to fight him, she could not fight him.
Because Odu did not want Ọrúnmìlà to suffer.
Otherwise, if they wanted to make Ọrúnmìlà suffer.
Odu, with the power of the bird, would fight the people.

When Odu finished speaking this way.
Ọrúnmìlà said, not bad.
When the time came Odu, said:
You Ọrúnmìlà, you will learn my taboo.
She said she wanted to tell her taboo.
She said she did not want her other wives to see her face.
She said that he should tell all his other wives not to look
   at his face.
Whoever looked at her face, she would fight this person.
She said she did not want anyone to look at her
   appearance.
Ọrúnmìlà says:
Great!
He then called all of his wives.
He prevailed over them.
The wives of Ọrúnmìlà would not look at Odu's face.
Odu told Ọrúnmìlà:
She said that for him she would do her job.
She said she would heal all things.
She said anything he did and went wrong, she would fix it.
She said that if he observed her taboo, all the things she
   did would be good.
Whoever would upset them would in turn disturb them.
If it were Oṣó (sorcerer), that he wanted to destroy.
She said she would leave him in nothingness.
Then he himself would be destroyed.
All your kids, who are Awo.
He will beg them to never dare to fiddle with Odu.
Because Odu is the power of Awo.
He said that if the Awo has Ifá, he will also have Odu.
The power that Odu gives you says so.
No woman should look at her shape.

From this day on, no babalawo (diviner) is complete without seeing Odu. He who has no Odu will not be able to consult Ifá. Any such babalawo who is initiated without this ritual is called Elegan. He will not be able to manipulate any sacred objects of Ifá for divination. Many aspiring diviners went to Nigeria and ended up as Elegan. Such novices made popular consultations that damaged the lives of many people because of their lack of Odu and authority. When a babalawo undergoes perfect ritual initiation and comes into Odu's possession as a protégé and initiate, Odu will never allow such a person to err or suffer. So be it![4] The foregoing paradigmatic story from Odù Ìrẹtẹ Ogbè instructs us that Odu is an enigma of power, alliance, and identity, through which Orunmila fulfills his mission of empowerment to his devotees. She must be revered and venerated to continue to benefit from her generosity, protection, and wisdom.

Ao Sabor de Oiá:
Of Deities and Their Artistic Rehumanizations

Whether it is in Africa or in the African diaspora, Oya is often acclaimed as one of the wives of Sango along with Osun and Oba. It is not unusual to come across myths, legends, or stories in popular culture about how Oya is related to Sango or the rest of Sango's wives.[5] Ao Sabor de Oiá (2003) reenacts the legacies of African heroic warrior women not as specifically tailored to the realities of African women per se but as modified by cultural plurality and religious intolerance that define the worlds of Salamita and Anselmo in the African diaspora. Because the plot in Ao Sabor de Oiá ultimately revolves around issues of identity, a Yoruba myth about Oya provides context for appreciating the shifting identities of the protagonists and antagonists alike.

In Yoruba Myths, Ulli Beier recounts the myth of the goddess Oya, who was originally described as an antelope but who occasionally sheds her antelope skin to assume that of a beautiful woman who one day intrigued a hunter named Sango:

> Oya was an antelope who transformed herself into a woman.
> Every five days, when she came to the market in town, she
> took off her skin in the forest and hid it under a shrub.

One day Shango [sic] met her in the market, was struck by her beauty, and followed her into the forest. Then he watched, as she donned the skin and turned back into an antelope.

The following day Shango hid himself in the forest, and when Oya had changed into a woman and gone to the market, he picked up the skin, took it home and hid it in the rafters.[6]

The rest of the story is equally significant, describing how Sango took Oya home and she bore him twins, which enraged the other two wives. Out of jealous rage, they reveal the secret of her skin and where to find it in the rafters. Oya quickly dons the skin and returns to the forest, never to be seen by Sango again. While Sango and Oya remain quite significant in Yoruba mythology, the lessons they provide their devotees may well be the balance between the physical and spiritual realms. Oya returns to the forest due to the betrayal of her trust in the rivaling household, while Sango commits suicide due to his inability to cope with the unusual burden of governance. In both cases, the moral lies in embracing both visible and invisible forces necessary to counter the excesses of choosing either path, which leads to destruction. By being united with the principle of balance and harmony, the excesses are contained, and each individual allies himself or herself with the principles of constraint in the heat of the moment so as not to make the wrong decision, leading to calamity.

Unlike the mysteries of Oya and Sango in Yoruba mythology, *Ao Sabor de Oiá* is divided into five lengthy stories within a story, as follows: (1) "The Woman of Fire"; (2) "The Hurt Bird"; (3) "The Rebirth of Fire"; (4) "The Return"; and (5) "In the Style of Oya." The novel benefits from an experienced storyteller and scriptwriter. Cléo Martins not only invokes suspense, passion, and complex plots, but she sees to it that her characters are so captivating that they turn the reader in their seats as they try to make sense of the riveting moments in which the characters find themselves as they struggle to survive passions that can mean either life, death, or freedom to escape the constraints of enclosure. Given that Cléo Martins spent some time at the Ilê Axê Opo Afonja, it is no coincidence that some of the characters in *Ao Sabor de Oiá* have similarities with such eminent personalities as Pai Agenor and Mãe

Stella, to whom the novel pays homage. Antônio Olinto, author of the famed *The Water House* (1970), notes how, when it comes to the novel of storyteller and scriptwriter Cléo Martins, "*Ao Sabor de Oiá* rekindles the importance of Yoruba culture in Brazilian culture and calls attention to the real bridge between two different worlds that we have seen in the course of the 20th century."[7] Likewise, the character who portrays an attorney, Sulamita Sulamita Verzeri de Paula Almada, is initiated into Candomblé and has a special rapport with Monk Beneditino Ancelmo. Thus, the writer blurs fiction and reality, creating a novel that has elements of fantasy, spirituality, hybridity, and magical realism.

Written as a five-part circular journey, the novel is also written in an epistolary format that dates from October 15, 1999, through October 26, 1999. A twelve-day odyssey from São Paulo (Brazil) through Mosteiro (Panamá), Salvador (Brazil), Curitiba (Brazil), London (United Kingdom), and back to São Paulo, among other locations, the journey is full of intrigues and digressions, and the global story is not without its localities for immersing and cleansing in spiritual encounters. In the "Foreword," the writer intimates about the context of the production of the novel, while also rendering gratitude to all those who were one way or the other involved in its gestation, especially Professor Agenor Miranda and Mãe Stella, the Iyalorixá (Priestess) of the Ilê Axé Opo Afonja: "I declare, reader, that this work was born out of my personal experience and emotions though it is far from being biographical, whether self or otherwise. Believe me if you can, but it is true, transparent, I confess, that no one put a spell on me for no spell catches me!"[8] With most works of spirituality, it is almost incumbent upon a writer so inspired to justify the context of nourishment for a creative work to establish not only credibility but also authenticity. While the latter idea is often critiqued as relative, it also has its place in a subject such as the sacred or the place of Candomblé in Brazilian literature. As a new voice of reason who chooses a credible spiritual leader such as famed Mãe Stella as her first reader and critic, the message is clear: any unwanted error has been sanitized to the degree that what is left is ample proof of mastery. As much as the subject is inspired by religiosity, especially the times and moments of goddesses such as Oya and Oba, one can only deduce the presence of a symbolic Sango to complete the equation, given that these are the wives of Sango and do not exist in a vacuum. The knowledge of Candomblé may not necessarily be vital to appreciating this novel, but it does help to connect the dots when it comes to the mysteries of characters and personalities within the novel.

Due to the "diaries" or epistolary mode, the five stories are presumably written by the same authorial or omniscient voice as it wonders through many cities, especially São Paulo, Salvador, Mosteiro, and London. At the core of many complex plots, which privilege the transformative agency that is Candomblé for all devotees, lies the magic of Candomblé as it transgresses the limits of inventiveness and mimesis. This raises the question about the double of the human spirit as it negotiates between physical and spiritual realms. Émile Durkheim in *The Elementary Forms of Religious Life* (2008) suggests that the double can be likened to a state of dreaming ("semi-invisible substance unavailable to direct experience" [53]), but he also questions the extent to which that state can travel back in time to gain validation:

> Our dreams often relate to past events; we see again what we saw or did when we were awake yesterday, the day before, during our youth and so on. These kinds of dreams are common and have a significant place in our nocturnal life. Now, the idea of the double cannot account for them. Even if the double can travel from one point to another in space, it is hard to see if it can travel back through time.[9]

If the double of our existence comes in the form of dreams, it is antithetical to daily existence, as Tish Warren observes in *Liturgy of the Ordinary* (2016). Warren opines, "The crucible of our formation is in the anonymous monotony of our daily routines."[10] In other words, the diary format is a testament to those experiences of the now, which thus become sacred, liturgic, or religious by virtue of their repetitiveness. This allows them to resonate with the profundity of their revelations as tangible living processes that are not reserved for a special nocturnal moment or escapade. The intensive movement from one location to another makes the need to document events even more crucial, as a moment can simply disappear like a flash while another could replace it with equal speed. Between the ordinary and the sacred, the sacred and the profane, there is a delicate hybrid moment of ecstasy or epiphany that defies comprehension. It is such magical moments that are not immune to errancy and fantasy, as the characters live the moment to the fullest without worrying about the aftermath. Having gone through many transformations herself, the writer has traversed spiritual immersions at the Casa Branca do Engenho Velho (Xangô), Ilê Axé Opo Afonja (Oxóssi), and with matriarchal mentors that helped her appreciate African goddesses that led her to Oya. In sharing the adventures of characters that see Oya as a nine-spirit being (Iansan or Iya Mesan, nine mothers) whose multiple identity seeks balance in the powers of her spiritual manifestations.

As a case study for the hybridization of Yoruba divinity and religiosity as represented by the wives of Xangô, Obá and Oya, Cléo Martins's novel engages Yoruba mythology and diaspora identities by locating interconnectedness between the continent and the diaspora. Nestor Canclini in *Hybrid Cultures* (2003) challenges the encroaching effects of globalization by suggesting that Latin America risks losing its cultural identity in the process. By privileging indigenous value systems, such as the virtues of religiosity (even when meshed with transmodern cultural circuits), Cléo Martins approximates tradition and modernity by teasing out what is hybrid in both forces of resistance and change. Deploying deconstructed religious precepts through an aesthetic maneuvering of cosmological symbologies, Cléo Martins invites the reader to appreciate hybridized Yoruba essences through literary art. Yet mythology collides with history and spirituality when it comes to Yoruba divinities. Myth carries the sacred character of ancient wisdom, where nature embodies the anxieties of humanity in their multiple manifestations. In so doing, natural cosmological phenomena become the ultimate cultural treasures through which the greatness of nations is appropriately measured. *Ao Sabor de Oiá*, by invoking the power of myth and mythmaking, reenacts symbologies of humanity and recuperates the innermost contradictions and sacredness of human nature. By deploying creative transcendence, the writer responds to the apprehensions of humanity with strength and vulnerability. The Yoruba cosmogony through the oral tradition as is manifest in divinatory chants or orikis of the deities produces ritualistic and cataclysmic archetypes that explain past events in their present representations. As a result, hybridizations are inevitable, given a range of shifting spontaneities and identities over space and time. *Ao Sabor de Oiá* manipulates sacred Yoruba myths by tapping into the decentralized Afro-diasporic spiritualities embodied in the personae of the female deities, or aiabás, who have now experienced existential hybridities through their transnational journeys and adaptations over the centuries.

Odu is the iconic multivalent character who opens the gates of knowledge for every being seeking oracular guidance from Orunmila and from Ifá. Yet, her symbolic function or mythic role is as important as her matriarchal presence, which shapes the many tensions that play out in the Orunmila household—a model structure that empowers both the grand priest as well as the initiated priests into the acts of divination. Likewise, in the domain of the sacred, or Candomblé, the aiabás, or female divinities, are the sacred queens whose revered religious identities are often invoked to counterbalance any negative forces of the profane world. These counter-hegemonic forces are also embodied by deities like Iemanjá, Nanã, Obá, Oiá, Oxum, and Euá. These female deities are foundational members of the mythic past that defines the Yoruba mythology. They are equally the domain of elements of nature, such as water, wind, fire, and earth, which impact the affairs of humanity as well as relate to their desires and interdictions. In the Yoruba world-view, there are over six hundred divinities. In Brazil, only sixteen are assembled in one Ilê Axê, or Candomblé, as syncretized entities due to religious syncretism over many centuries and as a measure of survival from slavery and resistance to the effacement of African religious cultures. As a result, instead of each terreiro being homogenic, they are rather heterogenic, as each assembles many deities into one religious entity; however, unlike the African setting, the divinities are region-specific. *Ao Sabor de Oiá* highlights personified divinities, such as Oxum, Oiá, and Obá, as interactive agencies, whose religious attributes define their actualized identities. These divinities reenact their own myths and histories as they occupy new roles and territories in the literary manifestation of transculturation proportions.[11] These entities struggle for survival in the cultural contact zone, which often leads to both dislocation and relocation as the reader verifies in the many references in the novel to the fictional Ilê Axê Saketê Avessan.[12]

In the realm of the first segment of the epistolary story, entitled "The Woman of Fire," *Ao Sabor de Oiá* seems to manifest autobiographical elements, especially since the author has passed through Ilê Axê Opo Afonja, and there are many similarities with some of the characters described in the novel.[13] However, the author warns us in the prologue that this is not the case when she observes, in the fictionalizing sense, the following: "Approaching the window, she understood, however speechless, that it was all something extraordinary: an eagle-pilgrim struggling for life."[14] The story alternates very frequently from location to location, such as from São Paulo, through the Beneditino Monastery in the interior of Paraná, to London, and to the capital of Bahia, Salvador. Most of the plot takes place between October 14 and 26, 1999. The thirteen days in which the action in the novel takes place may have mystical and numerical significance, but this is not explicitly revealed to the reader. Yet not much is left to the imagination, and some of the described events are likened to efforts to defamiliarize the routines and rituals of Candomblé, such as the mythologies of the orixás and the multivalent histories and memories of Yoruba ancient ways of life that have been preserved for posterity. The central plot structure revolves around the life and times of a young attorney, Sulamita de Almada, an Italian descendant who is a Reverend Sister in a Benedictine Convent and who finds herself impeded by Catholic rites to search for the sacred in the religion of the orixás. Here is a classic case of the conflicts of religious intolerance as opposed to religious syncretism.

From her protected and regimented life in the Catholic convent to her exciting and adventurous life once she meets the Iyialorixá Mãe Antônia da Anunciação, otherwise known as Mãe Totonha, Sulamita is never the same again. Possessed by Obá while in the interior, outside the serene ambiance of Candomblé, Sulamita is initiated in the Ilê Axé Saketê Avessan. thereafter becoming an iaô (wife) of Obá, a female orixá who is inspired by fire. She is a walking wind, a warrior woman, whom Cléo Martins describes as "an Amazonian warrior woman who lives in the interfacial zone of the encounter of non-mixing waters (the sea and the river) that produce delicious sounds."[15] Given her compassionate and fluid demeanor with everyone at the terreiro, the aiabá of Obá (Oba's wife) soon receives the title of maiê, whose function in the Candomblé hierarchy is to serve as personal assistant to the Iyalorixá (priestess), the one who controls the axé (power) within the house. Being white and educated, Sulamita, whose nickname is Obá Delé, is not totally well perceived by all the members despite having struck a powerful rapport with the biological granddaughter of Mãe Totonha, the veterinarian Alzira, to the extent that both are responsible for the gradually debilitating health of the priestess. The priestess's health is aggravated by the fact that the older daughter of the priestess, Alzira, otherwise known as Licinha de Oxum, has abandoned her religious heritage in Candomblé and is now a faithful believer and attendee of Neopentecostal Fogo de Betânia Church. The priestess often threatens to expel her own daughter from the terreiro. It is as if there was some form of "holy war" set off in the house. It is due to these tensions that the health of the priestess worsens.

Apparently, all of the aforementioned takes place during the Oxun festival, and Mãe Totonha thus requires even more serious attention as she is perturbed by her eldest daughter's ungrateful behavior. During a fire outbreak, in which Sulamita is overpowered by sleep, the priestess dies. Licinha de Oxum not only accuses Sulamita of killing her mother, but she promises to take some bold and intolerant steps to build what she calls a "real" Christian temple and destroy all the foundations of the orixás in the terreiro. Not only does Alzira, or Licinha, interfere with the funeral rites of Yoruba origin (ikú), but she leads an invasion of the cemetery by wearing black, a color that is prohibited in the ritual of leaving the ilê (the earth) and returning to the heavens (orum). As a result, the funeral rites (axexê) of Mãe Totonha are never completed. In view of these hurt feelings and the constant accusations by Licinha de Oxum that she is responsible for the death of the priestess, Sulamita is compelled to leave the Ilê Axé Saketê Avessan and move to São Paulo, where she suffers a mental breakdown. These flashes of memory take place on October 13, when Sulamita's monotonous life is interrupted by a deeply revelatory dream that connects her own Italian grandmother, Elba Lùcia, with Mãe Totonha, the Ialorixá. They are both wearing white and are accompanied by a young black woman with a large sword wearing a crown. The words she remembers most coming from the mouth of the priestess are "Obá Delé, my daughter, a warrior is never afraid of the struggle."[16]

As the novel progresses in its narrative journey, "The Hurt Bird" locates the reader within the Benedictine Monastery, where Brother Anselmo receives a visit from Alzira on the morning of October 15, 1999. The daughter of Oiá arrives desperate to complete the funeral rites (axexê) for Mãe Totonha, which were interrupted by the presence of devotees as well as by her verbal aggressions toward Sulamita. Bothered by her own conscience and the injustice committed against Sulamita, she wants Anselmo's spiritual help to be close to Sulamita again and complete the funeral rites, which include the selection of a new Iyalorixá. A year passes after the death of Mãe Totonha, and Alzira is now temporarily in a leadership position until the orixás declare a successor. For a novel that is not strictly about Candomblé but merely inspired by it, the fictionalized accounts in it are quite striking in detail and in their ability to gauge human behavior with such dexterity. The level of conflict between a spiritual mother and a rebellious daughter is sustained for quite a long time, carrying with it some degree of authenticity and curiosity in this riveting and touching story.

In returning to the narrative, the reader notes the families of Sulamita in Italy and her spiritual "family" in Brazil, which provide much-needed relief during moments of grief, stress, and confusion. Sulamita's mother, the ex-ambassador of Victória Regina, suddenly wakes up in the middle of the night on October 11 troubled by a dream. She tries to contact her daughter to no avail and, as a last resort, starts making plans to visit her in Brazil. In the meantime, in their effort to convince Alzira to complete the axexê (funeral rites) of Mãe Totonha and resist the encroaching influences of Pentecostals, the religious household seems to be on the path to reconciliation. The encounter between Alzira, Sulamita, and her mom who is visiting from London, signals the beginning of the end of the narrative. Sulamita pardons Alzira and returns to Salvador to fight to preserve the continuity of the Ilê Axé Saketê Avessan. The axexê ceremonies to complete the burial rites for Mãe Totonha resume, just as future deliberations about a selection of a new Iyalorixá are put into place.

With every beginning comes an end. The title story, "Ao Sabor de Oiá," is dedicated to the moment when the oracle announces through the power of divination that the house will become the responsibility of Licinha de Oxum, the long-standing iaô. Everyone is shocked that Licinha returns like a prodigal daughter to assume her responsibilities, even after abandoning them for a few days due to her confused state and conflict of interest. With the assistance of Victória Regina (daughter of Euá and deity of dreams) the aiabás Alzira de Oiá, Sulamita de Obá, and Licinha de Oxum divide the responsibilities of the house. If the thesis here is not in favor of hybridity, one cannot fully grasp Cléo Martins's approximation of Catholicism and African religious belief systems—not as a process of acculturation, as proposed by Fernando Ortiz, but more a hybridity à la Canclini.[17] Cléo Martins seeks to neutralize hierarchies, promote post-modern sacred-religious identities to include cultural identities, promote religiosity more as a personal spirituality than dogmatism—indeed as a personal choice and not a societal imposition—and reject all forms of fundamentalism and intolerance. Seen in the context of Yoruba sacred-ness, colonial religious beliefs cease being the mainstream religiosity but a hybridized consciousness in which universality may well be ambivalent because Africa has passed through the New World and vice versa. As a result, the violence of colonial syncretism is replaced by contemporary hybridity and the freedom to commingle and coparticipate with other religions in a framework of networks and solidarities without fear of losing any primordial essences. In this sense, Cléo Martins is against the idea of fixed religious discourse but rather open to transnational mobilities and ambivalent epistemic agencies toward ultimate diasporic fluidities.

Paradigmatically speaking, Cléo Martins theorizes, through fiction, that the best approach to Afro-Brazilian religiosity is to position the faith system as a fluid thought system that can easily be in conversation with multiple religious entities and identities without any sense of contradictions, conflicts, intolerance, or tensions. Such could be the experience of the Iyalorixá with the Benedictine Monk and the members of the Ilê Axé Saketê Avessan. In one of her moments of reflections about religion and the world we live in, especially after having been hurt by the accusation of being responsible for the death of the Iyalorixá Totonha, Sulamita de Obá weaves together an epistemological treatise that sounds more like an alter ego of Cléo Martins:

> The construction of a millennial synthesis—in the eyes of impossible humans; a seed of hope in a world desperately in need of hope.
>
> The daily reading of the diaries was overwhelming to her.
>
> Hunger, uneven income distribution, hate, religions as sources of division and the implantation of discord (the probable agents of the next world war); higher consumption of drugs, lack of morals in the social media, pedophilia now an issue at the Vatican; crisis in the Church, retrogression; distrust among families, increase in fundamentalist religious fanatics, lack of respect to the human body—and many other assaults on life.[18]

In this synthesis, issues coalesce for religion to tackle. Indeed, religion should not be seen as a means of promoting intolerance. Sulamita's argument, of course, is that with so many social issues oppressing the world, there is no room for religious fanaticism—only pragmatism. When seen as means to an end, if that end is defined as the well-being and happiness of humanity, religion provides a solution to world problems. Cléo Martins is adamant about ensuring world peace through religious coparticipation and solidarity. Her ideas move from the individual to the family to the universal. That Sulamita is first welcomed into Candomblé, rejected through a questionable excuse, and then reinserted into the same religious organization as a significant participant is not only a signal of hope but also of better things to come.

When it comes to the postmodern discourse that Cléo Martins advances, it can be summed up as the fact that there is a shift from the traditional religious ethos to the global or universal in the sense that the extended religious family need not be close but can be far-reaching, linking São Paulo to Salvador, Mosteiro, and London. The multivalent identities of Sulamita also echo the suggestion that identity cannot be fixed or unidimensional and must be open to new discoveries, multiplicities, and even reincarnations from past lives. Based on the attributes of her female orixá (Obá), Sulamita is ingenious, bold, courageous, and aggressive. While such a personality tends to achieve her ideals, she also experiences hurt and bitterness along the way and must be strong to overcome the odds. In its totality, *Ao Sabor de Oiá* raises several fluid issues that go against all forms of rigidity in favor of open-ended and flexible encounters.

Encantos de Oxóssi: Magical Healings Through Sacred Activation

If Oya or "Iya Mesan" (nine-person mother, Iansãn) embodies the tempestuous and the intrepid power of storms, Oxóssi is the impulsive, impatient, and multitasking hunter, who must do everything in his or her power not to miss the set target. The fluid quality of Oya as theorized in *Ao Sabor de Oiá* finds a contemporary ally in the "conquering" nature of Oxóssi, as manifest in *Encantos de Oxóssi* (2009). An oriki of Oxóssi states: "I am not about war, I am for peace / run away from a battle; never! / I overcome all obstacles astutely and passionately, / I am a virile warrior, an enchanted hunter, / In the ancestral land, In the ancestral land, / I am Oxóssi Matalambo!"[19] In this succinct oriki resides the summation of the attributes of Oxóssi. *Encantos de Oxóssi* deploys a double-pronged narrative structure that combines the poetic and the prosaic. In so doing, the writer communicates dense, esoteric, romantic, and political moments in poetry while reserving the more fluid issues of mundane proportions to the interlaced prose writing. Despite the title, the entire novel is not exclusively about Oxóssi; rather, the text focuses on many orixás, including Exu, Oxum, Ogum, Oya (Iansã), Xangô, and Oxumare (among others), and represents their vital interventions into the life and times of protagonist Dr. Renato. What both Oiá and Oxóssi have in common is aggression and resolve of purpose. Like Raul Longo's *Filhos de Olorum*, in which different orixás are used as icons to explicate the short stories, *Encantos de Oxóssi* weaves intersecting stories to give the reader a balanced perspective of Dr. Renato's life.

The author's preface notes his intent to document his memories of youthful dreams in a simple way, while inflecting them with the "peculiar language of the ancestors as inherited by certain religious mystics from Africa and as spoken by the men of the backlands and in conjunction with the Bahian way of speaking."[20] This alone goes beyond a folkloric ambition and is more of a blend of creative and spiritual spontaneities, through which such memories are recuperated in a meaningful way. For some, the process is soothing and romantic. For others, it is reflective of a traumatic past that needs to be revisited and exorcised. The field of psychoneuroimmunology (PNI) has revealed the connection between the mind and body to the degree that Dr. Pert argues, "In the end I find I can't separate brain from body. Consciousness isn't just in the head. Nor is it a question of the power of the mind over the body . . . because they're flip sides of the same thing. Mind doesn't dominate body, it becomes body."[21] But the healing virtue of balance in mind, body, and spirit is not limited to the creative experience alone but also resides in the harmony between the word and the thought behind that word. In the preface, Ildásio Tavares reminds the reader of such magisterial names of Latin American literature as Machado de Assis and Gabriel Garcia Marques, and he invokes the issues of myth, transcendence, fantasy, and fantastic realism, all of which come into unison in the world of the orixás, especially when humanity taps into their energy to make sense of their own confusion, as when one devotee of Candomblé understands Oxóssi as a knight mounted on a white horse who prescribes healing virtues to the sick. The first story, "Created as if by Enchantment," which is dedicated to Exu, has all the attributes of magical realism as Dr. Renato and wife, Dona Rosane, manipulate their dreams.[22] They consult with Father Mário de Oxóssi, the Candomblé priest, who confirms the value of the dreams and the need to conduct certain rituals as revealed by the dreams. Soon enough, Dona Rosane finds out that she is pregnant. As simple as this revelation seems, it is not simple for the couple, whose spiritual investment is such that they have to consult with a spiritual leader to confirm what they feel. They feel justified and relieved. Exu could have confused them by sowing doubts; rather, they all agree to follow the counsel of the babalorixá (priest).

In the second story, "Enchanted Friends," dedicated to Ibeji (twins), depicts shifting moments of sadness, joy, and torture, as two parents face the possibility of their daughter dying from a terminal disease. Their hope is restored through the divine intervention of Oxóssi and Oxalá after they take the child to the terreiro. In an epiphanic moment of sacred healing, a dialogue reveals the intensity of the process of invocation and restoration:

> Father Mário de Oxóssi, have mercy and heal my daughter! She seems to be under a demonic attack. I have done all I could do: prayers, cleansing baths, etc.
>
> Renatinho, appearing to be somewhat serious, orders:
> —Lay the sleeping girl here on the floor.
>
> Father Mário treats the child's requests, who takes off her shoes and he places his right foot on the head of the child, saying:
> —Wherever you came from, you will now return, for this I order in the name of my father Odé and the grace of Oxalá![23]

What appears to be a form of exorcism raises a few questions about the symbolism of placing the foot of Father Mário de Oxóssi on the child's head. One is compelled to invoke the issue of religious syncretism; yet, between Catholicism and African religion, the placing of the foot on the head sounds more like an abomination or what Catholicism rejects as a diabolic measure. This would amount to religious intolerance. Chynae may have seized this creative or poetic license to tolerate an action that is more acceptable in Candomblé than in Catholicism. He also confesses to his uncle, Renatinho, that while he understands all that is revealed or discussed, he is not sure where he has heard it. Father Mário reveals to the young man that he used to be an abiku (child born to die repeatedly), and whoever is good is born good. This episode explains why the story is entitled "Twins," for in Yoruba cosmology, twins are believed to be magical. If one twin dies, it represents a bad omen for the parents and society. The parents commission a wooden ibeji to represent the deceased twin, and the parents take care of the figure as if it were a real person. The parents then decorate the ibeji to represent their own status, using cowrie shells, beds, and coins. The firstborn of the twins is known as Taiwo while the second is called Kehinde. As an abiku, the anonymous child in the story appears to be traumatized by her deceased other, and that ghostlike child must be sent back to the world of the spirits. The title, "enchanted friends," is a curious manifestation of the bond and perhaps the curse on the child who does not die. It is as if the deceased child feels obligated to keep coming back to torment the child who is alive. In the final analysis, to be a twin is to live a double life: present with the living and yet sojourning with the ancestral in a kind of oscillating way of life that is beyond the twin's control.

When a career development opportunity to take a professional development course in São Paulo presents itself, Dr. Renato is compelled to leave Salvador da Bahia. The paternal grandparents then visit him in São Paulo in the fifth chapter (or story), "Paternal Grandparents's Visit," which is dedicated to "Oxum."[24] At the core of this story is the opportunity for the family to enjoy poetry as well as meet new members, such as Renatinho's girlfriend, Aninha. A traumatic revelation is discovered that the grandpa, Mário Alves, is hiding a secret: he suffers from prostate cancer, which could have been treated if he had been diagnosed sooner. After many months of treatment and poetry and guitar lessons, the grandfather decides to return to Salvador. Given the grandfather's illness, his dedicated grandson, Mário, decides to take his grandfather on a tour of major tourist attractions, such as Duque de Tororó, Lagoa de Abaeté, Santo Amaro, and Cachoeira. One of the greatest moments of this enchanting visit is Mário Alves's declamation of his poetry for all, especially the one entitled, "Song of Love": "To sing of love is magnificent / The sparrow may not possibly feel pain / for it mingles with thorns / Using its chest, when it sings: / A song of love."[25] The connection between the dedication of the chapter to Oxum may well reside in the historical places visited by the grandpa, as most of them deal with the river, and Oxum is the deity of the sweet rivers. Though this spiritual connection is more hybridized and symbolic than strictly religious, it does signal the soothing power of water, which somehow surrounds the whole of Bahia, hence the metaphoric nomination of the locale as "Bahia of All the Saints" to embody part of the sacredness of the state.

When taken as a conscious double-pronged writing that not only extols the virtues of Afro-Brazilian religiosity but also demystifies it by bringing other religious thought systems into conversation (such as

Catholicism and Spiritism), *Encantos de Oxóssi* advocates religious tolerance, pushes the boundaries of religious purity, and challenges stereotypes
about Afro-Brazilian culture, while also strongly promoting freedom of
spirituality. The "experimental novel" imaginatively combines poetry with
prose and deconstructs Émile Zola's naturalism by replacing the decadent
posture of humanism with limitless possibilities of hope and harmony.
The novel opens with the mystery of the white knight on a white horse,
a kind of spirit medium who often comes to the rescue at vital moments
in the novel by appearing to give advice or provide solace. It ends with
a celebration of Bahia and its magic and joyful moments, including
carnival and homages to Oxum and Oxóssi. Aside from following the
growth and development of the family of Dr. Renato, the reader also
gains insight into the lives of the members of his immediate family, as
well as members of his religious family. Some of the most memorable
moments in the novel can be found in chapter 12, "The Wedding of
the Enchanted," and chapter 13, "Matromonial Entanglements," when
Aninha and Renatinho get married with the support their two families.[26]
One may gesture a critical opinion that Chynae's novel is more romantic
and fantastic than realistic. This may not have been the intention of the
writer but the outcome of a double bind in Candomblé mythology and
the need of the writer to distance himself from any value judgment. The
result is a candid novel that leaves room for fantasy and magical realism
while at the same time exposing the dangers of not taking good care of
oneself and the benefits of absorbing the values of being in sync with
nature in order to be symbolically in harmony her positive attributes.

Conclusion

Cléo Martins's *Ao Sabor de Oiá* and Chynae's *Encantos de Oxóssi* open
unique windows into the diasporic possibilities of African religiosity as
processed through the empowering feminine principle. Whether Odu is
the mythic wife of Orunmila or the spiritual being (Àjé) that is endowed
with special esoteric powers to transform or manipulate the destinies of
men and women is not as pertinent as the female power she embodies.
The female deities encountered in both narratives include Oiá and Oxum,
and what they have in common transcends their associations with the
powerful Xangô deity and coalesces under the power to unleash natural
havoc on the environment based on their destructive energies. Through

duality and complementarity principles in Yoruba mythology, their energies are both creative and destructive. Though Oxóssi is a hunter and often tends to be male, it is not unusual for women to receive this deity as their chosen divinity, such as the case of the famed priestess of the Ilê Axê Opo Afonja, Mãe Stella de Oxóssi.[27] An àjé has the innate ability to perceive things beyond what the eye can see: indeed, she may be said to have a third vision. She is the ultimate source and plenitude of all actions. Anyone endowed with such a power has it for a lifetime and is seen as a powerful spiritualist who can diagnose ailments as well as treat and heal an ill-fated destiny.

The Yoruba word for a witch is àjé, but preferred euphemisms such as *awon iya wa* (our mothers) or *awon agbalagba* (the elders) are popular. The stereotypes held about witches by the Yoruba are similar to those in many other parts of Africa: they are believed to be active at night and are organized into an *egbe* or a society of mysterious initiates. An examination of a Yoruba sacred text, *Odu Ifa,* reveals àjé to be an endowment gifted to a female divinity. These female divinities often empower their daughters with àjé—that is, the spiritual and temporal power to dominate events in all realms of possibilities throughout Yoruba society. To seek the protection of the living, Ifa priests often invoke the power of Odu or Iyaami Osoronga:

> Ni won ba nkorin bayi pe / Iya kere e mo ohun mi o / Iyami Osonronga, / gbogbo ohun ti mba nwi / Ogbo lo ni e maa gbo dandan / Iyami Osoronga, / e mo ohun mi o / Iyami Osoronga, / igba lo ni ki e maa gba / Iyami Osoronga, / e mo ohun mi o / Iyami Osoronga, / oro ti okete ba ba le so / Ni le gbo dandan / Iyami Osoronga, / e mo ohun mi o / Iyami Osonronga, / gbogbo ohun ti mba ti nwi, / ni ko maa se / Iyami Osoronga / e mo ohun mi o.[28]

> (They started singing that / Young mother you will know my voice / Iyami Osoronga / every word that I speak / The ogbo leaf has said that you will understand it absolutely / Iyami Osoronga / you will know my voice / Iyami Osoronga / the calabash says that you will take it / Iyami Osoronga / you will know my voice / Iyami Osoronga, / the word that the okete rat speaks to the earth, the earth will hear it absolutely / Iyami Osoronga / you will know my voice / Iyami Osoronga

/ everything that I say, you will do / Iyami Osoronga / you
will know my voice.)

The knowledge of Odu or Iyami is the knowledge of the powers that
control the universe. That knowledge is vital for coping with the adversities of life. In identifying Odu, or "Our Mysterious Mother," one can pay
homage to her identity as a source of protection. In other words, it takes
identifying with Odu to solicit her protection. And, to offer protection,
Odu must also be able to identify her children. The issue of identity is a
point of departure to neutralizing negative forces. In Yoruba mythology,
for example, we say "mo ti mo oruko ti iku nje, iku o le pa mi," that is,
"I already know the name of death, it can no longer do me any harm."
This is a way of saying to death that if I can identify with you and pay
homage to you, you in turn have the responsibility to protect me. Both
narratives, Cléo Martins's *Ao Sabor de Oiá* and Chynae's *Encantos de
Oxóssi*, are enshrined within the cosmologies of Oiá and Oxóssi, and
the protagonists are aware of the powers of Oiá and Oxóssi as deities of
the winds and forests. Hence, at every moment of distress, they know
how to appease the deities and claim the blessings of Omoluabi, the
ultimate in Yoruba identitarian character.

Part III

Hybridities in Afro-Brazilian Culture

Chapter 9

Filhos de Gandhi and Cortejo Afro

Candomblé in the Carnivalesque Frame

This chapter compares an iconic carnival group, or afoxé, the Filhos de Gandhi (Sons of Gandhi) (1949), with a more contemporary and innovative bloco afro, Cortejo Afro (Black procession) (1998), with a keen eye toward demystifying the commingling of the sacred and the profane in carnivalesque cultural production. On the one hand, Filhos de Gandhi was founded in 1949 by a group of dock workers and was inspired by Gandhi's revolution in India. Unable to afford traditional carnival costumes, the members of the group got creative and adapted simple white sheets (stamped with the motifs of the group's theme for the year) and towels for their costumes. The Filhos de Gandhi, the largest carnival group on the circuit with over eight thousand revelers, parade through the streets of Salvador to a style of music called afoxé, a music derived from the Afro-Brazilian religion Candomblé. An all-male carnival organization, the Filhos de Gandhi takes to the streets wearing blue-and-white beaded necklaces that often give the air of a ritualized procession even within a profane celebration. Meanwhile, Cortejo Afro made its carnival debut in 1998 on the streets of Pirajá, a community in Salvador. The bloco is rooted in the spiritual guidance and principles of an established Candomblé house in Salvador, Ilê Axé Oyá. Cortejo Afro is artistic in its design and Afrocentric in its ideology. During the 2018 carnival, I interviewed the presidents of Filhos de Gandhi and Cortejo Afro: Gilsonei de Oliveira (the ex-president was Agnaldo Silva) and Alberto Pitta. Both resisted comparing the two organizations because they represent different principles and values.

233

While the comparative aspect of this chapter seeks to approximate the identity formation and sacred-profane dynamics of Afro-Bahian carnival, rather than to examine the religious reenactments, it nonetheless invokes Marc Cleiren's notion that "religion is not what it was for past generations. For most in the Western world, religion is no longer the widely shared and only source of truth, relied upon for answers to life's questions and an ultimate consolation. . . . The principles of self-preserving and self-transcendent orientation . . . give an illustration of the possible dynamics associated with individuals moving between groups, and how their identity is influenced."[1] Both Filhos de Gandhi and Cortejo Afro embody Cleiren's "self-preserving" and "self-transcendent" principles, given their organizational missions to preserve Afro-Brazilian religious traditions and their diasporic orientation, given their allusions to India, Africa, and Brazil as spaces that traversed violent histories but preserved their sense of dignity and pride. Such a political liberation of the spirit echoes the reversal and resilience that the carnivalesque engenders. The carnivalesque translates to a cultural mode in which the dominant power is subverted through humor and chaos. Mikhail Bakhtin's *Dostoevsky's Problem of Poetics* (1984) and *Rabelais and His World* (1984) describe the carnivalesque as a concept related to the Feast of Fools. Bakhtin argues that this medieval festival was originally held by the subdeacons of the cathedral as a way to escape the agonies of the year by wining and dining before the advent of Lent. Through Socratic dialogues and Menippean satire, everyone participates in carnival and engages in eccentric behavior that is befitting of inversion and the rituals of carnival. Through humor and the grotesque, a syncretic pageant is created that meshes the sacred with the profane. However, *Filhos de Gandhi* and *Cortejo Afro* diverge when it comes to the persistence of tradition and quest for innovation. Even when the politics of each group differs, their commonality lies in the shared value of promoting Afro-Brazilian identity in all its manifestations.

State of the Sacred-Carnivalesque

Many scholars and cultural insiders resist the temptation to assert what we have always suspected: sacred culture often makes its way into the domain of the popular. Henry Louis Gates Jr., in his "Celebrating Candomblé in Bahia," confirms what many carnival groups still deny today in Bahia.[2] But why the denial? As an Africa-derived religion, Candomblé represents the resilience of African people who were forcibly removed from the African continent and enslaved for centuries. Their religion was their saving grace, and they used it to counter the oppressive imposition of cultural values, such as the Catholic religion, and came out survivors. Religious syncretism helped preserve the African culture that Brazilian hegemonic culture tried to eliminate. Candomblé is everywhere in Brazil—masked, of course, under the pretenses of food, costumes, buildings, events, public ceremonies, and popular celebrations. Despite recent assaults on Afro-Brazilian shrines (terreiros) by extreme Pentecostals, including the destruction of religious paraphernalia, where individual devotees were made to swallow their religious beads and necklaces (as if the era of colonial-cum-police persecution of the nineteenth century were still in effect), Candomblé is still alive in Brazil. Gates synthesizes a rather problematic double-consciousness in the mindset of Brazilians—the implicit acceptance of a duality in Catholicism and Africa-derived orixá worship despite resistance from some intolerant quarters: "Many aspects of their various African heritages and cultures managed to survive with them. . . . Their orishas or deities would retain their African names, characteristics, and functions, but assumed new forms in the alien and hostile world of slavery in Latin America and the Caribbean. These manifestations of Ifa would come to be called Candomblé in Brazil."[3]

Yet, it is in Gates's cogent understanding of the function of carnival for the Brazilian black movement that I find even more compelling, especially his emphasis on the preservation of African heritage through carnival:

> The blocos afros are Afro-Brazilian cultural groups, Bahian carnival associations that celebrate and preserve Brazil's African heritage through music, dance, art, theater, and religious ceremony. Some of these groups flamboyantly define themselves through cross-dressing, a standard feature of carnivalesque ceremonies around the world; others don costumes directly informed by the elegant ceremonial dress of the Yoruba back on the continent. The female members of the blocos afros are often bedecked in gowns and head dresses that look as if they were tailored in Abeokuta, Nigeria rather than Rio.[4]

The African American critic is not alone in this observation that the religious has indeed meshed with the profane in the Brazilian melting pot. A few studies have emerged to uphold this creative fusion of Candomblé with the carnivalesque, including those by Ordep Serra, Liliane Santos, Janio Castro, Alberto Ikeda, Piers Armstrong, Karolina de Oliveira Rebouças, Isis McElroy, and Eduardo Davel and Renata Saback Rosa.[5] Each presents divergent perspectives on the intersection of the sacred with the profane, but this fluidity of the sacred-carnivalesque is not contradictory, having been true of the form since the antiquities. While these two contemporary carnival organizations under discussion share some characteristic semblances within this frame, they also diverge in terms of cultural politics, which makes a comparative analysis even more fascinating. The variety in the perspectives reassures curious minds that seemingly obvious observations may be hidden in plain sight to others due to a lack of cultural codes to decode what may not be meant for the naked eye.

Bahia has a unique location for the popularization of the sacred. The symbolic practices of Candomblé, as reenacted for tourists on the streets (for photo opportunities), by acarajé sellers on the street corners, as well as through the participation of Candomblé devotees in many religious processions or public parades, such as during national holidays, the Good End, Iemanjá, and Santa Bárbara feasts, are all conscripted in a larger public and social performance. These festivities constitute the means through which Black political and cultural groups advocate for the visibility of their otherwise marginalized religion (due to historical repressions), which struggles between religious syncretism and authenticity in the public space. The power of ritual structure that Candomblé commands allows for a preservation dynamic that also sustains its institutionalized force. As a result, Candomblé not only conserves the character of the spectacle but also empowers the popular ceremonies that define the Brazilian religious world. These festivities embody rich interfacial instrumentalities of Candomblé in relation to Brazilian society. It is thus interesting to analyze the real and symbolic dialogues between rituals of Candomblé and the discourses of the performative carnival groups who identify with their strategic identitarian platforms. From myths, deities, colors, and religious personalities in Brazilian history, the religious takes on new meaning as the festivities make the religion more dynamic and turn it into an agency of political force, change, and resilience.

The ensemble of works, which offers a conceptual review of the dynamics of the sacred in a tango with the profane, also systematically articulates the duality that makes up the singularity of the Bahian cultural tapestry. In *Rumores de Festa* (2009), Serra conducts a quadripartite study of the trio-elétrico (a high-tech mobile carnival-musical float)—the cycle of festivals in Bahia, the rounds of samba, and the triumph of the Amerindian—to prove his thesis that Bahian festivals originate from a sacred motif that has been reconfigured into popular culture. While Serra focuses on the specific festive and political scenario in Salvador-Bahia, Santos (2011) conducts a comparative analysis of two afoxé carnival groups, namely, Filhos de Gandhi (1949) in Salvador (Bahia) and Omo Oxum (2005) in Aracaju (Sergipe). Santos argues that the afoxés emerged in different but related historical contexts of repression. In the case of Bahia, Candomblé and related expressions of Blackness or Black religiosity were prohibited, and, thus, as a carnival group, Filhos de Gandhi was a masked means of protesting repression and ultimately found an alternative that preserves Black religiosity on the streets of Bahia. In the case of Sergipe, while Filhos de Gandhi emerged in 1949, Omo Oxum emerged in 2005 at a time when democracy was already better established in Brazil. Through a comparative, ethnographic, and archival research of the two entities, Santos surmises that the two cultural carnival organizations are resisting, self-legitimizing, and self-preserving entities who chose Black regality, courtship, and public procession to articulate their performative permanence as rooted forms of Black religious societies in the Brazilian public space.

While Serra and Santos articulate the contexts of the emergence of festivities in Salvador and Aracajú, Castro (2012) focuses on the reinvention of carnival as a profane extension of our Lady of conception (Iemanjá) in the city of Cachoeira. The merging of the sacred and the profane in the very case of Cachoeira is startling because there is already a history of religiosity pertaining to the famed annual celebration of the Sisterhood of Good Death in August. Castro points out that Cachoeira carnival ceases to take place on the streets and in a traditional city club, instead taking place in the context of the Our Lady of Ajuda festivity, in which the celebration is reinvented as a dynamic sociocultural festival that syncretizes the sacred and the profane. The result revitalizes the community, even if for a transient and political moment of unity and solidarity. As Castro confirms the emerging trends in the relocation of the sacred to the popular space and vice versa, one begins to also see the broader implications for Brazilian popular music because music is central to Brazilian festivities—whether sacred or otherwise. It is along these lines of reflection that Ikeda (2016) argues for the merging process of the Ijexá rhythm in Afro-Brazilian communities, especially regarding how the religious practices of Candomblé find their way not only into popular culture but also into the more enduring Brazilian popular music. As an interlude to this mapping of sacred-profane dynamics, Armstrong (1999) offers an incisive examination of carnival as an "aesthetic escape hatch." While not as emphatic on the sacred-profane duality, Armstrong nonetheless focuses on the dynamics and complexities of baianidade (Bahian identity), which tends to be more favorable to the convenience of miscegenation (as represented by the Olodum Carnival Organization) than to the emphasis on Negritude (as in the Ilê Aiyê carnival organization). Armstrong comes close to articulating the emerging trend when he contends, "At the same time, the experience of carnival, poised between *ritual and hedonism*, and including the fundamental feature of the expression of fantasy through disguise, also plays at the boundary between the collective and the individual, whether the former is defined in terms of a particular community or in gross terms of racial identity"[6] Even when deployed as an "escape hatch," carnival for many blocos afros and afoxés is a strategic performance of resistance and resilience; in this regard, the popularization of the sacred may well be understood as a political strategy of self-preservation and cultural-political participation.

Beyond the sacred-profane dynamics that most studies touch on either directly or tangentially, the analyses by Rebouças (2005), McElroy (2010), and Davel and Rosa (2017) delve into the musical, transdiasporic, and management factors that thrust the organizations into the global sphere. Though masking the more controversial issues of racism and political participation, the contributions offer novel ways of explicating organizations that may be torn between Afrocentric ideology and business pragmatism, given the need for survival even when there are no longer open governmental persecutions but rather financial constraints beyond carnival celebrations. Rebouças (2005) studies afoxé Filhos de Gandhi's fifty-five-year history (1949–2004) and its trajectory and relation with the Bahian re-Africanization processes of the 1970s, as well as the preservation of Afro-Brazilian identity. As the organization prepares for its seventieth anniversary, it is a good moment to assess its accomplishments and politics. Likewise, Cortejo Afro will soon celebrate its twentieth anniversary. It is perhaps an opportune moment to conduct this comparative analysis. While McElroy (2010) seeks to resolve her own critical perspective stemming from an autobiographical fascination with the group via their emblematic resonance with the nonviolence philosophy of the iconic Gandhi, she captures the sacred-profane dynamics of the group when she states, "I remember how when I later came across images of this semi-religious *carnaval* group, or *afoxé*, I was enchanted by what I perceived as beautiful, poetic, political, and 'carnivalistically' sacred."[7] Despite the relative novelty of Cortejo Afro in the context of pioneers, it is rewarding to see an article address its management structure, which also betrays part of its ideological mission. Meanwhile, Davel and Rosa (2017) deploy a tripartite model to study change in cultural contexts: (1) the symbolic value and symbolic consumption of cultural goods; (2) the challenges of cultural change; and (3) the management strategies of symbolic value for dealing with the challenges of cultural change in context. The cursory literature review affirms the sacred-profane dynamics of Black groups but also points in the direction of contradictions and cultural conflicts that emanate from a global perspective.

Filhos de Gandhi: Syncretism and Passive Politics

Filhos de Gandhi currently occupies a strategic place in Bahian pacification politics in the sense that it is not openly political and enjoys the benefit of parading Candomblé on the streets without any direct persecution from state authorities given its air of syncretism and passive politics. When compared to other more profane organizations, Filhos de Gandhi maintains its ritualistic and sacred characteristics by embodying the characteristics of a religious group even during carnival procession. Bahian carnival, in general, is unique for its street appeal when compared to the Rio carnival that takes place in a constrained location like the Sambódromo. Millions of revelers pack the narrow streets of Salvador to dance, sing, and make merry to the music of the blocos afros, afoxés, and trios elétricos. Yet, hidden under the merrymaking is a lot of history dating back to the nineteenth century, when Salvador had a mix of indoor and outdoor carnival parties. As early as the 1840s, Bahian elites enjoyed a splashy celebration called the *entrudo*. The festivity had been imported from Portugal and the Brazilian police did everything to banish it. As an alternative, carnival parades were first introduced in 1884. Ten years later, middle-class groups emerged but carnival remained a white festival until Afro-Brazilians organized their own groups known as afoxés.

As an afoxé, Filhos de Gandhi represents those carnival groups that bring Candomblé music, with its religious songs, dances, rhythms, and percussions, to the secular context of the street. The members play instruments like sekere and agogo. Though the afoxé groups started in Salvador, they have grown nationally, especially in cities such as Aracajú, Rio de Janeiro, Recife, and Fortaleza. In the past, members of afoxé groups were devotees of Candomblé but, nowadays, there are members of the organization that do not worship Candomblé. Adopting a nonviolent approach from the famous Mahatma Gandhi of India, now in the context of repression against Candomblé practices in Brazil, they applied and won a permit to parade peacefully without police interference. The organization was formed in 1949 by dock workers, and though it started with about one hundred participants, the group has grown to over fifteen thousand members and is known to have paved the way for the advent of the blocos afros. The carnival organization has won the respect of the public as one of the most respected institutions that promote black identity in Bahia. With some ambivalence, I read Filhos de Gandhi as a "passive" organization because this passivity in the context of creation may well be its strategy of survival and an opportunity to promote Afro-Brazilian religion in a strategic manner. While its passive politics has yet to change dramatically, there are indications that it cannot simply remain apolitical for too long, given the injection of new blood and young minds into the organization.

In *A Trajetória de Filhos de Gandhy* (2004) (Trajectory of Filhos de Gandhy), the Bahian Educational TV, in their series *Beleza Pura* (Total beauty), provides an overview of the origins and development of the carnival organization. Drawing upon comments from scholars such as Antônio Godi, Jaime Sodré, and Gilberto Gil, as well as a sampling of music recorded at the Concha Acústica and dedicated to the organization by popular musicians, such as "Axé da Lua" (Moon power) by Cacau da Bahia, "Ossain Irê" (All hail, healing goddess!) by Public Sunday, "Lenço Branco" (White handkerchief) by Boboco, "Filhos de Gandhi" by Edil Pacheco, and "Patuscada do Gandhi" (Gandhi's revel) by Gilberto Gil, among others, the video captures rare moments in the parades from 1983 through the 2000s. In addition, the video traces the history of the organization, the difficulties of Afro-Brazilians joining white elite groups, and the necessity of starting their own group in response to the prevailing racism of the time. Explaining the blue and white colors of Gandhi revelers' costumes as the colors of Ogum and Oxalá, respectively, the video highlights the characteristics of the organization, especially the percussion, songs, dances, and ijexá rhythms, which are "serene and not frenetic like *frevo* or thunderous like an *escola de samba*."[8] Gilberto Gil adds, rather emotively, "You feel all that tranquility, that shiver running through your body, taking hold of you. This is the spiritual side of *carnaval*, its balance."[9] Gil's emotive response is characteristic of how many perceive this uniquely sacred and profane organization as it leads revelers through the streets of Salvador, promoting peace and nonviolence. Other dissenting voices, however, feel the organization could do more to have a political impact in terms of moving toward political participation and agency.

Though the musical sample in A *Trajetória de Filhos de Gandhy* offers rare insights, with rare carnival footages, into the Gandhi organization as an icon, as a musical journey, and as a cultural phenomenon with reverberations throughout Brazil, a few famed tracks are not included, such as "Filhos de Gandhi" by Clara Nunes and "Filhos de Gandhi" by Gilberto Gil. However, these are quite intriguing and worthy of analysis. The homage by Nunes sounds like an oriki (praise-song) and enumerates the qualities of the group compared with other groups, such as Badauê, Ilê Aiê, Malê de Balê, and Ojú Obá. Nunes describes it as "a plaited sky / a sea of stars," the "fragility / of a suffered people," whose "rare beauty," "profound greatness," "daughters," and "grandchildren" have come to offer to Brazil a new ijexá rhythm through their music. What adds to the melody of the music is the fact that it is modeled after Filhos de Gandhi's unique liturgic rhythm that characterizes it as a pioneering afoxé. If Nunes enumerates other carnival groups to highlight the singularity *of Filhos de Gandhi*, Gil opts for the deities (Omolu, Ogum, Oxum, Oxumaré, Iansã, Iemanjá, chama Xangô, and Oxossi),calling them to assemble with everyone else to see the beauty of Filhos de Gandhi. So as not to leave anyone out of this rallying call, Gil also includes business entities, such as Ali Baba (nicknamed "the gentleman of Baghdad"), all God's children, and even "our Heavenly Father," who must all know that "on earth, it is carnival time," and it is time, indeed, to see Filhos de Gandhi. Both tracks, produced in different years by two iconic musicians, further highlight the significance of this famed organization to the world at large. What is commonly shared in the two musical tracks beyond their ijexá melody is the infusion of Yoruba words and names—which speaks to the pan-Yoruba roots of the organization and the strong influence of Candomblé in their carnival performance.

While there may be unpublished works that address Filhos de Gandhi as a separate entity or in comparison with other carnival groups, only a few published books are available for research. I have come to see in such rare books a gateway into the multiplicity of perspectives the organization engenders. Anísio Félix in *Filhos de Gandhi* (1987), Antônio Risério in *Carnaval Ijexá* (Ijexá carnival) (1981), and IPAC in *Desfile de Afoxés* (Parades by Afoxé groups) (2010), provide a panoramic history of the emergence of Afro-Bahian carnival by emphasizing the place of Filhos de Gandhi as well as other Yoruba-influenced groups such as Ilê Aiyê and Badauê, coupled with an anthology of Afro-Bahian musical poetry by such celebrities as Gilberto Gil, Caetano Veloso, and Paulinho Camafeu. The lack of critical works on these organizations is not due to lack of interest but rather because of the politics of publication as well as the need for potential authors to have assurance that the efforts would be worth their time. There is also ambivalence about the organization in terms of its neutral positioning when it comes to political agitation. The philosophy of peace that was negotiated since its formation in the mid-twentieth century may also explain the reluctance of the leadership to move beyond that "peaceful" and "passive" parade of an otherwise sacred organization on the street. Like many other more contemporary carnival groups, which have shifted their philosophies over time (in terms of marketing and survivalist strategies), including Olodum and Ilê Aiyê, Filhos de Gandhi may well be reaching a moment for rethinking its traditional position against politicization and social agitation.

Félix put together *Filhos de Gandhi* (1987) as a vital document for members and nonmembers alike. Indeed, it is a panoramic historical survey of the emergence of the organization. Yet, it is in this panorama that the full import of the organization lies, such as the circumstances of its emergence, its founding members, its development of different strategies and allegories, and ultimately how the organization moved from just a bloco or carnival group to a sacred-syncretized organization. Without any table of contents, this completely unpaginated book runs close to a hundred pages and is divided into two parts: "And the Dock Workers Created *Filhos de Gandhi*" and "Only the Makers Know How to Tell the History," which features sixteen depositions by founding members and a few ex-presidents. Coupled with a preface by Cid Teixeira, the book gives a firsthand primer into the beginnings of the afoxé group. Teixeira was a historian and an academic, whose collection of works *Salvador, Uma Viagem Fotográfica* (2017), edited by Fernando Oberlaender, was launched recently at the Shopping Barra. The collection, published by Caramurê Publicações, contains the works of the famed scholar, including *Vistas na Cidade da Bahia, Uma Visão Geral de Salvador*; *Cidade Alta*; *Cidade Baixa*; and *Transportes na Cidade da Bahia*. Teixeira's preface is incisive, as it captures the significance of the Gandhi organization as well as the value of Félix's efforts to reconstruct its history through the voices of past iconic members and leaders. The timing of the founding could not have been more opportune: dock workers were on strike against the economic recession in Brazil, Gandhi had been assassinated the year before, and there was a general atmosphere of tension and cumulative political agitations, leading to the creation of the group in 1949. Teixeira sums up the significance quite poetically:

> The rhythmic appeal was immense; the cultural heritage enormous, the stimulus, immeasurable. Time went by. There was a reward for the Afoxés and the Filhos de Gandhi collective who integrated themselves within the wave. They remain alive. The traditionalists complain of changes, the new blood comes with a carnivalesque delirium when admitted, the permanent investors take advantage, and the tourism-marketing industry exploits the situation. One thing is certain. The Filhos de Gandhi organization integrates itself more within the pulsating system than within the circulatory system of Bahian culture. It integrates itself from the heart. So quite visible, so well felt, so well documented, and so well analyzed by the text of Anísio Félix.[10]

While Teixeira's preface may have tried to give a balanced vision to the recurrent critiques that *the Filhos de Gandhi* organization is passive and apolitical, it does not lay these concerns to rest. Teixeira situates the organization within political agitations for change in Bahia, including the fact that some of the members joined the Brazilian Communist Party. This revelation is quite telling, but the organization today remains culturally and religiously symbolic rather than an effective, desirable, and pragmatic agent of change.

Of the fifty founding members of Filhos de Gandhi, only about a dozen are featured in this primer to the organization, including Djalma

Conceição, Lindolfo Ramos de Souza, Humberto Ferreira Café, Arivaldo Fagundes Perreira ("Carequinha"), Hamilton Ferreira Santos, Herondino Joaquim Ribeiro, Manoel Nicanor das Virgens, Manoel José dos Santos, Domiense Pereira Amorim, Eduarlino Crispiniano de Souza, Máximo Serafim Mendes, Nelson Ferreira dos Santos, Jaime Moreira de Pinho, Bráulino José do Bonfim, Hermes Agostinho dos Santos, and Almir Fialho. As much as these different perspectives document the individual experiences of the organization, praising it for creating a magical moment to register their aspirations and challenges, I find the deposition by Arivaldo Fagundes Pereira, otherwise known as "Carequinha," to be illustrative of balanced assessments of the organization. In addition to paying homage to its founding members, Pereira gives minute details of the dynamics of the group, including the achievements, challenges, joys, and frustrations regarding the group's current situation. He finds the younger generation more in charge than the elders, and the numbers of participants have increased dramatically—from a few hundred to thousands. Acknowledging the organization's religious syncretism as well as its nondiscriminatory policy, Pereira painstakingly and succinctly sums up his pride in an organization that does not perceive racial discrimination or choose to be conformist, tolerant, and passive despite racism:

> Everyone can parade with Gandhi; if not, we would be dealing with internal and external racism and we abhor this kind of thing. That is why Gandhi does not participate in the black movement. Besides, all classes of workers participate. We never had any separatism. . . . From the first year, we came out rather eclectic. No point discriminating or separating. If the movement did not start with poor and modest folks like the dock workers, we would not have been able to welcome people of all races. We are all brothers, children of God, whether Catholic, syncretic, or devotees of Candomblé.[11]

Beyond this official ideological position on syncretism within the group, Pereira celebrates how the people embrace each other and feel good when they see Gandhi parade on the streets of Salvador, from Terreiro de Jesus through Avenida Sete in Salvador. Seeing Brazilians, foreigners, Blacks, and whites filled with emotion meant for Pereira that Filhos de Gandhi is "in the blood of the people." Pereira also shares his music "Papai Ojô," which was eventually recorded by Gilberto Gil as "Batucada de Gandhi." Pereira provides vital information regarding the order of sacred songs that members sing during the carnival procession: opening with sacrifice to Exu, then chants for Ogunedé, Xangô, Yansã, Oxum, Sirê, and Oxalá, with which the processional singing ends. Overall, for Pereira, despite the organization's growth and disorganization, on the streets Gandhi is all about peace, joy, and respect to families. One could only wish this utopian vision of human solidarity was shared by all Brazilians. However, that is surely not the case.

In his own more theoretical vision, Risério in *Carnaval Ijexá* (1987) performs a conceptualization of the re-Africanization processes of the blocos afros and afoxés. Though the title leans more to the afoxés, the actual contents of the book are complimentary to both groups. Divided into twenty-one short chapters that appear to be previously published journal articles, this rich compendium highlights Afro-Bahian carnival. Of these chapters, three are particularly useful for our purposes: "Axé do Gandhi" (Gandhi's power), "Orixás no Carnaval" (Yoruba deities in carnival), and "Axé Odara" (Good energy), which constitutes a mini-anthology of Afro-Bahian poetry. *Carnaval Ijexá* synthesizes the journey of young Afro-Bahians in the process of reacting to the tense racial climate in Brazil only to find that white hegemony dominated freed slaves who were struggling to integrate into a racist society. Drawing upon the dynamic wave of the civil rights movement in the United States, as well as the resonant influence of Black Soul and Black Power movements on Afro-Ijexá sensibility, Risério dissects, in "Axé do Gandhi," how this outreach to ancestral Africa is an aftermath of feelings of alienation from Africa and oppression in the New World. The consciousness of Africanity, through gestures, attitudes, wearing of African clothes, plaiting hair, and inserting cowries within them, all speaks to identifying with Africa as a source of symbolic power and resistance to racism. Risério credits Gil for the major resurgence of Filhos de Gandhi when he returned from exile in the late 1970s. According to Gil:

> I went to meet with about twenty frustrated members of *Filhos de Gandhi* who had their instruments on the ground around Praça da Sé. They no longer had financial resources nor did they have the energy to continue being involved in Bahian carnival. I asked them to let me join the group. It

was like something devotional, a kind of promise, the will
to put my prestige on the line for a beautiful cause like the
afoxé. . . . And, last year (1980), they grew to be a thousand
members.[12]

Given the generosity of Gil, Risério compellingly associates the musician
with the Yoruba warrior deity Xangô, who is known to be in favor of
justice, dignity, and freedom.

Yet, it is not just with Filhos de Gandhi that Gil sacrificed his
reputation. When it comes to the appropriation of the orixás or the
sacred in Bahian carnival, Gil is a constant presence and advocate.
In "Orixás no Carnaval," Risério engages the musician and gets him
to comment on the relationship of Afro-Brazilians with their African
past as they employ their religious tradition to reconstitute daily rituals
and ceremonies through dance: "Supported by the religious tradition
of black Africa in its Western version, displaying dances, rhythms, and
chants from Yoruba liturgy, and at the same time, inserted within a
delirious context of carnival, the *afoxés* became free-moving entities
within a frontier, linking through initiate and mundane paths, the two
dialectically complementary worlds: the sacred and the profane."[13] While
membership requirements of Filhos de Gandhi used to be rigorous, with
the expectation that members would have some connection with Candomblé, times have changed. Nowadays, potential members are young,
flexible, and not necessarily associated with Candomblé. Risério calls
this antiquated expectation a "mystical transaction of the *afoxés*."[14] The
rites of passage of the organization also include a religious ceremony that
involves offering a sacrifice to Exú, after which the group begins singing
and dancing, thus initiating its carnivalesque peregrination through the
streets of Salvador. Beyond the Gandhi group, Risério also touches upon
other groups, such as Badauê, Ilê Aiyê, and Malê Debalê. These three
groups are also influenced by Candomblé in various degrees. While many
carnival groups continue to argue against the influence of the sacred,
I believe that there is enough evidence in their ritual performance to
indicate that sacredness is alive and well in carnival performance.

The closing section of *Carnaval Ijexá* is a befitting homage to
Afro-Bahian music and religiosity. It assembles a plethora of iconic
Afro-Bahian musicians, including Caetano Veloso, Gilberto Gil, Moraes
Moreira, and Paulinho Camafeu, among others. What the musical texts
have in common is the shared Yoruba religious rootedness, as Yoruba dei-

ties and words are evoked as a form of solidarity with the land of origins as well as the continuum that has been reconstructed and syncretized. Beyond celebrating carnival groups such as Filhos de Gandhi, Ilê Aiyê, Badauê (as in famed songs like "Ilê Aiyê" by Caetano Veloso, "Filhos de Gandhi" by Gilberto Gil, and "Magia Badauê" by Moa do Catendê), the texts also touch upon signs of re-Africanization, such as the plaiting of hair in "Beleza Negra" by Milton de Jesus and the valorization of the drum over electric guitars in "O bater do tambor" by Caetano Veloso. Of these encyclopedic poems, one is perhaps even more sensitive and electrifying than others. "Beleza Pura" by Caetano Veloso alternates material value with material culture and the beauty that transcends all. Veloso succeeds in enumerating values of Afro-consciousness, such as "black skin," "hair braiding," "elegance," and "culture," which money cannot easily buy. As a rich text on the uniqueness of Bahia as a melting pot of many cultures, Risério's *Carnaval Ijexá* singularly pays homage to carnival by highlighting its potential to be sacred, popular, and political in Bahia—while not neglecting the political and cultural movements of the United States that have influenced the Afro-Brazilian agitation for true "racial democracy."

As the most recent publication exclusively dedicated to afoxés, IPAC's *Desfile de Afoxés* (2010) provides a unique opportunity to access one of the most mysterious carnival organizations in Bahia. In its five-part structure, it brings together studies on methodology by Ednalva Queiroz, on historical analysis by Magnair Barbosa, and on ethnography by Nívea Alves dos Santos, as well as depositions provided by the main afoxé groups in Salvador and a declaration report on the preservation of afoxé parades as cultural patrimony of Bahia. This invaluable book also contains a DVD with the same title. The video showcases interviews with the historian Jaime Sodré and leaders of Filhos de Gandhi, Filhos de Congo, Filhas de Gandhi, Filhas de Oxum, Filhas de Olorum, Pai Burukô, and Afoxé Korin Efan, among others. The different organizations emphasize the connection they have with Candomblé as well as the significance of the creation of afoxés as the first stage of the re-Africanization process in Bahia. Afoxés were also noted as preserving entities when it comes to nature. The use of cheap lavender derived from alfazema (an aromatic plant of the lavandula type) during carnival also speaks to the appropriation of certain elements during carnival to pay homage to nature.

The methodology section accounts for the process that led to the application and approval of the carnival parades of Filhos de Gandhi as immaterial culture of Bahia through historical, symbolic, and documental approaches that involve archival research at the headquarters of main afoxés in Salvador as well as interviews with their leaders and with scholars of culture. It was remarkable to note in the historical study section the evolution of a dozen afoxé carnival groups, from Embaixada Africana (1895), Pândegos da África (1896), Império da África (1898), and Filhos da África (1895) through Filhos de Gandhi (1949). The study also reveals the racist pronouncements of Nina Rodrigues about African descendants, whom he referenced as "uncultured Africans who were enslaved in Brazil."[15] Rodrigues also denigrated the Afro-religious entities as inferior in comparison to Catholicism. Resultantly, these so-called enslaved Africans were not allowed to join the white elite carnival groups, and this event set the stage for starting their own Africa-derived groups such as the afoxés and, much later, the blocos afros. While the ethnographic study traces the Yoruba people, especially the Ijexá ethnic group, as having come in limited numbers from the present Ondo State of Nigeria, it also highlights their religious impact and how they deployed it to preserve their culture through myths and rites that solidified their vital force and dignity. To capture the totality of the value system of the Yoruba, the ethnography also involves interviews with the leadership of the afoxés to understand their own memories in the reconstruction of the cultural legacy of the afoxés. In its historical and documental value, *Desfile de Afoxés* promises to remain one of the essential references on older carnival groups, but it could have been enriched by gauging the perspectives of scholars outside of the limited administrative circuit of IPAC, such as Antônio Risério, João Reis, Jefferson Bacelar, Gilberto Gil, and Caetano Veloso, among others.

Contemporary Politics and Legacy

Filhos de Gandhi celebrated its seventieth anniversary in 2019, so it is a critical moment to assess its impact and legacy in the Afro-Brazilian community and, by extension, in Brazil. To project into the future, it is necessary to look to the past. The sixtieth anniversary was a cue to what was to come in 2019. Salvador holds a Guinness World Record for throwing the biggest street party on earth. From Terreiro de Jesus to Campo Grande and to Barra, thousands of Filhos de Gandhi merrymakers take to the streets, choreographed like a sea of flowing white cloth, and enchanting with song and dance for the orixás. As they bridge the sacred and the profane, they strategically circumvent the repression that had been rampant since the mid-nineteenth century against Black movements and Black political organizing. Dressed up to pay homage to their Indian patron, Gandhi, an icon of nonviolence, they manipulate African rituals by showcasing them on the streets of Salvador as if they were profane activities. For the most part, Filhos de Gandhi has maintained its message of peace as a philosophy of life, but within this apolitical stance lies subtle politicking to keep Afro-Brazilian culture alive. One point of criticism levied on the group over the years is its nonacceptance of women in their midst. This led a group of women to launch Filhas de Gandhi (1979).[16] Through symbolism of doves, goats, elephants, and Yoruba deities whose praise they sing, they air their consciousness of Indo-African identity, which signals the multicultural positioning of the group. By transforming the transnational into the local, Filhos de Gandhi appeals to all generations by representing something profound in Brazilian culture. The theme of the sixtieth anniversary was about how the world needs love. While this is a compelling message, it also limits the effectiveness of the group, as love is an emotion that cannot be accounted for, controlled, or quantified. Such strategy is not pragmatic, as it conditions the proponents to passivity that may not effect social change. In other words, Filhos de Gandhi must begin to rethink its strategy given the changing political times Brazil is facing.

Choosing the subtheme of "From the Sea Shores to the World," the sixty-ninth anniversary took place in 2018. With close to five thousand members, Filhos de Gandhi hit the streets of Salvador with yet another year of celebration of peace, love, and faith, traversing the Dodô Circuit (Barra-Ondina) on Monday, February 12, 2018, and returning to the Osmar Macedo Circuit (Campo Grande/Avenida) on Tuesday, February 13, 2018. For the first time in Gandhi's history, a symbol of a white dove, measuring six by five meters, was integrated into the procession. The president credited the dove to two artists from Rio de Janeiro and Paratins. Arany Santana, the state secretary of culture, made a striking comment about Gandhi: "*Filhos de Gandhi* patrimonially reclaimed *afoxé*. It is a resistant carnival group whose politics is the quest for peace."[17] Of the five thousand Gandhi revelers, about 15 percent were tourists— this is an indication that tourists are no longer satisfied with the same observatory position they have always had; they now want to be more involved and to gain a different experience through participation in the eccentricities of Bahian culture. The Bahian governor, Rui Costa, has promised to support the construction of a Gandhi memorial that will involve consolidating the major archives of the Gandhi organization, reconstructing its history, and commissioning a historian to execute the project. Another novelty in Bahia is the Casa de Carnaval (House of carnival), which opened in 2018 and houses memorabilia and publications on Afro-Bahian carnival.

In a regenerative moment, several iconic musicians, including Gil, Brown, and Vercillo, produced an album in conjunction with the Filhos de Gandhi. The artistic director of the organization, Carlinhos Brown, stated that the album contains twelve tracks in the ijexá rhythm, and it was meant to revitalize the organization before its seventieth anniversary.

The main theme of Gandhi's carnival in 2018, "African Diaspora: The Crossing Did Not Weaken Me, It Made Me Stronger," appeals to the apoliticism of the carnival group and is worth deconstructing for its symbolism. The African diaspora, the dispersal of millions of Africans and their enslavement in the New World, was a painful event. By taking up this subject from a new perspective, Filhos de Gandhi may be responding to the accusations that it is passive, peaceful, and apolitical and also missing vital opportunities to make itself relevant in Brazilian politics. As Arany Santana mentioned previously, the promotion of peace among all people may be political because the alternative is war and conflict. Yet, it is not sufficient to be symbolic but Filhos de Gandhi should put its prestige on the line for political causes that impact Afro-Brazilians, such as agitation for more political participation through education and reorientation. On the symbolic plane, the many icons can be approximated as follows: (1) Gilberto Gil is association with Ogum as a patron deity that becomes a central motif on the carnival costume; (2) an homage to Mahatma Gandhi is located directly under Gil as the symbolic Indian patron; (3) Xangô is located to the right of the design, with its double-edged axe enlarged for effect, while the symbol of justice lies right on top of the axe as a complementary motif of justice; and (4) on the left of the design is a cluster of images lined up diagonally, including a map of the African continent with the name of the association encircling it, a tortoise to symbolize age and wisdom, a mask referencing the ancestors, and a fish in a quadrangle with oceanic motifs behind it (as if it's swimming across the Atlantic or is the embodiment of waterine deities, such as Yemanjá and Oxum), as well as adinkra symbols that catch African motifs from whence they emerge. Surrounding the design is a total of seven white doves that may be interpreted as circling peace and announcing victory over the travails of the arduous journey across the Atlantic. In closing this segment with this textile-related analysis, one can surmise that Filhos de Gandhi's politics is more subtle and symbolic than aggressive and pragmatic. One would have to take more time to closely scrutinize what has worked for the organization in terms of political relevance and legacy in the course of its seventy years of integrating the sacred with the profane.

Cortejo Afro: Masking Politics, Embodying the Spirits

Every organization's mission statement is an ample indication of its philosophy of life. Cortejo Afro's politics lies in reaffirming values and aspects of black culture in Bahia while incorporating new elements to ensure the growth of local communities in the twenty-first century. The organization seeks to reinterpret the defining rhythms and beats that make Bahia unique in its ethical and aesthetic significance, especially within carnivalesque manifestations. As a bloco afro that emerged from the authentic setting of an Afro-religious temple, Ilê Axé Oyá, which is led by the Iyalorixá (priestess) Mãe Santinha, Cortejo Afro projects an image of a "vanguardist" establishment that enjoys setting the tone for other carnival groups. The organization is noted for its opulent costumes and exuberant choreography, which is rich in Africa-influenced movements. The president, artist, and designer, Alberto Pitta, has over thirty years of experience in creating images for Afro-carnival organizations. In particular, Pitta has fifteen years of experience as a producer for the Olodum carnival. By favoring Oxalá-derived colors of white and silver, the organization signals allegiance to the Yoruba supreme deity—who is dressed predominantly in white. Likewise, the introduction of the big umbrellas extols the virtues of African kingdoms in their exquisite beauty, such as the kingdoms of Benin, Songhai, Oyo, and Zulu, among others. As a testament to its growing fame and popularity, it has benefitted from special appearances by music stars, such as Caetano Veloso, Gerônimo, Arto Lindsay, Davi Moraes, Margareth Menezes, Daniela Mercury, Saulo, Gilberto Gil, and É o Tchan. As the organization promotes Afro-Brazilian culture through the appreciation of Yoruba deities, its broader politics lie in resistance to exclusionism by integrating Candomblé rhythms into popular music with an added creative value in its innovative costumes.

In other words, by masking politics, Cortejo Afro embodies the spirits of the African ancestors and their deities.

To ensure the celebration of its twentieth anniversary in 2018, Cortejo Afro made a passionate appeal to potential revelers to raise R$60,000 (reais), of which R$36,000 (61 percent) had been attained by February 16, 2018. As a last-resort marketing strategy, the advertising caption read: "Can you imagine *Cortejo Afro* not being able to parade to celebrate its 20th anniversary this year? It is important to keep the roots and essences of Afro-Bahian carnival groups alive. We are counting on you!" While it is not clear how often such desperate calls are made by carnival groups to the community, it shows the degree of financial struggle these groups experience every year—especially those who are yet to be solvent and established. The rewards, depending on contributions, are as follows: (1) a donation of R$10 gets acknowledgment on social media; (2) R$20 receives a digital "godfather" seal; (3) R$40 qualifies for entrance to the rehearsal of Cortejo Afro; (4) R$100 gets three tickets to a rehearsal of Cortejo Afro; (5) R$200 receives one carnival costume to parade with Cortejo Afro; (6) R$500 receives two carnival costumes to parade with Cortejo Afro, plus two meters of textile; (7) R$800 receives four carnival costumes to parade with Cortejo Afro, plus two meters of textile; (8) R$1,500 receives eight carnival costumes to parade with Cortejo Afro, plus two meters of textile; (9) R$3,000 receives a molded effigy of the organization plus four meters of textile assigned by Alberto Pitta; and (10) R$25,000 receives a 1x1-meter painting that is autographed by Pitta. This is a unique campaign that exposes some of the challenges faced by carnival organizations, including the very top players who enjoy funding from public and private organizations. Instead of protesting the lack of governmental funding, the organization opted for pragmatism by applying an aggressive business campaign strategy that yielded over half of the set goal—and that may have made a difference in celebrating its twentieth anniversary.

Negotiating Cultural and Professional Syncretism

It was a relief to see the organization successfully participate in the 2018 Afro-Bahian carnival despite financial challenges. Thematically inspired by the music of Caetano Veloso, specifically "Milagres do Povo" (Miracles of the people), the dancing sea of empowered bodies revitalized by the energy of the deities first appeared disorganized, then turned out to be professionally choreographed by a few excellent dancers that give the group an air of a well-rehearsed sacred bacchanal. Homage to the deities was obvious due to the dancing movements that captured their characteristics, as well as to the infusion of ijexá beats that echo orixá worship. The energy is transferred to the audience, as if exchanging a mutual moment of visitation from the deities. As the feeling of being possessed by spirits that find transient home to manifest their synergies of communication between the ancestral and the living, participants also preserve African heritage and African identities, which were eroded and syncretized over the years of repression and resistance in the New World. Ancestral bodies, now lacking physical bodies, find in human bodies an abode of visitation to commingle with the living. In other words, the dancing bodies during carnival procession are no longer ordinary human bodies but possessed sacred bodies. Mixing Candomblé with other Western traditions of modern dance and jazz, Clyde Morgan, a contracted Federal University of Bahia professor of dance, along with his group of disciples, they translated energies from African American dance moves into Bahian rhythmic swing. Known in Pirajá as a community-based entity with a religious penchant, Cortejo Afro embodies the best in religious syncretism as well as cultural hybridity as it unites two complementary and sometimes fluid poles of the sacred and the profane. The organization thus becomes a dancing spirit as well as a hybrid cross-over appeal for the younger generation.

Alberto Pitta is considered by Caetano Veloso to be "the most creative artist that is operating in this immense movement that fills the streets with the beauty of carnival. Pioneer of Afro-Bahian textiles, he is a thinker when it comes to the process that makes all of his characteristics as an artist fine and refined."[18] Pitta occupies a central place in the organization and marketing of Cortejo Afro, as an Afro-carnival organization that takes pride in the community of Pirajá and, by extension, Bahia. During his thirty years of creative artistic research, he has been involved in the creation of Afro-Bahian textiles for many carnival organizations, through symbols, African rootedness, and inspiration in the orixá tradition. Having grown up under the influence of Candomblé faith, he has been immersed in the values of Afro-Brazilian religiosity that has helped many Black cultural organizations resist discrimination and fight for cultural freedom and political participation. Such religious values that are predicated on political resistance and cultural syncretism permit Pitta the ability to interpret hidden sacred codes and symbols. Through his cultural activism in the artistic and cultural scene of the Afro-carnival organizations, such as the afoxés, blocos afros and blocos de índio, Pitta reenvisions the empowerment of Afro-Brazilian communities and individuals. For twenty years now, Pitta has focused on the artistic and conceptual production of the Cortejo Afro carnival organization. Beyond his active involvement in the Afro-Bahian carnival scene since the early 1990s, he has been invited to exhibit his artistic works in Germany, Angola, United States, England, France, and Brazil during national and international festivals. As an art educator, Pitta has contributed to the growth of the art scene in Bahia by working at the Odoyá Institute, where he teaches sculpture. At the Projeto Axé, he served as the secretary of art education, culture, and aesthetics.[19] Through the interface of syncretism and professionalism, Pitta succeeds in making himself a singular bridge between the many factions of Bahian cultural tapestry.

In an extensive interview conducted by "Nós Transatlânticos" (We the transatlantics), entitled "Cortejo Afro and the Rereading of African Heritage" (2016), Pitta provides a succinct background of the emergence of Cortejo Afro in the context of Candomblé and as a community project. The interview gives insight into the rebelliousness and social activism of the Pitta family as a whole. He traces his activism back to his grandfather who was an activist and was always under surveillance by the government. Because of this persecution, he lived a clandestine life to evade the probing eye of police and the government. Pitta inherited the militancy of his grandfather and the spiritual influence of his mother, Mãe Santinha (Anísia da Rocha Pitta e Silva), who is well respected in the community of Pirajá.[20] Pitta notes that the family moved from São Caetano, where the priestess set up her Candomblé house. Though the family had misgivings about that move from an urban to a rural area, in retrospect, Pitta feels that she was acting reasonably at the time. Thanks to that move, the family was able to build a fascinating structure that is similar to that of the Casa do Benin in Pelourinho, a complex structure with some African motifs in its architecture. It took a while to build, but it was well worth the effort. The creative artist hints at the unconscious modeling of its Cortejo Afro organization after that of Ilê Aiyê. He notes quite transparently that gone are the days of exclusively thinking of the organization as a "community project" in the context of the 1970s, when Ilê Aiyê was about community organizing and fighting racial discrimination. For Pitta, the Ilê Aiyê model was quite radical and was an entirely different mission. Pitta realized that Cortejo Afro was born within the entrepreneurial "show business" (performance) idea. He reminisces that when Mãe Hilda, Vovô's mother, chose to put her religious "throne" on top of the carnival float and sit through the street procession of Ilê Aiyê, it was a way to legitimize the Candomblé faith during carnival celebration. It was a radical gesture because Candomblé had existed before the advent of the carnival groups. Such a political gesture by Mãe Hilda was also a way to legitimize the mission of the Afro-Bahian carnival groups for cultural political participation through carnival. In sum, Cortejo Afro entered carnival as a form of business.

Though Cortejo Afro attempts to duplicate the efforts of Ilê Aiyê, it does recognize that contemporary politics calls for a different strategy, one in which business must be part of the ideological principle. Pitta confirms that fashion design was part of the attraction of Cortejo Afro. For this reason, artists such as Caetano Veloso, Margareth Menezes, and Daniela Mercury have enjoyed performing with the group. He sees Cortejo Afro as a vanguard organization falling somewhere between culture and religiosity. He also pays homage to his mother, whose patron deity is Iansã (Santa Barbara), the deity of the winds and tempest. Given that most blocos afros and afoxés were born within Candomblé, the faith has served as inspiration for aesthetic agency and social transformation. It is in this regard that Cortejo Afro is syncretized between religiosity and profanity and between community empowerment and a business enterprise. Alberto Pitta has said that Africans who were brought to Brazil were culturally and materially rich and not poor. In other words, it was the Portuguese who made Afro-Brazilians poor by exploiting their riches in Africa as well as exploiting their bodies and minds in the New World. The point here is that most people who parade with Cortejo Afro are from the lower classes and, though mostly uneducated, the signs and symbols on the creative costumes express a thousand words and relate to the daily lives of the revelers. They can feel beautiful and proud, just like Ilê Aiyê members feel a sense of human dignity through their participation in the organization. Invoking the image of the Navios Negreiros as conceived by Castro Alves (a nineteenth-century poet), Pitta suggests that the slave ship image is a double-edged metaphor: evoking both serpent and riches. On the one hand, the slave ship carried life and wealth (kings and queens); on the other, the journey was tortuous to the extent that some lost their lives to the "serpent" carrying them in its belly. "The slave ship is ultimately a symbol of dislocation," affirms Pitta. Fascinated by the accomplishments of Ilê Aiyê and drawing inspiration from its politics, the artist concludes with his admiration for the organization he seems to have modeled Cortejo Afro after: "Ilê Aiyê was not just a carnival organization when it started. It remains political in order to make Bahia what it is today; in essence, it is a group promoting Afro-Brazilian values and dignity. The re-Africanization of the city of Bahia through Ilê Aiyê makes Bahia very unique."[21] While there is a lot to compare between Cortejo Afro and Ilê Aiyê, the reluctance of the two organizations to see parallels makes such an effort a deferred dream in the immediate.

In her own study of race consciousness, diaspora, the place of Bahian identity in the consideration of Afro-Bahian carnival, and W. E. B. DuBois's theory of double consciousness, Deinya Phenix suggests that the influence of the blocos afros is not as radical as it was in the 1970s. They are now more cooperative as they compromise their ideals in exchange for funding from public and private organizations. Drawing upon the Duboisian sense of "contempt and pity" that comes from being torn between two selves, Phenix argues that Afro-carnival groups are constrained by funding and may actually have an ambiguous attitude toward their moral ideals and the financial realities that challenge their survival:

> As blocos afro have become more accepted and appreciated, they now have to be content with the 'contempt and pity' of Brazilian society in more integrated ways, like engaging the urban space that they previously were excluded from. In addition to carrying on the revolutionary musical and aesthetic activities of the cultural programs in support of Afro-Brazilian communities, they must now contend with increasing status and commercial value as blocos may respond to pressure toward more commercially viable presentation."[22]

When one contextualizes Cortejo Afro in this Duboisian theory of "double consciousness," one perceives the dilemma as cutting across all the carnival groups. On the one hand, Cortejo Afro, according to Pitta, is about taking personal aesthetics ("elegantly sophisticated" per their motto) that are inspired in Candomblé to the streets through exuberant textiles, choreographic movements, and Africa-derived music and percussion. On the other hand, the organization must deal with the business side of carnival in terms of economic survival. The contradiction comes from that very illusory idea that merely taking Africa-derived culture to the street changes the status quo of the people. Art may well be a way to improve self-esteem and change perceptions, but when the carnival is over the people return to their daily routine of deprivation, poverty, and struggle.

Returning to the 2011 carnival in which Cazuza and Gil participated as musical stars, Pitta evokes the slogan, "After the slave ships, other currents," to counter the trauma of the Atlantic crossing. Notwithstanding the sacrifice of depending on influential friends and donors to ensure the continuity of parading during carnival, Cortejo Afro seems to be satisfied with using art as an instrument of empowerment for the people. It is a way to confront the social inequalities that keep Afro-Brazilians timid, subdued, and marginalized. By developing a sense of community, as well as a sense of empowerment and pride, Cortejo Afro keeps hope alive when it comes to symbologies of freedom despite its pragmatic focus on finances.

Despite the accomplishments of Cortejo Afro, a homophobic segment of the community insinuates that it is a rallying point for the LGBTQ community in Salvador. While there is really no evidence of such a claim, publicity for the rehearsals leading to carnival in February 2018 states: "O ensaio da banda é reconhecido por ser um dos ensaios mais friendly da cidade e costuma ser *point de encontro do público LGBT*" (The rehearsal of the performing group is known for being one of the most friendly rehearsals of the city and normally serves as the *meeting point for the LGBTQ community*).[23] The addition of the "LGBTQ community" may well be a way of reaching out to a broader audience and the artistic community of Bahia, but it also signals an affective disposition toward the group. Regardless of the truth of that connection, it neither negates the contributions of Cortejo Afro to the promotion of Afro-Bahian rich culture nor does it represent a legitimate cause for concern. All human beings deserve to express themselves and participate in the defense of equal rights and should not be marginalized due to their sexual orientation. The sexual discrimination has implications for social acceptability and future dynamics. If there is a shared vision for cultural awareness, political participation, and equality among people, personal differences should not create divisions. The collective action against racial discrimination is the foremost mission of all race-conscious people. By reconciling differences, whether real or artificial, well-meaning individuals seek the good in every human being. The mission of Cortejo Afro is of a higher priority than the insinuation of homosexuality—which has neither impact nor implication for the cultural and political transformation of the Pirajá community that is primarily served by the organization.

Cultural Politics and Community Impact

The wave of cultural revitalization that hit the city of Salvador in the 1990s under the governorship of Antônio Magalhães also impacted neighboring communities of Bahia. At the time, Bahian leaders adopted a model that led to the forcible expulsion of the former dwellers of Pelourinho (a metropolitan cultural center). These people were depicted as derelicts and the dregs of the society: prostitutes, homeless people, and drunks. Governmental powerbrokers subsequently handed over the revitalized space to cultural entities with "touristic" and business interests, such as blocos afros (Filhos de Gandhi, Olodum, and Ilê Aiyê) and international cultural "houses" like Benin and Nigeria. The rationale of such a public policy may be pragmatic and commercial rather than political and cultural. While the strategies of social integration may have included culture, it is somewhat isolated and not all-inclusive because there are still communities suffering from poverty and neglect. Cortejo Afro, for example, provides workshops for the youngsters of Pirajá, who learn how to make carnival costumes. As a result, culture begins to be integrated with the politics of community development, which has concrete implications for individual professional growth, empowerment, and a sense of pride in Afro-Brazilian identity. As the motto of the organization aptly affirms: "O Cortejo Afro surgiu da necessidade de reafirmação dos valores e aspectos da cultura negra na Bahia, respeitando a diversidade e incorporando novos elementos visando o crescimento das comunidades do século XXI" (Cortejo Afro emerged from the necessity for the reaffirmation of aspects of Black cultural values in Bahia, respecting diversity and incorporating elements that seek development of twenty-first-century communities).[24] Cortejo Afro has done more than respond to concerns about the predominance of Axé music by reestablishing the African identity of carnival. It has, in addition to reinstating pride in African heritage, culture, and standards of beauty in the local celebration of carnival, contributed to the development of the Pirajá community through local development projects and activities.

' A close analysis of the trajectory of Cortejo Afro in Afro-Brazilian carnival reveals an inextricable relationship between cultural performance and social agency. In his own self-assessment as the president of the organization, Pitta situates his entry into the "business" as a passage via Olodum Afro-carnival group, which he left in 1997. The following year Cortejo Afro was formed. For Pitta, "From Paul Simon to Michael Jackson, I was directly part of the life, aesthetics, art, and culture of Olodum; learning and teaching young blacks in Pelourinho, including João Jorge, who was young at the time."[25] This assertion legitimizes Pitta's fifteen years of experience with Olodum and his decision to start Cortejo Afro based on his experience of artistic production for Olodum Carnival as director of art and aesthetics. It was somewhat of a social mobilization as well as a personal decision to help develop his community. Pitta regrets the organizational failure of a number of blocos afros and afoxés that led to their exit from the carnival circuits, but he recognizes it as part of the unforeseen consequences of any cultural enterprise that depends on public and private funding.

' In commemoration of its fifteenth anniversary, Cortejo Afro honored its mission to recuperate the lost colors of Afro-Bahian carnival. Unlike the era of the 1970s that Pitta recalls, when revelers remember each community decorating and cleaning their homes, as well as preparing for carnival, times have changed. Gone are the days of rushing into the streets with the expectation of seeing the fireworks that inaugurated the first parade of King Momo. Nowadays, however, Thursday is reserved for the coming out of the schools of samba, including Chiclete com Banana and Filhos de Bell, among others. Inspired by the deity of iron in Yoruba mythology, Ogum, Cortejo Afro chose the theme "men of steel" as a symbolic pretext to celebrate iron in Africa. The theme celebrates iron as it relates to technology and to the knowledge of African engineers, who have understood the utility of iron and steel since the fifteenth century. These were Afro-Brazilian ancestors or Bantu people. Reflecting on the aesthetic and community impact of Cortejo Afro during its fifteen years of existence, Pitta reminds us that it was the center of youth activity, despite their marginalized conditions:

> This is what *Cortejo* is about. It is a cultural organization (*bloco*) that is daring in artistic installations, in aesthetic interventions, in which the youths of the periphery appreciate what they see when *Cortejo* startles them in terms of

a unique way to parade. This touches me profoundly, as it touched people way back in the 1970s. Certainly, even if we cannot measure it precisely, I am sure the youths are touched because I understand that art is the singular means for us to improve our lives, our community.[26]

Cortejo Afro's priorities are as follows: (1) to seek inspiration in Afro-Brazilian religiosity; (2) to redefine Afro-Bahian carnival through artistic agency; (3) to connect artistic production with community development; (4) to empower the community through social transformation and growth; and (5) to invest in the youth as the key to the future through whom the politics of participation, cultural freedom, and economic access must be redefined and appropriated. The future starts today in the vision of Cortejo Afro. By targeting the youth and empowering them to feel self-esteem and pride, the organization aims at preparing them for a certain and fulfilling future.

When the association first began, the carnival project was the main attraction and was all about organizing things "on the go," often at the last minute. However, this fluid way of doing things is no longer tenable. As Pitta explains, Cortejo Afro spends about a million reais annually (about $330,000 US dollars) to hold the event. This may appear to be a lot of money for one carnival group, but it is barely enough—and, at times, not even enough for just the basic necessities. Such a figure is necessary because the audience that Cortejo Afro attracts is a mixed one: from the professor-academic, graduate students, and intellectuals to illiterates. As a result, not everyone has the same consumption power, and the organization must seek external grants to make ends meet by appealing to both public and private donors, like the Ministry of Culture and business enterprises. Such a dynamic approach requires a super-elaborated project in which the concept, the history, and the budget mesh with what Pitta calls the "Law of Incentive" to appeal to potential supporting agencies. There was a year in which the theme was "House, Meat, and Housing," in which the organization abolished the idea of the "chord" normally used to separate members from the public during carnival; instead, it was an artificial divide using artificial "closes" to keep people from joining from outside. This was a smart solution as the entity saved money by not having to hire security people to control the chords.

When it comes to marginalization, racial discrimination is not the only cause. At times, medical issues might also contribute to marginalization. One year, Cortejo Afro came up with the theme "Prayers, Blessings, and Sympathies," during which albinos were invited to be part of the parade. This idea came from the African legend that albinos were special beings dedicated to Oxalá (supreme deity). The organization, in its research, also found that albinoism (deficient melanin pigmentation) is a serious issue throughout Africa but especially in Angola. For some, the problem is so severe that some are only able to come out at night, for it is difficult to see during the day because of the sun and how it affects their skin due to their deficient melanin pigmentation. According to Pitta:

> I went to an association of albinos in Salvador and I was so surprised by what I saw. They told us stories about how there can never be two albinos in a bus. Have you ever seen two albinos in a bus? They say when one enters and finds that one albino was already in the bus, the other one gets out. And this calls attention to a number of issues. We started to find out that there were black and white albinos. Albinos who are children of black parents and albinos who are children of white parents. We found out a lot of things within this albino culture and we took our time to make this information public through carnival. *Cortejo Afro* took 30 albinos to the streets. People even thought they were Germans but I had to explain to them: "Oh no, they are not Germans, they are truly albinos."[27]

Such is the effort of the organization to touch the consciousness of people from all walks of life.

The variety of themes calls for a creative imagination. Beyond albinos, Amerindians have also been showcased to highlight the genocide perpetrated on their people in the Americas. This theme was an interesting celebration of the organization's tenth anniversary. During this period it was discovered that an Amerindian named Galdino was burned alive at a bus stop in Brasília by middle-class youngsters. The idea also paid homage to the Indian Carnival Groups (blocos de índios) by recuperating their history. The organization based its research on a book by Dee Brown, *Bury My Heart at Wounded Knee: An Indian History of the American West* (2007), which recounts the brutality of the Wild West in American history and how Native Americans suffered terribly under the colonial regime.

Pitta was enamored by the year 2009, when the organization's theme was "water." It was a rainy year, so the theme worked out as anticipated. People even found it hilarious and joked: "Pitta, for God's sake, do not name your theme for next year a 'stone'; for if it rained this way when it is water, imagine what can happen."[28] Based on the metaphor of water, the theme was better developed as, "The Door of No Return: The Ship's Umbilical, An African Odyssey," which was a way of speaking about the Atlantic passage of the slave ships. In other words, Cortejo Afro saw in the slave ship a symbol of dislocation. From that thematic treatment, the organization also addressed the Benin ethnic group, the Jeje. Using a serpent as metaphor, members all dressed in a serpent motif. It was quite elaborate and expensive. Unlike other organizations, which produce two-hundred-page research studies on their theme and distribute it to the public, Cortejo Afro talks *with* the people and, after gaining their insights, comes up with a related carnival theme. Thus, people's opinions matter a lot. On one occasion, the organization came up with the creative idea of using the body as a "textile." Other compelling themes include the 2012 event, when Caetano Veloso was honored with the focus of "Other Words." It was a moment to address the issue of the invisibility of Afro-carnival organizations. The 2013 theme was equally fascinating, "Iron and Steel Africa: Men of Steel," which paid homage to the iron deity, Ogun. These varied themes and the invitation of fashion designers, such as Paulo Borges and Mathew Barney, are ample indication that Cortejo Afro is gaining traction and attention as it evolves into a major national and international cultural organization.

Filhos de Gandhi and Cortejo Afro: Functional Religiosity

Though they have divergent missions when it comes to the politics of social transformation, both Filhos de Gandhi and Cortejo Afro share a vision of functional religiosity and community development. Beyond the surface, with the sacred-profane dynamics as contextualized within the carnival moment, one wonders if outside this ephemeral period there are long-term effects in terms of sustainable empowerment that derive from functional religiosity. Brian Christens (2012) has proposed "psychological empowerment" as a community approach to enhancing power and well-being.[29] Drawing upon studies that focus on processes through which individuals and community organizations take control of their destinies, the concept proposes that community participation leads to higher levels of mental health, as subjective well-being and concrete local transformations mesh to produce psychological empowerment. In the context of Filhos de Gandhi and Cortejo Afro, the question is: Does psychological empowerment suffice without participation beyond the carnivalesque moment? Filhos de Gandhi and Cortejo Afro derive symbolic satisfaction from being able to parade during the yearly carnival; they are proud to put thousands of people on the street to celebrate Afro-Brazilian culture through community-based causes or religiosity without compromising the sense of pride, even if they have to pursue funding from the very system that oppresses them. The irony in this negotiated or syncretic cultural redemption is the fact that, while religion provides psychological support and while culture provides emotional comfort, they only do so temporarily, while the very forces of marginalization and dispossession remain intact after the collective bacchanal. While the sacred enhances the profane in the process of neutralizing the negative effects of racial discrimination, these temporary measures only defer the social trauma of marginality until after each carnival event. As Candomblé becomes visible during carnival, it ceases to be invisible, but its sense of power remains symbolic. Both Filhos de Gandhi and Cortejo Afro have the potential to be more empowering, in the dynamic sense, and to move beyond the psychological.

Chapter 10

Give Us This Day Our Daily Acarajé

Acarajé: From Sacred to Secular

With its reputation as an ancestral-force food item, one that is an integral part of Brazilian culture itself, acarajé evokes African and Afro-Brazilian culture the way no other Brazilian food does, especially in Bahia, with its African heritage. Without intending to be parodic, it could be said that the notion of a divine provision of biblical manna for the children of Israel during their arduous forty-year ritualistic journey toward the metaphoric promised land does not even begin to equal the interesting transformation of an African culinary ritual art into a human consumable during its many centuries of adaptation and reinvention in the New World, especially in Brazil. While akara, a traditional Yoruba beancake that is fried in red palm oil, is still a staple food in Nigeria and in most parts of West Africa, it has circulated in Brazil through the Middle Passage and through subsequent ritual offerings to the Atlantic deities, such as Exu (Elegbaara, an agent of the crossroads), Iasān (Oya, or deity of strong winds), and Xangô (deity of thunder and fire), and there is still more than meets the eye in that magical transformation.[1] Through a diasporic, contextual historicization of the food itself, as well as an intersectional analytical approximation of its sacred significance and its communal mediation within the personal narrative *Dinha do Acarajé* (2009), this chapter argues that acarajé has been transformed and popularized from the sacred to the secular. This transformation occurred through the power of survival as well as through the inevitable commercialization of the ritual offering in the process of dynamic cultural continuity and retention.

265

Any casual observer in Salvador da Bahia, or in most cities of Brazil, will notice the baiana de acarajé on a street corner or, nowadays, in a business or restaurant setting, either selling acarajé or serving as "blax-ploited" local color in Bahia. It is rumored in some Candomblé quarters that professionals, such as teachers, nurses, attorneys, or entrepreneurs, may be requested by their orixá through divination to set aside some days in the week to sell acarajé to appease their deities, such as Yemoja, Oya, Oxum, Obatala, and Exu.[2] Deity-inspired food in general is referred to as comida de santo (saints' food); in addition to this general term, each food has its own ontology as well as referential divinity to which its offering is destined.[3] Offering food to the deities is a ritual practice, which is meant to invoke and provoke the deity in question into action by using the language of activation, or axé (vital force). This ritual language communicates to the spiritual realm a supplication for remedy on the earthly realm and serves as a transduction of the supplication for the receiving system on the otherworldly realm to quickly perceive the urgency. While Brazilian cuisine is influenced by its colonial history, beyond syncretized African and Portuguese practices, the main African ingredients of beans and seasoning spices have remained the same over centuries, from slavery to the present day, due to the religious context in which ritual foods have been preserved.

Many scholars have argued that the preservation of African ritual practices in Bahia had to do with the fact that Afro-Brazilian religion of Candomblé was deployed as an instrument of resistance and survival during slavery. Likewise, "African Bahian cuisine derives from the culinary practices performed in the terreiros (shrines). Orisas would be worshiped as ritual banquets as demanded by the cult, and each orisa has its own votive food."[4] As the most iconic Africa-derived dish in the comida de santo repertoire, especially in Bahian cuisine, acarajé has not only become a staple food for all Brazilians, alongside feijoada, but it has also assumed a vital place in Brazilian popular music and culture. It is the most popular street food sold by baianas de acarajé and often the subject of some of the most iconic Brazilian musicians of all time. Of the many songs that continue to promote the significance of acarajé in Brazilian culture, one cannot but be touched by the singularity of "A Preta do Acarajé" (The acarajé seller) by Dorival Caymmi. The singer is sensitive to the dedication and predicament of the seller, who wants to convince the potential buyer of the intrinsic value of the food as well as the labor, love, and sacrifice it takes to offer such a delicious and

Africa-infused food for all Brazilians: "No one wants to know the work involved / . . . / Everyone enjoys eating *acarajé* / Everyone enjoys eating *abará*."[5] In two movements, one contextualizing the melancholic tone of the seller as she markets her product on abandoned nocturnal streets and the other emphasizing the same qualities to the potential consumer, the song invokes the enchantment of acarajé for the people, who consume the food without knowing the intensity of labor that accompanies its preparation. It is indeed a cordial invitation to learn more about the mysteries and values of this typical Bahian food. If Dorival Caymmi extols the essential Bahia identity of acarajé without forgetting the labor of the producer and seller, then Jauperi in "Acarajé tem Dendê" (Acarajé embodies palm oil) plays with the idea of how the staple snack fits well with the festive ambience of the community. In the song, excessive heat and musicality surely call for equally excessive consumption of cold beer. In all its cultural significance, then, acarajé represents a vital culinary legacy of Africa in Bahia, which locals and visitors alike can celebrate while satisfying their human curiosities and hunger.

While a number of studies have addressed the cultural heritage impact and commercial potential of acarajé in Brazil, especially in more touristic spaces such as Salvador and Rio de Janeiro, only a few have engaged in the actual labor involved in its preparation, as described by Dorival Caymmi in his popular music.[6] Of such rare studies, IPHAN's *Ofício das Baianas de Acarajé* and Nina Bitar's *Baianas de Acarajé* constitute two of the most authoritative and exhaustive studies to give culinary art a definitive perspective. Beyond the documentary and archival value of the former, which reflects the diversity of its subject matter—ranging from the identitarian and historical contexts of the trade, the contemporary manifestation across the different races that make up Brazil, the dynamics and changes over the years, and the challenges of cultural preservation, Bitar's *Baianas de Acarajé* craftily shifts the focus from cultural heritage to the inextricable value of the cultural producer. In so doing, the author calls into question the limits of defining cultural heritage as material without paying attention to the human dimension. This fascinating ethnographic case study of four acarajé sellers in Rio de Janeiro attests to a subset of memories of Africa in Brazil, while also delineating such issues as the mystery and grace of the profession despite its popular dismissal as a "marginal" vocation, its cosmological linkages with Candomblé ritual practices, and its dispersal all over Brazil following a pattern of migrations from Salvador to the rest of the country. By the end of the author's careful presentation of each of the sellers, who hail from different locations in Rio de Janeiro, including Sônia (antiquities market in the center of Rio), Ciça (November 15th Square), Jay (Copacabana), and Nicinha (Ipanema Hippie Market), Bitar articulates the saintly nature of the food item, both as a historical offering to the deities and as a way of life for the sellers. Bitar also draws attention to the larger implication for family ties that the religious connections have managed to preserve to date. Nonetheless, Bitar makes the case for persistent zones of tension surrounding the sellers, who struggle to navigate the complex bureaucratic structures as they seek legitimacy for a trade that is often incorporated as an "intangible cultural material" despite the state's habit of exploiting it for touristic purposes. Unfortunately, to complicate life for these sellers, evangelicals have also entered into the acarajé business, branding theirs as "Bolinhos de Jesus" (Jesus's cakes). In responding to this interesting development, Jay, one of the sellers in Britar's study and the sole male seller in what is ordinarily a female profession, asks rhetorically: "If their *acarajé* belongs to Jesus, does that mean mine belongs to the devil?" In sum, the strength of the book lies in its advocacy for the acarajé seller, who it incorporates into Brazilian cultural and historical heritage.

Professionalization of the Baianas de Acarajé

One of the ways that the Brazilian government is working to ensure recognition, respect, and visibility for the sellers of acarajé is through incorporating sellers as an association (Associação das Baianas de Acarajé), as well as by granting them historical and cultural heritage since 2005. This validation, Scott Barton notes, is what makes street food in general appealing to both locals and tourists alike: "To this day, street food is part of everyday life. Ubiquitous across the urban landscape, on beaches, and in tourist areas throughout Bahia, street food is a key component for the informal sector of Brazil's urban economics. Through the sale of acarajé and other staples, the Baianas have systematically introduced and anchored local nutritional patterns to local groups and regional populations."[7] Acarajé has become a dynamic part of Brazilian cultural heritage over the years, and, to preserve this heritage, Afro-Brazilian communities have come together to demand the Brazilian government recognize an association to protect their interests and way of life when it comes to the knowledge of Afro-Brazilian cuisine. They contend that the street trade dates to the abolition of slavery, when liberated Afro-Brazilian women located themselves on street corners with their food trays, simultaneously fulfilling their religious obligations as mandated by their Candomblé rites, nurturing family ties that were fragmented by enslavement, and raising money for the survival of their newly formed family structures postslavery.[8]

In addition to safeguarding this cultural heritage, the proponents argue that the creation of an association has the potential to encourage the formation of additional Candomblé sororities and fraternities. Remarkably, with this exciting prospect of official recognition, their once-persecuted culinary business and religion has grown, and the number of filhas de santo (daughters of the saint) has risen within the terreiros, as many of these daughters have obligations (such as selling acarajé) to fulfill periodically. Ultimately, after some research was conducted by the National Center for Folklore and Popular Culture to quantify the number of baianas de acarajé, the Association of Acarajé and Mingau of the State of Bahia (ABAM) was created on April 11, 1992. The role of the association was to serve as a regulating body for the preservation of the African roots of the product, the professionalization of the activity, and the setting up of food hygiene and financial management courses to help Bahians better manage their businesses. Shortly after, in 2005, UNESCO declared baianas de acarajé an intangible cultural heritage of Brazil. Similarly, the State of Bahia Law No. 12, 206, of January 19, 2010, designated November 25 to commemorate the baianas, just like November 20 is set aside to commemorate the death of Zumbi dos Palmares, or the National Day of Black Consciousness. The current tourism around acarajé is not devoid of a deep historical context. The baianas de acarajé may well be referred to as the "face of Bahia" or, quite literally, the "postcard of Bahia" because they are seen all over Bahia, not only on a daily basis on the streets and beaches but also during many of the annual cycle of festivities (ciclo de festas), in which sacred ceremonies of the Afro-Brazilian religion Candomblé take to the streets to showcase their reverence for the Africa-derived saints (orixás). Yet, like other sacred art forms that were persecuted in the colonial times, like Candomblé (Afro-Brazilian religion) and capoeira (Afro-Brazilian martial art), the baianas de acarajé also faced persecution and state-sponsored violence. It was only during the Estado Novo (New state) regime of Getúlio Vargas, when the government felt the need to forge a national identity, that these Africa-derived identities became integrated and facilitated. Charged with the responsibility to officially recognize different aspects of Brazilian culture and society, the Institute of National Historic and Artistic Patrimony (IPHAN) set out to preserve, document, and professionalize many Brazilian cultural and historical entities, including the baianas de acarajé.

Though the baianas de acarajé struggle to balance tradition with modernity as they preserve Africa-derived cultural products while also resisting the appropriation of the same products by the tourism industry through controlling the terms and structures of its manifestation as a dynamic cultural and political agency, the cuisine itself suffers from a lack of standardization that the association is laboring to redress. Nonetheless, the baiana has been popularized in literature and culture, including Dorival Caymmi's song "O que é que a baiana tem" (What is the baiana made of?), in which Carmen Miranda performs the hyper-sexualized role of the baiana, her frenzied bodily movements encircled by different men, who identify, one at a time, what exactly the baiana has on her body (the enchanting white garb, the head tie, the many religious trinkets on her neck, the bangles, and the multicolored layers of a puffy skirt). The baiana has also been popularized in Aluísio Azevedo's O Cortiço (The slum), in which the author portrays the baiana as lazy, extroverted, and unscrupulous. The image of the baiana has since been steadily commercialized over the years by the tourism industry. It was against this conflated background that baianas came together to form their own association in 1992, with offices located in many cities, including Rio de Janeiro, Brasília, and Fortaleza. The Brazilian government further sponsored the incorporation of the acarajé-selling profession in 2004 through an association aimed at protecting its place within Brazilian cultural heritage. The main objectives of the association are (1) facilitate the process of obtaining official street vendor licenses; (2) collaborate with specific doctors, pharmacists, dentists, and grocery stores to establish agreements that will allow members to receive reduced rates for services; (3) design and offer cuisine-related courses on how to prepare acarajé, as well as courses in the English language to facilitate communication with tourists; (4) collaborate with the state government regarding opportunities for Afro-Brazilians to pursue college by paying the first two years of college tuition for the children of baianas; (5) regulate the traditional garb of the baianas within the religious symbolism of the product, including the mandatory use of the wooden table or tabuleiro, thus barring bars, restaurants, and, more recently, evangelicals, from competing; (5) ensure that baianas have official permission of FIFA to sell their product within the confines of the arenas during the World Cup.

Acarajé may have survived colonial persecution and may have transformed itself into a central palate in Afro-Brazilian cuisine and culture, but it has yet to overcome the colonial stigma as a by-product of the consistently persecuted Afro-Brazilian religion, Candomblé. This partly explains the constant efforts to exclude it from mainstream events, despite ambivalent governmental support for its cultural integration. A case in point stems from the struggle to sell acarajé during the recent World Cup of 2014. As Brazil prepared for the 2014 World Cup via the elimination process of the Confederations Cup of 2013, the International Federation of Football Association (FIFA) declared that selling acarajé was to be restricted to a two-kilometer radius from the stadiums. Acarajé vendors suffered in the twelve Brazilian World Cup cities because of these policies by FIFA. In Salvador, for example, baianas de acarajé were known to have previously sold their food item around the Fonte Nova Stadium. Because the city itself depends on about fifty thousand vendors to sustain its informal economy in the middle of high unemployment, municipalities were not as stringent about vending licenses. As a result, the entire city of Salvador was extremely dependent on this informal economy and could not afford the ban placed on the baianas de acarajé by FIFA. Using social media as an instrument of protest, baianas argued that restrictions were a form of cultural attack, using the hashtag "#NãoQueroMcDonalds, #QueroAcarajé" (I do not want McDonald's, I want acarajé). The campaign was quite effective, as Skari Ivester notes: "Baianas de acarajé are the first group of street vendors in the history of FIFA and the World Cup to have obtained permission to sell within the World Cup exclusive zone . . . Baianas de acarajé are now recognized as the culture of their nation and humanity. With as spirit of resistance and resilience—local and global, modern and traditional—they mobilize to protect their craft, based on the particular cultural space they occupy."[9] By framing the exclusion of the baianas from the World Cup arena as a form of cultural terrorism on the part of FIFA, and by sidestepping traditional media, which is usually biased against the Afro-Brazilian community and its religious ethos, the Association of Baianas de Acarajé was able to influence public opinion. The victory was not only a win for acarajé but a victory for the entire Afro-Brazilian cultural enterprise, which is determined to sell its cultural product to Brazil and the rest of the world without apology.

Framing the *Acarajé* Vendor
as a Matriarch in *Dinha do Acarajé*

Ubaldo Marques Porto Filho's *Dinha do Acarajé* celebrates a unique Afro-Brazilian community personality, the famous "Dinha" in Rio Vermelho, Salvador da Bahia. Born on May 20, 1951, and deceased on May 17, 2008, Lindinalva de Assis was only seven years old when she first found herself alongside her grandmother, Dona Ubaldina de Assis, selling acarajé. As fate would have it, she took over the business when she was ten years old after her grandmother became ill. Dinha's beginning was quite humble, and she lived in a modest house in Engenho Velho da Federação, a neighborhood that at the time was noted for its poverty, high crime rate, and gang-related violence following many centuries of deprivation after the abolition of slavery. With her business becoming increasingly successful, Dinha moved from the poor neighborhood to a more tourist-inclined and business-savvy environment in Rio Vermelho. Despite her small business, Dinha claimed to have used her limited resources over the years to train close to fifty extended family members and the community at large. She attributed her success to her just-plain-delicious acarajé, to human relations, and to her genuine friendships within the community—qualities that brought celebrities, such as Jorge Amado, Nizan Guanais, ex-soccer player Socrates, Dr. Diocletian, and Wilson Lins, to help her to better publicize her business through popular endorsements.

While the narrative is filled with anecdotes and family and community memories, especially those that linked Dinha with her ancestral past and how she came to be a guardian of the acarajé trade, there is one intriguing episode in *Dinha do Acarajé*. An aggressive competitor, Regina, who used to sell acarajé in the Graça neighborhood in Salvador, an area known for its affluent residents, decided to extend her business to Rio Vermelho, where Dinha was the only known presence. This perplexing situation caused a lot of ripples. The clientele became divided, the community was eager to see how the controversy would end, and the news media fueled the competition through provocative and sentimental headlines. Eventually, the stalemate was resolved when the two settled for a shared space, with each developing their customers over the years. Before Dinha's passage to join her ancestors, her daughter Claudia Assis, an accountancy graduate who was then thirty-nine years old (she turned fifty in 2019), took over from her mother, following the tradition of Dinha, who had taken over from her grandmother, making this a truly Bahian cultural narrative that embodies many generations and memories. Located at the crossroads of Federação and Barra, the matriarch's legacy is a restaurant known as Casa da Dinha (Dinha's house), which retains all the relics of the past and is imbued with a sense of hope for the future of the acarajé tradition.

There is an intricate relationship between African religiosity and matriarchy in the African diaspora, and most Afro-Brazilian women are connected to Candomblé in Brazil, regardless of whether their involvement is academic, superficial, or thorough. As part of a communal and self-empowering strategy, Afro-Brazilian women deploy sacred rituals to combat the enduring vestiges of racism, sexism, and patriarchy. Ruth Landes, J. Lorand Matory, and Cherise Sterling have examined the significance of matriarchy in Afro-Brazilian religious reality. While they agree on the centrality of Candomblé as the structuring core of the larger Afro-Brazilian culture, they differ in their varied understanding of how the supreme Iyalorixá, or Mãe-de-Santo, manipulates her spiritual and administrative leadership to address patriarchy, promote gender equality, and counter the larger societal penchant for racial and gendered discrimination. While Brazil may be far from the center of the food social movement, it has a longer history of European, African, Indigenous, and even Asiatic influences on its cuisine. Acarajé not only falls within the African influence on Brazilian cuisine but also reflects the legacy of slavery on the national consciousness, as all members of Brazilian society now find themselves sharing in the unique legacy of colonial migration and conquest. The inalienable presence of women is at the center of the process of preparing, consuming, and conserving acarajé. These are the same women who once struggled to feed their own children when they were mandated to feed the colonial master's children. These are the same women who once used their own milk to nourish the master's children, their breasts becoming saggy and dried up, while sacrificing the health of their own malnourished children. Despite today's globalized cultural consumption, acarajé continues to suffer persecution and discrimination, even despite popular and political efforts to preserve Afro-Brazilian cultural traditions. The Afro-Brazilian matriarchs, or baianas de acarajé, who feel the burden of such persecution the most, are not afraid to challenge postcolonial oppression when it comes to protecting the tradition and sale of acarajé.[10] Notwithstanding its maligning, acarajé has carved its well-deserved place in Brazilian gastronomy, as well as in global food studies.

The role of officially preserving the culture of acarajé must be credited to Afro-Brazilian matriarchs. Whether they are the vendors or the more-respected Iyalorixás (supreme religious female leaders of Candomblé houses or terreiros), Afro-Brazilian matriarchs are the ones with political agency, and they are not afraid to exercise that authority to demand recognition for an age-old Africa-derived palate. Drawing on Homi Bhabha and Stuart Hall, Cheryl Sterling (2012) engages the contradiction of how "public expression of cultural values, empowers the objectified Others to become sites of their own discourse." Sterling further deconstructs the role of the tourism industry in the exploitation of the baianas:

> In the tourist center of the city of Salvador, Pelourinho, rather than stressing its importance in the slavery narrative of Brazil. . . . new forms of exploitation occur and are condoned, from more explicit prostitution to its lesser forms of young, black women dressed in the elaborate Baiana costumes parade on the sidewalks and through the narrow streets soliciting customers for exclusive shops or posing for photographs with tourists for a fee.[11]

While Sterling questions state-sponsored touristic violence against the legacy of baianas, the cultural critic is also quick to observe that all is not lost. She writes, "The deeper knowledge that impels ritual behavior is still in the hands of those who are the keepers of these traditions." By "keepers," Sterling is referring to the Candomblé matriarchs, as well as to their stewards in the cultural realm, the baianas do acarajé. If acarajé is today the most consumed food by tourists in Salvador and throughout the major cities of Brazil, it is due to the resilience and determination of the guardians of tradition, both within the religious setting of Candomblé, where they are known as filhas de santo because acarajé may have once been dedicated to the deity Iasãn (as part of their rites of passage) and without the sacred sphere, where they become entrepreneurial agents of a religious product.

Notably, Dinha is called the "Queen of Acarajé" or the "Queen of the Baianas" by her many fans, including Nelson Costa Santana (Bambá), actor Alexandre Barillari, Fátima Mendonça (wife of then-Minister Jaques Wagner), first lady Maria Letícia Lula da Silva, famous boxer Popó, Axé, and singers such as Daniela Mercury, Margareth Menezes, and Carlinhos Brown, among other celebrities. Dinha has become a household name throughout Bahia. *Dinha do Acarajé* serves as a pioneering biographical work that sets in motion the recognition of other deserving acarajé vendors, who deserve to be documented as integral parts of Bahian cultural history. She is considered by many to be patient, cheerful, radiant, charismatic, and even magnetic in her determination to produce acarajé of the highest quality for public consumption; at the same time, she serves as a pioneer and pillar for those who come after her, ensuring that they emerge from their hitherto socially imposed invisibility to become visible and impactful participants in grand open markets, festivals, exhibitions, and regional and international conferences. As her biography confirms, Dinha is a great representative of Bahian gastronomy. The biographer Ubaldo Marques Porto Filho adopts a chronological plot structure to render for the reader the most intimate and transformative moments in the life of Dinha, from her place of origin in Santo Amaro to her stardom in Rio Vermelho, Salvador. In telling the story of Dinha, Porto Filho is also narrating the history of Afro-Brazilian cuisine, especially as it concerns the popularization of a sacred food item like acarajé. Through a painstaking ethnographic and archival methodology, mediated by poetic linear acrostics (D-I-N-H-A-D-O-A-C-A-R-A-J-É) that capture both her popularized name (Dinha do Acarajé), as well as her characteristics of a divine diva, including her persistent struggle and resolve coupled with her humble gallantry, Porto Filho remarkably details the epic journey of Dinha toward becoming an icon of Bahian culture. In twenty-four carefully interwoven chapters, Porto Filho traces the life of Dinha, creating a compelling genealogy that goes back three generations, from her grandmother's journey to the journey of her daughter, who now occupies the same seat despite her formal education as a trained accountant.

Tracing the origin and trajectory of Dinha from Santo Amaro to Salvador has its own intrigue. The intricate link between the three generations lies in the valued vending of acarajé, and it has turned out to be an against-all-odds family venture. Afro-Brazilian women who hail from Santo Amaro have historically been reputed to be good cooks, and, even if this may be derogatory in the context of slavery, it has taken on a new meaning in terms of job opportunities for those bent on leaving the rural ambience of the former colonial plantation for the urban reality of Salvador. They cling to that qualification with the marketing slogan: "I am from Santo Amaro and I am a good cook."[12] The biographer also notes the equally pioneering efforts of Maria de São Pedro (popularly called Cordolina), who was also from Santo Amaro and who was Dinha's grandmother of Dinha. Cordonlina opened a restaurant at the Mercado Modelo (Model Market at the Lower City) in 1969, which had a positive impact on Dinha. Though Cordolina had eight children with João de Santos, six of whom were boys, her two daughters, Ubaldina and Ester, ran away from home to settle in Rio Vermelho, where they found work as domestics and cleaners. Initially, Ubaldina had to contend with the complex reality of not being a devotee of Candomblé at a time when most acarajé vendors were expected to be daughters of the saint. Ubaldina had four daughters, and Rute de Assis was the eldest. When Rute was only fourteen years old, she became pregnant and was forced to become a baiana de acarajé within four years so she could keep her baby nourished. One day, after selling acarajé in Itapuã, she was the victim of a car accident. Three people, including Rute de Assis and her son, died, and an additional twenty-seven other passengers were injured. On May 20, 1951, Ubaldina's first granddaughter was born in Rio Vermelho, named Lindinalva de Assis, but called "Dinha." Dinha grew up acquiring intimate knowledge of the acarajé business through hands-on practical experience from her family predecessors. Through her family's hardships—she often did not take any vacation and overworked herself to sustain her family—Dinha did not have time to be a normal child. Despite these odds, and by gaining the admiration of local celebrities due to her delicious acarajé, Dinha became revered as the "Queen of Acarajé" and "Ambassador of Bahia," winning many prizes and awards. She went on to establish a restaurant known as Casa da Dinha (House of Dinha) as part of her legacy, which was to be inherited by her own daughter, who is now proud to continue Dinha's legacy.

Tradition and Continuity: The Future of Acarajé

With the ancestral passage of Dinha in 2008, Cláudia de Assis, her daughter, did not let the tradition die. Instead, she took over the reins of the sacred-secular business. Thus, a tradition that started seventy years ago with Dinha's grandmother, Ubaldina de Assis, has become a permanent family and community ritual throughout the Largo da Dinha, which was named in remembrance of Dinha, even though the traditional name was Largo de Santana in Rio de Vermelho. The future of acarajé is predictable, and a tradition that has been sustained for many centuries is not about to change except maybe to meet touristic demands. The "packaging" of acarajé, for example, is beginning to imitate that of McDonald's "sandwiches," with all the superficial vatapá, carurú, salad, and shrimp inserted in the middle, as opposed to the simple round dumpling in the West African original. The core change, however, is the shift from a required sacred obligation to commercial volunteerism. Traditionally, acarajé vendors were exclusively women, the filhas de santo, and they were initiated into Candomblé, including the cult of Xangô and Oiá (Iansã), and were expected to fulfill their "obligations" to their orixás, both during the colonial period and after the abolition of slavery, by preparing Afro-Brazilian snacks for sale on the streets in the evening hours. Through the investment of tourism in many Afro-Brazilian rituals and festivities, acarajé has become a staple cultural patrimony of Brazil and will remain so for many centuries to come. It has indeed become, by extension, a tourist attraction of the city of Salvador, and of many Brazilian cities, well beyond the exotic appropriation by the same tourist industry. The Memorial of Baianas de Acarajé, currently located in Pelourinho, is a living museum for the documentation of the historical archives of this ancestral art, which defies any drastic change in space and time. Registered by the National Institute of Artistic and Historical Heritage under the Ministry of Culture, this museum exhibits props, handicrafts, and some of the gastronomic instruments used by the baianas de acarajé. Though the tradition of passing the symbolic food tray from mother to daughter, as in the case of Dinha to her daughter Cláudia, has changed somewhat, the Culture Ministry now expects every baiana to be registered and licensed. The change is only a matter of protocol and formality rather than actual change in the tradition of product and marketing. In fact, two very famous baianas helped to keep the tradition going in the city of Salvador: Dinha in Rio Vermelho and Tânia Bárbara Neri in Farol da Barra.

While Bahia is reputed to be a major hub of tourism in Brazil, the same tourism industry represents Afro-Brazilian cultural relics as objects of exoticism, thus downplaying the role of resistance in the Afro-Brazilian population, which is responsible for the retention and preservation of Brazilian culture. Beyond being appropriated simply as a tourism vocation and location, Bahia represents a historic colonial setting, which has evolved into a cultural mecca that should be revered as one of the great locations of South America. Bahia holds the key to varied hidden treasures of historical significance—not as the colonizer would like to project and exploit them as part of a continuation of dispossession and disempowerment but as a living museum, where the traumas and trajectories of the Middle Passage are documented, synergized, and reinterpreted in an archive of memory and of vitality, where Afro-Brazilians work through the oppressive residuum of slavery's past. Acarajé and the baianas de acarajé should be considered embodied cultural heritages of Brazil. By celebrating Afro-Brazilian cultural heritage and by indicting the dominating arrogance of the slave master and Brazil's contradictory racial democracy, which determines the place of Brazil's original producers of culture, the Afro-Brazilians, baianas de acarajé challenge and redress the persistent process of objectification, exoticization, and exploitation, fighting for a more equitable stake in the national treasure. The symbolic representation of Afro-Brazilians only as local color during festivities and celebrations lacks the willpower to decisively move from strategic toleration to necessary political participation. It is about time Afro-Brazilians begin to enjoy the fruits of the labor that constructed Brazil and be given their well-deserved share of the daily bread that the Brazilian constitution in theory provides them.

Given the fact that culinary art is an integrative part of human activity and cultural-historical practice, the cooking and consumption of food items have become symbolic acts of culture conditioned by culture itself.[13] The gradual whitening of Brazilian culture and race is problematic because it resonates with the persistence of white superiority. Black social movements have made limited strides to challenge this whitening, but the objective of Brazilian hegemonic forces is to ensure that Afro-Brazilians and their culture are controlled by whites. By appropriating acarajé as a "Bolinho de Jesus," for example, evangelicals not only demonstrate their fanaticism and intolerance but they also "steal" from Afro-Brazilian culture. The result is that Afro-Brazilian community risks being dispossessed of its age-long heritage, through which many generations survived the economic hardships of slavery and beyond and through which they raised their children with the very minimum they could amass, using their creative acumen and selling Africa-derived snacks that they reinvented in the New World. Through religious syncretism, not only were affluent white Brazilians able to enter Candomblé and Umbanda settings to become leaders at the expense of long-standing Afro-Brazilians, who were the founders and nourishers of the value systems within Afro-Brazilian sacred structures, but evangelicals, with their religious fanaticism, were also able to demonize acarajé and appropriate this "satanic food," rebranding it as "Jesus Dumpling" to make it acceptable for a wider population. Afro-Brazilians must not only resist and challenge this arrogant cultural appropriation and assault, but they must also continue to lead their own heritage religions without the manipulation of Brazilian hegemonic forces. Acarajé should not be taken over by any religious or political group. It must retain its Africanness and religiosity without losing its market value.

Conclusion

As the sacred, the profane, and the syncretic interface, they no longer exclusively occupy unidimensional locations in ritual places, such as sacred groves, shrines, temples, or material embodiments of the supernatural. Hence, to understand the relocation of the sacred requires a close examination of the multiple sites of rituals, including their contexts, texts, and cultural performances. From activating the sacred in the Yoruba diaspora of Brazil; to exploring the sacred as a literary manifestation in the works of Mãe Stella de Oxóssi, Mãe Beata de Yemonjá, Mãe Valnizia Bianch, Pierre Verger, Jorge Amado, Vasconcelos Maia, Abdias Nascimento, Nelson Rodrigues, Zora Seljan, Dias Gomes, Raul Longo, Robson Pinheiro, Cléo Martins, and Chynae; to celebrating Candomblé in cultural hybridities as manifest in Afro-Brazilian carnival performances of Filhos de Gandhi, Cortejo Afro, and the appropriation of acarajé in Brazilian culinary repertoire, this book has argued that African divinities have been culturally hybridized in Brazil through multiple media. What used to be exclusively sacred manifests profanely as strategies of historical preservation, cultural resistance, and political negotiation. Through the comparative prisms of numerous cultural productions, this study has engaged the creative tensions, intrigues, provocations, invocations, resilient adaptations, and political musings that constitute the new stylistic strategies deployed by Afro-Brazilian cultural producers to challenge and make sense of Brazil's problematic racial democracy.

The central motif in this study for the relocation of the sacred to the profane was the confrontational dialogue with political hegemony, where "hegemony" is not necessarily the domain of the ruling elite but rather a site of exclusive religious dominion. By appropriating the sacred within the profane, the marginalized deactivate their sense

281

of powerlessness and activate the power of the sacred. Brazil, as with other sites of Afro-Atlantic migration, is a locale where the divinities that accompanied the enslaved through the Middle Passage continue to seek redress for the tortuous experiences of slavery and its aftermath. While the first step in self-preservation involves reclaiming religiosity as a weapon of therapeutic self-defense, the second step involves the appropriation of the sacred in the popular frame both to challenge its marginality as well as to integrate it as part of the larger Brazilian culture. By analyzing Afro-Brazilian religiosity through expressive cultures, this study has revisited the unique contributions of the three intertwined cultures and races (namely, the indigenous, the Afro-descendant, and the European), while privileging the Afro-Brazilian in light of their marginality and relative continuous persecution by fanatical groups, such as Pentecostals. Through appropriations, readaptations, hybridizations, and cultural syncretizations, the Brazilian colonial experience has morphed into a strategic process of miscegenation, one that has ultimately transformed Brazil into a unique multicultural, multidimensional, and yet problematically "segregated" country.

Of the many controversial terms in Brazilian intellectual discourse, syncretism is perhaps the most problematic, after miscegenation, hybridity, and racial democracy. Contrary to popular assumptions, all religions are syncretic because they represent a huge synthesis that integrates several elements to form a new whole. Afro-Brazilian cultures perceive syncretism to be a combination of popular Catholicism and Afro-Brazilian religions. In other words, the domain of religion is indeed a meeting point of different traditions. The logic of popular practice in religion contradicts the intellectual logic that questions how religious practices shift and adapt to new milieus. By their very performative nature, art and religion are indeed inseparable. With art, aesthetics, music, dance, painting, sculpture, and literature, it is difficult to claim purity because the idea of syncretism commonly recalls mixture, pollution, confusion, and a synthesis of contradictory elements. While syncretism suggests the imposition of the religion of the colonizer on the colonized, and thus tends to be condemned by Afro-Brazilian religious leaders and militants, Afro-Catholic adherents include African para-liturgical elements in their ceremonies as they compete to increase their diminishing population of Afro-Brazilian adherents. The re-Africanization movement of the 1970s also critiqued Afro-Brazilian syncretism, making the case for a negation of the naïve acceptance of an oppressive confusion between African orixás and Catholic saints. Through an examination of representative works in which syncretism is manifest or relocated, this study has not only highlighted how religiosity is manipulated politically but also how marginalized religions have been popularized in the name of strategic self-preservation.

In the so-called pluralist or mythic racially democratic society, the discussion of minority rights tends to exclude the need to distinguish Afro-Brazilian orixás and Catholic saints. Contrary to popular opinion, syncretism is present in traditional Afro-Brazilian religious entities, such as the Casa das Minas. Ferretti, for example, categorizes syncretism in four hypothetical types: (1) separation or nonsyncretism; (2) mixture or fusion; (3) parallelism or juxtaposition; and (4) convergence or adaptation. It is thus quite difficult to narrow the definition of syncretism to a rigid classification, and its state is constantly shifting. Because there are many similar characteristics between the all-white Catholic saints and the Afro-Brazilian orixás who are usually attributed to them, coupled with the overlap between the calendars of both religions, syncretism is almost inevitable. To the degree that tradition and syncretism do mix, they are not necessarily contradictory but complementary. Every religion is a living, contradictory culture and not a rigorously organized approach to deity worship that is strictly codified without flexibility. As a result, many world festivals evolved from religious practices. It is thus advisable not to dismiss the syncretism of Afro-Brazilian religious practitioners.

Likewise, festivals and folkloric activities often translate the syncretic into popular religiosity. Ultimately, Afro-Brazilian religious practices often find themselves in possessed bodies, sacred places, chants, texts, liturgical ceremonies, and profane performances. Afro-Brazilian syncretism, as manifested in the chapters of this book, reflects a transcultural device to retain the African culture that the enslaved struggled to sustain through many strategic negotiations with the oppressing colonizer. In the postabolition era, the manifestations of syncretism remain constant and even more vibrant, given the freedom to be creative without the attendant pressure of the repressive instrumentality of the colonial state that existed before the abolition of slavery.

By identifying Bahia as one of the major zones for the activation of the sacred, this book has projected the "Black Rome" as the heart and roots of the Brazilian nation, even as it visibly betrays its African influence in every facet of life. From its colonial and religious foundations, sacredness, dialectics of the sacred and the profane, ritual structures and strictures, and its profanation of the sacred, to its Afro-carnival groups and their emblematic hybridities, Bahia is a quintessential zone of miscegenation and syncretism with cogent political implications for cultural resistance. The second chapter situated the "colonial gaze" of Pierre Verger as he captures as well as preserves Yoruba ritual altars through his photography and anthropology. The third chapter celebrated the creative contributions of matriarchs and Iyalorixás, such as Mãe Stella de Oxóssi, Mãe Beata de Yemonjá, and Mãe Valnizia Bianch, as living museums of Afro-Brazilian religiosity. The fourth chapter focused on two feminine water spirits, namely Iemanjá and Oxum, as they are innovatively interpreted in two works by Jorge Amado and Vansconcelos Maia, where the deities dominated natural phenomena. The fifth chapter attempted the theoretical extermination of the miscegenation thesis by examining two plays by Abdias Nascimento and Nelson Rodrigues, where the Blackness of the protagonists is contested. The sixth chapter examined Yoruba mythology in the dramas of Zora Seljan and Dias Gomes, especially as it relates to the temperaments of both deities, Xangô and Iansã. The seventh chapter compared Umbanda and Candomblé to approximate the power of Spiritism and African ancestry as they coalesce in codified sacred rituals in the works of Raul Longo and Robson Pinheiro. The eighth chapter located Odu as the deity of divination while privileging Oya and Osossi as river and hunting personalities in the works of Cléo Martins and Chynae, respectively. The ninth chapter studied two Afro-Bahian carnival groups, separated by fifty years, but which share a unique sacredness that manifests on the streets through the creative choreography of Afro-Brazilian religion with festive profanity for the purpose of self-preservation and cultural politics. The final chapter revisited acarajé as a once-sacred offering that has been hybridized as a popular food item in Brazil. Through these extensive textual, performative, and cultural ritualizations, which are unified in their syncretism and hybridity, the power of preservation and cultural resistance comes alive. *Relocating the Sacred* has highlighted the various ways in which Brazilian cultural producers document relocated sacredness, while also setting the stage for further studies on the syncretic nature of Afro-Brazilian religious practices as a whole.

Notes

Introduction

1. The Yoruba people are one of the largest ethnic groups in southwestern Nigeria and are also found in Benin and Togo due to migrations, trade, and resettlements. They are a fascinating group due to their strong orisa religion that believes in the power of ase (or "life force," "spiritual life cycle," or the "after-life") and interconnectedness with deities, which have the power to regulate the lives and destinies of their worshippers. Due to the history of Atlantic slavery, the Yoruba religious and cultural traditions made their way to the Caribbean and the Americas, including Cuba, Trinidad, and Brazil. For more information about the Yoruba, see, for example, William Bascom, *The Yoruba of Southwestern Nigeria* (Prospect Heights, IL: Waveland, 1969). On Yoruba spiritual identity, see Toyin Falola and Ann Genova, eds., *Orisa: Yoruba Gods and Spiritual Identity in Africa and the Diaspora* (New Jersey: Africa World, 2005).

2. For a detailed analysis of the major Yoruba deities, see Robert Farris Thompson, "Portraits of Major Orisha," in *Flash of the Spirit: African and Afro-American Art and Philosophy* (New York: Vintage, 1983), 18–99. In the specific Brazilian context, see also Pierre Fatumbi Verger, *Orixás: Deuses Iorubás na África e no Novo Mundo* (Salvador: Corrupio, 2002); Reginaldi Prandi, *Mitologia dos Orixás* (São Paulo: Companhia das Letras, 2001); and Agnes Mariano, Aline Queiroz, Dadá Jacques, and Mauro Rossi, eds., *Obarayi: Babalorixá Balbino Daniel de Paula* (Salvador: Editora Barabô, 2009).

3. See, for example, Sérgio Figueiredo Ferretti, *Repensando o Sincretismo* (São Paulo: EDUSP, 1995); José Carlos Pereira, *Sincretismo Religioso and Ritos Sacrificiais: Influências das Religiões Afro no Catolicismo Popular Brasileiro* (São Paulo: Editora Zouk, 2004); and Neil Turner, *Religious Syncretism in Brazil: Catholicism, Evangelicalism and Candomblé* (Grin: Verlag, 2011).

4. For an application of this concept to textual analysis, see my unpublished essay, "Afro-Spiritual Identities: Self and Other in Muniz Sodré's A *Lei do Santo* and Ernesto Veras' *Portas Fechadas*," 2020, typescript.

5. Claudia Moser and Cecelia Feldman, eds., *Locating the Sacred: Theoretical Approaches to the Emplacement of Religion* (Oxford: Oxbow, 2014), 1–12.

6. Vijay Agnew, "The Quest for the Soul in the Diaspora," in *Diaspora, Memory, and Identity: A Search for Home*, ed. Vijay Agnew (Toronto: University of Toronto Press, 2005), 268–90.

7. Rachel E. Harding, *A Refuge in Thunder: Candomblé and Alternative Spaces of Blackness* (Bloomington: Indiana University Press, 2000), 135.

8. For a detailed analysis of how Yoruba and African plants have been used for healing and public health research on both sides of the Atlantic, see, for example, Pierre Fatumbi Verger, *Ewé: The Use of Plants in Yoruba Society* (Salvador: Odebrecht, 1997); and Anna Pagano, "Afro-Brazilian Religions and Ethnic Identity Politics in the Brazilian Public Health Arena," *Heath, Culture, and Society* 3, no. 1 (2012): 1–30.

9. Heather Shirey, "Transforming the Orixás: Candomblé in Sacred and Secular Spaces in Salvador da Bahia, Brazil," *African Arts* 42 (2009): 62–79.

10. In response to Pentecostal religious intolerance and physical attacks against Candomblé in the last twenty years, leaders and devotees of Candomblé have now begun a process of insisting on African authenticity. By removing Catholic saints from their terreiros and no longer masking themselves under colonial syncretism as a measure of survival, they launch a political statement about their freedom of expression. See Anadelia A Romo, *Brazil's Living Museum: Race, Reform, and Tradition in Bahia* (Chapel Hill: University of North Carolina Press, 2010), 61–66. Romo notes that the sense of African pride was perhaps "most developed in the realm of Candomblé, where claims of African authenticity were the ultimate praise for a *terreiro*, or house of worship. . . . Eugênia Ana Santos (known more commonly as Aninha and Martiniano Eliseu do Bonfim (known as Martiniano) reinforced each other's legitimacy. Together they increased the status of African connections and of religious practice centered on ideas of African authenticity" (61).

11. Patrick A. Polk, "Introduction: Have You Been to Bahia?," in *Axé Bahia: The Power of Art in an Afro-Brazilian Metropolis*, ed. Patrick A. Polk, Robert Conduru, Sabrina Gledhill, and Randal Johnson (Los Angeles: Flower Museum at UCLA, 2017), 12–53. For other works on Afro-Brazilian art history, see: Niyi Afolabi, Márcio Barbosa, and Esmeralda Ribeiro, eds., *The Afro-Brazilian Mind: Contemporary Afro-Brazilian Literary and Cultural Criticism* (New Jersey: Africa World, 2008); Emanoel Araújo, ed., *A Ancestralidade dos Símbolos* (São Paulo: MASP, 2018); Emanoel Araújo, ed., *Brazilian Sculpture: An Identity in Profile* (São Paulo: Ministry of Culture, 1997); Emanoel Araújo, *Esculturas, Relevos, Monoprints* (Salvador: Best Editora, 1991); Emanoel Araújo, ed., *A Mão Afro-Brasileira: Significado da Contribuição Artística e Histórica* (São Paulo: TENENGE, 1988); Emanoel Araújo, ed., *Textos de Negros e Sobre Negros* (São Paulo: Museu Afro-Brasil, 2011); Kimberly L. Cleveland, *Black Art in Brazil: Expressions of*

Identity (Gainesville: University Press of Florida, 2013); Roberto Conduru, *Arte Afro-Brasileira* (Belo Horizonte: C/Arte Editora, 2007); Goya Lopes and Gustavo Falcón, *Imagens da Diaspora* (Salvador: Solusluna, 2010); Abdias Nascimento, *Orixás: Os Deuses Vivos da África* (Rio de Janeiro: IPEAFRO, 1995); Mikelle Smith Omari-Tunkara, *Manipulating the Sacred: Yoruba Art, Ritual, and Resistance in Brazilian Candomblé* (Detroit: Wayne State University Press, 2005); Adriano Pedrosa and Tomás Toledo, eds., *Afro-Atlantic Histories* (São Paulo: MASP, 2020); Deoscoredes Maximiliano dos Santos and Juana Elbein dos Santos, eds., *Autos Coreográficos: Mestre Didi, 90 Anos* (Salvador: Corrupio, 2007); and Jaime Sodré, *A Influência da Religião Afro-Brasileira na Obra Escultórica do Mestre Didi* (Salvador: EDUFBA, 2005).

12. Some examples of CDs and DVDs acquired while on research visits to Brazil in the last ten years include Milton Nascimento's *Missa dos Quilombos* (1997), Richard Serraria et al.'s *Alabê Ôni* (2018), Sergio d'Ogun's *Alafia* (2017), Fabiana Cozza's *Canto Sagrado* (2019), Mãe Carmen's *Obatala* (2019), Hank Schroy and Alabês do Ilê Oxumare's *A Orquestra do Candomblé da Nação Ketu* (2011), and Ilê Omolu Oxum's *Cantigas e Toques para os Orixás* (2004).

13. At its Video Library, the Bahian TVE (Educational TV) has for public consultation several fascinating documentaries (in DVD format) on Candomblé houses as well as on Afro-Bahian carnival groups, named the "Project of Cultural Mapping and Landscaping of Bahia" series. See, for example, *Ilê Axé Bahia: A Saga dos Orixás* (Salvador: TVE, 2002), and *Gaiaku Luiza: Força e Magia dos Voduns* (Salvador: TVE, 2004), which demonstrate the extent to which the State of Bahia is equally invested in the preservation of relocated sacred African heritage in Brazil through the electronic and digital media.

14. Christopher Dunn, "Afro-Bahian Carnival: A Stage for Protest." *Afro-Hispanic Review* 11, no. 1–3 (1992): 11–20. For other works on carnival where African religious influence is pronounced and articulated, see also Niyi Afolabi, *Ilê Aiyê in Brazil and the Reinvention of Africa* (New York: Palgrave, 2016); Claudia Alexandre, *Orixás no Terreiro Sagrado do Samba: Exu & Ogum no Candomblé do Vai-Vai* (Rio de Janeiro: Griot Editora, 2021); Rita Amaral and Wagner Gonçalves Silva, "Foi Conta para Todo Canto: As Religiões Afro-Brasileiras nas Letras do Repertório Musical Brasileiro," *Afro-Ásia* 34 (2006): 189–235; Nelson Cerqueira, ed., *Carnaval da Bahia: Um Registro Estético* (Salvador: Omar G, 2002); Larry Crook, "Black Consciousness, *Samba-Reggae*, and the Re-Africanization of Bahian Music in Brazil," *The World of Music* 35, no. 2 (1993): 90–108; Daniel Crowley, *African Myth and Black Reality in Bahian Carnival* (Los Angeles: UCLA Museum of Cultural History, 1981); Milton Cunha, *Carnaval é Cultura: Poética e Técnica no Fazer Escola de Samba* (São Paulo: SENAC, 2015); Eliana Dumêt, *O Maior Carnaval do Mundo: Salvador da Bahia* (Salvador: Editora Palloti, 2004); Christopher Dunn, "Seeking the Orixás in Brazilian Popular Music," in *Axé Bahia: The Power of Art in an Afro-Brazilian*

Metropolis, ed. Patrick A. Polk, Robert Conduru, Sabrina Gledhill, and Randal Johnson (Los Angeles: Flower Museum at UCLA, 2017), 180–91; Frederico A. R. C. Mendonça, ed., *Desfile de Afoxés* (Salvador: IPAC, 2010); and Raquel Turetti Scotton and Sônia Côrrea Lages, "Ogum, a Voz do Gueto: Orixá do Rap e da Rima nas Letras de Criolo e Emicida," *PLURA: Revista de Estudos de Religião* 11, no. 1 (2020): 169–86.

15. For a more detailed description and analysis of Africa-derived religiosities as artistic expressions of popular culture and Afro-Brazilian identity, see, for example, Clarissa Amaral, *African Heritage Tourism in Bahia* (Salvador: Secretariat of Tourism for the State of Bahia, 2009); Paloma Jorge Amado Costa, *A Comida Baiana de Jorge Amado* (Rio de Janeiro: Record, 2003); T. J. Desch-Obi, *Fighting for Honor: The History of African Martial Art Traditions in the Atlantic World* (Columbia: University of South Carolina Press, 2008); Jane Fajans, *Brazilian Food: Race, Class, and Identity in Regional Cuisines* (London: Berg, 2012); Frederico A. R. C. Mendonça, *Festa da Boa Morte* (Salvador: IPAC, 2011); Floyd Merrell, *Capoeira and Candomblé: Conformity and Resistance through Afro-Brazilian Experience* (Princeton, NJ: Markus Wiener, 2005); João Carlos Cruz de Oliveira, *Terreiros de Candomblé de Cachoeira e São Félix* (Salvador: IPAC, 2015); Tereza Paim and Sonia Robatto, *Na Mesa da Baiana: Receitas, Histórias, Temperos e Espírito Tipicamente Baianos* (São Paulo: Editora SENAC, 2018); and Palo Ribeiro, *Arte de Capoeira* (Salvador: TVE Bahia, 2009 [DVD]).

16. I deploy Afro-spiritual identity here more as a subject, rather than object, following Robert Rogers's understanding of the conceptualization of selfhood and otherhood as integrative processes through which boundaries are potentially neutralized. See Rogers, *Self and Other: Object Relations in Psychoanalysis and Literature* (New York: New York University Press, 1991), 33–35.

17. Stephen Selka, *Religion and the Politics of Ethnic Identity in Bahia, Brazil* (Gainesville: University Press of Florida, 2007), 112.

18. Selka, *Religion and the Politics*, 75. For a further analysis of Candomblé as an "alternative space of blackness," see also Michel Agier, "Between Affliction and Politics: A Case Study of Bahian Candomblé," in *Afro-Brazilian Culture and Politics: Bahia 1790s to 1990s*, ed. Hendrik Kraay (Armonk: M.E. Sharpe, 1998), 134–57; and Rachel Harding, *A Refuge in Thunder* (Bloomington: Indiana University Press, 2000).

19. Vagner Gonçalves da Silva, "Religion and Black Cultural Identity: Roman Catholics, Afro-Brazilians and Neopentecostalism," *Vibrant* 11, no. 2 (2014): 210–46.

20. Gonçalves da Silva, "Religion and Black Cultural Identity," 218.

21. Stefania Capone, *Searching for Africa in Brazil: Power and Tradition in Candomblé* (Durham, NC: Duke University Press, 2010), 254.

22. David T. Haberly, *Three Sad Races* (Cambridge: Cambridge University Press, 2010 [1983]).

23. Racial democracy may be defined as Brazil's official claim of racial harmony due to facile race mixture. The concept was advanced by Gilberto Freyre in the 1930s through his classic and contentious *The Masters and the Slave* (1933), in which he argued that miscegenation was a positive process between the three races (European, African, and Amerindian) that created Brazilian character and identity. By not factoring how race mixture has marginalized the Afro-Brazilian population, the concept has come under scrutiny by leaders of Black social movements, who see it as a pretext for continued or veiled racism. In the Afro-Brazilian religious realm, racial democracy is contested, as it is seen as similar to religious syncretism, through which Candomblé devotees were able to preserve their Africa-derived religion during enslavement and that they now feel was repressive of their true African identity. By challenging racial democracy and religious syncretism, Candomblé worshippers feel they should be free to venerate African deities without necessarily equating them with Catholic saints through syncretism. Race mixture and religious syncretism should not continue to be an excuse for racial oppression and marginalization but should also accommodate Africa-derived religions and identities to proclaim their Africanness and political power without fear or shame.

24. For a detailed discussion on the persistence of coloniality in religious syncretism, see, for example, Raimundo C. Barreto, "Racism and Religious Intolerance: A Critical Analysis of the Coloniality of Brazilian Christianity," *Mission Studies* 38 (2021): 398–423; Cláudio Márcio do Carmo and Célia Maria Magalhães, "Sincretismo e Questão Racial: Relações Lexicais e Representações Conflitantes em Dois Jornais e Duas Revistas Impressas Brasileiras." *DELTA* 26, no. 1 (2010): 25–57; Paulo Montero, "Syncretism and Pluralism in the Configuration of Religious Diversity in Brazil," *Mecila Working Papers Series* 4 (2018): 1–20; and Jim Wafer and Hédimo Rodrigues Santana, "Africa in Brazil: Cultural Politics and the Candomblé Religion," *Folklore Forum* 23, no. 1–2 (1990): 98–114.

Chapter 1

1. Góes Calmon, Francisco Marques de, *Vida Econômica-Financeira da Bahia* (Salvador: Governo do Estado da Bahia, 1979); and Luís Henrique Dias Tavares, *História da Bahia* (Salvador: Civilização Brasileira, 2001 [1959]).

2. For an insightful exploration of the nexus between religion and Afro-Brazilian identity and politics, see Stephen Selka, *Religion and the Politics of Ethnic Identity in Bahia, Brazil* (Gainesville: University Press of Florida, 2007), 48–72, 120–52.

3. While African influence is visible all over Bahia, the influence of the Yoruba of West Africa is more pronounced due to the religious and cultural relics in Candomblé as well as in culinary heritage. For an authoritative study

on the Yoruba contributions to transatlantic communities, see Kamari Maxine Clarke, *Mapping Yoruba Networks: Power and Agency in the Making of Transnational Communities* (Durham: Duke University Press, 2004). For a detailed study of Afro-Bahian culinary traditions, see Jailson de Andrade et al., eds., *Atlas da Culinária na Baía de Todos os Santos* (Salvador: EDUFBA, 2013).

4. Rex Nettleford pronounced this statement during his delivery as Keynote Speaker at the First International Conference on Caribbean Studies in the Bahamas in 2001.

5. See Caetano Veloso, "Céu da Bahia," Musica.com, accessed August 3, 2017, https://www.musica.com/letras.asp?letra=1177618.

6. See Gerônimo, "É d'Oxum," Jellynote (accessed August 3, 2017), https://www.jellynote.com/en/guitar-chords/geronimo/e-doxum.

7. For the most comprehensive, detailed, and illustrated book on popular festivals, see Nelson Varón Cadena, *Festas Populares da Bahia, Fé, e Folia* (Salvador: Edição do Autor/Assembléia Legislativa da Bahia).

8. For a comprehensive structural analysis of Candomblé, see Roger Bastide, *O Candomblé da Bahia: Um Rito Nagô* (São Paulo: Companhia das Letras, 2009 [1958]). For an authoritative analysis of the origins, traditions, continuity, and diversity of Candomblé in Brazil, see also Aulo Barretti Filho, ed., *Dos Yoruba ao Candomblé Ketu* (São Paulo: EDUSP, 2010).

9. Mikelle Smith Omari-Tunkara, *Manipulating the Sacred: Yoruba Art, Ritual, and Resistance in Brazilian Candomblé* (Detriot: Wayne State University Press, 2005).

10. For a detailed appreciation of the blend of the sacred and profane (including pertinent interviews with the sisters and the Catholic priest in the ritual) when it comes to the preservation and popularization of the sisterhood through tourism, see the State TV's DVD production, *Festa da Boa Morte* (Salvador: TVE, 1994).

11. See, for example, Secretaria de Turismo do Estado da Bahia, *Turismo Étnico Afro na Bahia* (Salvador: Secretaria de Turismo do Estado da Bahia, 2009), 71–74; Claudius Portugal, *Magica Bahia* (Salvador: Fundação Jorge Amado, 1997), 69–92; and Jorge Amado, *Bahia de Todos os Santos* (Rio de Janeiro: RECORD, 1977), 177–87.

12. For a detailed analysis of this event, see Cheryl Sterling, "A Bença [sic]: The Blessings of the Bando de Teatro Olodum," in *African Diaspora in Brazil*, ed. Fassil Demissie (New York: Routledge, 2014), 71–92.

13. For a more detailed discussion of the multiple agencies of Yemoja in Africa and the African diaspora, see Henry Drewal, ed., *Sacred Waters: Arts for Mami Wata and Other Divinities in Africa and the Diaspora* (Bloomington: Indiana University Press, 2008); and Solimar Otero and Toyin Falola, *Yemoja: Gender, Sexuality, and Creativity in the Latina/o and Afro-Atlantic Diasporas* (Albany: State University of New York Press, 2013).

14. Elizabeth Isichei, "Mami Wata, Water Spirits, and Returners in and Near the Igbo Culture Area," in *Sacred Waters: Arts for Mami Wata and Other Divinities in Africa and the Diaspora*, ed. Henry Drewal (Bloomington: Indiana University Press, 2008), 242. See also Armando Vallado, *Iemanjá:A Grande Mãe Africana no Brasil* (Rio de Janeiro: Pallas, 2008); and Lloyd Weaver and Olukunmi Egbelade, *Yemoja: Maternal Divinity, Tranquil Sea, and Turbulent Tides* (Brooklyn: Athenia Henrietta, 1999).

15. Cheryl Sterling, *African Roots, Brazilian Rites* (New York: Palgrave, 2012), 73.

16. Sônia Ivo, "Iconografia," *Festa de Santa Bárbara* (Salvador: IPAC, 2010), 41–42.

17. Nívea Alves dos Santos, "O Culto a Santa Bárbara na Bahia," in *Festa de Santa Bárbara* (Salvador: IPAC, 2010), 45.

18. Carla Bahia, "A Festa de Santa Bárbara no Pelourinho," in *Festa de Santa Bárbara* (Salvador: IPAC, 2010), 66.

19. Dias Gomes, *Journey to Bahia* (Washington, DC: Brazilian American Cultural Institute, 1962), 32.

20. Dias Gomes, *O Pagador de Promessas* (Rio de Janeiro: Bertrand, 1997), 15.

21. João Cezar de Castro Rocha, "A Guerra de Relatos no Brasil: Contemporâneo ou A 'Dialética da Marginalidade'" (Oxford: Oxford Working Papers, Center for Brazilian Studies, 2004), 153–84.

missing note 22?

23. Dias Gomes, *Journey to Bahia* (Washington, DC: Brazilian American Cultural Institute, 1962), 9.

24. Eduardo de la Fuente, "'Profane' Rather Than 'Secular': Daniel Bell as Cultural Sociologist and Critic of Modern Culture," *Thesis Eleven* 118, no. 1 (2013): 105–115.

25. Mattijs van de Port, *Ectastic Encounters: Bahian Candomblé and the Quest for the Really Real* (Bloomington: Indiana University Press, 2011), 133.

26. Ruth Landes, *The City of Women* (Alberquerque: University of New Mexico Press, 1947), 101–102.

27. Niyi Afolabi, *Ilê Aiyê in Brazil and the Reinvention of Africa* (New York: Palgrave, 2016).

28. Cheryl Sterling, *African Roots, Brazilian Rites* (New York: Palgrave, 2013), 108.

29. Angela Schaun, *Práticas Educomunicativas: Grupos Afro-Descedentes, Salvador-Bahia: Ara Ketu, Ilê Aiyê, Olodum, Pracatum* (Rio de Janeiro: MAUAD, 2002), 155.

30. Kwame Dixon, *Afro-Politics and Civil Society in Salvador da Bahia, Brazil* (Gainesville: University Press of Florida, 2016), 39.

31. Daniela Mercury, "Chame Gente," Letras (accessed July 16, 2017), https://www.letras.com.br/daniela-mercury/chame-gente.

32. For a more detailed study of the groups, as individual organizations and as collectives, see, for example, IPAC, *Desfile de Afoxés* (Salvador: IPAC, 2010); Nelson Cerqueira et al., *Carnaval da Bahia: Um Registro Estético* (Salvador: Fundação do Estado da Bahia, 2002); and Eliana Dumêt, *O Maior Carnaval do Mundo: Salvador da Bahia* (Salvador: Omar G., 2004).

33. Stefania Capone, *Searching for Africa in Brazil* (Durham, NC: Duke University Press, 2010), 122.

34. Michael Hanchard, *Orpheus and Power* (Princeton, NJ: Princeton University Press, 1994), 164–67.

Chapter 2

1. "Andrew" was the name assigned to the typical Nigerian in radio propaganda during the 1980s that targeted those youngsters who were desperately frustrated with living in Nigeria after many years of restless efforts to make positive headway in their own country and were contemplating going overseas for better opportunities.

2. Pierre Verger, *Ewe: The Use of Plants in Yoruba Society* (Salvador: Odebrecht, 1995).

3. Roger Bastide, *The African Religions of Brazil: Towards a Sociology of the Interpenetration of Civilizations*, trans. Helen Sebba (Baltimore: Johns Hopkins University Press, 1978); J. Lorand Matory, *Black Atlantic Religion: Tradition, Transnationalism, and Matriarchy in the Afro-Brazilian Candomblé* (Princeton: Princeton University Press, 2005); Paul Christopher Johnson, *Secrets, Gossip, and Gods: The Transformation of Brazilian Candomblé* (New York: Oxford University Press, 2002); Stefania Capone, *Searching for Africa in Brazil: Power and Tradition in Candomblé* (Durham: Duke University Press, 2010); Luis Nicalau Parés, *The Formation of Candomblé: Vodum History and Ritual in Brazil* (Chapel Hill: University of North Carolina Press, 2013).

4. Bastide, *The African Religions of Brazil*, 381.

5. J. Lorand Matory, "In-Depth Review: *The Formation of Candomblé: Vodun History and Ritual in Brazil*, by Luis Nicolau Parés," *Scholarly Exchange* (2015): 610.

6. Matory, *Black Atlantic Religion*, 613.

7. Johnson, *Secrets, Gossip, and Gods*, 151–78.

8. Pierre Verger, *Trade Relations Between the Bight of Benin and Bahia from the 17th to 19th Century*, trans. Evelyn Crawford (Ibadan: Ibadan University Press, 1976); Verger, *Orixás* (Salvador: Corrupio, 2002 [1951]); Verger and Carybé, *African Legends of the Orishas* (Salvador: Corrupio, 2006); Verger, *Notas Sobre o Culto aos Orixás e Voduns na Bahia de Todos os Santos no Brasil*, trans. Carlos

Eugenio de Moura (São Paulo: EDUSP, 1999 [1957]); Verger, *Fluxo e Refluxo* (Salvador: Corrupio, 1987 [1968]); and Verger, *Artigos* (Salvador: Corrupio, 1992).

9. Jérôme Souty, *Pierre Fatumbi Verger: Du regard détaché à la connaissance initiatique* (Paris: Maisonneuve & Larose, 2007); Jean-Pierre Le Bouler, *Pierre Fatumbi Verger: um homem livre*, trans. Fábio Araújo, Anamaria Morales, Márcia Caffé, and Dominique Lurton (Salvador: Fundação Pierre Verger, 2002); Cida Nóbrega and Regina Echeverria, *Verger: Um Retrato em Preto e Branco* (Salvador: Corrupio, 2002); Ângela Lühning, ed., *Verger/Bastide: Dimensões de uma amizade*, trans. Rejane Janovitzer (Rio de Janeiro: Bertrand Brasil, 2002).

10. Wole Soyinka, *Death and the King's Horseman* (New York: Norton, 2003).

11. Ana Lucia Araujo, "Pierre Fatumbi Verger: Negotiating Connections Between Brazil and the Bight of Benin," *Luso-Brazilian Review* 50, no. 1 (2013): 113–39.

12. Cited in Nóbrega and Echeverría, *Verger*, 355.

13. See Cynthia Garcia, "To and From Bahia and Back," *NewCityBrazil*, May 10, 2016, accessed October 15, 2018, https://www.newcitybrazil.com/2016/05/10/to-and-from-bahia-and-back-a-review-of-the-photographs-of-pierre-verge-at-the-new-galeria-marcelo-guarnieri-rio-de-janeiro/.

14. See Pierre Verger, *Orixás*, 27–28. Verger may have used the racist voice of Nina Rodrigues to justify his own fetish perspective but what both have in common is the delegitimization of African religiosity and their representation of ancient religious traditions as lesser when compared to the Catholic faith. By distinguishing between Catholic practices and African fetishes, Verger condescendingly suggests that the Catholic faith is far superior to the African religion because it was a matter of the new one desiring to be considered equal to the old. Not only is Verger apparently mistaken and racist, but his entire effort to educate his readers about the commonality of both Brazilian and African ritual cultures is defeated by his colonial mentality. Laying the blame of his prejudice on the influence of Nina Rodrigues may not do justice to the age-old racism of the time during which Verger was postulating about the crossroads and controversies of African-derived religions in Brazil.

15. Verger and Carybé, *African Legends of the Orishas*, 7.

16. João Martinho Braga de Mendonça, "Visual Anthropology in Post-Colonial Worlds: 'What Has Gone Wrong,'" *Vibrant* 9, no. 2 (2012): 213–52.

17. Braga de Mendonça, "Visual Anthropology," 218.

18. Rosane Andrade, *Fotografia e Antropologia: Olhares Fora-Dentro* (São Paulo: Estação Liberdade, 2002), 49. For a more detailed analysis devoted to Candomblé, see also Lisa Castillo, "Icons of Memory: Photography and Its Uses in Bahian Candomblé," *Stockholm Review of Latin American Studies* 4 (2009): 11–23.

19. See, for example, Paul Hartman, *A Memoir on the Physical Review* (College Park, MD: American Institute of Physics, 2008 [1994]).

20. Pierre Verger, "Notes sur le Culte des Orisa et Vodun: à Bahia, la Baie des Tous les Saints au Brésil," *Mémoires de l'IFAN*, no. 51 (1957); Verger, *Retratos da Bahia, 1946 a 1952* (Salvador: Corrupio, 1980); Verger, *Le Messager/ The Go-Between: Photographies 1932–1962* (New York: Powerhouse, 1981).

21. Verger, *Retratos da Bahia*.

22. Pierre Verger, *Dieux d'Afrique* (Paris: Revue Noire, 1995).

23. Verger, *Ewe*, 276–77. Translation of verse 27 of the Ogbe turupon, being the incantation prescribed for remedying barren women.

24. Castillo, "Icons of Memory." For a more detailed study, see also Lisa Earl Castillo, "The Elusive Limits of the Secret: Afro-Brazilian Religion in the Photography of Pierre Verger," in *O Brasil de Pierre Verger*, ed. Alex Baradel (Salvador: Fundação Pierre Verger, 2006), 203–31.

25. Nina Rodrigues, *O Animismo Fetichista dos Negros Baianos* (Rio de Janeiro: Civilização Brasileira, 1935 [1896]); Ruth Landes, *The City of Women* (Albuquerque: University of New Mexico Press, 1994); Juana Elbein dos Santos, *Os Nagô e a Morte* (Petrópolis: Vozes, 1986); Susan Sontag, *On Photography* (New York: Picador, 1977); Roland Barthes, *Camera Lucida: Reflections on Photography* (New York: Hill and Wang, 1980).

26. See Wole Soyinka, *Myth, Literature, and the African World* (Cambridge: Cambridge University Press, 1990). For an analogy between theory and praxis, see also Soyinka, *Death and the King's Horseman*.

27. There are many versions to this episode. One is speculative at best, given that this version is only supported by another version that also needs verification and given that it circulates in a context where the collaborators are either out of the loop by way of passage to the beyond, avoid the controversy, or prefer to not problematize further what was a rather traumatic experience. An informal interview with Dr. Lisa Earl Castillo in Salvador da Bahia, Brazil, in December 2017, reveals that a version was told to her by Professor João Reis, who states that it was actually Professor Olabiyi Yai who had attempted to recover the Ife Head from Carybé's house and not Wole Soyinka. How the said Ife Head ended up with Wole Soyinka and back in Ile-Ife, Nigeria, is another puzzling story. In any case, the fact here is that some Yoruba Royal Head was duly recovered from Bahia (perhaps from the homes of Afro-Brazilian enthusiasts such as Pierre Verger and Carybé) and returned to Nigeria. This caused pandemonium in Nigeria and resulted in a Soyinka-led campaign to deport Pierre Verger from Nigeria. The connections between the deportation and recuperation of deemed "stolen" artifacts are as puzzling as the "original" story itself.

28. Wole Soyinka, *Death and the King's Horseman*, 3.

29. Simon Gikandi, "Introduction," in *Death and the King's Horseman*, Wole Soyinka (New York: Norton, 2003), xvii.

30. Duro Ladipo, *Three Yoruba Plays* (Ibadan: Mbari, 1964).

31. Wole Soyinka, *The Lion and the Jewel* (Oxford: Oxford University Press, 1962). While a comedy, the play may also be read as a situation in which the colonizer, figured as the Lion, is preying on the Jewel, which signifies either the African nation or, in specific terms, Nigeria. In this metaphoric context, I am inferring that the controversy between Pierre Verger and Wole Soyinka may well be interpreted as a dilemma of Nigeria returning to the abode of the Lion (Pierre Verger) to retrieve her Jewel, the Yoruba royal crowns.

Chapter 3

1. Rachel E. Harding, *A Refuge in Thunder: Candomblé and Alternative Spaces of Blackness* (Bloomington: Indiana University Press, 2000), 104–146.

2. This movement was spearheaded by Mãe Stella of Ilê Axé Opo Afonja, but some adherents of Candomblé still secretly attend Catholic masses, the same way evangelicals privately attend Candomblé rituals. For a more detailed analysis of these contradictions, see Stephen Selka, *Religion and the Politics of Ethnic Identity in Bahia, Brazil* (Gainesville: University Press of Florida, 2007), 73–96.

3. Luis Nicolau Parés notes that "the 1920s and early 1930s are remembered as a period of strong police repression of Candomblé." For a more detailed analysis, see Luis Parés, "The Nagôization Process in Bahian Candomblé," in *The Yoruba Diaspora in the Atlantic World*, ed. Toyin Falola and Matt Childs (Bloomington: Indiana University Press, 2004), 195.

4. Parés, "The Nagôization Process in Bahian Candomblé," 196. See also Luis Nicolau Parés, *The Formation of Candomblé: Vodum History and Ritual in Brazil* (Chapel Hill: University of North Carolina Press, 2013), 35–66, 159–207.

5. João Reis, "Candomblé in Nineteenth-Century Bahia: Priests, Followers, Clients," in *Rethinking the African Diaspora: The Making of a Black Atlantic World in the Bight of Benin and Brazil*, ed. Kristin Mann and Edna G. Bay (New York: Routledge, 2001), 118. For more incisive historical and critical analyses of the leadership of one of the oldest and famed Candomblé temple in Bahia, Ilê Axé Opo Afonja, see, for example, Opo Afonja, *Políticas de Acautelamento do IPHAN: Ilê Axé Opo Afonja* (Salvador: IPHAN, 2015); Mestre Didi, *História de Um Terreiro* (Salvador: Cathargo & Forte, 1994); Vera Felicidade de Almeida Campos, *Mãe Stella de Oxóssi: Perfil de Uma Liderança Religiosa* (Rio de Janeiro: Zahar, 2003); and Maria das Graças de Santana Rodrigué, *Ori Apere: O Ritual das Águas de Oxalá* (São Paulo: Selo Negro, 2001).

6. See, for example, Jocélio Teles dos Santos, ed., *Mapeamento dos Terreiros de Salvador* (Salvador: Centro de Estudos Afro-Orientais-UFBA, 2008).

7. Denise da Fonseca and Sonia Giacomini, ed., *Presença do Axé* (Rio de Janeiro: PALLAS & PUC Editora, 2013), 163.

8. For a more in-depth yet descriptive analysis of the way of life in a Candomblé temple, see, for example, Rita Amaral, *Xirê: O Modo de Crer e de Viver no Candomblé* (Rio de Janeiro: PALLAS, 2005).

9. Mãe Valnizia Bianch, *Reflexões*, trans. Rachel Harding (Salvador: Edição do Autor, 2019), 79. Mãe Valnizia is the Iyalorixá of the Terreiro do Cobre, a Candomblé temple in Salvador da Bahia. Her temple is one of the oldest in Bahia. It constitutes, like many others, a politically and socially engaged ritual institution whose members are engaged in Afro-Brazilian human and civil rights organizing through which they demand respect for and recognition of Afro-Brazilian religious traditions. While not every Candomblé temple is written about, the inner workings as well as the African "tales" that form the moral template for organizing and continuity are embedded in those that are written about. See, for example, Everaldo Conceição Duarte, *Terreiro do Bogum: Memórias de Uma Comunidade Jeje-Mahi na Bahia* (Lauro de Freitas: Solisluna, 2018); Raul Lody, *Santo Também Come* (Rio de Janeiro: PALLAS, 2012); Erisvaldo Pereira dos Santos, *Formação de Professores e Religiões de Matrizes Africanas* (Belo Horizonte: Nandyala, 2015); and Teresinha Bernardo, *Negras Mulheres e Mães: Lembranças de Olga de Alaketu* (Salvador: PALLAS, 2019).

10. For insights into the organization, stratification, seniority, and hierarchy in Candomblé, see, for example, Vivaldo da Costa Lima, "Organização do Grupo de Candomblé: Estratificação, Senioridade, and Hierarquia," in *Culto aos Orixás*, ed. Carlos Eugênio Marcondes de Moura (Rio de Janeiro: PALLAS, 2004), 79–132. For insights into leadership style and hierarchy in the Santa Bárbara Vírgem temple in Sergipe-Aracaju, see also Dijna Andrade Torres, *Mulher Nagô: Liderança e Parentesco no Universo Afro-Brasileiro* (Curitiba: Appris Editora, 2015). Similar studies regarding leadership styles can be located in the memories of Olga de Alaketu as contained in Teresinha Bernardo, *Negras, Mulheres e Mães* (Rio de Janeiro: PALLAS, 2003). Olga de Alaketu indeed celebrates the power of women when she notes: "Look, my daughter, in my house only a woman can be a queen. In fact, you know why? Because she has more power" (148).

11. Succession of priestesses in Ilê Axé Opo Afonja to date includes Mãe Aninha (1909–1938); Mãe Bada de Oxalá (1939–1941); Mãe Senhora (1942–1967); Mãe Ondina de Oxalá (1969–1975); Mãe Stella de Oxóssi (1976–2018); and Ana de Xango (2018–Present). For specific insights into Mãe Stella's leadership style, see, for example, Vera Felicidade de Almeida Campos, *Mãe Stella de Oxóssi: Perfil de Uma Liderança Religiosa* (Rio de Janeiro: Jorge Zahar, 2003).

12. For more insights into her early life in the Ilê Axé Opo Afonja, see, for example, *Estrela Azul: Mãe Stella @ 60 Anos* (Salvador: TVE, 1999), DVD. See also *A Cidade de Mulheres* (Salvador: Casa de Cinema/Petrobras, 1999), DVD.

13. For a more detailed description of Oxóssi, see Pierre Verger, *Orixás: Deuses Iorubás na África e no Novo Mundo* (Salvador: Corrupio, 2002), 112–14. In Verger's synthesis of Osoosi's qualities and characteristics, he states: "The

archetype of Osoosi is that of a smart person, quick, always alert and constantly in motion. They are full of initiatives, new discoveries and activities. They have a sense of responsibility and of taking care of the family. They are generous, hospitable, and friendly; but they are also apt at changing residences as they pursue new ways of life even if to their own detriment, and at times with a penchant for a calm and harmonious domestic life" (114).

14. Jaime Sodré, "Ialorixá, O Poder Singular Feminino," in *Faraimará: O Caçador Traz Alegria*, ed. Cléo Martins and Raul Lody (Rio de Janeiro: PALLAS, 1999), 261. For another befitting homage on her investiture into the Bahian Academy of Letters, see also Myriam Fraga, "Mãe Stella de Oxóssi, Odé Kaiodé: Saudação à Acadêmica," *Revista de Academia de Letras da Bahia* 52 (2014): 351–62.

15. For insights on the definition of the symbolism of Oxóssi in Candomblé and in Umbanda, see, for example, Margaret Souza, *Oxóssi: Senhor das Matas* (Fortaleza: Published by author, 2017), 15. The author states, "Oxóssi is a hunter of lost souls, of children who lost their path in the course of evolution" (15).

16. Ubiratan Castro de Araújo, "O Símbolo Mais Puro," in *Osóòsi: O Caçador de Alegrias*, Mãe Stella de Osóòsi (Salvador: Fundação Pedro Calmon, 2011), 7.

17. Mãe Stella de Osóòsi, *Osóòsi: O Caçador de Alegrias* (Salvador: Fundação Pedro Calmon, 2011), 10.

18. Osóòsi, *Osóòsi: O Caçador de Alegrias*, 11.

19. Osóòsi, *Osóòsi: O Caçador de Alegrias*, 65.

20. Osóòsi, *Osóòsi: O Caçador de Alegrias*, 74.

21. Osóòsi, *Osóòsi: O Caçador de Alegrias*, 79.

22. See for example, Felipe Fanuel Xavier Rodrigues, "O Contexto Religioso na Literatura de Maya Angelou e Mãe Beata de Yemonjá," *XII Congresso Internacional da ABRALIC* (UFPR, Curitiba, 2011), 1–8; and Assunção de Maria Souza e Silva, "Por dentro do *Caroço de Dendê*: A Sabedoria dos Terreiros de Mãe Beata de Yemonjá," *Revista África e Africanidades* 2, no. 8 (2010): 1–8. See also Stella Guedes Caputo and Malisa Passos, "Cultura e Conhecimento em Terreiros de Candomblé: Lendo e Conversando com Beata de Yemonjá, *Currículo sem Fronteiras* 7, no. 2 (2007): 93–111.

23. CRIOULA, "Mãe Beata de Iemanjá e a fé que nos move," *CRIOULA*, May 26, 2018, https://CRIOULA.ORG.BR/CATEGORY/ARTIGOS.

24. Elina Harktikainen, "A Politics of Respect: Reconfiguring Democracy in Afro-Brazilian Religious Activism in Salvador, Brazil," *American Ethnologist* 45, no. 1 (2018): 95.

25. Cited in Haroldo Costa, *Mãe Beata de Yemonjá: Guia, Cidadã, Guerreira* (Rio de Janeiro: Garamond, 2010), 149.

26. Marcos Serra, *30 Anos do Ilê Omiojuarô: Ancestralidade, Educação, Arte e Ativismo nas Redes de Mãe Beata de Iyemonjá* (Salvador: Novas Edições Acadêmicas, 2015), 93.

27. Vânia Cardoso, "Introduction," in *Caroço de Dendê:A Sabedoria dos Terreiros*, Mãe Beata de Yemonjá (Rio de Janeiro: PALLAS, 2008), 14.

28. Zeca Ligeiro, "Preface," in *Caroço de Dendê:A Sabedoria dos Terreiros*, Mãe Beata de Yemonjá (Rio de Janeiro: PALLAS, 2008), 19.

29. Júlio Braga and Mãe Beata de Yemonjá, *Caroço de Dendê:A Sabedoria dos Terreiros* (Rio de Janeiro: PALLAS, 2008), 1, 129.

30. Braga and Yemonjá, *Caroço de Dendê*, 97.

31. Braga and Yemonjá, *Caroço de Dendê*, 121.

32. Braga and Yemonjá, *Caroço de Dendê*, 122.

33. Valnizia Bianche, *Reflexões: Escritas de Mãe Valnizia Bianch* (Salvador: Edição do Autor, 2019), 14.

34. Bianche, *Reflexões*, 66.

35. Bianche, *Reflexões*, 71.

36. Cléidiana Ramos and Meire Oliveira, "Preface," in *Reflexões: Escritas de Mãe Valnizia Bianch*, Valnizia Bianche (Salvador: Edição do Autor, 2019), 11.

37. Rachel Elizabeth Harding, "Valnizia Bianche," in *Reflexões: Escritas de Mãe Valnizia Bianch*, Valnizia Bianche (Salvador: Edição do Autor, 2019), 15.

38. Bianche, *Reflexões*, 51.

39. Bianche, *Reflexões*, 19.

40. Reginaldo Prandi, *Mitologia dos Orixás* (São Paulo: Companhia das Letras, 2001), 515.

Chapter 4

1. Gal Costa, "É d'Oxum," Suas Letras, accessed December 25, 2017, http://www.suasletras.com/letra/Gal-Costa/e-D-oxum/20494.

2. Pai Cido de Osun Eyin, *Candomblé: A Panela do Segredo* (São Paulo: Editora Arx, 2002), 199, my translation.

3. Cheryl Sterling, *African Roots, Brazilian Rites* (New York: Palgrave, 2012), 79.

4. Pierre Verger, *Notas sobre o Culto dos Orixás* (Rio de Janeiro: Pallas, 2002), 301–304, my translation.

5. Lydia Cabreara, *Iemanjá & Oxum* (São Paulo: Edusp, 2002), 53.

6. Rowland Abiodun, "Hidden Power," in *Osun Across the Waters*, ed. Joseph Murphy and Mei-Mei Sanford (Bloomington: Indiana University Press), 26.

7. Jorge Amado, *Sea of Death*, trans. Gregory Rabassa (Dartmouth, MA: Tagus, 2013), v.

8. Patrícia Trindade Nakagame, "Jorge Amado e o Sentido Plural de Revolução," *Miscelânia* 20 (2016): 216, my translation.

9. Amado, *Sea of Death*, 130.

10. Amado, *Sea of Death*, 53.

11. Amado, *Sea of Death*, 230.

12. For a more detailed analysis of this complex relationship between Guma and Iemanjá, see Jaques Salah, *A Bahia de Jorge Amado* (Salvador: Casa de Palavras, 2008), 145–48.

13. Bobby J. Chamberlain, *Jorge Amado* (Boston: Twayne, 1990), 97.

14. Chamberlain, *Jorge Amado*, 10.

15. Amado, *Sea of Death*, vii.

16. Amado, *Sea of Death*, 15.

17. Amado, *Sea of Death*, 58.

18. Amado, *Sea of Death*, 62.

19. Amado, *Sea of Death*, 17.

20. Alice Raillard, *Conversando com Jorge Amado* (Rio de Janeiro: Record, 1990), 163.

21. Lícia Soares de Souza, "Forças e Fragilidades de Porto dos Milagres: Adaptação Televisiva de *Mar Morto*," in *Jorge Amado: Leituras e Diálogos em Torno de Uma Obra*, ed. Rita Olivieri-Godet and Jacqueline Penjon (Salvador: Fundação Casa de Jorge Amado, 2004), 271.

22. Jorge Amado, *Sea of Death*, 145.

23. Vasconcelos Maia, *O Leque de Oxum* (Salvador: Assembléia Legislativa do Estado da Bahia, 2006), 32, my translation.

24. The 2006 edition contains five chronicles beyond the main novella, *O Leque de Oxum*, while the 1961 edition contains three short stories, namely, "Antes do Segundo marcado" (Before the set moment); "A Confissão" (Confession); and "Preto e Branca" (Black man and white woman).

25. Pierre Verger, "How Olokum Became Water Goddess," *Lendas Africanas dos Orixás* (Salvador: Corruprio, 2011), 60.

26. Diedre Badejo, *Osun Seegesi: The Elegant Deity of Wealth, Power and Femininity* (Trenton, NJ: Africa World, 1996), 80.

27. Ívia Alves, "Vasconcelos Maia: Desdobramento de Um Tema." *Letra Viva* 8 (1988): 13.

28. Vasconcelos Maia, *O Leque de Oxum* (Salvador: Assembléia Legislativa do Estado da Bahia, 2006), 85, my translation.

Chapter 5

1. This accusation is problematic as it speaks to a nonculpable, consensual act, rather than an afterthought, and both Virgínia and Margarida can use such accusations as excuses to get rid of the black men in their lives after their "bodies" have been used and abused in the name of love and pleasure. In the case of Virgínia, specifically, it is important for her to see Ismael as a rapist because she does not want the mixed-race offspring that might come of

the sexual relation. In fact, in addition to this psychological rejection of the "black angel," Virgínia's next cathartic moment is to kill the offspring herself by drowning one after the other.

2. For a comparative analysis of data on racial identity and political behavior, see Gladys L. Mitchell-Walthour, *The Politics of Blackness* (Cambridge: Cambridge University Press, 2018), 93–143.

3. Gilberto Freyre, *The Masters and the Slaves* (New York: Knopf, 1946); Homi Bhabha, *The Location of Culture* (New York: Routledge, 1994); Carl Degler, *Neither Black nor White* (Madison: University of Wisconsin Press, 1986).

4. *Sortilégio* (Black mystery) by Abdias do Nascimento and *Anjo Negro* by Nelson Rodrigues were first part of the production of the TEN, Teatro Experimental do Negro, which was quite powerful in the mid-1940s in terms of the promotion of black consciousness and pride.

5. France W. Twine, *Racism in a Racial Democracy: The Maintenance of White Supremacy in Brazil* (New Brunswick, NJ: Rutgers University Press, 1998), 98. For an additional study of the Bahian case study of racial relations, see also Thales de Azevedo, *As Elites de Cor numa Cidade Brasileira* (Salvador: EDUFBA, 1996).

6. Christen Smith, *Afro-Paradise: Blackness, Violence, and Performance in Brazil* (Chicago: University of Illinois Press, 2016), 5.

7. Carl Degler, *Neither Black nor White* (Madison: University of Wisconsin Press, 1986), 213.

8. Abdias do Nascimento, "Sortilege II: Zumbi Returns," trans. Elisa Larkin Nascimento, in *Crosswinds: An Anthology of Black Dramatists the Diaspora*, ed. William B. Branch (Bloomington: Indiana University Press, 1993), 243.

9. Leda Martins, "A Ritual Choreography: The Orishas' Steps in *Sortilégio*," *Callaloo* 18, no. 4 (1995): 869.

10. Martins, "A Ritual Choreography," 867.

11. Wole Soyinka, *Myth, Literature and the African World. London* (Cambridge: Cambridge University Press, 1976).

12. Nascimento, "Sortilege II: Zumbi Returns," 210.

13. Ruy Castro, *O Anjo Pornográfico; A Vida de Nelson Rodrigues* (São Paulo: Companhia das Letras, 1992), 203.

14. Femi Ojo-Ade, "Preface," in *Home and Exile: Abdias Nascimento, African Brazilian Thinker and Pan African Visionary*, ed. Femi Ojo-Ade (Trenton, NJ: Africa World Press, 2014), xv.

15. Elisa Larkin Nascimento, *The Sorcery of Color: Identity, Race, and Gender in Brazil* (Philadelphia: Temple University Press, 2007), 208–226.

16. The title is my translation. For the original, see José Endoença Martins, "A Negritice e Comunidade Imaginada de Afro-Brasileiros na Literatura," *Terra Roxa e Outras Terras: Revista de Estudos Literários* 15 (2009): 1–12.

17. José Endoença Martins, "A Negritice e Comunidade Imaginada de Afro-Brasileiros na Literatura," *Terra Roxa e Outras Terras: Revista de Estudos Literários* 15 (2009): 4.

18. Roberto Fernández Retamar, *Caliban e Outros Ensaios* (São Paulo: Busca Vida, 1988).

19. Nascimento, "Sortilege II: Zumbi Returns," 239.

20. Sandra Richards, "Constructions of Afro-Brazilian Identity in the Theatre of the 1950s: The Cases of Dora Seljan and Abdias do Nascimento," *The Journal of Afro-Latin American Studies and Literatures* 3 (1995): 159.

21. Richards, "Constructions of Afro-Brazilian Identity," 160–61.

22. Elisa L. Nascimento. *The Sorcery of Color: Identity, Race, and Gender in Brazil* (Philadelphia: Temple University Press, 2007), 213.

23. Nascimento. *The Sorcery of Color*, 218.

24. Nascimento, *The Sorcery of Color*, 223.

25. Femi Ojo-Ade, ed., *Home and Exile: Abdias Nascimento: African Brazilian Thinker and Pan African Visionary* (Trenton, NJ: Africa World Press, 2014), 1–15.

26. Katherine McKittrick, *Demonic Grounds: Black Women and the Cartographies of Struggle* (Minneapolis: University of Minnesota Press, 2006), 46.

27. See Fred Clark, *Impermanent Structures* (Chapel Hill, NC: Studies in the Romance Languages and Literatures, 1991), 99.

28. Clark, *Impermanent Structures*, 99.

29. Nelson Rodrigues, "Black Angel [*Anjo Negro*]," in *The Theater of Nelson Rodrigues II*, ed. Joffre Rodrigues (Rio de Janeiro: Ministério da Cultura, 2001), 205.

30. Valdemar Valente Junior, "O Demônio e o Anjo: Personagens Negras e Idéia de Preconceito Racial no Teatro Brasileiro," *Todas as Letras* 17, no. 2 (2015): 214.

31. Henrique Buarque de Gusmão, "Nelson Rodrigues Leitor de Gilberto Freyre: O Projeto Teatral Rodriguiano em Aliança com a Sociologia Freyreana," *Sociedade e Estado* 23 (2008): 107.

32. For an in-depth understanding of the Oedipus complex and its bearing on the burden of Ismael, see René Girard, *Violence and the Sacred* (New York: Johns Hopkins University Press, 1977), 169–92.

33. Girard, *Violence and the Sacred*, 39–67.

34. Julee Tate, "Dangerous Games: The Female Character in Afro-Brazilian Theater," *Marvels of the African World: African Cultural Patrimony, New World Connections, and Identities* (Trenton, NJ: Africa World Press, 2003), 308.

Chapter 6

1. Claudia Moser and Cecilia Feldman, *Locating the Sacred: Theoretical Approaches to the Emplacement of Religion* (Oxford: Oxbow, 2014), 1.

2. The Yoruba pantheon consists of over two hundred male and female orisas. The male òrìṣà (orisas) include Aganju (volcanoes, wilderness and rivers); Babalu Aye (orisa of the Earth and strongly associated with infectious diseases

and healing); Erinle (orisa of medicine, healing, and comfort and a physician to the gods); Esu (trickster); Ibeji (twins); Obatala (creator of human bodies and of spiritual purity and moral uprightness); Oduduwa (deity of humans); Ogun (orisa who presides over iron, fire, hunting, politics, and war); Oko (agriculture); Osanyin (the forest); Osumare (divine rainbow serpent linked with creation and procreation); Osoosi (hunt and forest); Sango (thunder and lightning); and Sopona (smallpox). The female òrìṣà include Aja (the forest, the animals within it, and herbal healing); Aje (wealth); Ayao (air); Egungun-oya (divination); Mawu (creator goddess, associated with the sun and moon); Nana Buruku (androgynous Supreme Creator); Oba (first wife of Sango and deity of domesticity and marriage); Olokun (patron deity of the descendants of Africans in the diaspora); Osun (orisa who presides over love, intimacy, beauty, wealth, and diplomacy); Oya (deity of the Niger River, associated with wind, lightning, fertility, fire, and magic); and Yemoja (a mother goddess, patron deity of women and the Ogun river). For rigorous interrogations of these deities in their global contexts, see Pierre Verger, *Orixás Deuses Iorubás na África e no Novo Mundo* (Salvador: Corrupio, 2002); and Toyin Falola and Ann Genova, eds., *Orisa: Yoruba Gods and Spiritual Identity in Africa and the Diaspora* (Trenton, NJ: Africa World Press, 2005).

3. For a detailed study of this deity, see Solimar Otero and Toyin Falola, *Yemoja: Gender, Sexuality, and Creativity in the Latina/o and Afro-Atlantic Diasporas* (Albany: State University of New York Press, 2013), 215–66; see also Armando Vallado, *Iemanjá: A Grande Mãe Africana do Brasil* (Rio de Janeiro: PALLAS, 2002), 1–53.

4. Michel Despland, *Bastide on Religion: The Invention of Candomblé* (London: Equinox, 2008), 77.

5. I invoke "musicscape" here as a theoretical loan term from Arjun Appadurai, even though it would stand in closer proximity with "Ethnoscape." In "Disjuncture and Difference in the Global Cultural Economy," Appadurai lays out his meta theory of disjuncture. He identifies five disjunctive yet interrelated global cultural flows to complicate the idea that the new global cultural economy is complex, overlapping, and disjunctive: (1) ethnoscapes: the migration of people across cultures and borders; (2) mediascapes: use of media that shapes the way we understand our imagined world; (3) technoscapes: cultural interactions due to the promotion of technology; (4) financescapes: the flux capital across borders; and (5) ideoscapes: the global flow of ideologies. Appadurai, *Modernity at Large: Cultural Dimensions of Globalization* (Minneapolis: University of Minnesota Press, 1996), 32.

6. Antônio Olinto, "The Survival of the Gods," in Zora Seljan, *The Story of Oxala* (London: Rex Collins, 1977), ii.

7. Olinto, "The Survival of the Gods," iii.

8. See Joseph Campbell, *The Power of Myth* (New York: Anchor, 1991), 164.

9. Sandra L. Richards, "Constructions of Afro-Brazilian Identity in the Theatre of the 1950s: The Case of Zora Seljan and Abdias do Nascimento," in *Transatlantiques: Atlantic Cross-Currents*, ed. Susan Andrade, E. Julien, Micheline Rice-Maximim, and A. Songolo (Trenton, NJ: Africa World Press, 2001), 135.

10. Ali Mazrui, *The Africans: The Triple Heritage* (New York: Little, Brown, 1986), 56.

11. Robert Lima, "Xangô and Other Yoruba Deities in the Plays of Zora Seljan," *Afro-Hispanic Review* 11, no. 1–3 (1992): 26.

12. Zora Seljan, *As Três Mulheres de Xangô e Outras Peças Afro-Brasileiras* (São Paulo: Instituição Brasileira de Difusão Cultural, 1958), 10.

13. Reginaldi Prandi, *Mitilogia dos Orixás* (São Paulo: Companhia das Letras, 2001), 28. My translation of original Portuguese. This authoritative book includes an overview of myths and orixás, occasionally referencing the deities that also feature in Cuban Santería, as well as an extensive compilation of each orixá's orikis, from which to select. Most of these poems (orikis) are in Portuguese and must be translated to be accessed by the non-Portuguese speaker.

14. Prandi, *Mitilogia dos Orixás*, 295.

15. Zora Seljan, *Três Mulheres de Xangô* (Rio de Janeiro: Sociedade Brasileira de Autoes Teatrais, 1978), 15.

16. Seljan, *Três Mulheres de Xangô*, 135.

17. Seljan, *Três Mulheres de Xangô*, 42.

18. Elaine Graham, "What We Make of the World," in *Between the Sacred and Profane: Researching Religion and Popular Culture*, ed., Gordon Lynch (New York: I. B. Taurus, 2007), 69.

19. Aristotle, *Arte Poética*, trans. Pietro Nassetti (São Paulo: Martin Claret, 2007), 30.

20. Anatol Rosenfeld, *O Mito e o herói no Moderno Teatro Brasileiro* (São Paulo: Perspectiva, 1996), 60.

21. Dias Gomes, *O Pagador de Promessas* (Rio de Janeiro: Bertrand Brasil, 1989), 100.

22. Gomes, *O Pagador de Promessas*, 143.

23. Gomes, *O Pagador de Promessas*, 148.

24. Gomes, *O Pagador de Promessas*, 98.

25. Gomes, *O Pagador de Promessas*, 145.

26. For a more detailed analysis of axé as agency of resistance, see Mikelle Smith Omari-Tunkara, *Manipulating the Sacred* (Detroit: Wayne State University Press, 2005), 1–25.

Chapter 7

1. Owe Wikstrom, "Liturgy as Experience: The Psychology of Worship: A Theoretical and Empirical Lacuna," in *The Problem of Ritual*, ed. Tore Ahlback

(Stockholm: The Donner Institute for Religious and Cultural History, 1993), 83.

2. While the controversy does not degenerate to the extent of scholarly dishonesty, Mircea Eliade is accused of having inadvertently ignored the contribution of Durkheim and his *Sacred and the Profane* (1957) by basically neglecting his concrete contribution to the discourse on the sacred and the profane. Durkheim theorizes on the sacred-profane dichotomy in his *Elementary Forms of Religious Life* (1912), but Eliade makes it look as if he alone is the first to make the discovery.

3. Excerpts from Fr. Mark Daniel Kirby's (Priest of the Diocese of Tulsa) "The Proper Chants of the Paschal Triduum in the Graduale Romanum: A Study in Liturgical Theology" (PhD diss., Oxford University, August 2002), https://www.catholicculture.org/culture/library/view.cfm?recnum=9557.

4. Kirby, "Proper Chants of the Paschal Triduum."

5. Mattijs van de Port, *Ecstatic Encounters: Bahian Candomblé and the Quest for the Really Real* (Amsterdam: Amsterdam University Press, 2011), 41.

6. This reference also alludes to the "Uncle Tom" character in African American experience.

7. Robson Pinheiro (with the Spirit Ângelo Inácio), *Tambores de Angola* (São Paulo: Casa dos Espíritos, 1998), 127. This is my translation of corrupted Portuguese (creole as used in the text) that I have rendered in Pidgin English. One notices the corruption of not only syntax but also of grammar. This creative incorporation of the popular language of the elder, who may have had little to no formal education, is commendable. It lends credence to the power and actions of the Umbandist Spirit worker while at the same time debunking the claim that the faith is only for a bourgeois clientele.

8. Mary Del Priore, *Do outro Lado* (São Paulo: Planeta, 2014), 48.

9. Iracilda Gonçalves, *Psicografia: Verdade ou Fé?* (João Pessoa: Editora Universitária UFPB, 2010), 172.

10. Robson Pinheiro, *Os Espíritos em Minha Vida* (Contagem, MG: Casa dos Espíritos Editora, 2008), 190–93. Translation from the Portuguese is mine.

11. Pinheiro, *Tambores de Angola*, 164.

12. Pinheiro, *Tambores de Angola*, 164–65.

13. André Pinheiro, *Revista Espiritual de Umbanda: Representações, Mito Fundador e Diversidade do Campo Umbandista*, in *Espiritismo e Religiões Afro-Brasileiras*, ed. Artur Isaia and Ivan Manoel (São Paulo: Ed. Unesp, 2012), 225.

14. Pinheiro, *Os Espíritos em Minha Vida*, 248.

15. Pinheiro, *Os Espíritos em Minha Vida*, 250.

16. "Instituto Robson Pinheiro," Instituto Robson Pinheiro (accessed on February 5, 2018) https://www.robsonpinheiro.com.br/. Translation is mine.

17. "Instituto Robson Pinheiro."

18. Raul Longo, *Filhos de Olorum: Contos e Cantos de Candomblé* (Rio de Janeiro: PALLAS, 2011), 9. My translation.

19. See Longo, *Filhos de Olorum.*

20. For a more elaborate analysis of ritual as it develops into popular performance, see, for example, Victor Turner, *From Ritual to Theatre: The Human Seriousness of Play* (New York: Paj, 1982).

21. See the subtitle of *A Refuge in Thunder* (Bloomington: Indiana University Press, 2002).

22. Longo, *Filhos de Olorum,* 9.

23. Catherine Bell, *Ritual Theory, Ritual Practice* (Oxford: Oxford University Press, 2009), 3.

24. Bell, *Ritual Theory, Ritual Practice.*

25. Longo, *Filhos de Olorum,* 9.

26. Clifford Geertz, *Myth, Symbol, and Culture* (New York: Norton and Co., 1974), 75.

27. Longo, *Filhos de Olorum,* 13.

28. Longo, *Filhos de Olorum,* 14.

29. Longo, *Filhos de Olorum,* 16.

30. Longo, *Filhos de Olorum,* 17.

31. Nana (Buruku) is the female Supreme Being in the West African traditional religion of the Fon people (Republic of Benin), the Akan people (Republic of Ghana), and the Ewe people (Republic of Togo). She is the most influential deity in West African theology. In Dahomey mythology, Nana Buluku is the mother Supreme Creator who gave birth to the moon spirit Mawu, the sun spirit Lisa, and the universe. After giving birth to these, she retired and left the matters of the world to Mawu-Lisa, according to the Fon mythology. She is the primary creator, Mawu-Lisa the secondary creator, and the theology based on these is called "Vodun," "Voodoo," or "Vodoun."

In Candomblé, Iansan is known as Oya, Iyá Mésàn, or most commonly, as Iansã, derived from the Yoruba Yánsán. In Yoruba religion, she commands winds, storms, and lightning. She is the queen of the River Niger and the mother of nine. She is an invincible warrior. Attributes of Iansã including great intensity of feeling, sensation, and charm. Another ability attributed to Iansã is control over the mysteries that surround the dead. Iansã is syncretized with Santa Bárbara. In the Candomblé nação (association) of Angola Congo, Iansã is associated with the color red.

Ogun is the god of war and metals. In Yoruba religion, Ogun is a primordial orisa who first appeared as a hunter. He was the husband of Oya. He is said to have been the first Orisa to descend to the realm of Ile Aiye (Earth), to find suitable place for future human life. In some traditions he is said to have cleared a path for the other gods to enter Earth using a metal ax and with the assistance of a dog. To commemorate this, one of his praise names, or oriki, is Osin Imole or the "first of the primordial Orisa to come to Earth."

Yemoja (Yoruba: Yemọja) is a major water deity from the Yoruba religion. She is an orisa and the mother of all orisas, having given birth to the fourteen Yoruba gods and goddesses. She is often syncretized with either Our Lady of Regla in the Afro-Cuban diaspora or various other Virgin Mary figures of the Catholic Church, a practice that emerged during the era of the transatlantic slave trade. Yemoja is motherly, strong, and protective, and she cares deeply for all her children, comforting them and cleansing them of sorrow. She is said to be able to cure infertility in women, and cowrie shells represent her wealth. She does not easily lose her temper, but, when angered, she can be quite destructive and violent, as the flood waters of turbulent rivers.

Esu or Exú (Yoruba: Èṣù) is an orisa in the Yoruba religion of the Yoruba people (originating from Yorubaland, an area in and around present-day Nigeria). As the religion has spread around the world, the name of this orisa has varied in different locations, but the beliefs remain similar. Esu partially serves as an alternate name for Elegua, the messenger for all orisas, and that there are 256 paths to Eleggua—each one of which is an Esu. It is believed that Esu is an orisa like Eluggua, but there are only 101 paths to Esu according to Ocha, rather than the 256 paths to Eleggua according to Ifá. Esu is known as the "Father who gave birth to Ogboni," and he is also thought to be agile and always willing to rise above any challenge.

Ṣàngó (Yoruba language: Ṣàngô, from "shan," to strike; he is also known as Changó or Xangô in Latin America, as well as Jakuta or Badé) is an orisa. He is syncretized with either Saint Barbara or Saint Jerome. Historically, Sango is a royal ancestor of the Yoruba as he was the third Alafin (king) of the Oyo Kingdom prior to his posthumous deification. Ṣàngó has numerous manifestations including Airá, Agodo, Afonja, Aganju, Lubé, and Obomin. He is considered one of the most powerful rulers in Yorubaland and is noted for his anger.

Babalú-Ayé (Yoruba: Ọbalúayé, meaning "Father, Lord of the Earth") is an orisa strongly associated with infectious diseases and healing in Yoruba cosmology, including the body, wealth, and physical possessions. In West Africa, he was strongly associated with epidemics of smallpox, leprosy, influenza, ebola, and HIV/AIDS. Although strongly associated with illness and disease, Babalú-Ayé is also the spirit that cures these ailments. Both feared and loved, Babalú-Ayé is sometimes referred to as the "Wrath of the Supreme God" because he punishes people for their transgressions. People hold Babalú-Ayé in great respect and avoid calling his actual name, because they do not wish to invoke epidemics.

Osun (known as Ochún or Oxúm in Latin America), also spelled Ọṣun, is an orisa, a spirit, a deity, or a goddess that reflects one of the manifestations of God in the Ifá and Yoruba religions. She is one of the most popular and venerated orisas. Osun is the deity of the river and fresh water, luxury and pleasure, sexuality and fertility, and beauty and love. She is connected to destiny and divination. She is the patron saint of the Osun River in Nigeria, which bears her name. The river has its source in Ekiti State, in the east of Nigeria, and passes through the city of Osogbo, where Osun-Oshogbo, the principal sanctuary of the deity, is located. Osun is honored at the Osun-Osogbo Festival, a two-week-long annual festival that usually takes place in August at the Osun-Osogbo Sacred Grove on the banks of the river.

Osumare (known as Ochumaré or Oxumaré in Latin America) is an orisa. Osumare is the god of the rainbow in Yoruba mythology, and Osumare also means rainbow in the Yoruba language.

32. See Sidney M. Greenfield and A. F. Droogers, eds., *Reinventing Religions: Syncretism and Transformation in Africa and the Americas* (Lanham, MD: Rowland & Littlefield, 2001).

33. The vivid presence of the Baiana in national culture makes it conducive as another element of national integration, and it has become a representation of the sacred and profane without any contradiction, especially in Bahia. Given its appropriate symbolism in both spaces as an agency for cultural preservation and touristic entertainment, especially as "ushers" in tourism shops and as "photo-ops" volunteers for commercializing gains, it is no longer unusual to encounter the sacred in the secular zone.

34. The process of religious syncretism in Brazil also involved violence, violations, and impositions. In the first instance, African magical knowledge system was repressed, ridiculed, stereotyped, and condemned as "witchcraft" before Afro-Brazilians were converted to Catholicism through a process of convergence with religious ceremonies that also involved the enslaved population and dramatizations of religious or biblical stories. Beyond the era of masking and negotiation with the instruments of state power and religion, especially after the abolition of slavery in 1888, Afro-Brazilians started to feel free to elaborate and standardize their Candomblé religion but not without persistent persecutions that continue today. For a comparative elaboration of Candomblé, see, for example, Vagner Gonçalves da Silva, *Candomblé e Umbanda* (São Paulo: Editora Ática, 1994), 129–33. For more insightful studies of resistance against assimilationist approaches within Candomblé, see also Carlos Eugênio Marcondes de Moura, ed., *Candomblé: Religião do Corpo e da Alma* (Rio de Janeiro: PALLAS, 2004), 103–38; Rita Amaral, *Xirê! O Modo de Crer e de Viver no Candomblé* (Rio de Janeiro: PALLAS, 2005), 29–56; and Vivaldo da Costa Lima, *Lessé Orixá: Nos Pés do Santo* (Salvador: Corrupio, 2010), 221–29.

Chapter 8

1. Odu is at once the sacred name of every Ifá priest as well as the mythical wife of Orunmila, otherwise known as Olofin. She is regarded as the mother of all Ifá priests' wives. For a more detailed description of Odu and the

patakis about her attributes, cleansings, spells, orikis, songs, and sacred stories, see Baba Raul Canazares, *Oya: Santeria and the Orisha of the Winds* (New York: Original, 2006), 1–33. See also Reginaldo Prandi, *Mitologia dos Orixás* (São Paulo: Companhia das Letras, 2001), 362–65.

2. Oya is defined as the wind that turns into fire. She is a force that moves rapidly and often generates heat in the process of such dynamic movement that can easily turn into a thunderbolt. She is the wind that nourishes the fire. However, the wind or the physical element represents the spiritual domain that balances the harmonious duo of wind and air. In the ancestral realm, Egúngún is the wind within the earth, the one that speaks like the wind. The wind is the portent of the empyrean wisdom that links ancestral wisdom with that hidden within the earth.

Oxóssi is a hunter and is one of the four orixás known as the "hunting ones," or warriors, with Eleggua, Ogun, and Osun, in both Afro-Cuban Santeria and Afro-Brazilian Candomble religions. These orixás work together for their followers' spiritual development. Oxóssi is characteristically the spirit associated with the hunt, forests, animals, and wealth. He is also the spirit of meals because he provides food for the devotees. He is associated with lightness, astuteness, wisdom, and craftiness in the hunt. He is, above all, the orixá of contemplation who loves the arts. He hunts with a bow and arrow (called an ofá), hunting for good influences and positive energies.

3. Cited in Biodun Adediran, ed., *Cultural Studies in Ife: Selections from the 1993–94 Seminar Papers of the Institute of Cultural Studies* (Ile Ife: Obafemi Awolowo University, 1995).

4. Adediran, *Cultural Studies in Ife.*

5. See, for example, *Oya Oriri* (2007 [2016]), a movie that reenacts the powers of Sango, the downfall and suicide of Sango, and the aftermath that leads to Oya becoming a river. Another is *Três Mulheres de Xangô* (1978) (Three Women of Xangô) by Zora Seljan, where the same myth is elaborated as a play but with a different bent and climax.

6. Ulli Beier, "Oya," in *Yoruba Myths* (Cambridge: Cambridge University Press, 1960), 33.

7. See editorial comments at "Livro: Ao Sabor de Oiá," Estante Virtual (accessed March 11, 2018), https://www.estantevirtual.com.br/livros/cleo-martins/ao-sabor-de-oia/2687576950.

8. Cléo Martins, *Ao Sabor de Oiá* (Rio de Janeiro: PALLAS, 2003), 8.

9. Émile Durkheim, *The Elementary Forms of Religious Life* (Oxford: Oxford University Press, 2008), 53.

10. Tish Harrison Warren, *Liturgy of the Ordinary: Sacred Practices in Everyday Life* (Dreamers Grove, IL: Intervarsity, 2016), 34.

11. Fernando Ortiz, *Contrapunto Cubano dal Tabaco y el Azucar* (Caracas: Biblioteca Ayaeucho, 1987).

12. Mary Louise Pratt, *Imperial Eyes: Travel Writing and Transculturation* (New York: Routledge, 1992).

13. Original title is "A Madonna de Fogo," which translates as "The Woman of Fire." Martins, *Ao Sabor de Oiá*, 17–52.

14. Martins, *Ao Sabor de Oiá*, 16.

15. Martins, *Ao Sabor de Oiá*, 24.

16. Martins, *Ao Sabor de Oiá*, 20.

17. See Ortiz, *Contrapunto Cubano dal Tabaco y el Azucar*; and Néstor Garcia Canclini, *Hybrid Cultures: Strategies for Entering and Leaving Modernity* (Minneapolis: University of Minneapolis, 2003).

18. Martins, *Ao Sabor de Oiá*, 69.

19. Chynae [Raymundo Adães Motta], *Encantos de Oxóssi* (Lauro de Freitas, BA: Livro-com, 2009), 173.

20. Chynae, *Encantos de Oxóssi*, 15–16.

21. Candace Pert, "Your Body is Your Subconscious Mind: Mind-Body Medicine Becomes the Science of Psychoneuroimmunolgy (PNI)," Healing Cancer, http://www.healingcancer.info/book/export/html/34.

22. Chynae, *Encantos de Oxóssi*, 17–24.

23. Chynae, *Encantos de Oxóssi*, 32.

24. Chynae, *Encantos de Oxóssi*, 49–58.

25. Chynae, *Encantos de Oxóssi*, 57.

26. Chynae, *Encantos de Oxóssi*, 119–26, 127–38.

27. For a biographical study of this major personality in Candomblé, see, for example, Vera Felicidade de Almeida Campos, *Mãe Stella de Oxóssi: Perfil de Uma Liderança Religiosa* (Rio de Janeiro: Zahar, 2003). See also Maria Stella de Azevedo Santos, *Meu Tempo É Agora* (Salvador: Assembléia Legislativa do Estado da Bahia, 2010).

28. Fategbe Fatunmbi, "Iyaami Osoronga," Scribd (accessed March 16, 2018) https://www.scribd.com/doc/281807467/Iyami-Osoronga.

Chapter 9

1. Marc Cleiren, "Identity Under Pressure: Motivation and Emotional Dynamics in Cultural and Religious Groups," in *Emotions and Religious Dynamics*, ed., Douglas J. Davies and Nathaniel A. Wayne (London: Ashgate, 2013), 121–22.

2. Henry Louis Gates Jr., "Celebrating Candomblé in Bahia," *The Root*, February 16, 2010, https://www.theroot.com/celebrating-candomble-in-bahia-1790878635.

3. Gates, "Celebrating Candomblé in Bahia."

4. Gates, "Celebrating Candomblé in Bahia."

5. See Ordep Serra, *Rumores da Festa: O Sagrado e o Profano na Bahia* (Salvador: Editora da Universidade da Bahia, 2009); Janio Roque Barros de Castro, "A Reinvenção do Carnaval na Extensão Profana da Festa de Nossa Senhora da Ajuda na Cidade de Cachoeira, No Recôncavo Baiano," *Textos Escolhidos de Cultura e Arte* 9, no. 1 (2012): 154–67; Alberto Ikeda, "O Ijexá no Brasil: Rítmica dos Deuses nos Terreiros, nas Ruas e Palcos da Música Popular," *Revista USP* 111 (2016): 21–36; Piers Armstrong, "The Aesthetic Escape Hatch: Carnaval, blocos afro and the Mutations of baianidade under the Signs of Globalisation and re-Africanisation," *Journal of Iberian and Latin American Studies* 5, no. 2 (1999): 65–98; Karolina de Oliveira Rebouças, "Afoxé Filhos de Gandhi: 55 Anos de Música Afro-Brasileira o Tempo dos Tempos," Senior Thesis, University of Uberlandia, 2005; Isis Costa McElroy, "A Transdiasporic Paradigm: The *Afoxé Filhos de Gandhy*," *Afro-Hispanic Review* 29, no. 1 (2010): 77–100; and Eduardo Davel and Renata Saback Rosa, "Gestão, Cultura e Consumo Simbólico no Cortejo Afro," *Revista Pensamento Contemporâneo em Administração* 13 (2017): 13–30.

6. Armstrong, "The Aesthetic Escape Hatch," 91. My emphasis.

7. McElroy, "A Transdiasporic Paradigm," 77.

8. Chris McGovern and Ricardo Pessanha, *The Brazilian Sound: Samba, Bossa Nova and the Popular Music of Brazil* (Philadelphia: Temple, 1998), 122. My emphasis.

9. McGovern and Pessanha, *The Brazilian Sound*, 122.

10. Anísio Félix, *Filhos de Gandhi: A História de Um Afoxé* (Salvador: Gráfica Central, 1987), 9. My translation. All subsequent translations are mine.

11. Félix, *Filhos de Gandhi*, 30.

12. Antônio Risério, *Carnaval Ijexá* (Salvador: Corrupio, 1981), 53.

13. Risério, *Carnaval Ijexá*, 55.

14. Risério, *Carnaval Ijexá*, 56.

15. IPAC, *Desfile de Afoxés* (Salvador: IPAC/Fundação Pedro Calmon, 2010), 14.

16. The need to create a carnival group that caters exclusively for women, mothers, and lovers of the original Filhos de Gandhi, led to the creation of the first female afoxé in Brazil on July 2, 1979. According to Glicélia Vasconcelos, the sixty-nine-year-old founding member, the group was the initiative of a former director of Filhos de Gandhi, the deceased Gilberto Nonato Sacramento, otherwise known as "Negão." Interview with Glicélia Vasconcelos, February 2, 2018.

17. Interview with Arany Santana, February 10, 2018.

18. See "Alberto Pitta," Cortejo Afro (accessed April 20, 2018) http://www.cortejoafro.com.br/alberto-pitta/.

19. Axé Project was founded as a nongovernmental organization in 1990, with a mission to ensure basic human rights, particularly those of children and adolescents who have been challenged by lack of a social structure

and ended up on the streets. Axé Project started by providing education for children struggling to make a living in the streets of Salvador, in addition to fighting for their rights. Its activities have been expanded to include outreach efforts to families of such children, as a measure to reintegrate them back into the family structure, as well as a strategic outreach to those children who are not yet living on the streets and to organizations with similar objectives and interests, so that experiences are shared for the betterment of the mission of Axé Project. Three units are involved in its communication chain—(1) street education; (2) education units; and (3) advocacy efforts—all of which help to solidify the mission of the organization.

20. The mother of Alberto Pitta was the matriarch and priestess of Ilê Axé Oyá in Pirajá. She passed on in 2015 at ninety years old.

21. Alberto Pitta, "*Cortejo Afro* and the Rereading of African Heritage" (Salvador: Nós Transatlânticos, 2016), DVD.

22. Deinya Phenix, "Race Consciousness, Diaspora, and *Baianidade*: Observations from an Epic Global Party," *Consciousness, Literature and the Arts* 17, no. 1 (2016): 14.

23. http://viajay.com.br/blog/visualizar/cortejo-afro-divulga-incio-de-ensaios-de-vero-em-salvador (accessed April 20, 2018). My emphasis.

24. "Histórico," Cortejo Afro (accessed April 21, 2018), http://www.cortejo afro.com.br/historico/.

25. Alberto Pitta, "Experiências do Cortejo Afro no Carnaval de Salvador" in *Políticas e Gestão da Cultura: Diálogos entre Universidade e Sociedade*, ed., Clelia Nero Côrtes, Alice Lacerda, Renata Leah, and Ricardo Soares (Salvador: EDUFBA, 2017), 210.

26. Pitta, "Experiências do Cortejo Afro no Carnaval de Salvador," 211.

27. Pitta, "Experiências do Cortejo Afro no Carnaval de Salvador," 212.

28. Pitta, "Experiências do Cortejo Afro no Carnaval de Salvador," 213.

29. Brian D. Christens, "Targeting Empowerment in Community Development: A Community Psychology Approach to Enhancing Local Power and Well-Being," *Community Development Journal* 47, no. 4 (2012): 538–54.

Chapter 10

1. For its basic preparation in the Brazilian context, see Manuel Querino, *A Arte Culinária na Bahia* (Salvador: Papelaria Brasileira, 1928); Vivaldo da Costa, *A Anatomia do Acarajé e Outros Escritos* (Salvador: Corrupio, 2010), 153–79; Neil Lopes, *Enciclopédia Brasileira da Diáspora Africana* (São Paulo: Selo Negro, 2004), 28; Josmara B. Fregoneze, Marilene Jesus da Costa, and Nancy de Souza, *Cozinhando História: Receitas, Histórias e Mitos de Pratos Afro-Brasileiros* (Salvador: Fundação Pierre Verger, 2011), 36–43; and Hermelinda Lys Carneiro

de Andrade, *A Cozinha Baiana no Restaurante Senac do Pelourinho* (Salvador: SENAC, 2008), 20. Preparation in the Nigerian or West African context is similar except Brazilians often add shrimp, hot pepper, blended salad, and other traditional supplements as a form of local appetizing trademark. Acarajé serves as both a religious offering to the deities in the Afro-Brazilian religion of Candomblé and as street snack. Originally brought by enslaved peoples from West Africa, it is prepared with mashed black-eyed peas seasoned with salt and chopped onions, which are then molded into small ball shapes and deep-fried in palm oil in front of customers. In Brazil, it is served split in half and stuffed with spicy pastes made from shrimp, ground cashews, palm oil, and other ingredients. Acarajé can also come in a second form, called abara, where the mashed black-eyed peas are boiled instead of deep fried.

2. The ritual offering is a tradition that originates from the African continent and is not unique to Bahia in the African diaspora. For example, in June 2019, the inhabitants of Ile-Ife made akara (similar to acarajé) to feed the Yoruba deities, the diviners (babalawos), devotees, and the people in general to honor Yemoja, Oya, Osun, and Obatala. While there is no singular explanation for the etymology of acarajé in Brazil, it is generally understood that it is a corruption of the original Yoruba word akara (noun meaning the staple food that is common in West Africa, referring to black-eyed bean cake) and jé (the verb referring to the act of eating). It may well be that, in the course of Afro-Brazilian religious devotees offering each other akara, both words became merged over the centuries. It is also suggested by the Anthropology Professor Vivaldo da Costa Lima of the Federal University of Bahia, Brazil, that the word derives from the Yoruba egungun (masquerading or ancestral) society, where the devotees consumed akara egbe (that is, akara of the egungun society eaten during their masking traditions or outings) that was later corrupted to akara-jé because Brazilians found it difficult to pronounce the monosyllabic "gb" sound that does not exist in Portuguese as it does in Yoruba. Interview with Professor Vivaldo da Costa Lima was granted in July 2003 in Salvador.

3. For a detailed analysis of 150 food items offered to the Afro-Brazilian deities, see Raul Lody, *Santo Também Come* (Rio de Janeiro: PALLAS, 2012), 59–90.

4. Guilherme Radel, *A Cozinha Africana da Bahia* (Salvador: Lei de Incentivo à Cultura, 2006), 59. For additional analysis of the significance of acarajé in Brazilian culture, see also Vivaldo da Costa Lima, *A Anatomia do Acarajé e os Outros Escritos* (Salvador: Corrupio, 2010).

5. See Dorival Caymmi, "A Preta do Acarajé," Letras, accessed December 1, 2019, https://www.letras.mus.br/dorival-caymmi/1117681/. The song not only focuses on acarajé but also draws attention to its steam-cooked variation (as opposed to fried) called abará.

6. See, for example, Vivaldo da Costa Lima, *A Anatomia do Acarajé* (Salvador: Corrupio, 2010); Carolina Fonseca, "Baianas do Acarajé: Patrimônio *Urbano* Imaterial?," *IV NENECULT: Encontro de Estudos Multidisciplinares em Cultura* (Salvador: UFBA, May, 28–30, 2008), 1–14; Roberta Guimarães, "Objetos, Sistema Culinário e Candomblé: O Patrimônio das 'Baianas de Acarajé,'" *Religião e Sociedade* 32, no. 1 (2012): 233–37; Daniel Bitter and Nina Bitar, "Comida, Trabalho e Patrimônio: Notas sobre o Ofício das Baianas de Acarajé e das Tacazazeiras," *Horizontes Antropológicos* 18, no. 38 (2012): 213–36; Denise Botelho, "Gastronomia Afro-Religiosa: Profissionalização de Mulheres Negras de Axé," *Linhas Críticas* 23, no. 52 (2017): 665–76; Patrícia Rodrigues de Souza, "Food in African Brazilian Candomblé," *Religion and Food* 26 (2015): 264–80; and Antonio Walter Ribeiro de Barros Junior and Felipe Modolo, "O Ritual do Acarajé : Entre o Sagrado e o Profano: Uma Análise da Comida de Santo nas Práticas Comerciais Contemporâneas," *Revista Empreenda-Unitoledo* 2, no. 2 (2018): 186–208. Though not germane to the current study, the elegant outward appearance of the baianas is also labor intensive beyond the preparation of the food. In addition to the painstaking work, every baiana de acarajé takes time to dress up with pride as a typical baiana, a cultural image that is also religiously derived, as it replicates the ambience of the sacred associated with the devotees of Candomblé, hence the sight of the white outfit that often accompanies the dress code of this cultural vendor. For more insights on the language of dress and fashion of the baiana, see, for example, Kelly Mohs Gage, "*Moda da Bahia*: An Analysis of Contemporary Vendor Dress in Salvador," *Fashion Theory* 20, no. 2 (2016): 153–79; and Marcos Rezende, ed., *Mulheres de Axé* (Salvador: Kawo-Kabiyesile, 2015).

7. Scott Alves Barton, "FIFA vs. As Baianas de Acarajé and the Politics of the Cultural Imaginary," in *Urban Foodways and Communication: Ethnographic Studies in Intangible Cultural Food Heritages Around the World*, ed. Casey Man Kong Lum and Vager Marc de Ferrière (New York: Rowman and Littlefield, 2016), 127. See also Anderson Carigé, "Baiana de Acarajé: De Personagem Cantada a Profissão," in *Imagens da Cidade da Bahia*, ed., Délio José Ferraz Pinheiro and Maria Auxiliadora da Silva (Salvador: EDUFBA, 2007), 67–77. While Barton praises the baianas for their courageous resolve to challenge the marginalization of their cultural product during the World Cup, Carigé provides a synthesis and analysis of the significance of the baianá, while urging further studies on the complex cultural, gendered, and enterprising phenomenon, especially in Bahia.

8. Traditionally, the selling of acarajé has always been the economic activity of many Afro-Brazilian women after the abolition of slavery. At least 70 percent of Afro-Brazilian women who are members of the Association of the Baianas de Acarajé are not only from Bahia but are also the sole heads of their families. See, for example, Roger Sansi, *Fetishes & Monuments: Afro-Brazilian*

Art and Culture in the 20th Century (New York: Berghahn, 2007), 75–77. For a perusal of a general introduction intended for young minds and general readers, where the significance of the "baiana table" containing different products sold by the baiana is highlighted, see Sonia Rosa, *O Tabuleiro da Baiana* (Rio de Janeiro: PALLAS, 2009). A tabuleiro refers to the wooden board or glass box where the baianas display different food items for sale, such as the classical acarajé (fried bean dumpling, which is ground, seasoned with pepper, vatapá, caruru, dried shrimp and salad, and fried in boiling palm oil).

9. Sukari Ivester, "Culture, Resistance and Policies of Exclusion at World Cup 2014: The Case of the 'Baianas do Acarajé,'" *Journal of Policy Research in Tourism, Leisure & Events* 10 (2015): 9–10.

10. For a more detailed analysis of hegemonic threats against acarajé in the local and global worlds, see, for example, Lígia Santos, *O Corpo, O Comer, e a Comida* (Salvador: EDUFBA, 2008); and Lígia Santos, "Acarajé, Dendê, Modernidade, e Tradição no Contexto Soteropolitano" in *Dendê: Símbolo e Sabor da Bahia*, ed., Raul Lody (São Paulo: SENAC, 2009), 81–92. Some of the criticism levied against acarajé is the claim that it is fattening due to the high cholesterol associated with palm oil.

11. Cheryl Sterling, *African Roots, Brazilian Rites* (New York: Palgrave, 2012), 56.

12. Ubaldo Marques Porto Filho, *Dinha do Acarajé* (Salvador, UMPF, 2009), 15.

13. See Claude Lévi-Strauss, *Antropologia Estrutural* (São Paulo: Cosac Naify, 2008).

Bibliography

Adediran, Biodun. *Cultural Studies in Ife: Selections from the 1993–94 Seminar Papers of the Institute of Cultural Studies*. Ile-Ife: Obafemi Awolowo University, 1995.

Adegbindin, Omotade. *Ifá in Yoruba Thought System*. Durham, NC: Carolina Academic Press, 2014.

Afolabi, Niyi. "Afro-Spiritual Identities: Self and Other in Muniz Sodré's *A Lei do Santo* and Ernesto Veras' *Portas Fechadas*." Unpublished manuscript, 2020, typescript.

———. "Axé: Invocation of Candomblé and Afro-Brazilian Gods in Brazilian Cultural Production." In *Fragments of Bone: New-African Religions in a New World*, edited by Patrick Bellegarde-Smith, 108–123. Urbana: Illinois University Press, 2005.

———. *Ilê Aiyê in Brazil and the Reinvention of Africa*. New York: Palgrave, 2016.

———. "Milton Nascimento's *Missa dos Quilombos*: Musical Invocation, Race, and Liberation." In *Migrations and Creative Expressions in Africa and the African Diaspora*, edited by Toyin Falola, Niyi Afolabi, and Aderonke Adesanya, 65–79. Durham: Carolina Academic Press, 2008.

Afolabi, Niyi, Márcio Barbosa, and Esmeralda Ribeiro, eds. *The Afro-Brazilian Mind: Contemporary Afro-Brazilian Literary and Cultural Criticism*. Trenton, NJ: Africa World Press, 2008.

Afonja, Opo. *Ilê Axé Opô Afonja: Políticas de Acautelamento do IPHAN*. Salvador: IPHAN, 2015.

Agier, Michel. "Between Affliction and Politics: A Case Study of Bahian Candomblé." In *Afro-Brazilian Culture and Politics: Bahia 1790s to 1990s*, edited by Hendrik Kraay, 134–157. Armonk, NY: M. E. Sharpe, 1998.

———. "Racism, Culture and Black Identity in Brazil." *Bulletin of Latin American Research* 14, no. 3 (1995): 245–64.

Agnew, Vijay. "The Quest for the Soul in the Diaspora." In *Diaspora, Memory, and Identity: A Search for Home*, edited by Vijay Agnew, 268–290. Toronto: University of Toronto Press, 2005.

Albuquerque, Wlamyra R. de. *O Jogo da Dissimulação: Abolição e Cidadania Negra no Brasil*. São Paulo: Companhia das Letras, 2009.

Alexandre, Claudia. *Orixás no Terreiro Sagrado do Samba: Exu and Ogum no Candomblé do Vai-Vai*. Rio de Janeiro: Griot Editora, 2021.

Almeida Campos, Vera Felicidade de. *Mãe Stella de Oxóssi: Perfil de Uma Liderança Religiosa*. Rio de Janeiro: Zahar, 2003.

Alonso, Miguel. *The Development of Yoruba Candomblé Communities in Salvador, Bahia, 1835–1986*. New York: Palgrave, 2014.

Alvarez, Sonia E. Evelina Dagnino, and Arturo Escobar, eds. *Cultures of Politics, Politics of Cultures: Re-Envisioning Latin American Social Movements*. Boulder, CO: Westview, 1998.

Alves, Ívia. "Vasconcelos Maia: Desdobramento de Um Tema." *Letra Viva* 8 (1988): 7–17.

Amado, Jorge. *Bahia de Todos os Santos*. Rio de Janeiro: Record, 1977.

———. *Jorge Amado: 100 Anos Escrevendo o Brasil*. Salvador: Casa das Palavras, 2013.

———. *Jorge Amado: Cacau: A volta ao Mundo em 80 Anos*. Salvador: Casa das Palavras, 2014.

———. *Jorge Amado: Literatura e Política*. Salvador: Casa das Palavras, 2015.

———. *Mar Morto*. Rio de Janeiro: Record, 2004 [1936].

———. *Mar Morto*. São Paulo: Companhia das Letras, 2008 [1933].

———. *Sea of Death*. Dartmouth: Tagus, 1984.

Amaral, Clarissa, ed. *African Heritage Tourism in Bahia*. Salvador: Secretariat of Tourism for the State of Bahia, 2009.

Amaral, Rita. *XIRÊ! O Modo de Crer e de Viver no Candomblé*. Rio de Janeiro: PALLAS, 2005.

Amaral, Rita, and Vagner Gonçalves Silva. "Foi Conta para Todo Canto: As Religiões Afro-Brasileiras nas Letras do Repertório Musical Brasileiro." *Afro-Ásia* 34 (2006): 189–235.

———. "Religiões Afro-Brasileiras e Cultura Nacional: Uma Etnografia em Hipermídia." *Caderno Pós Ciências Sociais* 3, no. 6 (2006): 107–130.

Andrade, Hermelinda Lys Carneiro de. *A Cozinha Baiana no Restaurante Senac do Pelourinho*. Salvador: SENAC, 2008.

Andrade, Jailson de, Vanessa Hatje, and Gal Meirelles e Núbia Ribeiro, eds. *Atlas da Culinária na Baía de Todos os Santos*. Salvador: EDUFBA, 2013.

Andrade, Rosane. *Fotografia e Antropologia: Olhares Fora-Dentro*. São Paulo: Estação Liberdade, 2002.

Andrews, George Reid. "Brazilian Racial Democracy, 1900–90: An American Counterpoint." *Journal of Contemporary History* 31, no. 3 (1996): 483–507.

Araujo, Ana Lucia. "Pierre Fatumbi Verger: Negotiating Connections Between Brazil and the Bight of Benin." *Luso-Brazilian Review* 50, no. 1 (2013): 113–139.

Araújo, Emanoel, ed. *A Ancestralidade dos Símbolos.* São Paulo: MASP, 2018.

———. *Brazilian Sculpture: An Identity in Profile.* São Paulo: Ministry of Culture, 1997.

———. *Esculturas, Relevos, Monoprints.* Salvador: Best Editora, 1991.

———, ed. *A Mão Afro-Brasileira: Significado da Contribuição Artística e Histórica.* São Paulo: TENENGE, 1988.

———, ed. *Textos de Negros e Sobre Negros.* São Paulo: Museu Afro-Brasil, 2011.

Araújo, Ubiratan Castro de. "O Símbolo Mais Puro." In *Osóòsi: O Caçador de Alegrias,* Mãe Stella de Osóòsi. Salvador: Fundação Pedro Calmon, 2011.

Aristóteles. *Arte Poética.* Translated by Pietro Nassetti. São Paulo: Martin Claret, 2007.

Armstrong, Piers. "The Aesthetic Escape Hatch: *Carnaval, blocos afro* and the Mutations of *baianidade* under the Signs of Globalisation and re-Africanisation." *Journal of Iberian and Latin American Studies* 5, no. 2 (1999): 65–98.

———. *Cultura Popular na Bahia: Estilística Cultural Pragmática.* Feira de Santana: Editora UEFS, 2001.

———. "Popular Sovereignty, Bakhtin and the Sea in Jorge Amado's Religion." *Studies in Latin American Popular Culture* 26 (2000): 129–150.

Azevedo, Ricardo. *Axé-Music: O Verso e o Reverso da Música que Conquistou o Planeta.* Salvador: Empresa Gráfica da Bahia, 2007.

Azevedo, Thales de. *As Elites de Cor numa Cidade Brasileira.* Salvador: EDUFBA, 1996.

Azevedo Santos, Maria Stella de. *Meu Tempo É Agora.* Salvador: Assembléia Legislativa do Estado da Bahia, 2010.

Bacelar, Jefferson, and Cláudio Pereira, eds. *Vivaldo da Costa Lima: Intérprete do Afro-Brasil.* Salvador: EDUFBA, 2007.

Badejo, Diedre. *Osun Seegesi: The Elegant Deity of Wealth, Power and Femininity.* Trenton, NJ: Africa World Press, 1996.

Bakhtin, Mikhail. *Problems of Dostoevsky's Poetics.* Translated by C. Emerson. Minneapolis: University of Minnesota Press, 1984.

———. *Rabelais and His World.* Translated by H. Iswolsky. Bloomington: Indiana University Press, 1984.

Baradel, Alex, ed. *O Brasil de Pierre Verger.* Salvador: Fundação Pierre Verger, 2006.

Barcellos, Mario Cesar. *Os Orixás e a Personalidade Humana.* Rio de Janeiro: Pallas, 2010.

Barreto, Raimundo C. "Racism and Religious Intolerance: A Critical Analysis of the Coloniality of Brazilian Christianity." *Mission Studies* 38 (2021): 398–423.

Barretti Filho, Aulo. *Dos Yoruba ao Candomblé Ketu: Origens, Tradições e Continuidade.* São Paulo: EDUSP, 2010.

Barros, José d'Assunção. *A Construção Social da Cor: Diferença e Desigualdade na Formação da Sociedade Brasileira.* Petrópolis: Vozes, 2009.

Barthes, Roland. *Camera Lucida: Reflections on Photography*. New York: Hill and Wang, 1980.

Barton, Scott. "FIFA vs. As *Baianas de Acarajé* and the Politics of the Cultural Imaginary." In *Urban Foodways and Communication: Ethnography Studies in Intangible Cultural Food Heritages around the World*, edited by Casey Man Kong Lum and Marc de Ferrière le Vayer, 121–138. Lanham: Rowman and Littlefield, 2015.

Bascom, William. *The Yoruba of Southwestern Nigeria*. Prospect Heights, IL: Waveland, 1969.

Bastide, Roger. *The African Religions of Brazil: Toward a Sociology of the Interpenetration of Civilizations*. Translated by Helen Sebba. Baltimore: Johns Hopkins University Press, 1978.

———. *Brasil: Terra de Contrastes*. São Paulo: Difel, 1980.

———. *O Candomblé da Bahia: Um Rito Nagô*. São Paulo: Companhia das Letras, 2009 [1958].

Belier, Ulli. *Yoruba Myths*. Cambridge: Cambridge University Press, 1960.

Bell, Catherine. *Ritual Theory, Ritual Practice*. Oxford: Oxford University Press, 2009.

Bell, Daniel. *Divinations: Theopolitics in the Age of Terror*. Sydney: Cascade Books, 2017.

Bernardo, Teresinha. *Negras Mulheres e Maes: Lembranças de Olga de Alaketu*. Salvador: PALLAS, 2019.

Bhabha, Homi. *The Location of Culture*. New York: Routledge, 1994.

Bianch, Valnizia. *Reflexões: Escritas de Mãe Valnizia Bianch*. Translated by Rachel Harding. Salvador: Edição do Autor, 2019.

Bitar, Nina. *Baianas de Acarajé: Comida e Patrimônio no Rio de Janeiro*. Rio de Janeiro: Editora Aeroplano, 2011.

Bitter, Daniel. "Comida, Trabalho e Patrimônio: Notas sobre o Ofício das Baianas de Acarajé e das Tacacazeiras." *Horizontes Antropológos* 18, no. 38 (2012): 213–236.

Boff, Adriane. *O Namoro Está no Ar . . . Na Onda do Outro: Um Olhar Sobre os Afetos em Grupos Populares*. Santa Cruz do Sul, RS: EDUNISC, 1998.

Botelho, Denise M. "Gastronomia Afro-Religiosa: Profissionalização de Mulheres Negras de Axé." *Linhas Críticas* 23, no. 52 (2017): 664–76.

Braga, Júlio. *Oritamejí: O Antropólogo na Encruzilhada*. Feira de Santana: Editora Universitária de Feira de Santana, 2000.

Brookshaw, David. *Raça e Cor na Literatura Brasileira*. Porto Alegre: Mercado Aberto, 1983.

Brower, Keith H., Earl. E. Fitz, and Enrique Martínez-Vidal, eds. *Jorge Amado: New Critical Essays*. New York: Routledge, 2001.

Brown, Diana DeGroat. *Umbanda: Religion and Politics in Urban Brazil*. New York: Columbia University Press, 1994.

Brown, Kimberly Juanita. "Black Rapture: Sally Hemings, Chica da Silva, and the Slave Body of Sexual Supremacy." *Women's Studies Quarterly* 35, no. 1/2 (2007): 45–66.

Butler, Kim D. *Freedoms Given, Freedoms Won*. New Brunswick, NJ: Rutgers University Press, 1998.

Cabral, Sérgio. *As Escolas de Samba do Rio de Janeiro*. Rio de Janeiro: Lumiar Editora, 1996.

Cabrera, Lydia. *Iemanjá e Oxum*. São Paulo: EDUSP, 2002.

Cadena, Nelson V. *Festas Populares da Bahia, Fé, e Folia*. Salvador: Edição do Autor / Assembléia Legislativa da Bahia, 2015.

Calvo-González, Elena, and Luciana Duccini. "On 'Black Culture' and 'Black Bodies': State Discourses, Tourism and Public Policies in Salvador da Bahia, Brazil." In *Tourism, Power and Culture: Anthropological Insights*, edited by Donald V. L. Macleod and James G. Carrier, 134–52. Bristol: Channel View, 2010.

Campbell, Joseph. *The Power of Myth*. New York: Anchor, 1991.

Campos, Vera Felicidade de Almeida. *Mãe Stella de Oxóssi: Perfil de Uma Liderança Religiosa*. Rio de Janeiro: Zahar, 2003.

Canclini, Néstor Garcia. *Hybrid Cultures: Strategies for Entering and Leaving Modernity*. Minneapolis: University of Minneapolis, 2003.

Candemil, Luciano da Silva. "Panorama das Pesquisas sobre a Música do Candomblé." *Opus* 25, no. 1 (2019): 94–120.

Canizares, Baba Raul. *Oya: Santeria and the Orisha of the Winds*. New York: Original, 2006.

Capone, Stefania. "The 'Orisha Religion' between Syncretism and Re-Africanization." In *Cultures of the Lusophone Black Atlantic*, edited by Nancy Priscilla Naro, Roger Sansi-Roca, and David H. Treece, 219–232. New York: Palgrave Macmillan, 2007.

———. *Searching for Africa in Brazil: Power and Tradition in Candomblé*. Durham: Duke University Press, 2010.

Caputo, Stela Guedes. "Cultura e Conhecimento em Terreiro de Candomblé: Lendo e Conversando com Mãe de Yemonjá." *Currículo sem Fronteiras* 7, no. 2 (2007): 93–111.

Carmen, Mãe. *Obatala: Uma Homenagem a Mãe Carmen*. São Paulo: GEGE, 2019.

Carmo, Cláudio Márcio do, and Célia Maria Magalhães. "Sincretismo e Questão Racial: Relações Lexicais e Representações Conflitantes em Dois Jornais e Duas Revistas Impressas Brasileiras." *DELTA* 26, no. 1 (2010): 25–57.

Carneiro, Édison. *Candomblés da Bahia*. Rio de Janeiro: Civilização Brasileira, 1976.

———. *Candomblés da Bahia*. Salvador: Museo do Estado da Bahia, 1948.

Carvalho, José Jorge de. "Afro-Brazilian Music and Rituals: From Traditional Genres to the Beginnings of Samba." Unpublished manuscript, 1999.

―――. "The Multiplicity of Black Identities in Brazilian Popular Music." In *Black Brazil: Culture, Identity, and Social Mobilization*, edited by Larry Crook and Randal Johnson, 261–296. Los Angeles: UCLA Latin American Center, 1999.

―――. "Violence and Chaos in Afro-Brazilian Religious Experience." *Systèmes de Pensées en Afrique Noire* 16 (2004): 111–48.

Carvalho, Manoel José Ferreira de, and Edvard Passos. *A Cidade Efêmera do Carnaval*. Salvador: EDUFBA, 2016.

Carvalho, Murilo, et al. *Artistas e Festas Populares*. São Paulo: Brasiliense, 1977.

Carvalho, Silvania Capua. *Narrativas da Ancetralidade: O Mito Feminino das Águas em Mia Couto*. Curitiba: Appris, 2015.

Castillo, Lisa Earl. "Icons of Memory: Photography and its Uses in Bahian Candomblé" *Stockholm Review of Latin American Studies* 4 (2009): 11–23.

―――. "The Elusive Limits of the Secret: Afro-Brazilian Religion in the Photography of Pierre Verger." In *O Brasil de Pierre Verger*, edited by A. Baradel, 203–231. Salvador: Fundação Pierre Verger, 2008.

―――. *Entre a Oralidade e a Escrita: a Etnografia nos Candomblés da Bahia*. Salvador: Editora da Universidade Federal da Bahia (Edufba), 2008.

Castillo, Lisa Earl, and Luis Nicolau Parés. "Marcelina da Silva: A Nineteenth-Century Candomblé Priestess in Bahia." *Slavery and Abolition* 31, no. 1 (2010): 1–27.

Castro, A. A. "Axé Music: Mitos, Gestão e World Music." In *A Larga Barra da Baía: Essa Província no Contexto do Mundo*, edited by M. Moura, 196–237. Salvador: EDUFBA, 2011.

Castro, Janio Roque Barros de. "A Reinvenção do Carnaval na Extensão Profana da Festa de Nossa Senhora da Ajuda na Cidade de Cachoeira, No Recôncavo Baiano." *Textos Escolhidos de Cultura e Arte* 9, no. 1 (2012): 154–67.

Castro, Ruy. *O Anjo Pornográfico; A Vida de Nelson Rodrigues*. São Paulo: Companhia das Letras, 1992.

Castro Rocha, João Cezar de. "A Guerra de Relatos no Brasil: Contemporâneo ou A "Dialética da Marginalidade." In *Oxford Working Papers*, 153–84. Oxford: Center for Brazilian Studies, 2004.

Cerqueira, Nelson, ed. *Carnaval da Bahia: Um Registro Estético*. Salvador: Fundação do Estado da Bahia, 2002.

Chamberlain, Bobby J. *Colóquio Jorge Amado: 70 Anos de Mar Morto*. Salvador: Casa de Palavras, 2008.

―――. *Jorge Amado*. Boston: Twayne, 1990.

Christens, Brian D. "Targeting Empowerment in Community Psychology Approach to Enhancing Local Power and Well-Being." *Community Development Journal* 47, no. 4 (2012): 538–54.

Clark, Fred M. *Impermanent Structures: Semiotic Readings of Nelson Rodrigues' Vestido de Noiva, Álbum de Família, and Anjo Negro*. Chapel Hill: University of North Carolina Press, 1991.

Clarke, Kamari Maxine. *Mapping Yoruba Networks: Power and Agency in the Making of Transnational Communities*. Durham: Duke University Press, 2004.

Cleiren, Marc. "Identity Under Pressure: Motivation and Emotional Dynamics in Cultural and Religious Groups." In *Emotions and Religious Dynamics*, edited by Douglas J. Davies and Nathaniel A. Wayne, 121–152. London: Ashgate, 2013.

Cleveland, Kimberly L. *Black Art in Brazil: Expressions of Identity*. Gainesville: University Press of Florida, 2013.

Collins, John F. *Revolt of the Saints: Memory and Redemption in the Twilight of Brazilian Racial Democracy*. Durham, NC: Duke University Press, 2015.

Conduru, Roberto. *Arte Afro-Brasileira*. Belo Horizonte: C/Arte Editora, 2007.

Cordovil, Daniela. "Espiritualidades Feministas: Relações de Gênero e Padrões de Família entre Adeptos da Wicca e do Candomblé no Brasil." *Revista Crítica de Ciências Sociais* 110 (2016): 117–40.

———. "Sexualidade, Gênero e Poder: Uma Análise de Participação Feminina em Políticas Públicas para Afroreligiosos em Belém, Pará." *PLURA: Revista de Estudos de Religião* 4, no. 2 (2013): 149–63.

Costa, Haroldo. *Mãe Beata de Yemonjá: Guia, Cidadã, Guerreira*. Rio de Janeiro: Garamond, 2010.

Costa, Paloma Jorge Amado. *A Comida Baiana de Jorge Amado*. Rio de Janeiro: Record, 2003.

Costa Lima, Vivaldo da. *Lessé Orixá: Nos Pés do Santo*. Salvador: Corrupio, 2010.

Couto, Edilece Souza. *Tempo de Festas: Homenagens a Santa Bárbara, Nossa Senhora da Conceição e Sant'Ana em Salvador (1860–1940)*. Salvador: Editora da Universidade da Bahia, 2010.

Cozza, Fabiana. *Canto Sagrado*. São Paulo: Governo do Estado, 2019, compact disc and DVD.

Crook, Larry. "Black Consciousness, *Samba-Reggae*, and the Re-Africanization of Bahian Music in Brazil." *The World of Music* 35, no. 2 (1993): 90–108.

Crowley, Daniel. *African Myth and Black Reality in Bahian Carnival*. Los Angeles: UCLA Museum of Cultural History, 1984.

Cruz, Ricardo. *A Vingança de Xangô*. São Paulo: Biblioteca 24 Horas, 2014.

Cunha, Milton, ed. *Carnaval é Cultura: Poética e Técnica no Fazer Escola de Samba*. São Paulo: SENAC, 2015.

DaMatta, Roberto. *Carnival, Rogues, and Heroes: An Interpretation of Brazilian Dilemma*. Notre Dame, IN: Notre Dame University Press, 1990.

Dantas, Beatriz G. *Vovó Nagô e Papai Branco: Usos e Abusos da África no Brasil*, Rio de Janeiro: Graal, 1988.

Dantas, Marcelo. *Olodum: De Bloco Afro a Holding Cultural*. Salvador: Edições Olodum, 1994.

Davel, Eduardo, and Renata Saback Rosa. "Gestão, Cultura e Consumo Simbólico no Cortejo Afro." *Revista Pensamento Contemporâneo em Administração* 13 (2017): 13–30.

Degler, Carl. *Neither Black nor White*. Madison: University of Wisconsin Press, 1986.

Del Priore, Mary. *Do outro Lado*. São Paulo: Planeta, 2014.

Dempsey, Genevieve. "Captains and Priestesses in Afro-Brazilian Congado and Candomblé." *Ethnomusicology* 63, no. 2 (2019): 184–221.

Desch-Obi, T. J. *Fighting for Honor: The History of African Martial Art Traditions in the Atlantic World*. Columbia: University of South Carolina Press, 2008.

Despland, Michel. *Bastide on Religion: The Invention of Candomblé*. London: Equinox, 2008.

Didi, Mestre. *História de Um Terreiro Nagô*. São Paulo: Carthago & Forte, 1994.

Dixon, Kwame. *Afro-Politics and Civil Society in Salvador da Bahia, Brazil*. Gainesville: University Press of Florida, 2016.

D'Ogun, Sérgio. *Aláfia: Tambores de Ase*. São Paulo: NaMusic, 2017, compact disc.

Dorsey, Lilith. *Orishas, Goddesses, and Voodoo Queens: The Divine in the African Religious Traditions*. Newburyport, MA: Weiser, 2020.

Drewal, Henry, ed. *Sacred Waters: Arts for Mami Wata and Other Divinities in Africa and the Diaspora*. Bloomington: Indiana University Press, 2008.

Drewal, Margaret Thompson. *Yoruba Ritual: Performers, Play, Agency*. Bloomington: Indiana University Press, 1999.

Duarte, Everaldo Conceição. *Terreiro do Bogum: Memórias de Uma Comunidade Jeje-Mahi na Bahia*. Lauro de Freitas: Solisluna, 2019.

DuBois, W. E. B. *The Souls of Black Folk*. New York: Dover, 2016.

Dumêt, Eliana. *O Maior Carnaval do Mundo: Salvador da Bahia*. Salvador: Editora Palloti, 2004.

Dunn, Christopher. "Afro-Bahian Carnival: A Stage for Protest." *Afro-Hispanic Review* 11, no. 1–3 (1992): 11–20.

———. "Seeking the Orixás in Brazilian Popular Music." In *Axé Bahia: The Power of Art in an Afro-Brazilian Metropolis*, edited by Patrick A. Polk, Robert Conduru, Sabrina Gledhill, and Randal Johnson, 180–191. Los Angeles: Flower Museum at UCLA, 2017.

Durkheim, Émile. *The Elementary Forms of Religious Life*. Oxford: Oxford University Press, 2008.

Eliade, Mircea. *O Mito do Eterno Retorno*. Translated by M. Torres. Lisboa: Edições 70, 1985.

———. *O Sagrado e o Profano: A Essência das Religiões*. Translated by Rogério Fernandes. São Paulo: Martins Fontes, 1992.

———. *The Sacred and the Profane: The Nature of Religion*. Victoria: Harcourt, 1987 [1959].

Ericson, David F., ed. *The Politics of Inclusion and Exclusion: Identity Politics in Twenty-First Century America*. London: Routledge, 2011.

Fajans, Jane. *Brazilian Food: Race, Class, and Identity in Regional Cuisines*. London: Berg, 2012.

Falola, Toyin, and Ann Genova, eds. *Orisa: Yoruba Gods and Spiritual Identity in Africa and the Diaspora*. Trenton, NJ: Africa World Press, 2005.

Farias, Edson. *Ócio e Negócio: Festas Populares e Entretenimento, Turismo no Brasil*. Curitiba: Appris, 2011.

Félix, Anísio. *Filhos de Gandhi: A História de Um Afoxé*. Salvador: Gráfica Central, 1987.

Ferreira, Celça. "Matriarcas Negras em *Tenda dos Milagres* (1977): Uma Análise da Interseção entre Gênero e Raça no Cinema Brasileiro." *E-Compós* 17, no. 2 (2014).

Ferretti, Sérgio Figueiredo. *Repensando o Sincretismo*. São Paulo: EDUSP, 1995.

Fischer, Tânia. *O Carnaval Baiano: Negócios e Oportunidades*. Brasília: Sebrae, 1996.

Fonseca, Denise Pini Rosalem, and Sônia Maria Giacomini. *Presença do Axé: Mapeando Terreiros no Rio de Janeiro*. Rio de Janeiro: PALLAS, 2013.

Foucault, Michel. *A Ordem do Discurso*. São Paulo: Edições Loyola, 2011.

Fraga, Myriam. "Mãe Stella de Oxóssi, Odé Kaiodé: Saudação à Acadêmica." *Revista de Academia de Letras da Bahia* 52 (2014): 351–362.

Fraga, Myriam, Aleilton Fonseca, and Evelina Hoisel. *Jorge Amado nos Terreiros da Ficção*. Salvador: Casa das Palavras, 2012.

Fregoneze, Josmara B., Marilene Jesus da Costa, and Nancy de Souza. *Cozinhando História: Receitas, Histórias e Mitos de Pratos Afro-Brasileiros*. Salvador: Fundação Pierre Verger, 2011.

Freitas, Miranda Joseania. "O Carnaval Afro-Brasileiro em Salvador: Patrimônio da Cultura Brasileira." *VIII Congresso Luso-Afro-Brasileiro de Ciências Sociais* (2004): 1–18.

Freud, Sigmund. "Beyond the Pleasure Principle." In *ESB*, vol. XVIII, 17–85. Rio de Janeiro: Imago, 1976.

———. "The Negative." *ESB*, vol. XIX, 295–300. Rio de Janeiro: Imago, 1976.

———. "Project for a Scientific Psychology." In *Standard Brazilian Edition of the Complete Psychological Works of Freud*, vol. I, 387–529. Rio de Janeiro: Imago, 1976.

Freyre, Gilberto. "Casa-Grande e Senzala." In *Intérpretes do Brasil*, vol. 2, 121–645. Rio de Janeiro: Nova Aguilar, 2002.

———. *The Masters and the Slaves*. New York: Knopf, 1946.

Fromont, Cécile, ed. *Afro-Catholic Festivals in the Americas: Performance, Representation, and the Making of Black Atlantic Tradition*. University Park: Penn State University Press, 2021.

Fuente, Eduardo de la. " 'Profane' rather than 'Secular': Daniel Bell as Cultural Sociologist and Critic of Modern Culture," *Thesis Eleven* 118, no. 1 (2013): 105–115.

Funari, Pedro Paulo, and Sabdra Pelegrini. *Patrimônio Histórico e Cultural*. Rio de Janeiro: Zahar, 2006.

Gage, Kelly Mohs. "*Moda da Bahia*: An Analysis of Contemporary Vendeor Dress in Salvador." *Fashion Theory* 20, no. 2 (2016): 163–79.

Gates, Henry Louis. *The Signifying Monkey: A Theory of African American Literary Criticism*. New York: Oxford University Press, 2014.

Geertz, Clifford. *Interpretation of Cultures*. New York: Basic, 1973.

———. *Myth, Symbol, and Culture*. New York: W. W. Norton, 1974.

Girard, René. *Violence and the Sacred*. New York: Johns Hopkins University Press, 1977.

Gleason, Judith. *Oya: In Praise of the Goddess*. Boston and London: Shambhala, 1987.

Góes Calmon, Francisco Marques de. *Vida Econômica-Financeira da Bahia*. Salvador: Governo do Estado da Bahia, 1979.

Gomes, Dias. *Journey to Bahia*. Washington: Brazilian American Cultural Institute, 1962.

Gomes, Dias. *O Pagador de Promessas*. Rio de Janeiro: Bertrand, 1997 [1959].

Gonçalves, Iracilda. *Psicografia: Verdade ou Fé?* João Pessoa: Editora Universitária UFPB, 2010.

Gondin, Airton Barbosa. *Seu Guia no Candomblé*. Salvador: Gondin, 2003.

Gonzalez, Lélia. *Festas Populares no Brasil/Popular Festivals in Brazil*. São Paulo: Index, 1987.

Graham, Elaine. "What We Make of the World." In *Between the Sacred and Profane: Researching Religion and Popular Culture*, edited by Gordon Lynch, 63–81. New York: I. B. Taurus, 2007.

Greenfield, Sidney M., and A. F. Droogers, eds. *Reinventing Religions: Syncretism and Transformation in Africa and the Americas*. Lanham, MD: Rowland and Littlefield, 2001.

Gusmão, Henrique Buarque de. "Nelson Rodrigues Leitor de Gilberto Freyre: O Projeto Teatral Rodriguiano em Aliança com a Sociologia Freyreana." *Sociedade e Estado* 23 (2008): 89–112.

Haberly, David T. *Three Sad Races*. Cambridge: Cambridge University Press, 2010 [1983].

Hall, Stuart. *Da Diáspora: Identidades e Mediações Culturais*. Belo Horizonte: UFMG, 2003.

Hanchard, Michael. *Orpheus and Power*. Princeton, NJ: Princeton University Press, 1994.

Harding, Rachel E. *A Refuge in Thunder: Candomblé and Alternative Spaces of Blackness*. Bloomington: Indiana University Press, 2000.

Hartikainen, Elina. "A Politics of Respect: Reconfiguring Democracy in Afro-Brazilian Religious Activism in Salvador, Brazil." *American Ethnologist* 45, no. 1 (2018): 87–99.

Herskovits, Melville J., and Frances S. Herskovits. *Dahomean Narrative: A Cross Cultural Analysis*. Evanston, IL: Northwestern University Press, 1958.

Hita, Maria Gabriela. *A Casa das Mulheres n'Outro Terreiro*. Salvador: EDUFBA, 2014.

Ickes, Scott. *African-Brazilian Culture and Regional Identity in Bahia, Brazil*. Gainesville: University Press of Florida, 2013.

Ikeda, Alberto T. "O Ijexá no Brasil: Rítmica dos Deuses nos Terreiros, nas Ruas e Palcos da Música Popular." *Revista USP* 111 (2016): 21–36.

IPAC. *Desfile de Afoxés*. Salvador: IPAC/Fundação Pedro Calmon, 2010.

Irmões Vitale, *Álbum de Carnaval e Outras Festas Populares: Junina, Natal, Reveillon*. São Paulo: Irmões Vitale, 2004.

Ivester, Sukari. "Culture, Resistance and Policies of Exclusion at World Cup 2014: The Case of the 'Baianas do Acarajé.'" *Journal of Policy Research in Tourism, Leisure and Events* 10 (2015): 1–11.

Iwashita, Pedro. *Maria e Iemanjá: Análise de Um Sincretismo*. São Paulo: Edições Paulinas, 1991.

Jesus Barreto, José de. *Candomblé da Bahia*. Salvador: Solisluna, 2010.

Johnson, Paul Christopher. *Secrets, Gossip, and Gods: The Transformation of Brazilian Candomblé*. Oxford: Oxford University Press, 2005.

Jones, Joni L. "Yoruba Diasporic Performance: The Case for a Spiritually and Aesthetically-Based Diaspora." In *Orisa: Yoruba Gods and Spiritual Identity in Africa and the Diaspora*, edited by Toyin Falola and Ann Genova, 321–31. Trenton, NJ: Africa World Press, 2005.

Joseph, May, and Jennifer Natalya Fink, eds. *Performing Hybridity*. Minneapolis: University of Minnesota, 1999.

Keisha-Khan, Perry Y. "Geographies of Power: Black Women Mobilizing Intersectionality in Brazil." *Meridians: Feminism, Race, Transnationalism* 14, no. 1 (2016): 94–120.

Kirby, Fr. Mark Daniel (Priest of the Diocese of Tulsa). *The Proper Chants of the Paschal Triduum in the Graduale Romanum: A Study in Liturgical Theology*. PhD diss., Oxford University, 2002.

Lacan, Jacques. *The Seminar, Book 20: More, Still*. Rio de Janeiro: Jorge Zahar, 1985.

Ladipo, Duro. *Three Yoruba Plays*. Ibadan: Mbari, 1964.

Landers, Jane G., and Barry M. Robinson, eds. *Slaves, Subjects, and Subversives: Blacks in Colonial Latin America*. Albuquerque: University of New Mexico Press, 2006.

Landes, Ruth. *The City of Women*. Albuquerque: University of New Mexico Press, 1994.

Le Bouler, Jean-Pierre. *Pierre Fatumbi Verger: Um homem livre*. Translated by Fábio Araújo, Anamaria Morales, Márcia Caffé, and Dominique Lurton. Salvador: Fundação Pierre Verger, 2002.

Lehtonen, Mikko. *Cultural Analysis of Texts*. London: Sage, 2000.

Lévi-Strauss, Claude. *Antropologia Estrutural*. São Paulo: Cosac Naify, 2008.

Lima, Élida Regina Silva de. "Mulheres de Axé: A Liderança Feminina nos Terreiros de Candomblé." In *Perspectivas Feministas de Gênero: Dasafios no Campo da Militância e das Práticas*, 3591–3600. Recife: Universidade Rural de Pernambuco, 2014.

Lima, Robert. "Xangô and Other Yoruba Deities in the Plays of Zora Seljan." *Afro-Hispanic Review* 11, no. 1–3 (1992): 26–33.

Lima, Vivaldo da Costa. "Organização do Grupo de Candomblé: Estratificação, Senioridade, and Hierarquia." In *Culto aos Orixás*, edited by Carlos Eugênio Marcondes de Moura, 79–132. Rio de Janeiro: PALLAS, 2004.

Lima, Vivaldo da Costa. *A Anatomia do Acarajé e Outros Escritos*. Salvador: Corrupio, 2010.

Lloyd Weaver, Olorunmi Egbelade. *Maternity Divinity, Yemonja: Tranquil Sea, Turbulent Tides: Eleven Yoruba Tales*. Brooklyn, NY: Athelia Henrietta Press, 1998.

Lody, Raul. *Santo Também Come*. Rio de Janeiro: PALLAS, 2012.

———, ed. *Influências: Olhar a África e ver o Brasil*. São Paulo: Companhia Editora Nacional, 2005.

Longo, Raul. *Filhos de Olorum: Contos e Cantos do Candomblé*. Rio de Janeiro: PALLAS, 2011.

Lopes, Ângela Leite. *Nelson Rodrigues: Trágico então Moderno*. Rio de Janeiro: Editora UFRJ/Tempo Brasileiro, 1993.

Lopes, Goya, and Gustavo Falcón. *Imagens da Diaspora*. Salvador: Solusluna, 2010.

Lopes, Kleyde. *O Olodum do Pelourinho*. Salvador: Empresa Gráfica da Bahia, 1996.

Lourdes Siqueira, Maria de. *Saberes Africanos no Brasil*. Belo Horizonte: Mazza, 2010.

Lühning, Ângela, ed. *Pierre Verger: Repórter Fotográfico*. Rio de Janeiro: Bertrand, 2004.

———, ed. *Verger-Bastide: Dimensões de uma amizade*. Translated by Rejane Janovitzer. Rio de Janeiro: Bertrand Brasil, 2002.

Lühning, Angela. "Pierre Fatumbi Verger e sua Obra." *Afro-Ásia* 21–22 (1998–1999): 315–364.

Lynch, Gordon, ed. *Between Sacred and Profane: Researching Religion and Popular Culture*. London and New York: I. B. Taurus, 2007.

Maia, Vasconcelos. *O Leque de Oxum*. Salvador: Assembléia Legislativa do Estado da Bahia, 2006 [1958].

Malhadas, Daisi. *Tragédia Grega: O Mito em Cena*. São Paulo: Ateliê Editorial, 2003.

Malisse, Stéphane Rémy. "Um Olho na Mão: Imagens e Representações de Salvador nas Fotografias de Pierre Verger." *Afro-Ásia* 24 (2000): 325–66.

Mariano, Agnes, Aline Queiroz, Dadá Jacques, and Mauro Rossi, eds. *Obarayi: Babalorixá Balbino Daniel de Paula*. Salvador: Editora Barabô, 2009.

Marió, Estanslão Gacitúa, and Michael Woolock, eds. *Social Exclusion and Mobility in Brazil*. Washington: World Bank, 2008.

Martins, Cléo. *Ao Sabor de Oiá*. Rio de Janeiro: PALLAS, 2003.

Martins, Cléo, and Raul Lody, ed. *Faraimará, O Caçador Traz Alegria: Mãe Stella, 60 Anos de Iniciação*. Rio de Janeiro: PALLAS, 1999.

Martins, José Endoença. "A Negritice e Comunidade Imaginada de Afro-Brasileiros na Literatura." *Terra Roxa e Outras Terras: Revista de Estudos Literários* 15 (2009): 1–12.

Martins, José Pedro Soares. *Festas Populares do Brasil/Popular Festivals of Brazil*. São Paulo: Editora Komedi, 2010.

Martins, Leda. "A Ritual Choreography: The Orishas' Steps in *Sortilégio*." *Callaloo* 18, no. 4 (1995): 863–70.

Martins, Patrícia. *Ofício das Baianas de Acarajé: Trajetória e Desdobramento de Um Plano de Salvaguarda*. Brasília: Instituto do Patrimônio Histórico e Artístico Nacional, 2010.

Martins, Tamires Praga, and Tito Lolola Caravalhal. "O Matriarcado e a Resistência das Mulheres Negras em (Com)unidades Baianas: Dos Quilombos à Periferia." *Revista Três Pontos* 13, no. 1 (2017): 36–45.

Mason, John. *Ounje Fun Orisa: Cooking for Selected Heads*. New York: Yoruba Theological Archministry, 1999.

Matory, J. Lorand. *Black Atlantic Religion: Tradition, Transnationalism, and Matriarchy in the Afro-Brazilian Candomblé*. Princeton, NJ: Princeton University Press, 2005.

———. "In-Depth Review: *The Formation of Candomblé: Vodun History and Ritual in Brazil*, by Luis Nicolau Parés." *Scholarly Exchange* (2015): 610.

Mazrui, Ali. *The Africans: The Triple Heritage*. New York: Little Brown & Co, 1986.

McElroy, Isis Costa. "A Transdiasporic Paradigm: The *Afoxé Filhos de Gandhy*." *Afro-Hispanic Review* 29, no. 1 (2010): 77–100.

McGovern, Chris, and Ricardo Pessanha. *The Brazilian Sound: Samba, Bossa Nova and the Popular Music of Brazil*. Philadelphia: Temple University Press, 1998.

McKittrick, Katherine. *Demonic Grounds: Black Women and the Cartographies of Struggle*. Minneapolis: University of Minnesota Press, 2006.

Mendes, Miriam Garcia. *A Personagem Negra no Teatro Brasileiro*. São Paulo: Editora Ática, 1979.

———. *O Negro e o Teatro Brasileiro*. São Paulo: Editora Hucitec, 1993.

Mendonça, Frederico A. R. C., ed. *Desfile de Afoxés*. Salvador: IPAC, 2010.

———, ed. *Festa da Boa Morte*. Salvador: IPAC, 2011.

Mendonça, Gardênia Serafim de. "A Cozinha Baiana e a Influênicia da Cultura Africana em Sua Composição." *Revista Pensar Gastronomia* 1, no. 2 (2015): 1–26.

Mendonça, João Martinho Braga de. "Visual Anthropology in Post-Colonial Worlds: 'What Has Gone Wrong.'" *Vibrant* 9, no. 2 (2012): 213–52.

Meneguel, Cinthia Rolim de Albuquerque. "Tabuleiros das Meninas e o Acarajé: O Ponto que Conquistou os Festivais Gastronômicos de São Paulo." In *Alimentação e Cultura: Processos Sociais*, edited by M. Oliveira, E. Vanzella, and A. Brambilla, 419–444. João Pessoa: Editora do CCTA, 2019.

Merrell, Floyd. *Capoeira and Candomblé: Conformity and Resistance through Afro-Brazilian Experience*. Princeton, NJ: Markus Wiener, 2005.

Mitchell-Walthour, Gladys L. *The Politics of Blackness*. Cambridge: Cambridge University Press, 2018.

Montero, Paulo. "Syncretism and Pluralism in the Configuration of Religious Diversity in Brazil." *The Mecila Working Papers Series* 4 (2018): 1–20.

Montes, M. L., and E. Araújo, eds. *Negro de Corpo e Alma: Mostra do Descobrimento*. São Paulo: Associação Brasil 500 Anos Artes Visuais/Fundação Bienal, 2000.

Moraes Filho, Mello. *Festas e Tradições Populares do Brasil*. São Paulo: EDUSP, 1979.

Moser, Claudia, and Cecilia Feldman, eds. *Locating the Sacred: Theoretical Approaches to the Emplacement of Religion*. Oxford: Oxbow, 2014.

Motta, Gilson. *O Espaço da Tragédia na Cenografia Brasileira Contemporânea*. São Paulo: Perspectiva, 2011.

Moura, Carlos Eugênio Marcondes de. *Candomblé, Religião de Corpo e Alma: Tipos Psicológicos nas Religiões Afro-Brasileiras*. Rio de Janeiro: PALLAS, 2000.

———. *Culto aos Orixás: Voduns e Ancestrais nas Religiões Afro-Brasileiras*. Rio de Janeiro: PALLAS, 2010.

———. *Culto aos Orixás*. Rio de Janeiro: PALLAS, 2004.

Murphy, Joseph M., and Mei-Mei Stanford. *Osun Across the Waters: A Yoruba Goddess in Africa and the Americas*. Bloomington: Indiana University Press, 2001.

Nakagame, Patrícia Trindade. "Jorge Amado e o Sentido Plural de Revolução." *Miscelânia* 20 (2016): 210–24.

Nascimento, Abdias do. "African Culture in Brazilian Art." *Journal of Black Studies* 8, no. 4 (1978): 389–422.

———. *Mixture or Massacre: Essays on the Genocide of a Black People*. Translated by Elisa Larkin Nascimento. Dover, MA: Majority, 1989.

———. *Orixás: Os Deuses Vivos da África*. Rio de Janeiro: IPEAFRO, 1995.

———. *Sitiado em Lagos: Autodefesa de Um Negro Acossado pelo Racismo*. Rio de Janeiro: Nova Fronteira, 1981.

———. *Sortilégio II*. Rio de Janeiro: Paz e Terra, 1979.

———. "Sortilege II: Zumbi Returns." Translated by Elisa Larkin Nascimento. In *Crosswinds: An Anthology of Black Dramatists in the Diaspora*, edited by William B. Branch, 203–250. Bloomington: Indiana University Press, 1993.

Nascimento, Elisa Larkin. *O Sortilégio da Cor: Identidade, Raça e Gênero no Brasil*. São Paulo: Selo Negro, 2003.

————. *The Sorcery of Color: Identity, Race, and Gender in Brazil.* Philadelphia: Temple University Press, 2007.

Nascimento, Milton, Pedro Casadaliga, and Pedro Tierra. *Missa dos Quilombos.* São Paulo: Polygram/Grupo Nascimento, 1997, compact disc.

Nóbrega, Cida e Echeverria, Regina. *Verger: Um Retrato em Preto e Branco.* Salvador: Corrupio, 2002.

Ojo-Ade, Femi, ed. *Home and Exile: Abdias Nascimento, African Brazilian Thinker and Pan African Visionary.* Trenton, NJ: Africa World Press, 2014.

Olajubu, Oyeronke. "Seeing Through a Woman's Eye: Yoruba Religious Tradition and Gender Relations." *Journal of Feminist Studies in Religion* 20, no. 1 (2004): 41–60.

Olinto, Antônio. *The Water House.* New York: Carroll and Graf, 1970.

Oliveira, Altair B. *Cantando Para os Orixás.* Rio de Janeiro: PALLAS, 2012.

Oliveira, João Carlos Cruz de. *Terreiros de Candomblé de Cachoiera e São Félix.* Salvador: IPAC, 2015.

Oliveira Rebouças, Karolina de. "Afoxé Filhos de Gandhi: 55 Anos de Música Afro-Brasileira o Tempo dos Tempos." Senior Thesis, University of Uberlandia, 2005.

Omari-Tunkara, Mikelle Smith. *Manipulating the Sacred: Yoruba Art, Ritual, and Resistance in Brazilian Candomblé.* Detroit: Wayne State University, 2005.

Omoteso, Ebenezer. "A Study of Intertextuality and Mythology in Jorge Amado's *Mar Morto.*" *Estudos Portugueses e Africanos* 30, no. 5 (1997): 6–14.

Ortiz, Fernando. *Contrapunto Cubano dal Tabaco y el Azucar.* Caracas: Biblioteca Ayaeucho, 1987.

Ortiz, Renato. *A Moderna Tradição Brasileira: Cultura Brasileira e Indústia Cultural.* São Paulo: Brasiliense, 1988.

Osóòsi, Mãe Stella de, and Graziela Domini. *Odu Adajo: Coleção de Destinos.* Salvador: Assembléia Legislativa do Estado da Bahia, 2013.

Osóòsi, Mãe Stella de. *Estrela Azul: Mãe Stella @ 60 Anos.* Salvador: TVE, 1999. DVD.

————. *Osóòsi: O Caçador de Alegrias.* Salvador: Fundação Pedro Calmon, 2011.

Osun Eyin, Pai Cido de. *Candomblé: A Panela do Segredo.* São Paulo: Editora Arx, 2002.

Otero, Solimar, and Toyin Falola, eds. *Yemoja: Gender, Sexuality, and Creativity in the Latino/a and the Afro-Atlantic Diasporas.* New York: State University of New York, 2013.

Pagano, Anna. "Afro-Brazilian Religions and Ethnic Identity Politics in the Brazilian Public Health Arena." *Heath, Culture, and Society* 3, no. 1 (2012): 1–30.

Paim, Tereza, and Sonia Robatto. *Na Mesa da Baiana: Receitas, Histórias, Temperos e Espírito Tipicamente Baianos.* São Paulo: SENAC, 2018.

Palmie, Stephan. "The Cultural Work of Yoruba-Globalization." In *Christianity and Social Change in Africa: Essays in Honor of John Peel*, edited by Toyin Falola, 43–82. Chapel Hill: Carolina Academic Press, 2005.

Paranhos, Adalberto. "A Invenção do Brasil como Terra do Samba: Os Sambistas e sua Afirmação Social." *História* 22, no. 1 (2003): 81–113.

Parés, Luis Nicolau. "The 'Nagôization' Process in Bahian Candomblé." In *The Yoruba Diaspora in the Atlantic World*, edited by Toyin Falola and Matt D. Childs, 185–208. Bloomington: Indiana University Press, 2004.

———. *The Formation of Candomblé: Vodun History and Ritual in Brazil*. Translated by Richard Vernon. Chapel Hill: University of North Carolina Press, 2013.

Patrocínio Luz, Narcimária Correia do. *Itapuã da Ancestralidade Africano-Brasileira*. Salvador: EDUFBA, 2012.

Paula, Babalorixá Balbino Daniel de. *Obaràyí*. Salvador: Barabô, 2009.

Pedrosa, Adriano, and Tomás Toledo, eds. *Afro-Atlantic Histories*. São Paulo: MASP, 2020.

Penner, Hans H. "Language, Ritual, and Meaning." *Numen* 32 (1985): 1–16.

Pereira, Amauri Mendes, and Joselina da Silva, eds. *O Movimento Negro Brasileiro: Escritos sobre os Sentidos da Democracia e Justiça Social no Brasil*. Belo Horizonte: Nandyala, 2009.

Pereira, Edmundo, and Gustavo Pacheco, ed. *Ilê Omolu Oxum: Cantigas e Toques para os Orixás*. Rio de Janeiro: Museu Nacional, 2004.

Pereira, José Carlos. *Sincretismo Religioso and Ritos Sacrificiais: Influências das Religiões Afro no Catolicismo Popular Brasileiro*. São Paulo: Editora Zouk, 2004.

Phenix, Deinya. "Race Consciousness, Diaspora, and *Baianidade*: Observations from an Epic Global Party." *Consciousness, Literature and the Arts* 17, no. 1 (2016): 1–17.

Pinheiro, André. "Revista Espiritual de Umbanda: Representações, Mito Fundador e Diversidade do Campo Umbandista." In *Espiritismo e Religiões Afro-Brasileiras*, edited by Artur Cesar Isaia and Ivan Aparecido Manoel. São Paulo: Ed. UNESP, 2012.

Pinheiro, Délio José Ferraz, and Maria Auxiliadora da Silva, eds. *Imagens da Cidade da Bahia*. Salvador: EDUFBA, 2007.

———, eds. *Visões Imaginárias da Cidade da Bahia*. Salvador: EDUFBA, 2004.

Pinheiro, Robson (with the Spirit Ângelo Inácio). *Tambores de Angola*. São Paulo: Casa dos Espíritos, 1998.

———. *Os Espíritos em Minha Vida*. Contagem, MG: Casa dos Espíritos Editora, 2008.

Pinto, Valdina Oliveira, and Rachel Harding. "Afro-Brazilian Religion, Resistance, and Environment Ethics." *Worldviews* 20 (2016): 76–86.

Pitta, Alberto. "*Cortejo Afro* and the Rereading of African Heritage." Salvador: Nós Transatlânticos, 2016. DVD.

———. "Experiências do Cortejo Afro no Carnaval de Salvador." In *Políticas e Gestão da Cultura: Diálogos entre Universidade e Sociedade*, edited by Clelia

Nero Côrtes, Alice Lacerda, Renata Leah, and Ricardo Soares, 209–215. Salvador: EDUFBA, 2017.

Polk, Patrick A. "Introduction: Have You Been to Bahia?" In *Axé Bahia: The Power of Art in an Afro-Brazilian Metropolis*, edited by Patrick A. Polk, Robert Conduru, Sabrina Gledhill, and Randal Johnson, 12–53. Los Angeles: Flower Museum at UCLA, 2017.

Port, Mattijs van de. *Ecstatic Encounters: Bahian Candomblé and the Quest for the Really Real*. Bloomington: Indiana University Press, 2011.

———. "Visualizing the Sacred: Video Technology, 'Televisual' Style, and the Religious Imagination in Bahian Candomblé." *American Ethnologist* 33, no. 3 (2006): 444–61.

Porto Filho, Ubaldo Marques. *Dinha do Acarajé*. Salvador: UMPF, 2009.

Portugal, Claudius, ed. *Magica Bahia*. Salvador: Fundação Jorge Amado, 1997.

Prado, Décio de Almeida. *O Teatro Brasileiro Moderno*. São Paulo: Perspectiva, 1975.

Prandi, Reginaldo. "African Gods in Contemporary Brazil: A Sociological Introduction to Candomblé Today." *Ibero-Amerikanisches Archiv*, 24, no. 3–4 (1998): 327–52.

———. *Mitologia dos Orixás*. São Paulo: Companhia das Letras, 2001.

———. *Os Candomblés de São Paulo*. São Paulo: Editora HUCITEC, 1991.

Radel, Guilherme. *A Cozinha Africana da Bahia*. Salvador: Lei de Incentivo à Cultura, 2006.

Raillard, Alice. *Conversando com Jorge Amado*. Rio de Janeiro: Record, 1990.

Rappaport, Roy A. *Ecology, Meaning, and Religion*. Berkeley: North Atlantic, 1979.

Reis, João José. "Candomblé in Nineteenth-Century Bahia: Priests, Followers, Clients." In *Rethinking the African Diaspora: The Making of a Black Atlantic World in the Bight of Benin and Brazil*, edited by Kristin Mann and Edna G. Bay, 116–134. New York: Routledge, 2001.

Retamar, Roberto. *Caliban and Other Essays*. Minneapolis: University of Minnesota Press, 1989.

Rezende, Marcos, ed. *Mulheres de Axé*. Salvador: Editora Kawo-Kabiyesile, 2013.

Ribeiro, Palo. *Arte de Capoeira*. Salvador: TVE Bahia, 2009, DVD.

Richards, Sandra L. "Constructions of Afro-Brazilian Identity in the Theatre of the 1950s: The Cases of Dora Seljan and Abdias do Nascimento." *The Journal of Afro-Latin American Studies and Literatures* 3 (1995): 140–65.

———. "Constructions of Afro-Brazilian Identity in the Theatre of the 1950s: The Case of Zora Seljan and Abdias do Nascimento." In *Transatlantiques: Atlantic Cross-Currents*, edited by Susan Andrade, Eileen Julien, Micheline Rice-Maximin, and Aliko Songolo, 129–146. Trenton, NJ: Africa World Press, 2001.

Rio, João do. *As Religiões do Rio*. Rio de Janeiro: Organizações Simões, 1951.

Risério, Antônio. *Carnaval Ijexá*. Salvador: Corrupio, 1981.

Rocha, Fernando de Sousa. "Nelson Rodrigues through the Keyhole; And What We Saw There." *Luso-Brazilian Review* 47, no. 1 (2010): 71–88.

Rodrigeus, Raimundo Nina. *O Animismo Fetichista dos Negros Bahianos*. Rio de Janeiro: Civilização Brasileira, 1935.

Rodrigué, Maria das Graças de Santana. *Orí Àpéré Ó: O Ritual das Águas de Oxalá*. São Paulo: Selo Negro, 2001.

Rodrigues, Felipe Fanuel Xavier. "Affirming Yoruba Ancestry through Afro-Brazilian Literature." In *The Yoruba in Brazil, Brazilians in Yorubaland: Cultural Encounter, Resilience, and Hybridity in the Atlantic World*, edited by Niyi Afolabi and Toyin Falola, 319–336. Durham, NC: Carolina Academic Press, 2017.

———. "O Contexto Religioso na Literatura de Maya Angelou e Mãe Beata de Yemonjá." *XII Congresso Internacional da ABRALIC* (2011): 1–8.

———. "Reimaginando a Herança Africana em Contos." *Matraga* 26, no. 48 (2019): 635–53.

Rodrigues, João Jorge. *Música do Olodum: Revoluação da Emoção*. Salvador: Fundação Gregório de Mattos, 2002.

Rodrigues, João Jorge, and Nelson Mendes. *Olodum: Carnaval, Cultura, Negritude: 1979–2005*. Salvador: Fundação Cultural Palmares, 2005.

Rodrigues, Nelson. "Anjo Negro." In *Nelson Rodrigues: Teatro Completo*, edited by Sábato Magaldi, 125–192. Rio de Janeiro: Nova Fronteira, 1981.

———. "Black Angel [Anjo Negro]." In *The Theater of Nelson Rodrigues II*, edited by Joffre Rodrigues, 201–273. Rio de Janeiro: Ministério da Cultura, 2001.

———. *Os Africanos no Brasil*. São Paulo: Companhia Editora Nacional, 1977.

Rodrigues, Nina. *O Animismo Fetichista dos Negros Baianos*. Rio de Janeiro: Civilização Brasileira, 1935 [1896].

Rogers, Robert. *Self and Other: Object Relations in Psychoanalysis and Literature*. New York: New York University Press, 1991.

Rolim, Iara C. P. "O Olho do Rei: Imagens de Pierre Verger." Master's Thesis in Anthropology, University of Campinas, São Paulo, 2002.

———. "Primeiras imagens: Pierre Verger entre burgueses e infreqüentáveis." PhD diss., University of São Paulo, 2009.

Romo, Anadelia A. *Brazil's Living Museum: Race, Reform, and Tradition in Bahia*. Chapel Hill: University of North Carolina Press, 2010.

Rosenfeld, Anatol. *O Mito e o herói no Moderno Teatro Brasileiro*. São Paulo: Perspectiva, 1996.

Salah, Jaques. *A Bahia de Jorge Amado*. Salvador: Casa de Palavras, 2008.

Sansi, Roger. *Fetishes and Monuments: Afro-Brazilian Art and Culture in the 20th Century*. New York: Berghahn, 2007.

Sansone, Lívio. *Memórias da África: Patrimônios, Museus e Políticas das Identidades*. Salvador: EDUFBA, 2012.

Santana, Hédimo R., and James Wafer. "Africa in Brazil: Cultural Politics and the Candomblé Religion." *Folklore Forum* 23, no. 1/2 (2002): 98–114.

Santos, Deoscóredes Maximiliano dos (Mestre Didi). *Contos crioulos da Bahia: Creole Tales of Bahia.* Salvador: Núcleo Cultural Níger Okàn, 2004.

———. *História de um Terreiro Nagô.* São Paulo: Max Limonad, 1988.

Santos, Deoscoredes Maximiliano dos, and Juana Elbein dos Santos, eds. *Autos Coreográficos: Mestre Didi, 90 Anos.* Salvador: Corrupio, 2007.

Santos, Erisvaldo Pereira dos. *Formação de Professores e Religiões de Matrizes Africanas: Um Diálogo Necessário.* Belo Horizonte: Nandyala, 2015.

Santos, Eufrázia Cristina Menezes. "Performances Culturais nas Festas de Largo da Bahia." *Encontro Anual da Anpocs* 30 (2006): 1–32.

Santos, Jean Carlo Silva dos, and Eliane Di Diego Antunes. "Relações de Gêneros e Liderança nas Organizações: Rumo a Um Estilo Andrógino de Gestão." *Gestão Contemporânea* 10, no. 14 (2013): 35–60.

Santos, Jocélio Teles dos, ed. *Mapeamento dos Terreiros de Salvador.* Salvador: Centro de Estudos Afro-Orientais-UFBA, 2008.

———. "A Mixed-Race Nation: Afro-Brazilians and Cultural Policy in Bahia, 1970–1990." In *Afro-Brazilian Culture and Politics: Bahia 1790s–1990s,* edited by Hendrik Kraay, 117–33. Armonk, NY: M. E. Sharpe, 1998.

Santos, Juana Elbein dos. *Os Nagô e a Morte.* Petrópolis: Vozes, 1986.

Santos, Lígia Amparo da Silva. "Acarajé, Dendê, Modernidade, e Tradição no Contexto Soteropolitano." In *Dendê: Símbolo e Sabor da Bahia,* edited by Raul Lody, 81–92. São Paulo: SENAC, 2009.

Santos, Maria Stella de Azevedo. *Meu Tempo é Agora.* Curitiba: CENTRHU, 1995.

———. *Meu Tempo é Agora.* Salvador: Assembléia, 2010.

———. *Opinião, Santos, Maria Stella de Azevedo: Um Presente de A TARDE para a História.* Salvador: A TARDE, 2012.

Saueressig, Simone. *A Estrela de Iemanjá.* São Paulo: Cortez, 2009.

Schaun, Angela. *Práticas Educomunicativas: Grupos Afro-Descedentes, Salvador-Bahia: Ara Ketu, Ilê Aiyê, Olodum, Pracatum.* Rio de Janeiro: MAUAD, 2002.

Schneider, Andreas, Linda E. Francis, Herman W. Smith. "Measurement of Cultural Variations in the Sacred and the Profane." *Journal of Integrated Social Sciences* 3, no. 1 (2013): 130–56.

Schroy, Hank, Bira Reis, and Alabês do Ilê Oxumaré. *A Orquestra do Candomblé da Nação Ketu.* Salvador: NewRitual, 2011.

Scotton, Raquel Turetti, and Sônia Côrrea Lages. "Ogum, a Voz do Gueto: Orixá do Rap e da Rima nas Letras de Criolo e Emicida." *PLURA: Revista de Estudos de Religião* 11, no. 1 (2020): 169–86.

Secretaria de Turismo do Estado da Bahia. *Turismo Étnico Afro na Bahia.* Salvador: Secretaria de Turismo do Estado da Bahia, 2009.

Sekoni, Ropo. *Folk Poetics: A Sociosemiotic Study of Yoruba Trickster Tales*. Westport, CT: Greenwood, 1994.

Seljan, Zora. *Três Mulheres de Xangô*. Brasília: Instituto Nacional do Livro, 1978.

———. *Iemanjá e Suas Lendas*. São Paulo: Global Editora, 2017.

———. *The Story of Oxalá*. London: Rex Collins, 1978.

Selka, Stephen. *Religion and the Politics of Ethnic Identity in Bahia, Brazil*. Gainesville: University Press of Florida, 2007.

Serra, Marcos. *30 anos do Ilé Omiojuaró: Ancestralidade, Educação, Arte e Ativismo nas Redes de Mãe Beata de Iyemonjá*. Salvador: Novas Edições Acadêmicas, 2015.

Serra, Ordep J. T. *Águas do Rei*. Petrópolis: Vozes, 1995.

———. *Rumores da Festa: O Sagrado e o Profano na Bahia*. Salvador: Editora da Universidade da Bahia, 2009.

Serraria, Richard, Pingo Borel, Mimmo Ferreira, and Kako Xavier. *Alabê Ôni*. Salvador: AlabeOni, 2018.

Shirey, Heather. "Candomblé Beads and Identity in Salvador da Bahia." *Nova Religio: The Journal of Alternative and Emergent Religions* 16, no. 1 (2012): 36–60.

———. "Transforming the Orixás: Candomblé in Sacred and Secular Spaces in Salvador da Bahia, Brazil." *African Arts* 42 (2009): 62–79.

Siderer, Anna. "The Legacy of Pierre Fatumbi Verger in the Whydah Historical Museum (Benin): Development of an Ambivalent Concept of Hybridity." *History in Africa* 40 (2013): 295–312.

Silva, Aguinaldo, and Ricardo Linhares. *Porto dos Milagres*. Rio de Janeiro: Rede Globo, 2001.

Silva, Vagner Gonçalves da. *Candomblé e Umbanda: Caminhos da Devoção Brasileira*. São Paulo: Editora Ática, 1994.

———. "Religion and Black Cultural Identity: Roman Catholics, Afro-Brazilians and Neopentecostalism." *Vibrant* 11, no. 2 (2014): 210–246.

Silverstein, Leni. "Mãe de Todo Mundo—Modos de Sobrevivência nas Comunidades de Candomblé da Bahia." *Religião e Sociedade* 4 (1979): 43–169.

Siqueira, Maria de Lourdes, ed. *Imagens Negras: Ancestralidade, Diversidade e Educação*. Belo Horizonte: Mazzas, 2006.

Smith, Christen. *Afro-Paradise: Blackness, Violence, and Performance in Brazil*. Chicago: University of Illinois Press, 2016.

Sodré, Jaime. *A Influência da Religião Afro-Brasileira na Obra Escultórica do Mestre Didi*. Salvador: EDUFBA, 2005.

Sodré, Muniz. *A Lei do Santo: Contos*. São Paulo, Editora Malê, 2016.

———. *Pensar Nagô*. Petrópolis: Vozes, 2017.

Soler, Isabel. "O Destino é o Mar." *Cuadernos Hispanoamericanos* 633 (2003): 33–41.

Sontag, Susan. *On Photography*. New York: Picador, 1977.

Sousa Junior, Vilson Caetano. *Na Palma da Minha Mão: Temas Afro-Brasileiros e Questões Contemporâneas*. Salavdor: EDUFBA, 2011.

Souty, Jérôme. "Comme un seul homme: Pierre Fatumbi Verger." *L'Homme* 38, no. 147 (1998): 221–36.

———. *Pierre Fatumbi Verger: Du regard détaché à la connaissance initiatique*. Paris: Maisonneuve & Larose, 2007.

Souza, Licia Soares de. "Forças e Fragilidades de Porto dos Milagres: Adaptação Televisiva de *Mar Morto*." In *Jorge Amado: Leituras e Diálogos em Torno de Uma Obra*, edited by Rita Olivieri-Godet and Jacqueline Penjon, 265–277. Salvador: Fundação Casa de Jorge Amado, 2004.

Souza, Margaret. *Oxóssi: Senhor das Matas*. Fortaleza: Kindle, 2017.

Souza, Patricia Rodrigues de. "Food in African Brazilian Candomblé." *Religion and Food* 26 (2015): 264–80.

Soyinka, Wole. *Death and the King's Horseman*. New York: W. W. Norton, 2003.

———. *The Lion and the Jewel*. Oxford: Oxford University Press, 1962.

———. *Myth, Literature and the African World*. London: Cambridge: Cambridge University Press, 1976.

Staal, Frits. "The Meaninglessness of Ritual." *Numen* 26 (1979): 2–22.

———. *Rules without Meaning: Ritual, Mantras and the Human Sciences*. New York: Peter Lang, 1993.

———. "The Search for Meaning: Mathematics, Music, and Ritual." *American Journal of Semiotics* 2 (1984): 1–57.

Sterling, Cheryl. *African Roots, Brazilian Rites: Cultural and National Identity in Brazil*. New York: Palgrave, 2012.

———. "Bençá [sic]: The Blessings of the Bando de Teatro Olodum." In *African Diaspora in Brazil*, edited by Fassil Demissie, 71–92. New York: Routledge, 2014.

———. "Finding Africa in the Dances of the Gods." In *Migrations and Creative Expressions in Africa and the African Diaspora*, edited by Toyin Falola, Niyi Afolabi, and Aderonke Adesanya, 47–63. Durham, NC: Carolina Academic Press, 2008.

Stoll, Sandra. *Espiritismo à Brasileira*. São Paulo: Editora da Universidade de São Paulo, 2003.

Suárez, Farid Leonardo. "The Contested Candomblé Cult Matriarchate." In *The Yoruba in Brazil, Brazilians in Yorubaland: Cultural Encounter, Resilience, and Hybridity in the Atlantic World*, edited by Niyi Afolabi and Toyin Falola, 337–56. Durham, NC: Carolina Academic Press, 2017.

T'Osun, Babalorisa Mauro. *Irin Tite: Ferramentas Sagradas dos Orixas*. Rio de Janeiro: Pallas, 2014.

Tabacof, Germano. *Bahia: A Cidade de Jorge Amado*. Salvador: Casa de Palavras, 2000.

Tannenbaum, Frank. *Slave and Citizen*. Boston: Beacon Press, 1992.

Tate, Julee. "Dangerous Games: The Female Character in Afro-Brazilian Theater."
    In *Marvels of the African World: African Cultural Matrimony, New World
    Connections, and Identities*, edited by Niyi Afolabi, 301–315. Trenton, NJ:
    Africa World Press, 2003.

Teixeira, Cid. *Salvador, Uma Viagem Fotográfica*, edited by Fernando Oberlaender.
    Salavdor: Caramurê, 2017.

TEN. *Dramas para Negros, Prólogo para Brancos*. Rio de Janeiro: Teatro Exper-
    imental do Negro, 1961.

Theodoro, Mário, ed. *As Políticas Públicas e a Desigualdade Racial no Brasil: 120 Anos
    Após a Abolição*. Brasília: Instituto de Pesquisa Econômica Aplicada, 2008.

Thompson, Robert Farris. *Flash of the Spirit: African and Afro-American Art and
    Philosophy*. New York: Vintage, 1983.

Tishken, Joel E. *Sango in Africa and the African Diaspora*. Bloomington: Indiana
    University Press, 2009.

Torres, Dijna Andrade. *Mulher Nagô: Liderança e Parentesco no Universo Afro-
    Brasileiro*. Curitiba: Appris Editora, 2015.

Turner, J. Michael. "Manipulação da Religião: O Exemplo Afro-Brasileiro."
    Cultura 6, no. 23 (1976): 56–63.

Turner, Neil. *Religious Syncretism in Brazil: Catholicism, Evangelicalism and Can-
    domblé*. Berlin: Verlag, 2011.

Turner, Victor, ed. *Celebration: Studies in Festivity and Ritual*. Washington, DC:
    Smithsonian, 1982.

———. *From Ritual to Theatre: The Human Seriousness of Play*. New York: PAJ,
    1982.

TVE Educadora. *Gaiaku Luiza: Força e Magia dos Voduns*. Salvador: TVE, 2004.

———. *Ilê Axé Bahia: A Saga dos Orixás*. Salvador: TVE, 2002.

Twine, Francine. *Racism in a Racial Democracy*. New Brunswick, NJ: Rutgers
    University Press, 1998.

Valente, Waldemar Jr. "O Demônio e o Anjo: Personagens Negras e Idéia de
    Preconceito Racial no Teatro Brasileiro." *Todas as Letras* 17, no. 2 (2015):
    208–217.

Vallado, Armando. *Iemanjá: A Grande Mãe Africana do Brasil*. Rio de Janeiro:
    PALLAS, 2002 and 2005.

Van de Port, Mattijs. "Candomblé in Pink, Green and Black: Re-Scripting the
    Afro-Brazilian Religious Heritage in the Public Sphere of Salvador, Bahia."
    Social Anthropology 13, no. 1 (2005): 3–26.

———. "Visualizing the Sacred: Video Technology, 'Televisual' Style, and the
    Religious Imagination in Bahian Candomblé." *American Ethnologist* 33,
    no. 3 (2006): 444–61.

Vargas, Jackson de. *Cânticos dos Orixás no Batuque do Rio Grande do Sul*. Guaíba,
    RS: Self-published, 2018.

Vaughan, Patrícia Anne. "O Mar como Metáfora nos Romances *Mar Morto* e *O Velho e o Mar* Na Peça Teatral *Riders to the Sea*." *Revista de Letras* 19, no. 1–2 (1997): 98–104.

Veras, Ernesto. *Portas Fechadas*. Copell, TX: Edições Lexicon Brasiliensis, 2017.

Verger, Pierre. *50 anos de fotografia*. Salvador, Corrupio, 1982.

———. *Bahia Africa Bahia*. São Paulo: Pinacoteca do Estado, 1996.

———. *Bahia and the West African Trade (1549–1851)*. Ibadan: Institute of African Studies/Ibadan University Press, 1964.

———. *Brasil África Brasil: 90 anos*. São Paulo: Pinacoteca do Estado, 1992.

———. *Dieux d'Afrique*. Paris: Revue Noire, 1995.

———. *Ewé: O uso das plantas na sociedade Iorubá*. Introduction by Jorge Amado, illustrations by Carybé. São Paulo: Companhia das Letras, 1995.

———. *Ewe: The Use of Plants in Yoruba Society*. Salvador: Odebrecht, 1995.

———. *Flux et reflux de la traité des nègres entre la golfe de Bénin et Bahia de Todos os Santos du XVIIe au XIXe siècle*. Paris: La Haye, Mouton & Co., 1968.

———. *Fluxo e Refluxo*. Salvador: Corrupio, 1987 [1968].

———. *Lendas Africanas dos Orixás*. Salvador: Corrupio, 2011.

———. *O Mensageiro: Fotografias 1932–1962*. Salvador: Fundação Pierre Verger, 2003.

———. *Le Messager/The Go-Between: Photographies 1932–1962*. New York: Powerhouse, 1981.

———. *Notas Sobre o Culto aos Orixás e Voduns na Bahia de Todos os Santos no Brasil*. Translated by Carlos Eugenio de Moura. São Paulo: EDUSP, 1999 [1957].

———. "Notes sur le Culte des Orisa et Vodun: à Bahia, la Baie des Tous les Saints au Brésil." *Mémoires de l'IFAN*, no. 51 (1957).

———. *O Olhar viajante de Pierre Fatumbi Verger*. Introduction by Gilberto Sá, translated by Christopher Peterson. Salvador: Fundação Pierre Verger, 2002.

———. *Orixás: Deuses Iorubás na África e no Novo Mundo*. Salvador: Corrupio, 2002.

———. *Retratos da Bahia, 1946 a 1952*. Salvador: Corrupio, 1980.

———. *Saída de Iaô: Cinco Ensaios sobre a Religião dos Orixás*. São Paulo: Axis Mundi Editora and Fundação Pierre Verger, 2002.

———. "Une sortie de 'iyawo dans un village nagô au Dahomey.'" *Études Dahoméennes* 6 (1951): 11–26.

———. *Trade Relations Between the Bight of Benin and Bahia from the 17th to 19th Century*. Translated by Evelyn Crawford. Ibadan: Ibadan University Press, 1976.

Verger, Pierre, and Carybé. *Lendas Africanas dos Orixás*. Salvador: Corrupio, 1992.

———. *African Legends of the Orishas*. Salvador: Corrupio, 2006.

Verger, Pierre Fatumbi, and Enéas Guerra Sampaio. *Oxossi, O Caçador*. Translated by Maria Aparecida da Nóbrega. Salvador: Corrupio, 1961.

———. *Mensageiro entre Dois Mundos*. Directed by Lula Buarque de Hollanda. Rio de Janeiro, Conspiração Filmes, 1998.

Vianna, Hermano. *O Mistério do Samba*. Rio de Janeiro: Jorge Zahar Editor, Editora UFRJ, 1995.

Wafer, Jim. *The Taste of Blood: Spirit Possession in Brazilian Candomblé*. Philadelphia: University of Pennsylvania Press, 1991.

Wafer, Jim, and Hédimo Rodrigues Santana. "Africa in Brazil: Cultural Politics and the Candomblé Religion." *Folklore Forum* 23, no. 1–2 (1990): 98–114.

Walker, Sheila. *African Roots/American Culture*. New York: Roman and Littlefield, 2001.

Wallace-Sanders, Kimberly. *Mammy: A Century of Race, Gender, and Southern Memory*. Ann Arbor: University of Michigan Press, 2008.

Warren, Tich Harrison. *Liturgy of the Ordinary: Sacred Practices in Everyday Life*. Dreamers Grove, 2016.

Weaver, Lloyd, and Olukunmi Egbelade. *Yemonja: Maternal Divinity, Tranquil Sea, Turbulent Tides*. Brooklyn, NY: Athelia Henrietta, 1999.

Weber, Max. *The Sociology of Religion*. Boston, MA: Beacon Press, 1993.

Wikstrom, Owe. "Liturgy as Experience: The Psychology of Worship: A Theoretical and Empirical Lacuna." In *The Problem of Ritual*, edited by Ahlback Tore, 83–100. Stockholm, Sweden: The Donner Institute for Religious and Cultural History, 1993.

William, Rodney. *Apropriação Cultural*. São Paulo: Sueli Carneiro/Pólen, 2019.

Williams, Raymond L. *The Postmodern Novel in Latin America: Politics, Culture, and the Crisis of Truth*. New York: St. Martin's Press, 1995.

Xavier, Ismail. *Sertão Mar: Glauber Rocha e a Estética da Fome*. São Paulo: Brasiliense, 2000.

Yevington, Kevin A. *Afro-Atlantic Dialogues: Anthropology in the Diaspora*. Santa Fé: SAR, 2006.

———. "The Anthropology of Afro-Latin America and the Caribbean: Diasporic Dimensions." *Annual Review of Anthropology* 30 (2001): 227–60.

Yemonjá, Mãe Beata de. *Caroço de Dendê: A Sabedoria dos Terreiros*. Rio de Janeiro: PALLAS, 2008.

Zweig, Susan. *Brasil, País do Futuro*. Translated by Odilon Gallotti. Rio de Janeiro: Ridendo Castigat Mores, 2001.

Index

Abiodun, Rowland, 114
acarajé, 1–2, 10, 27, 109, 265–79,
    311n1; and Afro-Brazilian
    heritage, 268–70, 276–78, 312n2;
    appropriation of, 276–79; baianas
    de, 10, 27, 109, 266, 269–71,
    273–76, 313n6, 313n8; and labor,
    266–68; and persecution, 271;
    standardizing, 270–71; and tourism,
    270–71, 307n33. See also cuisine
"Acarajé tem Dendê" (Jauperi), 267
access, 21–22, 51–52, 56–60, 64–65,
    68–69, 259–60
acculturation, 5, 53–54, 222–23
activism, 79–80, 93–94, 99–102,
    137–38, 173–74, 192–93, 253–55
adura (prayer), 90
afoxés, 9–10, 20–21, 26, 42–43, 162,
    183, 233, 237–40, 245–48, 255–56.
    See also blocos afros; carnival
Africanism, Africanity, Africanness,
    20, 26; and Brazilian identity,
    11–14, 26–27, 269–70; and
    carnival, 245–46, 250–53, 255–60;
    and hybridization, 19–20; as plural,
    4; and preserving African value
    systems, 31–32, 44–45, 102–3,
    136, 183, 246; reenacting, 9–10;
    and syncretism, 13–14. See also
    Blackness; Yoruba

agbada (Yoruba garb), 27
Agnew, Vijay, 5
agogô (musical instrument), 44
àjé (witch, spiritual being), 228–29
akara (Yoruba beancake), 2, 265–66,
    312n2. See also acarajé
Alabama, O (newspaper), 82–83
albinoism, 260–61
Alves, Castro, 86, 255
Alves, Miriam, 166
Amado, Jorge, 29–30, 33, 57, 61,
    76, 110–11; bibliography, 115; A
    Descoberta da América pelos Turcos,
    123; imprisonment, 115; Mar
    Morto (Sea of death), 109–10,
    114–25
Amaralina (neighborhood), 84–85
ancestrality, 8, 101–2, 115–16,
    125–28, 130–31, 144–45, 161–62
Andrade, Jorge, 166
Andrade, Mário de, 128
Andrade, Rosane, 66
Angola ethnic group, 7, 82–83
Aninha, Mãe (Eugênia Anna
    Santos), 86
anthropology, 14–15, 40–42, 52–53;
    and colonial researchers, 56–57,
    59–60, 76; visual, 49–50, 60–61,
    64–71, 76–77. See also Verger,
    Pierre

Antunes, Elaine, 85
Appadurai, Arjun, 302n5
appropriation, 13–14, 20, 187–88, 191–92, 246, 270, 276–79, 281–82
Ara Ketu (People of Ketu), 2, 9–10, 26
Araujo, Ana Lucia, 61
Araújo, Ubiratan Castro, 35, 86, 88
Ariel (metaphor), 143–45
Aristotle, 172–73
Armstrong, Piers, 236, 238
Arte Poética (Aristotle), 172–73
assimilation, 53–54, 90, 115–17, 124–25, 138–40, 144–45, 154–55, 192, 204, 307n34
Assis, Lindinalva de (Dinha do Acarajé), 272, 274–76; legacy, 274–76
Associação das Baianas de Acarajé, 268–69
Association of Acarajé and Mingau of the State of Bahia, 269
authenticity, 4–5, 9, 11–15, 18, 53–57, 71, 76–77, 80–82, 90, 183, 216–17, 227–28, 251–52, 286n10. See also under Candomblé
axé (music, vital force), 8–9, 26, 43–44, 46, 146–48, 161–62, 179–80, 200–201, 204–5, 220–21, 245, 258, 266
Axé Bahia: The Power of Art in Afro-Brazilian Metropolis, 7–8
Axé Project, 310n19
Axévier, 166
axexê (funeral rites), 221–22
Azevedo, Aluísio, 270

baba eguns (ancestors), 127–28, 130–33
babalawo (Ifá priest), 51–52, 56–60, 63–64, 68–69, 208–14
babalorixás (priests), 161–62, 225–26

Babalú-Ayé (orisa of infectious diseases and healing), 305n13
Badauê (Power of unity), 2, 241–42, 246–47. See also afoxés
Badejo, Diedre, 129
Bahia: African presence in, 26–27, 193–94, 287n13; Afro-Brazilian identity, 12–14, 125–26, 238, 240, 277–78, 283–84; backlands, 196; as "Black Rome," 7–8; and carnival, 9, 239–40, 242, 247; as cultural cradle of Brazil, 26–28, 109–10; cycle of festivities, 109–10; and dialectic between sacred and profane, 10–11, 29–32, 39–41, 160–61, 236–37, 283–84; history of, 25–26, 28–29; industry, 26–27; LGBTQ community in, 257–58; as living museum, 40; representations of, 116; Yoruba influence on, 289n24. See also carnival; Candomblé; Yoruba
Bahia, Carla, 35
Bahian Educational TV, 240–41, 287n13
Bakhtin, Mikhail, 234
Bantu ethnic group, 80–81
Bárbara, Santa, 10, 34–37, 47, 175–78. See also Iansã
Barney, Mathew, 262
Barthes, Roland, 71
Bascom, William, 56–57
Bastide, Roger, 7, 41, 52–54, 56–59, 76, 161
"bater do tambor, O" (Veloso), 247
beauty, 29–30
Beier, Ulli, 214–15
"Beleza Negra" (Jesus), 247
Beleza Pura (Total beauty), 240–41
Bell, Catherine, 193–94
Bell, Daniel, 39
belonging, 11–12, 20, 84–85

Bethânia, Maria, 29
Bhabha, Homi, 3, 136, 274
Bianch, Mãe Valnizia (Flaviana
    Maria da Conceição Bianchi), 79,
    84–85, 100–105, 296n9; *Reflexões:
    Escritas de Mãe Valnizia Bianch*, 79,
    100–101
Bishof, Werner, 67
Bitar, Nina, 267–68
Black Experimental Theater (Teatro
    Experimental do Negro), 136–37,
    139–40, 143–44, 147–48, 166
Blackness: and Afro-Brazilian
    identity, 144–45, 147–48; in
    Bahia, 30; and blindness, 148–49;
    in Candomblé, 20–21, 40; and
    carnival, 238, 245–46; and culture,
    43; and discrimination, 3; erasure
    of, 137–41; and femininity,
    149–50; and hybridity, 19–20,
    127–28; in literature, 110–11; and
    marginalization, 156–57; and pride,
    150–51; rejecting, 135–37, 141–42,
    148–49, 153–56; and religion,
    11–14, 237; and social injustices,
    102; and writing, 110–11. *See also*
    Africanism; race
"Black Rome." *See under* Bahia
blindness, 148–50, 154–55
blocos afros, 239–10, 20–21, 42–43,
    45–46, 109, 183, 235–36, 240,
    248, 251–52, 255–58. *See also*
    afoxés; carnival
blocos de índios (Indian Carnival
    Group), 261
body: and desire, 120–21, 135–36;
    female, 149–50; and mind, 225–26;
    possessed, 46–47; and ritual,
    193–94
Borges, Paulo, 262
bossa nova, 161–62. *See also* music
Braga, Júlio, 96

Brazilian Communist Party (Partido
    Comunista Brasileiro), 110–11, 243
Brazilian Federation of Spiritists, 187
Brown, Carlinhos, 29, 44, 250
Brown, Dee, 261
Buarque, Chico, 166
Butler, Kim, 138

Cabrera, Lydia, 114
Cachoeira, Bahia, 10–11, 31, 116,
    227, 237–38
Caderno da Bahia group, 111,
    127–28
Caliban (metaphor), 143–45
Callado, Antônio, 166
Camafeu, Paulinho, 242
Campbell, Joseph, 89, 164
Canclini, Nestor, 218
Candemil, Luciano da Silva, 9
Candomblé, 1–2, 26; and Afro-
    Brazilian identity, 5–6, 11–13,
    125–26, 191–92; and anthropology,
    14–15; artistry of, 7–8; and
    authenticity, 13–15, 71, 81–82,
    87, 201, 286n10; and Blackness,
    20–21, 40, 237; and carnival,
    43–45, 240–42, 247, 252–57,
    262–63; and Catholic Church, 19,
    28–29, 226–28, 283, 286n10; circle
    dance, 5–6; and citizenship, 42;
    and cuisine, 265–66, 268–70, 276–
    79; defamiliarizing, 220, 227–28;
    devotees of, 181; differences among
    nations, 7; and divinity worship,
    33; and enslavement, 5; and
    festivities, 236; and gender, 85,
    97–100, 110, 141–42, 207–8, 214,
    219; history of, 5, 52–53, 80–83;
    and hybridization, 40–42, 53, 101–
    2, 222–24; and Ilê Axês (houses),
    6, 83–85, 184; and initiation, 89,
    130–31; internationalization of, 57,

Candomblé *(continued)*
64; and interpenetration of culture,
53–54; and literature, 114–16,
126–30, 216–17, 221–22; as living
religion, 52–55, 103–4; magic of,
217–18; and matriarchy, 79–80,
82–85, 100–101, 104–5, 273–74;
and mythology, 42, 87–92, 95–100,
133, 167, 305n31; organization of,
220–21, 296n10; origins of, 60–61;
and parity, 21; persecution of,
62–63, 81–84, 94, 101–5, 132–33,
141–42, 159–60, 191–93, 203–4,
240, 248, 270, 278–79, 295n31;
popularization of, 192–93, 202–3,
235, 265–66; and race, 202–3; and
ritual, 58, 91–92, 146–47, 161–63;
rural settings of, 81–82; and sacred,
141, 167–68, 178–80; in Salvador,
6–7; and secrecy, 55–56; and
survival of African cultural values,
165, 183, 203–5, 234–35, 246,
266–67, 289n23; and syncretism,
172, 200–201, 223–24; temples, 87,
176–78, 200–201; and vital force,
160–61; as weapon of resistance
during slavery, 55–56, 80–81, 161.
See also carnival; orisas; Yoruba
capitalism, 37, 180
capoeira, 8, 10–11, 26–29, 109,
178–79
Capone, Stefania, 11–12, 14–15, 47,
52, 55–56
Cardoso, Vânia, 96
Carnaval carioca (Rio de Janeiro), 9
Carneiro, Édison, 14, 81
carnival, 2–4, 8, 109, 162–63; and
Afro-Brazilian heritage, 235–36,
242, 245–46, 248–49, 255–56,
258–60, 262–63; and Amerindians,
261; and Blackness, 8, 246–49;
and commercialization, 45; and

gender, 310n16; and identity, 234;
and politics, 234, 236, 250–57;
and race, 42–43, 238–41, 244–45,
247–48; and relation between
sacred and profane, 9–10, 42–44,
46, 233–35, 237–39, 251–53,
262–63; social projects, 43–46; and
youth, 310n19. *See also* afoxés;
blocos afros; Cortejo Afro; Filhos
de Gandhi
carurú, 34–35, 103–4, 178, 276–77.
See also cuisine
Carvalho, José Jorge de, 9
Carybé (Héctor Julio Páride
Bernabó), 8, 57, 61, 63–64, 76,
166–67
Casa Branca do Engenho Velho, 100,
218
Casa de Oxumarê, 100
Castillo, Lisa Earl, 71
Castro, Janio, 236–38
Catholicism: and Candomblé, 12–14,
19–20, 55–56, 172, 175–76,
222–23, 226–28, 234–35, 248, 283,
286n10, 293n14; fixed religiosity
of, 140–41; and profane, 33; and
repression of African religions,
28–29, 33, 36, 46–47, 80–82,
159–60; and slavery, 18–19. *See
also* Candomblé
Caymmi, Dorival, 266–67, 270–71
characterization, 116–17, 121
Christens, Brian, 262–63
Chynae (Raymundo Adães Motta),
207–8; *Encantos de Oxossi*
(Enchantments of Oxóssi), 207–8,
224–30
Cidade de Deus (dir. Meirelles and
Lund), 37–38
citizenship, 5–6, 20, 42–43, 137–38,
147–48, 150–51
Clark, Fred, 152

class: and carnival, 239–40, 243–45, 255–56; and race, 137–38, 152; struggle, 124–25. *See also* gender; race
Cleiren, Marc, 234
Collins, John F., 20, 40
colonialism, 2–3, 20, 25–28, 56–57, 164–65, 197–98, 281–82, 289n24; as mentality, 51, 59–60, 72–74, 76–77; and religion, 28–29, 33, 80–81
comida de santo (saints' food), 266. *See also* acarajé; cuisine
communism, 115
Conceição, Joanice Santos, 31
Conduru, Roberta, 7–8
Conselheiro, Antônio, 29
Contos Crioulos da Bahia (Didi), 125–26
Cordovil, Daniela, 85
Cortejo Afro (Black procession), 44–46, 233–34, 238–39, 251–63; and culture, 58–59, 259–60; finances, 252, 260; and LGBTQ community in Salvador, 257–58; organizing, 262; politics of, 251–57; religious values of, 253–56; and social issues, 260–61; and youth, 258–60. *See also* carnival; Filhos de Gandhi
Cortiço, O (Azevedo), 270
cosmology, 9–10, 16–17, 60–61, 62, 64, 112–13, 116, 119, 127–30, 159, 179–80, 183, 189, 194, 207–8, 218, 226–27, 230, 267–68
Costa, Gal, 111–12
Costa, Harold, 93–94
creolization, 110–11. *See also* hybridization
CRIOULA, 93
crônicas (chronicles), 127–28
cuisine, 26; and Afro-Brazilian culture, 265–71, 276–79, 312n2;

and gender, 273–76; and labor, 266–67; ontology of, 266; and religiosity, 10, 34–35; and tourism, 269–71, 276–78. *See also* acarajé; tourism
culture: Afro-Brazilian, 163, 258; diasporic, 5, 26, 60–61; and identity, 8–14, 19–20, 218, 258; location(s) of, 3–4; and politics, 21–22, 40, 43–44; preserving, 90, 119–20; and pride, 11–12; and race and racism, 3–4, 30–31, 41–42, 136; and religion, 222–23; and sacred, 3–4, 18–19, 38–39, 41, 46–47, 111–12, 160–61; and secrecy, 55–56
Cuti, 166

Davel, Eduardo, 236, 238–39
Davis, Angela, 183–84
death (motif), 31–32, 117–19, 131, 149–50, 154–55
Death and the King's Horseman (Soyinka), 51, 58–59, 72–74
Degler, Carl, 136–38
demonic ground, 149–50
Dempsey, Genevieve, 85
dialogue, 54–55
diary, 216–18
diaspora, African, 3–5, 9–10, 45, 54–57, 112–13, 163–65, 198, 201–2, 207–8, 214, 218, 250–51, 255–57, 273; and carnival, 45, 250–51, 255–57; and food, 265–66; and gender, 149–50, 207–8, 228–29, 273; and hybridization, 218, 228–29; and violence, 149–50. *See also* Middle Passage; slavery; Yoruba
Didi, Mestre (Deoscoredes Maximiliano dos Santos), 59, 80, 95, 125–26

Dinha do Acarajé (Porto Filho),
265–66, 272, 274–75
Dique do Tororó, 7
divination, 56–57, 64–65, 68–71,
87–88, 146–47, 208–14, 218–19,
222–23, 266
Dixon, Kwame, 43
Dodô and Osmar, 44
double consciousness, 256–57
drama, 139–41; and Afro-Brazilian
identity, 143–46; and centrality of
orisas, 166–67, 179–80; and Greek
theater, 148–49, 153, 172–73;
"mythological theatre," 163–64,
167–70; and racial discourse,
146–49; and religious syncretism,
164–65; and rituals, 163–64; and
shock, 152; and staging, 150–51
dreams, 217, 221–26
Du Bois, W. E. B., 144
Dunn, Christopher, 9
Durkheim, Émile, 39, 182, 217,
304n2

Echeverría, Regina, 60
"É d'Oxum" (Gerônimo), 111–12
education: and Candomblé, 202–3;
and community development,
45–46, 94–95, 250–51; lack of,
101–2; and social mobility, 150–51,
154
egbomi (initiate), 100–101
egun (ancestors), 47, 127, 130–31
egungun (masquerading or ancestral),
126–28, 131–32, 312n2
Eliade, Mircea, 32, 89, 110, 114,
172, 174–78, 182, 304n2
equality, 39, 43, 85, 93–94, 137–38,
142, 145–46, 193, 202–3, 257–58,
273–74; inequality, 16, 43, 102,
137–38, 147–48, 152, 198, 257

Esu, Exu, Exú, Eleggua (God of the
crossroads), 2, 14–15, 97–98, 127,
140–41, 225–26, 305n13
ethnicity, 11–12, 19, 53–54, 137–38,
150–51, 161–62
ethnography, 14–15, 40–42, 51–54,
60–61, 137; and access, 56–59,
64–65; and photography, 58,
62–63, 71
Evangelicalism: and Bolinhos de
Jesus (Jesus's cakes), 268, 278–79;
and Candomblé, 12–13, 81, 83–84,
94, 101–2, 192–93, 203–4, 235,
286n10; and spiritism, 188. *See also*
Candomblé; Catholic Church
exceptionalism, 149–50
exoticism, 40–41, 53–54, 59–60, 68,
276–78

fallen black angel, 138–41, 147, 157
Falola, Toyin, 113
family, 71, 84–85, 90–91, 97, 103–4,
118, 148–49, 223–24, 227–28,
267–69
fanaticism, religious, 13–15, 79–80,
83–84, 101, 104–5, 192–93,
223–24, 278–79, 281–82. *See also*
Evangelicalism
favela (slum), 37–38, 83–84, 188
Feiticeiro, O (Marques), 82
Feldman, Cecilia, 4–5, 160
Félix, Anísio, 242
feminism, 85, 165–66, 183–84
Ferretti, Sérgio Figueiredo, 283
Festa da Boa Morte (Good Death
Festival), 10
Festa de Yemanjá, Iemonjá
(Yemonja's Feast), 7–8, 30, 33–34,
162–63
Festa de Santa Bárbara, 10–11, 30,
34–35

FESTAC '77 (Second World Black and African Festival of Arts and Culture), 144, 162

festivals: and celebration, 127, 131–32, 162–63, 236; cycle of, 30, 35, 109–10, 113; as hybrid social structure, 18–19; as popular religiosity, 283. *See also* carnival

fetish, 63, 129–30, 168–69, 293n14

FIFA. *See* International Federation of Football Association

filhas/filhos de santo (children of the saint), 120 141–42, 269

Filhos de Gandhi (Children of Gandhi), 2, 9–10, 26, 44, 162, 233, 234, 237–51, 262–63; and Afro-Brazilian heritage, 245–46; anniversary, 248–50; history of, 242–44; legacy, 248–49; and pacifism, 239–40; politics of, 250–51; as religious group, 239–41; research on, 242. *See also* carnival

Filhos de Gandhi (Félix), 242–43

"Filhos de Gandhi" (Gil), 241

"Filhos de Gandhi" (Nunes), 241

folklore, 59–60, 62–63, 88–89, 166–67, 199–200, 204–5, 225, 283

Fon ethnic group, 80–83

Fonseca, Denise Rosalem da, 83–84

fragmentation, 140–41, 146–47

Frank, Robert, 67

freedom: of choice, 37; creative, 181, 187, 199, 201, 283; religious, 187, 192–93, 199, 222–23, 227–28; and resisting oppression, 197–98, 253–54; from slavery, 10–11, 137–38. *See also* racial democracy myth

French Scientific Research Center (IFAN), 66, 71

Frevo carnaval, 9

Freyre, Gilberto, 19–20, 53, 136–37, 156, 289n23

Fuente, Eduardo de la, 39

Fundação Pierre Verger (Pierre Verger Foundation), 51, 60–62, 64–65, 76–77

fundamentalism, 222–24. *See also* Evangelicalism; fanaticism

Gandhi, Mahatma, 44, 240, 250. *See also* Filhos de Gandhi

Gantois, Mãe Menininha do, 29–30

Garcia, Cynthia, 62

Gates, Henry Louis, Jr., 98, 234–36

gaze: colonial, 55, 58–61, 72; photographic, 59–60, 71, 76–77

Geertz, Clifford, 194–95

gender: and Afro-Brazilian religion, 84–85, 88, 141–42, 163, 165–70, 179–80, 207–8, 214, 219, 228–29; and Atlantic feminine deities, 110, 112–14, 128–30, 157–58; and baianas de acarajé, 270–71, 313n8; and carnival, 248–49, 310n16; and race, 79–80, 146–50; and religion, 83–84, 160, 273–74; in sacred rites, 42, 83. *See also* acarajé; Candomblé; matriarchy

Gerônimo, 1–2, 29–30, 111–12

Giacomini, Sônia Maria, 83–84

Gikandi, Simon, 74

Gil, Gilberto, 6, 29, 44, 61, 76, 162, 183–84, 240–42, 244–46, 250

Girard, René, 157

Gledhill, Sabrina, 7–8

globalization, 3, 12–13, 218, 273–74, 302n5

Godi, Antônio, 240

Gomes, Dias, 35–38, 47, 166; biography, 171; O *Pagador de Promessas* (Payment as pledged/

Gomes, Dias (continued)
    Journey to Bahia), 35–38, 47, 159,
    171–80
Gomes, Luciano, 45–46
Gonçalves, Iracilda, 187–88
Graden, Dale, 82
Gusmão, Henrique Buarque de, 156

Haberly, David T., 19–20
Hall, Stuart, 274
Harding, Rachel, 5, 40, 80–82,
    100–103, 184
Hartikainen, Elina, 94
Hausa ethnic group, 82–83
hegemony, 3, 14–15, 44–45, 104–5,
    144–48, 155–56, 191–92, 201–4,
    219, 234–35, 245–46, 278–79,
    281–82
Herskovits, Frances S., 7, 19
Herskovits, Melville J., 7, 19, 41, 53,
    56–57, 61
hierophany, 174–76
Hinduism, 5
Hita, Maria, 80, 84–85
hybridity, hybridization, 3–4, 9–10,
    19–22, 27, 30–32, 35–38, 110–11,
    127–28, 136, 188, 222–23; cultural,
    34–35, 125, 164; and diaspora,
    218; and relationship between
    sacred and profane, 32–33; and
    survival of African cultural values,
    46–47, 83, 109–10, 115–16,
    222–23

Iansã, Iansan, Iyá Mésàn, Oya
    (Goddess of winds, storms, and
    lightning), 10, 34–37, 47, 118,
    159, 161, 163, 165–70, 172,
    176–80, 255, 305n13. See also
    Bárbara, Santa
Ibeji (twins), 225–27
identity, 2–3; Afro-Brazilian, 116–17,
    125–26, 143–48, 183, 214–16,

288nn16; benefits of, 20; and
    carnival, 234, 238, 256–58; and
    countering oppression of slavery,
    80–81; crisis of, 4; and culture,
    8–11, 218; ethnoreligious politics
    of, 11–12; and gender, 84–85; and
    multiplicity, 224; negotiating, 5–6,
    19–20; and race, 11–12, 136, 153,
    238. See also class; gender; race
Iemanjá. See Yemonjá
Ifá, 51–52, 68–70, 208–14, 219
IFAN. See French Scientific Research
    Center
Igbo Odu, Igbodu (forest or womb of
    secrets), 209–10
Ijexá rhythm, 44–45, 238, 241–42,
    250. See also music
Ikeda, Alberto, 236, 238
Ilê Aiyê (House of the World), 1–2,
    9–10, 19–20, 26, 42–45, 254–56
Ilê Axé Opô Afonja, 2, 79, 85–87,
    111, 215–16, 218–20, 229, 296n11
Ilê Axé Oyá, 251–52
Ilê Omiojuarô, 79, 93–95
IMF. See International Monetary
    Fund
incest, 148–49, 151
inclusion, 102–3, 132–33, 135–37
indigenous Amerindians, 261
inequality. See under equality
Institute for Artistic and Cultural
    Patrimony (IPAC), 31, 35, 242,
    247
International Federation of Football
    Association (FIFA), 271
International Monetary Fund (IMF),
    50
intolerance, 36, 80, 83–84, 101, 159,
    192–93, 222–23, 286n10
IPAC. See Institute for Artistic and
    Cultural Patrimony
IPHAN. See National Institute of
    Historic and Artistic Heritage

Isichei, Elizabeth, 34
Islam, 164–65
itan (histories), 90
Ivester, Skari, 271
iyalorixás (priestesses), 82, 84–86,
    100–101, 141–42, 162
Iyami Agba (feminine divinity), 89

Jackson, Michael, 45
Jamaica, Beto, 45–46
Jauperi, 267
Jeje ethnic group, 7, 54–55, 262
Jesus, Carolina Maria de, 37–38
Jesus, Milton de, 247
Johnson, Paul Christopher, 52, 55–56
Johnson, Randal, 7–8
Jung, Carl, 89
Junior, Sousa, 41–42

Kardec, Allan, 185–90
Kirby, Father Mark Daniel, 182–83
Kuti, Fela, 183–84

labor and laborers: and Afro-
    Brazilians, 28–29, 277–78, 313n6;
    and economics, 84, 203; and food,
    266–68, 313n6; and gender, 313n6;
    industrial, 20; slave, 28–29
Ladipo, Duro, 74
Landes, Ruth, 7, 14, 41–42, 71, 80,
    85, 273
Lavagem do Bomfim (Washing of the
    Good-End Church), 8, 10
Le Bouler, Jean-Pierre, 60–61
LGBTQ community, 257–58
liberation, 13–14, 16–17, 45–46,
    55–56, 146–48, 185–86, 197, 234,
    268–69. See also freedom
Ligeiro, Zeca, 96
Lima, Élida Regina Silva de, 85
Lima, Jorge de, 166
Lima, Robert, 165
Lima, Vivaldo da Costa, 82

Lion and the Jewel, The (Soyinka),
    75, 295n31
literature, 3–4; and popularizing
    African mythology, 115–16, 126–
    27, 194, 216–17; and psychological
    development, 116; and sacred,
    114–15
liturgy, 182–83
Livro de Espíritos, O (Kardec),
    187–88
local color, 121
Lody, Raul, 87–88
Longo, Raul, 181; Filhos de Olorum
    (God's children), 181, 191–205
Lühning, Ângela, 60

macumba, 167
Magalhães, Antônio, 258
magical realism, 111, 117, 126–27,
    225–26, 228
Maia, Carlos Vasconcelos, 110–11,
    125–32; bibliography, 111; O Leque
    de Oxum (Oxum's mirror), 109–11,
    125–32
Mami Wata. See Yemonjá
Mar Morto (Amado), 33
marginalization, 20, 116–17, 133,
    139–40, 156–57; and dialectic of
    sacred and profane, 37–38, 281–82;
    and medical conditions, 260–61
Marley, Bob, 183–84
Marques, Xavier, 82
Martins, Cléo, 87–88, 207–8; Ao
    Sabor de Oiá (In the Style of Oya),
    207–8, 214–24, 228–30
Martins, José, 143–45
Martins, Leda, 140–41
mata atlântica (Atlantic Forest), 26
Matory, J. Lorand, 52, 54–55, 80, 85,
    113, 273
matriarchy, 79–80, 84–85, 217–19,
    272–74, 283–84. See also gender
Matta, Roberto da, 40

Mazrui, Ali, 165
McElroy, Isis, 236, 238–39
McKittrick, Katherine, 148–49
Mead, Margaret, 65
medicine, traditional, 64–65, 68–71,
    286n8
medium, spirit, 184–85
Memorial of Baianas de Acarajé, 277
memory, 4–6, 8–10, 20–21, 32–33,
    41–42, 52–55, 61–65, 88, 96,
    100–104, 111–12, 121, 142, 160–
    62, 183–84, 191, 202–3, 207–8,
    219–20, 267–68, 272–73, 277–78
Mendonça, João Martinho Braga de,
    65
Menezes, Bezerra de, 187
Menezes, Margaret, 29
Mercado de Santa Bárbara, 34–35
Mercury, Daniela, 29–30, 44
Middle Passage, 3, 6, 10, 53, 112,
    255–57, 262, 265–66, 277–78,
    281–82. See also slavery
Miranda, Carmen, 270
miscegenation, 135–39, 148–51,
    157–58, 183–84, 281–82, 289n23.
    See also hybridity and hybridization
Missa dos Quilombos (Nascimento),
    18–19
modernism, 110–11, 126–27; and
    regionalism, 127–28, 132–33
modernity, modernization, 20, 133; as
    corrosive, 79–80
Moraes, Vinicius de, 166
Moreno, Tatti, 7
Morgan, Clyde, 253
Moser, Claudia, 4–5, 160
motherhood, 33–35, 84–85, 98–100,
    103–4, 112–13, 118–21, 125,
    128–30, 175–76, 201–2. See also
    matriarchy
mulatto (figure), 83, 118, 125, 137–38

multiculturalism, 28, 40, 136,
    248–49, 281–82. See also racial
    democracy myth
Murphy, Joseph M., 114
music, 8–9; and Afro-Brazilian
    identity, 161–63, 183–84; and
    carnival, 240–42, 246–47, 250;
    and dialectic between sacred
    and profane, 182–83, 237–38;
    and liberation, 46; popular, 8–9,
    162–63, 202–3, 237–38, 240–41,
    251–52, 266–68; preservation of,
    8–9, 44; and religion, 161–63.
    See also bossa nova; Ijexá rhythm;
    samba
Muzenza, 44–46. See also carnival
Myth, Literature, and the African
    World (Soyinka), 60, 141, 145–46
mythology, 42, 87–92, 97–100,
    114–15, 146, 159, 199–200; and
    culture, 218; and gender, 219;
    Greek, 148–49; and history, 90–91,
    104–5; and morality, 95–97; and
    nation, 166–67; popularizing,
    115–16, 133; recuperating, 116–17;
    and theater, 163–64

Nagô nation, 7, 14, 53–55, 82–83.
    See also Yoruba
Nakagame, Patrícia Trindade, 117–18
Nanã, 110, 219
Nana Buruku (Supreme Being), 63,
    301n2, 305n13
Nascimento, Abdias, 135–36, 166;
    and gender, 146–48; Mixture or
    Massacre?, 144; name, 143; Pan-
    African consciousness of, 143–44;
    Sitiado em Lagos, 144; Sortilégio,
    146–48; Sortilégio II, 135–48,
    157–58
Nascimento, Elisa, 143–44, 147–48

Nascimento, Milton, 18–19
nation: and carnival, 9–11; and culture, 26–27, 115–17, 269–71, 273–74, 277–78, 307n33; history of, 28–29, 273–74; participation in, 11–12, 20, 116–17, 137–38, 143–47, 183–84, 277–78; and ownership of heritage, 74–75; and racial democracy myth, 137–38, 143–49, 183–84, 277–78; and religion, 203–4, 218, 222–23, 273–74, 277–78; and transnationalism, 52–56, 166–67, 222–23. See also acarajé; Amado, Jorge; race; racial democracy myth; Yoruba
National Center for Folklore and Popular Culture, 269–70
National Institute of Historic and Artistic Heritage (IPHAN), 87, 267, 269–70
Neopentecostalism. See Evangelicalism
Nettleford, Rex, 28
new man (figure), 118
Nigeria, 2, 8–9, 34, 50–52, 57–59, 64–65, 72–77, 265
Nossa Senhora do Rosário dos Pretos (Pelourinho), 34–35
Nunes, Clara, 241

Obá (deity of the stormy rivers), 159, 163, 165–66, 168–70, 179–80, 195–200, 214, 220–21
Oba Waja (Ladipo), 74
Obatala (God of divination), 2, 167, 210
Odu, 208–14, 219, 228–30, 307n1
Oduduwa (God of creation), 89
Oedipus Rex (Sophocles), 148–49
Ogum, Ogun (God of iron, justice, metals, and war), 2, 90–91, 118, 210, 250, 262, 305n13

Ojo-Ade, Femi, 143, 148
Okambi (Progenitor or Child of Okan), 2
Olinto, Antônio, 163–64, 216
Oliveira, Altair B., 41
Oliveira, Diogo Luís de, 29
Oliveira, Gilsonei de, 233
Olodum (Celebrant), 2, 9–10, 19–20, 26, 42–45
Olodumaré, 5, 210
Olokum, 128–29
Olorum, 97
Omo Oxum (afoxé), 237
Omolu, 91
oral tradition, 79–80, 96–97, 104–5, 111, 218
orikis (ritualistic praises), 90, 113, 193–94, 224–25, 241
orin (songs of praise), 90
Orisanla (Supreme being), 89
orisas, orixás (deities), 2, 5, 42; appropriation of, 246; artistic representations of, 7–8; in Brazilian culture, 115–16, 219–20; characteristics of, 167–68; feminine deities, 112–14; and food, 265–68; and gender, 112–14, 207–8; interacting with, 159, 162; interventions in human life, 225–26; literary representations of, 109–10, 126–31, 133, 140–41, 144–45, 157–58, 166–67, 179–80, 191, 193–205; oracular culture of, 49, 63; pantheon, 89–92, 110, 112–13, 160–61, 164–67, 265–66, 301n2, 305n13, 308n2; and relocation, 6–7; reverence for, 269–70; studies of, 42; transatlantic tradition of, 62–63, 112–13; veneration of, 81
Orixás Theater, 171. See also Seljan, Zora

Orun (other world), 131

Orunmila (Father of Divination), 2, 209–11, 219, 228–29

Osanyin, 90

Osoosi, Oxóssi, (forest and hunting deity), 79, 87–92, 207–9, 224–26, 228, 230, 296n13, 308n2

Osóòsi: O Caçador de Alegrias (Stella de Oxóssi), 79

Osumare, Ochumaré, Oxumaré (God of the rainbow), 305n13

Osun, Ochún, Oxúm (Deity of the river and fresh water, sexuality and fertility) 1–2, 112–13, 159, 163, 165–70, 179–80, 199–200, 227–29, 214, 305n13; representations of, 109–12, 114, 126–33

Otero, Solimar, 113

Our Lady of Conception. *See* Virgin Mary

ownership, 15–16, 30–31, 50–51, 62–63, 72–73, 76–77

Oxalá, 79, 101–2, 131, 146, 226, 251–52

Oxóssi, Mãe Stella de (Maria Stella de Azevedo Santos), 79, 85–92, 104–5, 215–16, 229; initiation and training, 87; legacy, 87–88; *Meu Tempo é Agora*, 86–87; nursing education, 86; *Odu Adajo/Ofun: Coleção de Destinos*, 86–87; *Ososi: O Caçador de Alegrias*, 86–92

Oxum Abalo, 167

Oya (Goddess of the wind and river), 2, 207–9, 214–16, 224–25, 228–30, 308n2

pacifism, 239–40

Palmares, Zumbi dos, 269

paranormal, 184–86, 190–91

Parés, Luis Nicolau, 52, 54–55, 82

Pentecostalism. *See* Evangelicalism

Pereira, Arivaldo Fagundes ("Carequinha"), 243–44

performance, 3–4, 9–10, 20–22, 31–32, 39–42, 68–70, 83–84, 91–92, 136, 146–47, 161, 167–68, 236–38, 246, 259, 282–84

Phenix, Deinya, 256–57

Philip, Marlene, 149–50

photography, 49–50, 57; ethics of, 65–66, 71; as ethnography, 51–52, 58, 60–69; and gaze, 59–61, 76; as memory, 61–62. *See also* anthropology, visual

Pierson, Donald, 41

Pinheiro, Robson, 181; conversion, 188; criticism of, 189–90; legacy of, 190–91; *Tambores de Angola* (Drums of Angola), 181, 184–91, 203–5

Pitta, Alberto, 233, 251–57, 259, 262

Pivin, Jean-Louis, 67

planalto, 26

plantation economy, 25–26, 28–29

pluralism, 21, 214, 283. *See also* racial democracy myth; syncretism

PNI. *See* psychoneuroimmunology

poetry, 94–98, 224–28, 242

politics: and Afro-Brazilian access to participation, 21–22; and carnival, 9–10, 234–36, 238–43, 248–62; and culture, 40, 42–43, 47, 273–74; and identity, 11–12, 19–20; and liberation, 13–14, 197; and sacred, 3–4, 5–6, 9–10, 40, 80–81, 93–95, 197–203, 281–84

Polk, Patrick A., 7–8

popular, popularization, 21–22, 28, 141, 159–63, 171–72, 191–93, 234–38, 265–66, 282–83. *See also* profane; sacred

Port, Mattijs van de, 41, 183
Porto dos Milagres (Port of miracles),
    123–25
Porto Filho, Ubaldo Marques, 272,
    274–76
poverty, 38, 84–85, 102–4, 135–36,
    193–94, 256–57, 272
Prandi, Reginaldo, 41, 167–68
"Preta do Acarajé, A" (Caymmi),
    266–67
primitive, 90–91
profane, profanation, 32, 34–35,
    37–39, 114, 116, 119, 176–78,
    182, 202–3, 217–18, 233, 235–37,
    262–63, 281. *See also* popular;
    sacred
psychoanalysis, 155–57
psychography, 187–89
psychology: of leadership, 84–85; in
    literature, 111, 116; and race, 135–
    36, 139–40, 147–49, 153, 155–56,
    203–4; and religion, 203–4, 262–63
psychoneuroimmunology (PNI), 225
purity. *See* authenticity

"que é que a baiana tem, O"
    (Caymmi), 270
Querino, Manoel, 59

race: in Brazil, 3–4, 21, 41–42;
    and carnival, 244–45; and
    culture, 3–4, 41–43, 278–79; and
    dehumanization, 141–42; and
    discrimination, 3–4, 44–45, 111,
    183–84; and equality, 141, 193–94,
    238–39; and fragmentation,
    140–41; and gender, 146–48;
    and hierarchy, 135–40, 146–47,
    150–55, 248; and identity, 11–14,
    19–20, 238; and mixture, 11–12,
    14–15; and oppression, 136–38;
    and racism, 9–10, 71, 79–80,
    102; and religion, 151; and sexual
    orientation, 257–58; and trauma,
    156–57. *See also* class; gender;
    identity
racial democracy myth, 3–4, 14–15,
    19–22, 135–38, 140–41, 144,
    146–52, 154–55, 157–58, 183–84,
    283, 289n23
rage, 159–60
Ramos, Arthur, 53
Ramos, Graciliano, 128
Rastafarianism, 46
re-Africanization movement, 13–15,
    20, 30–31, 44–45, 47, 57, 63, 81,
    138–39, 204, 238–39, 245–47,
    282–83, 295n2
Rebouças, Karolina de Oliveira, 236,
    238–39
Refavela (Gil), 162
Reis, João, 82–83
religion: and activism, 102;
    and fanaticism, 80; and
    interpenetration of civilizations,
    53–54; as live dialogue, 54–55;
    and persecution, 79–80; and
    racial identity, 11–15, 20, 136;
    and racism, 151; and resistance to
    social oppression, 164–65, 183–84;
    and ritual, 194–95; and social
    inclusion, 132–33; and syncretism,
    282–83. *See also* Candomblé;
    Evangelicalism; ritual; sacred
religious studies, 52–53
relocation, 3–4, 6–7; and mixture,
    10–11; and preservation of
    Afro-Brazilian culture, 4–6, 281;
    problematic side of, 7, 21; and
    sacred, 8–9, 81, 167–68
resistance, 3–5, 16, 19–20, 28–31, 37,
    40, 44–46, 53–56, 73–74, 109–10,

resistance (continued)
161, 183–84, 191–92, 197, 201–3,
219, 238, 245–46, 251–53, 266–67,
271, 277–78, 281, 284. See also
politics; survival
Retamar, Roberto, 144
Richards, Sandra, 143–44, 146–47
Rio de Janeiro, 10, 14, 83–84, 93,
137, 267–68; and macumba, 167
Risério, Antônio, 242, 245–46
ritual, 3–4; in absence of religious
stricture, 38; and body, 193–94;
commercialization of, 31; and
context, 160–61; and food, 266;
location of, 4–5; and music, 8–9;
performances, 20–21, 91–92; and
political engagement, 31–32;
public/private nature of, 40; and
relationship between sacred and
profane, 32–33, 194–95; religious,
18–19; as resistance, 30–31;
ritualizations, 18–19, 28; structures
and strictures, 36
ritual drama, 139–41, 144–46
Rocha, João Cesar de Castro, 37–38
Rodrigues, Nelson, 135–36; aesthetics
of shock, 152; Anjo Negro, 135–37,
142–43, 148–158
Rodrigues, Raymundo Nina, 14, 53,
58–59, 71–76, 82, 248, 293n14
Romo, Anadelia A., 40
Rosa, Guimarães, 128
Rosa, Renata Saback, 236, 238–39
Rosenfeld, Anatol, 172–73
Roustaing, Jean-Baptiste, 187
Rumores de Festa (Serra), 237

sacred: and affirmation of racial
identity, 20–21, 30–31; artistry
of, 7–9; and carnival, 233,
262–63; and challenging racism,
3; and culture, 41, 46–47;
documentation of, 9; domain
of, 7–8; and freedom, 181; and
gender, 273–74; hybridization of,
3–4; and imagination, 40–41;
and literary, 114–15; and liturgy,
182; and political agency, 281–82;
and popular, 3–4, 20–22, 27–28,
31, 101–5, 109–12, 114–16, 141,
160–63, 171–72, 191–92, 202–3,
234–35, 237–38, 265–66, 282–83;
and poverty, 37–38; preservation
of Afro-Brazilian cultural values,
104–5; and profane, 32, 34–43,
116, 119, 167–68, 174–80,
217–18, 233, 235–37, 262–63, 281;
relocation of, 3–4, 81, 159–61; and
resistance to slavery, 80–81; and
ritual, 18–19, 194–95; and social,
40, 203; space of, 4–5, 6, 174–76,
179–80, 182; and state cultural
formation, 25–28; therapeutic,
181, 185–86, 189–90. See also
Candomblé; religion; ritual
sailors, 114–15, 119–21
Saint-Léon, Pascal, 67
Salvador da Bahia, 6–8, 26; as
African Brazil, 27–28; and
carnival, 248–49; cultural
revitalization, 258–59; and
history of Candomblé, 161–62;
informal economy of, 271; and
popularization of sacred, 111–13;
and sea, 119–20
samba, 10, 26, 28–29, 46, 161–62.
See also music
Sanford, Mei-Mei, 114
Sangalo, Ivete, 29
Sansi, Roger, 7
Santana, Arany, 250
Santos, Antônio Carlos dos
("Vovô"), 1
Santos, Jean, 85

Santos, Joel Rufino dos, 166
Santos, Juana Elbein dos, 59, 61, 71, 76
Santos, Liliane, 236–37
Santos, Nívea Alves dos, 35
São Francisco River, 26
Saueressig, Simone, 41
Schaun, Angela, 43
Schneider, Andreas, 39
sea, 115–16; in Afro-Brazilian mythology, 114–15; representations of, 115–23
second-tier foreign exchange market (SFEM), 50
secrecy, 55–56, 81
secular, secularization, 38–39; and profane, 38–39; and ritualizations, 18–21. See also profane; sacred
Sekoni, Ropo, 98
Seljan, Zora, 146; Afro-dramas of, 163–64; bibliography, 164, 166–67, 170–71; biography, 163–64, 170–71; and centrality of orisas, 166–67; The Story of Oxalá, 163; Três Mulheres de Xangô (Three wives of Sango), 159, 163–70, 179–80
Selka, Stephen, 7, 11–13
SEPPIR. See Special Secretary for the Promotion of Racial Equality
Serra, Marcos, 93–95
Serra, Ordep, 40, 236–37
sertão region, 26
sexuality, 113; and racism, 147–48; as self-negation, 135–36
SFEM. See second-tier foreign exchange market
Shirey, Heather, 6–7
Silva, Agnaldo, 233
Silva, Vagner Gonçalves da, 11–13
Silveira, Renato da, 82
Simon, Paul, 45

Sisterhood of Good Death, 31
slavery, 20; and Afro-Brazilian inclusion, 132–33, 137–38; and Bahia, 25; and Catholic Church, 18–19; and diversity of African ethnic groups, 53–54; and identity, 20; influence on cultural formations, 29, 31; legacy of, 68, 150–51; memory of, 4; and naming, 143; and oral tradition, 6; and preservation of African religious cultures, 3, 5–6, 11–12, 46–47, 53, 80–81, 104–5, 112–13, 116–17, 161–62, 165, 183, 192, 195–96, 203–4, 219, 255–56, 265–66, 268–69, 277–78, 281–82; and slave ship, 255–57, 262; violence of, 185–86, 196–98; and Yoruba diaspora, 285n1
Smith, Christen, 137
soap opera, 123–25
Soares, Arlete, 61, 63–64
social mobilization, 12–13
sociology, 40–41, 52–53; cultural, 39; and sacred, 40. See also anthropology
Sodré, Jaime, 88, 240
Sontag, Susan, 71
Sousa, Tomé de, 29
Souty, Jérôme, 60
Soyinka, Wole, 49–51, 58–60, 62–63, 72–76, 141, 145–46, 294n27
space: and Blackness, 20–21, 40; of sacred, 6, 18–19, 32–33, 174–80, 182
Special Secretary for the Promotion of Racial Equality (SEPPIR), 83–84
spiritism, 181, 184–91, 202–3, 227–28; history of, 187–88; and hybridity, 188
Staal, Frits, 194–95

stereotypes, 116, 121, 151
Sterling, Cheryl, 31, 40, 42–43, 113, 273–74
storytelling, 79, 95–97, 114–15, 215–16. *See also* oral tradition
Strahan, Ian, 28
string stories, 121
suicide, 165–66
survival, 3–4, 11, 14, 19–20, 37–38, 46–47, 52–55, 61, 76, 82–85, 102–4, 112–13, 119–20, 126, 154–55, 163–65, 183, 192, 197–98, 203–4, 219, 234–35, 238–42, 256–57, 265–69, 271, 278–79, 286n10
symbolism, 87–92, 116, 148–49, 175–76, 226–27
syncretism, 3, 5, 21, 129–30, 281, 283; and "co-existence," 52–53, 58–60, 63; and coloniality, 294n24; and conflict, 21; and racial heritage, 11–12, 14–15, 19–20; rejecting, 13–14; religious, 33–36, 50, 53–55, 80–81, 87, 102–3, 112–13, 115–16, 130–33, 160–61, 164–65, 172, 179, 200–201, 203–4, 219, 226, 234–35, 244–45, 278–79, 282–83, 289n23; violence of, 222–23, 307n34

Tailors' Revolt of 1798, 29
Tannenbaum, Frank, 137–38
Tarde, A (newspaper), 87–88, 101
Tatau, 45–46
Tate, Julee, 157–58
Tavares, Ildásio, 225
Teixeira, Cid, 242–43
Telles, Jocélio, 82
terreiro (temple), 5, 33, 79, 81–84, 94–95, 176–78; organization of, 87
Terreiro do Gantóis, 100
Terreiro Pilão do Cobre (Copper Pestle Temple), 79, 100–101

tolerance, religious, 21, 227–28
tourism, 30, 109, 307n33; and carnival, 44; and cuisine, 269–71, 274, 276–78; and hybridization, 27; and plantation economy, 28; and sacred, 31–32
Trajetória de Filhos de Gandhy, A (Trajectory of Filhos de Gandhi), 240–41
translation, 69–70, 72
transnationalism, 9, 52–55, 143–44, 218, 222–23, 248–49
trauma, 156–57; and healing, 225
trickster (figure), 97–98
Tunkara, Omari, 31
Twine, France, 137

Umbanda, 53, 55–56, 181, 183–85, 202–3; and "Caboclo das Sete Encruzilhadas" (Mixed-race Brazilian of Seven Crossroads), 188; cosmology of, 189–90; epistemology of, 187–88; and hybridity, 188; and survival of African cultural values, 203–5
UNESCO. *See* United Nations Educational, Scientific and Cultural Organization
Unified Black Movement (Movimento Negro Unificado), 47, 94
United Nations Educational, Scientific and Cultural Organization (UNESCO), 269
Universal Control of Spiritist Teachings (CUEE), 187–88
urban, 84–85

Vallado, Antônio, 113
Vargas, Getúlio, 269–70
Veloso, Caetano, 29–30, 44, 183–84, 242, 247, 253, 262

Verger, Pierre, 41, 49–52, 82, 113,
128–29; biography, 51–52; colonial
mentality of, 59–60, 68–73;
documentation of Candomblé
in Bahia, 57; fetish perspective,
293n14; legacy of, 61–64, 66–
68, 76–77, 296n13; on Osoosi,
296n13; as photographer, 62–63,
65–67, 71; place in broader
African religious world, 52–53;
research, 50–51, 60–61; and
questions of access, 56–59, 64–65,
68–71; and Soyinka, 58–59, 72–77,
294n27
Verger, Pierre, works of: *African
Legends of the Orishas*, 60, 63–64;
Artigos, 60; *Dieux d'Afrique*, 63,
66–67; *Ewé: The Use of Plants in
Yoruba Society*, 60, 64–65, 68–69;
Fluxo and Refluxo, 60, 68; *Indiens
pas morts*, 66–67; *Le Messager/The
Go-Between: Photographies 1932–
1962*, 67; *Notas Sobre o Culto aos
Orixás e Voduns*, 60; "Notes sur le
culte des Orisá et Vodun à Bahia,
la Baie de tous les Saints, au Brésil
et à l'ancienne Côte des Esclaves
en Afrique," 67; *Orixás: Deus
iorubas na África e no Novo Mundo*,
60, 63, 67; *Retratos da Bahia, 1946
a 1952*, 67; *Trade Relations Between
the Bight of Benin and Bahia*, 60,
64–65
violence, 102; and diaspora,
149–50; police, 183–84; and
racial oppression, 150–51; sexual,
151–52, 156–57, 299n1
Virgin Mary (Our Lady of
Conception), 10–11, 31, 33–34,
46–47, 110, 112–13, 129–30,
175–76, 237–38, 305n31. *See also*
Bárbara, Santa; Osun; Yemonjá

Wafer, Jim, 7
War of the Canudos (1897), 29
Warren, Tish, 217
water (motif), 110
Weber, Max, 39
West, Cornel, 144
whiteness, 135–36; desiring, 150–51,
153–55; and racial supremacy, 3,
137, 141, 149–50
Wikstrom, Owe, 182
wisdom, 70–71, 79, 101, 104–5,
209–10, 218, 250–51, 308n2;
sacred, 93–100
World Cup, 271, 313n7
writing, 110–11

Xamã (Ajẹ), 91–92
Xangô, Sango (Deity of thunder), 2,
118, 126–27, 130–33, 159–61, 163,
165–66, 168–70, 179–80, 195–200,
214–16, 228–29, 250, 305n13
Xango, Mãe Ana de (Ana Verônica
Bispo dos Santos), 86
Xavier, Chico, 187–88
Xirê (ritual performance), 92

Yemonjá, Yemoja, Iemojá, Yemanjá
(Sea goddess or mermaid),
2, 8, 10, 27, 33–34, 42, 79,
98–100, 111–13, 160–61, 201–2,
305n13; celebration of, 237–38;
representations of, 109–10, 113–16,
118–21, 124–25, 129–30, 133
Yemonjá, Mãe Beata de (Beatriz
Moreira Costa), 79, 83–84,
93–100, 104–5; biography, 93;
Caroço de Dendê, 79, 95–100;
legacy, 93–95; mother of, 98–100
Yoruba, 285n1; in Afro-Brazilian
culture, 1–2, 111–12, 125–26,
289n24; and Blackness, 20–21;
and Candomblé, 82–83; and

Yoruba (*continued*)
colonialism, 2–3; cosmology of,
119, 127–30, 179–80, 207–10,
226–27; and cuisine, 312n2;
diaspora in Bahia, 25–27; and
gender, 210–11, 219, 228–30; and
ìgbà of Odu, 210–11; initiation,
51–52, 68–69; isolation of, 56–57;
language, 2; and liturgy, 8–9;
medicine, 64–65, 68–71, 286n8;
musical tradition of, 44, 161–62;
mythology, 87–89, 146, 163–65,
191, 195–96, 214–15, 218–19,
228–30, 259–60; national cultural
history of, 73–74, 76–77; oral
tradition, 114–15; orisa oracular
culture of, 49, 62–63; pantheon,
33, 63, 89–90, 160–61, 165–70,
199–200, 251–52, 285n2, 301n2,
305n31; preserving culture of,
219–20, 248, 265–66; primitive
history of, 90–91; and relationship
between sacred and profane,
32–33, 222–23; and religion,
246–47; relocation of, 5; sacred
rituals of, 2–3; and syncretism,
3–4, 33–35; transatlantic networks
of, 54–55, 60–61, 63, 68, 80–81.
See also Africanism; Candomblé;
orisas

Zola, Émile, 228